D0143282

SOCRATES
AND THE
STATE

SOCRATES
AND THE
STATE

Richard Kraut

PRINCETON UNIVERSITY PRESS

Princeton, New Jersey

Published by Princeton University Press, 41 William
Street, Princeton, New Jersey 08540

In the United Kingdom: Princeton University Press,
Guildford, Surrey

Library of Congress Cataloging in Publication Data will
be found on the last printed page of this book

ISBN 0-691-07666-9
ISBN 0-691-02241-0 (pbk.)

Publication of this book has been aided by a grant from the
Publications Program of the National Endowment
for the Humanities

This book has been composed in Linotron Bembo type

Clothbound editions of Princeton University Press books
are printed on acid-free paper, and binding materials are
chosen for strength and durability. Paperbacks, although
satisfactory for personal collections, are not usually
suitable for library rebinding

Printed in the United States of America by Princeton
University Press, Princeton, New Jersey

For Susan

CONTENTS

IV

CITIZENS AND OFFSPRING

V

PRIVATE PERSONS AND GENERALIZATION

VI

DOKIMASIA, SATISFACTION, AND AGREEMENT

VII

SOCRATES AND DEMOCRACY

VIII

DEFINITION, KNOWLEDGE, AND TEACHING

APPENDIX

ACKNOWLEDGMENTS

I WISH to express my gratitude to the Center for Hellenic Studies, in Washington D.C., where I wrote a first draft of Chapters I-VI, and developed the ideas for VII and VIII. My research there was also supported by a Fellowship from the American Council of Learned Societies. Chapters VII and VIII slowly improved because I was able to read a short version of them at the Great Expectations Bookstore, in Evanston, Illinois, and to the philosophy departments of Indiana University, the University of Wisconsin, the University of Chicago, Temple University, Northwestern University, and Marquette University. The University of Illinois at Chicago gave me a Short Research Leave to produce a final draft of the entire manuscript, and the Philosophy Department relieved me of my teaching responsibilities for a term. Without so much institutional support, this book probably would never have been written; at any rate, it would certainly have been far worse than it is.

As I worked on this project, many individuals helped me generously with advice, criticism, and encouragement. In particular, I would like to mention Jan Bremmer, Peter Burian, Susan Cole, Kathleen Cook, John Deigh, Gerald Dworkin, David Gallop, Joan Kung, Ian Mueller, Gregory Vlastos, and Charles Young. I am especially grateful to John Deigh, who spotted many philosophical weaknesses in the first draft and helped me repair the damage. And I would also like to express my appreciation for the work of Pansy Moy, who provided valuable secretarial assistance in the production of a finished manuscript.

To Gregory Vlastos, I owe my deepest debt and give my warmest thanks. Since my days as a graduate student, he has been encouraging my work, criticizing my ideas, and serving as an example of how much can be accomplished in teaching and scholarship. What follows is an attempt, however deficient, to live up to the high standard he sets.

ABBREVIATIONS

Aristotle

E.E.	*Eudemian Ethics*	*Pol.*	*Politics*
N.E.	*Nicomachean Ethics*	*Rhet.*	*Rhetoric*

Plato

(titles of spurious or doubtful works are bracketed)

Alc. I	*[Alcibiades* I]	*H. Mi.*	*Hippias Minor*
Ap.	*Apology*	*La.*	*Laches*
Charm.	*Charmides*	*Lys.*	*Lysis*
Cleit.	*[Cleitophon]*	*Phd.*	*Phaedo*
Def.	*[Definitions]*	*Protag.*	*Protagoras*
Euphr.	*Euthyphro*	*Rep.*	*Republic*
Euthyd.	*Euthydemus*	*Symp.*	*Symposium*
Grg.	*Gorgias*	*Tht.*	*Theaetetus*
H. Ma.	*Hippias Major*		

Xenophon

Ap.	*Apology*	*Mem.*	*Memorabilia*
Lac. Pol.	*Constitution of the Lacedaimonians*	*Oec.*	*Oeconomicus*

SOCRATES
AND THE
STATE

I

PRELIMINARIES

1

Synopsis

THIS STUDY has two aims. The first is to understand the political theory Socrates adopts when he refuses, in Plato's *Crito*, to escape from jail.[1] The second is to put this dialogue into a broader context, by examining the general political orientation ascribed to Socrates not only in the *Crito* but throughout Plato's early works. Let me describe these two projects in greater detail.

The contents of the *Crito* are of course well known. Socrates is in prison, having been condemned to death for corrupting the young and introducing new gods. As he awaits the day of his execution, he is visited by his friend Crito, who urges him to flee. Socrates agrees to consider the proposal, and he reminds Crito of a basic point they have accepted many times in the past: injustice must never be done, not even in response to injustice. It is on the basis of this principle that Crito's offer is to be evaluated. If escape is just, Socrates will flee; if unjust, he will remain and accept his punishment. At this point, the conversation is taken over by the personified Laws of Athens. Their

---

[1] I believe (and I hope this study will show) that giving an interpretation of the *Crito* is a worthwhile project whether or not this dialogue is a historically accurate account of the philosophy of Socrates. But I also think that the dialogue has at least this much historical accuracy: the opportunity to escape from jail certainly existed, and since Socrates did not take advantage of it, he must have had his philosophical reasons. The *Crito* gives us those reasons, as Plato understood them, and as we shall see, the portrait of Socrates that emerges from this dialogue fits neatly with the portrait we find in other early Platonic dialogues. This way of reading the *Crito* allows for the possibility that neither Crito nor any other admirer actually pleaded with Socrates to escape, since they already knew the arguments he would have given against such a plan of action. There is of course no way to rule out this possibility; and surely it is improbable

speech, barely interrupted by questions, forms the philosophical heart of the dialogue, and it will be the main focus of this study: Chapters II through VI are devoted to this part of the *Crito*. The Laws put forward a theory of political loyalty, and from their general principles they infer that Socrates would be doing a great injustice were he to escape from jail. Socrates applauds their argument, the conversation ends, and several days later he dies.

What are we to make of the philosophy that led him to his death? The first aim of this study is to answer that question.

that Socrates first started thinking about legal-philosophical issues after he was sentenced to death. On the other hand, a person like Crito might have hoped that Socrates would reconsider his attitude toward disobedience; after all, he is always willing to reexamine his philosophical ideas. So something like the conversation we find in the *Crito* might well have occurred; at a minimum, it is roughly the conversation that would have occurred, had an offer to escape been made. Compare Allen's treatment of this issue, *Socrates and Legal Obligation*, p. 66. More generally, I take it that in the *Apology*, the *Crito*, and the other early dialogues, Plato is trying to give a roughly accurate portrait (not a word-for-word transcription) of what Socrates said. See Allen, ibid., pp. 33-36, for a defense of the "essential accuracy" of the *Apology*. See too Vlastos, "The Paradox of Socrates," pp. 3-4. After a general review of the evidence, Lacey concludes: "The early Plato is rightly regarded as our main source . . ." for the philosophy of Socrates. See "Our Knowledge of Socrates," p. 49. The same view is defended by Guthrie, *A History of Greek Philosophy* (hereafter cited as *History*), Vol. III, pp. 325-377; see esp. p. 350. For further discussion, see Ch. VII nn. 7, 15. Though Xenophon and Plato overlap considerably in their portraits of Socrates, Plato is to be followed wherever they conflict, for reasons well stated by Vlastos, ibid., pp. 1-3. On the issue of disobedience, it cannot be decided whether Xenophon and Plato ascribe the same views to Socrates until we look carefully at the relevant texts. For Xenophon's account of Socrates' attitude toward obeying the law, see *Mem*. I ii 9, I ii 41-47, III iii 9, IV iv 12-19; these passages require interpretation, but I will not undertake that task in this study. I consider the following Platonic works (in alphabetical order) to be unquestionably early, and therefore especially reliable as sources for the philosophy of Socrates: *Ap.*, *Charm.*, *Crito*, *Euthyd.*, *Euphr.*, *Grg.*, *H. Ma.*, *H. Mi.*, *Ion*, *La.*, *Lys.*, and *Protag.* I believe that certain parts of the *Meno* are Socratic (the search for definition, the unteachability of virtue), others Platonic (the doctrine of recollection, the sufficiency of true belief for virtue). See VIII.12 for further discussion. (Throughout this study, a Roman numeral followed by an Arabic numeral is a reference to chapter and section. For example, VIII.12 is Chapter VIII Section 12. By contrast, Ch. VIII n. 12 is footnote 12 of Chapter VIII.) I take Book I of the *Republic* (but not the rest) to be a portrait of Socrates, whether it was written independently or as part of the larger work. For my understanding of Socrates, I do not rely on dialogues (e.g. *Alc.* I and II, *Cleit.*, *Minos*) whose Platonic authorship is not generally acknowledged. But if these works are genuine, as some scholars think, they provide further support for my interpretation. See Ch. VII nn. 43, 77.

More specifically, in Chapters II through VI I shall be concerned with the following issues.

(A) It is difficult, when reading the *Crito*, to resist the impression that its political philosophy is offensively authoritarian. It seems to exaggerate the need for law and order, and it leaves too little room or perhaps none at all for dissent and disobedience. Citizens are turned into slaves of the state, and they must obey their city's orders as children obey their parents.[2] Just as Socrates must accept his punishment despite its injustice, so too must all citizens submit to the city's orders, however deficient they may be.[3] And if anyone happens to be dissatisfied with the way Athens conducts its legal business, he ought to pack up his belongings and leave.[4]

I will argue that this impression of the dialogue is deeply mistaken. If we read the speech of the Laws carefully, we will see that they do not severely limit the citizen's opportunities for dissent and disobedience. As we will discover, the *Crito* is not

---

[2] Thus Woozley, *Law and Obedience*, pp. 62-75; Santas, *Socrates*, pp. 21-26; Young, "Socrates and Disobedience," pp. 16-17, 21-22.

[3] Thus Romilly, *La loi dans la pensée grecque*, p. 130; Dybikowski, "Socrates, Obedience, and the Law: Plato's *Crito*," p. 529; A. Barker, "Why Did Socrates Refuse to Escape?" p. 25; Grote, *Plato, and the Other Companions of Socrates* (hereafter cited as *Plato*), Vol. I, pp. 302-304; Greenberg, "Socrates' Choice in the *Crito*," pp. 61-63; Martin, "Socrates on Disobedience to Law," pp. 35, 38; Adkins, *Merit and Responsibility*, pp. 263-264; and A. E. Taylor, *Plato*, p. 168. Friedländer, *Plato*, Vol. II, p. 176, takes the *Crito* to be saying not that unjust laws must always be obeyed, but that ". . . justice is shown in its concrete embodiment . . . in the specific laws of the city of Athens." This seems to mean that there can be no such thing as an unjust law. E. Barker, *The Political Thought of Plato and Aristotle*, p. 52, also adopts this interpretation. All of these scholars agree that according to the Laws citizens can never justifiably disobey the city. So too Young, "Socrates and Disobedience," esp. p. 24, n. 18, though he argues that the unconditional opposition of the Laws to disobedience is not really accepted by Socrates. Maier, *Sokrates*, p. 409, takes the *Crito* to assert the ". . . natürlichen Überordnung des Staatsganzen über das Individuum. . . ." On pp. 411 and 416, Socrates becomes a proto-Kantian: he insists on inner freedom and outward subordination to the state. For notable attempts to show that the speech of the Laws leaves some small room for disobedience, see Allen, *Socrates and Legal Obligation*, pp. 86, 109-113; Santas, *Socrates*, Ch. I, esp. pp. 43-56; Vlastos, "Socrates on Political Obedience and Disobedience," esp. pp. 530-534; Wade, "In Defense of Socrates," esp. pp. 314, 317-318, 324-325; Woozley, "Socrates on Disobeying the Law," esp. pp. 307-308; and Woozley, *Law and Obedience*, esp. pp. 28-40.

[4] The dialogue is so interpreted by Vlastos, "Socrates on Political Obedience and Disobedience," pp. 525-526; and Woozley, *Law and Obedience*, p. 81.

a one-sided plea for authority, civic stability, and the supremacy of the state. It is more accurately viewed as an attempt to strike a fair balance between the needs of citizens and the needs of their city. The Laws are trying to reconcile two antagonistic ideas: (a) citizens owe a certain form of loyalty to the state, and without such loyalty the state cannot survive; (b) there is a moral standard by which a city is to be judged, and when it fails to meet that standard, the citizen must disobey. Because the *Crito* tries to fit these two ideas together, its political philosophy cannot be summed up by means of simple formulas. It does not turn the individual into a servant of the state, in any significant sense; it does not demand blind obedience; and it does not tell the citizen to "love it or leave it." Despite initial appearances and despite the consensus of scholars, it is an exaggeration to portray the *Crito* as one of the most severe documents in the history of legal thought.[5] It is more moderate than its readers have realized.

(B) We should always distinguish the quality of a philosophical argument from the plausibility or truth of its conclusions. For example, we can concede that Hobbes argues in a masterly way for his theory of the state, even though we reject his authoritarianism. Similarly, the speech of the Laws might be carefully reasoned, even if the legal principles they advocate are unpalatable. But in fact the *Crito* has not received high marks for philosophical rigor. Grote characterized it as a "rhetorical harangue."[6] Vlastos complains that "time and again we see the diction running to hyperbole and the thought blown about by gusts of feeling."[7] Santas concedes that Plato "over-argued and

---

[5] Thus Allen, *Socrates and Legal Obligation*, p. 105: "Few documents in the history of Western legal and moral philosophy have pitched the obligations of citizenship so high. . . ." I have not been able to find a single writer who would disagree with this assessment, as I do. Even those (cited in n. 3 above) who think that the dialogue leaves some room for disobedience would accept Allen's statement. I am of course not saying that the *Crito*'s legal philosophy is beyond criticism. On the contrary, see III.2 (the citizen may have too much discretion), V.8 (weaknesses of the parent-city analogy), and VI.13 (objections to the argument from agreement).

[6] *Plato*, p. 302.

[7] "Socrates on Political Obedience and Disobedience," p. 519.

overstated Socrates' loyalty to the city. . . ."[8] Greenberg, citing
the analogy made by the Laws between parents and the city,
confesses that he "hardly knows where to begin in outraged
protest at this argument. For the most part it is not an argument
at all. To be against it is like being against motherhood and in
favor of sin."[9] In a recent book-length study of the *Crito*, Woozley
found that the most he could say in its favor was that its arguments "are interestingly bad rather than uninterestingly
good."[10] Young suggests that since Crito is too stupid to com-
prehend a good argument against escape, the Laws are forced
to give a weak argument—one that Socrates does not really
endorse.[11]

Again, I wish to defend an alternative: I believe that the *Crito*
is as careful a dialogue as Plato wrote. The speech of the Laws
is of course filled with emotion, but when we take their argument apart and examine it line by line, we can see how ingenious and well-constructed it is. They state their points carefully
and anticipate objections. Putting together a series of sensible
principles they arrive at a powerful conclusion. The *Crito* deserves a higher reputation than it currently enjoys as a sophisticated piece of reasoning.

So much then for the first aim of this study. In Chapters VII
and VIII, I turn to my second goal, which is to understand the
politics of Socrates as they are presented throughout Plato's early
works. The main issues I will discuss are these.

(C) During the fifth and fourth centuries, Athens was an extreme democracy. Every adult male citizen could vote in the
Assembly, and that body had supreme political authority. Thus
the laws gave great power to the majority, and Socrates believed that this group lacked the wisdom necessary to use its
power well. We need look no farther than the *Crito* to see his
hostility to democracy. He tells his friend that medical and moral

---

[8] *Socrates*, p. 55.
[9] "Socrates' Choice in the *Crito*," p. 64.
[10] *Law and Obedience*, Preface.
[11] "Socrates and Disobedience," pp. 6-9. See McLaughlin, "Socrates on Political Disobedience," for a reply to Young's paper.

decisions should be treated alike: we should pay attention to the advice of the trained expert, and disregard the views of the many (47a2–d5). Remarkably, Socrates excludes the possibility that the many might have or develop moral expertise. Later in the dialogue, he says that most men will always reject his principle that injustice must never be done (49c10–d5). And if we turn to the *Apology*, we find him telling the jury that ". . . no man will be spared if he genuinely opposes you or any other great number (*plēthos*) and prevents many unjust and illegal things from happening in the city . . ." (31e1–4).[12] Socrates believes that most people are and always will be corrupt. They will advocate injustice in certain circumstances, and they will act unjustly. Since the many are inevitably corrupt, and since the laws of Athens give power to the many, we should expect Socrates to declare himself deeply dissatisfied with his native city. But, mysteriously, he concedes that he has the opposite attitude. For in the *Crito*, the Laws argue that he has been greatly satisfied with the way Athens is governed, and they say that this satisfaction amounts to an implicit agreement to obey the city's orders. Socrates does not protest, as we might have expected he would, that in fact he has been highly critical of rule by the many. Why not? Why does he admit that he is more pleased than any other citizen with the laws of Athens? What was it about those laws that so greatly satisfied him? Why does he prefer the Athenian legal system to any other, in spite of the fact that other cities gave far less power to the many?

I know of no satisfactory treatment of this issue, and in fact there has been little recognition that there is a problem to be solved. Scholars have seized on one passage or another, but they have not tried to see the whole of Socratic politics in focus. Popper calls him a good democrat;[13] Wood and Wood, at the other extreme, consider him an aristocratic partisan.[14] As a third

[12] All translations are my own, unless otherwise indicated. Burnet's edition of Plato's works is used throughout.

[13] *The Open Society and Its Enemies*, Vol. I (hereafter cited as *The Open Society*), pp. 128, 191, 194, 305 n. 53.

[14] *Class Ideology and Ancient Political Theory* (hereafter cited as *Class Ideology*), pp. 95–97. So too Winspear and Silverberg, *Who Was Socrates?* pp. 57, 70–71, 84.

alternative, we might think that Socrates was too apolitical and confused to develop a coherent stance toward Athenian democracy. I will argue, however, that none of these alternatives is correct. The early dialogues, as I read them, portray a cogent and sympathetic critic of his city's political system. Just as Socrates was no simple authoritarian or naive individualist in his attitude toward civil orders, so he was neither entirely opposed nor entirely friendly to Athenian democracy. He valued the extraordinary freedom his native city gave its citizens, though he condemned its egalitarian way of making law.[15]

(D) Are there significant differences between the politics of Socrates and those of Plato's *Republic*? One way of contrasting them is to portray Socrates as an upholder of autonomous choice, Plato as an oppressive authoritarian. According to this picture, Plato wants the state to mold the individual's conception of virtue, whereas Socrates thinks we should discover the proper conception of the virtues on our own. That is why he refuses to tell his interlocutors the answers to the definitional questions he raises, and masks his moral expertise behind an ironic profession of ignorance: he wants us to discover satisfactory definitions for ourselves. Similarly, he refuses to call himself a teacher of virtue because that might lead to false expectations in his listeners. They would consider him a dogmatic purveyor of moral advice, and would fail to realize that Socrates takes himself to be a very different sort of teacher—one who improves his audience by asking questions and challenging them to think for themselves. Since Socrates views himself as a moral expert, the early dialogues are to be read as a dramatic portrayal of the limited role such expertise should play in social life. As Vlastos puts it, ". . . the role of the specialist and the expert," accord-

---

[15] It is sometimes said that Socrates affirmed his loyalty to Athens in the *Crito* because of the city's democratic constitution. Thus Santas, *Socrates*, p. 38; Popper, *The Open Society*, pp. 194, 305 n. 53. I will argue against this interpretation in Chapter VII. According to Socrates, as I understand him, no special legitimacy is conferred upon a statute merely because it has been adopted by a majority. Nor does the *Crito* claim that since Socrates could have tried to change the law if he did not like it, he ought to obey it; so I will argue in Chapter III. For a defense of the view that there is more reason to obey the laws of a democracy than those of an undemocratic country, see P. Singer, *Disobedience and Democracy*.

ing to Socrates, "should be to offer guidance and criticism, to inform and clarify the judgment of the layman, leaving the final decision up to him."[16] The contrast with Plato's philosopher-king could not be greater: the latter accepts power, gives commands, and expects obedience; Socrates, on the other hand, sees no possible value in combining moral expertise with political office, and he therefore withdraws from the legal institutions of his city. He is an apolitical, antiauthoritarian thinker.[17]

I will argue that this approach to the early dialogues should be rejected. Socrates, as I understand him, did not take himself to be a moral expert or a teacher of virtue, in any sense. On the contrary, he thought it a serious possibility that virtue cannot be taught, and his doubts about teachability sustained his satisfaction with Athenian democracy. He had no answers to the definitional questions he asked; in fact, he thought that at best answers were a long way off, and at worst they were beyond the powers of human discovery. But he also believed that if the science of ethics is ever discovered, those few who master it would be entitled to take command, and all others ought to obey. So, on my reading of the early dialogues, the moral authoritarianism of the *Republic* is something Plato inherited from Socrates. In spite of the fact that Socrates was greatly satisfied with the Athenian legal system, and preferred it to Sparta and Crete, the *Republic* describes the sort of state he would have infinitely preferred to all others.

[16] "The Paradox of Socrates," p. 20.

[17] Each part of this interpretation has its adherents, though not everyone who accepts one part is committed to the whole. The view that Socrates has concealed definitions is found in Cornford, *Plato and Parmenides*, p. 245; Versényi, *Socratic Humanism*, p. 118; and Teloh, *The Development of Plato's Metaphysics*, (hereafter cited as *Plato's Metaphysics*), p. 46. For the view that Socrates takes himself to be a teacher, see Teloh, ibid., p. 51; Devereux, "Nature and Teaching in Plato's *Meno*"; Crombie, *An Examination of Plato's Doctrines*, Vol. I, p. 222. Popper, *The Open Society*, p. 306 n. 55, says that Socrates ". . . fought for freedom . . . and died for it." His Socrates is an "anti-authoritarian" (p. 129) who was "betrayed" (p. 194) by Plato. Vlastos, "The Paradox of Socrates," p. 21, says that Socrates' method is the expression of his "vision of human freedom." He also suggests (pp. 12-14) that Socrates hides his views so that his interlocutors will make their own moral discoveries. So too Teloh, ibid., pp. 61-64. Gulley, *The Philosophy of Socrates*, p. 176, takes Socrates to believe that education is a matter of individual encounters, whereas Plato assigns the primary responsibility for education to the state.

2
An inconsistent Socrates?

According to one common interpretation of the *Crito*, the Laws leave no room whatsoever for justified disobedience. Rather, they require "absolute submission," "blind obedience," "strict and complete compliance."[18] The problem for such an interpretation is that it makes Socrates contradict himself. He says that we must never do what is unjust, a point made more forcefully in the *Crito* than anywhere else (49a4–b8). What if a law or an order requires the citizen to perform an act that he correctly believes is unjust? If Socrates is committed to blind obedience, then the act must be done. If he calls upon us never to act unjustly, then the act must not be done. Obviously, a Socrates who will always obey the city, no matter what it commands, is an inconsistent Socrates.

The contradiction can be avoided by a philosopher who believes that somehow or other law and virtue cannot conflict. Such a doctrine might be attractive to Thrasymachus, since he wants to recognize no standard of justice other than the decrees of a particular city.[19] But Socrates is worlds apart from such a position. He thinks there is an objective standard of justice;[20] this means that it is possible for human beings to make mistakes about what is just; and obviously if those who have political power go wrong about justice, they will make defective laws.[21]

---

[18] "Absolute submission" is Grote's phrase (*Plato*, p. 303), "blind obedience" (une obéissance aveugle") Romilly's (*La loi dans la pensée grecque*, p. 130), and "strict and complete compliance" A. E. Taylor's (*Plato*, p. 168).

[19] See *Rep.* 338c1–339b8. Note especially 339b7–8: justice is obedience to the rulers. Socrates immediately forces Thrasymachus to abandon this extreme position. *Tht.* 175c–177d also rejects the doctrine that whatever a city establishes as just really is just for it. For philosophical treatments of Thrasymachus and further references to the philosophical literature, see Irwin, *Plato's Moral Theory*, p. 289 n. 23; Annas, *An Introduction to Plato's Republic*, pp. 34–49, 57–58.

[20] I take it to be an uncontroversial matter that Socrates has an objective conception of ethics. That is, he assumes that there are independent truths about the good, and that we must come to know them if we are to become virtuous. The craft analogy of Plato's early dialogues and the search for definitions presuppose the objectivity of ethics.

[21] The point is well put by Allen, *Socrates and Legal Obligation*, p. 89: "The Biblical injunction that thou shalt not follow a multitude to do evil is one which Socrates would most emphatically have accepted . . . and it is deprived of meaning if what the multitude do, when organized, is by definition good."

The possibility that moral blindness might coincide with political power is for Socrates no merely theoretical possibility. As we have seen, he insists that the democratic majority and the politicians of Athens have no moral expertise. If a law or decree has been adopted by a large popular vote, that does not give Socrates the slightest reason for thinking that it is a good or a just decision. Accordingly, he is the last person in the world who would have been surprised at the existence of unjust legislation and unjust commands in Athens. We should expect his objective conception of ethics and his contempt for the many to lead him to the conclusion that sometimes in a democracy a virtuous man will have to disobey his city's commands. And that is precisely what he does say, in the *Apology*. He assures the jury that if they were to order him to give up his philosophical mission, he would disobey them (29b9–d5). Furthermore, democracies are not the only political systems in which a virtuous citizen might have to defy the state. He reminds his audience that when he was commanded by the Thirty Oligarchs to bring in Leon of Salamis to be executed, he merely walked away, because he thought their order impious and unjust (32c4–e1). Evidently, Socrates was clearheaded enough to see that you cannot be unconditionally committed both to justice and to obedience. He insists that when an order calls upon a citizen to act in a way that conflicts with virtue, he must refuse.

None of this shows, of course, that the *Crito*, like the *Apology*, recognizes the need for disobedience. That issue can only be resolved by an examination of the text. Nonetheless, the evidence of the *Apology* forces the responsible reader to adopt a certain interpretive policy toward the *Crito*. Suppose, when we turn to the speech of the Laws, we find certain ambiguities: certain statements might be taken to mean that disobedience is sometimes justified, or they might also be given a more authoritarian interpretation. Should this occur, we will have good reason to adopt the more permissive reading. If possible, the *Crito* ought to be interpreted in a way that makes it consistent with the *Apology* and the other early Platonic dialogues.[22]

[22] It might be objected that the *Crito*'s apparent authoritarianism is consistent

3
Philosophy banned

It could be argued that in the *Apology* Socrates is not nearly so
defiant of authority as I have made him out to be. Consider his
statement that he would disobey the court were it to order him
to abandon philosophy:

> . . . Suppose you should say to me, "Socrates, for now we
> will not be persuaded by Anytus, but instead we will re-
> lease you—on this condition, however, that you no longer
> spend your time on inquiry or philosophy. But if you should
> be caught doing this, you will die." If, as I say, you were
> to release me on these terms, I would say to you, "I have
> the utmost regard and affection for you, Athenian gentle-
> men, but I will obey the god rather than you, and so long
> as I breathe and am able, I shall not cease from philoso-
> phizing. . . . (29c5–d5)

Socrates is certainly threatening to disobey[23]—but would he be
violating a legal command?[24] If the order to give up philosophy

---

with the authoritarianism of the *Republic*, and that the former work should
therefore be considered a middle dialogue, or at least a transitional work. According to this hypothesis, the *Crito* represents Plato's quarrel with Socrates,
rather than the latter's quarrel with himself; and therefore there is no reason to
try to interpret the speech of the Laws in a way that makes it consistent with
the *Apology*'s tolerance for disobedience. In reply: The *Republic* never suggests
that citizens owe absolute obedience to their city, whatever the merit of its
political leaders. Rather, the *Republic*'s claim is that in a philosophical state,
governed by moral experts, the rulers must always be obeyed. So if the *Crito*
advocates unconditional obedience to the rulers of one's native city, regardless
of the wisdom of those rulers and regardless of the content of their orders, then
it is expounding a political philosophy that is far more authoritarian and morally objectionable than anything we find in the *Republic*. I see no good reason
to read the *Crito* as Plato's move away from Socrates. The common view among
scholars, that this dialogue belongs squarely in the early period, is surely correct. For a useful survey, see Ross, *Plato's Theory of Ideas*, pp. 1–2.

[23] Contrast Woozley, *Law and Obedience*, pp. 44–46. He suggests that Socrates
is merely telling the jury that he will not be persuaded by them. Against this,
see my review, "Plato's *Apology* and *Crito*: Two Recent Studies" (hereafter
cited as "Two Recent Studies"), pp. 658–659.

[24] The issue was raised by Brickhouse and Smith in a paper read to the 1981
Western Division meeting of the American Philosophical Association. ". . . We
show that the jury directive Socrates vows to disobey would have been illegal,
a legal fact which has gone wholly unnoticed in the vast literature on the issue."

is *illegal*, then perhaps our passage tells us less than we had thought.

Two uncontroversial points about Athenian law are relevant at this point.

(A) There was no fixed penalty attached to certain crimes, including those of which Socrates was accused. In such cases, the appropriate form of punishment had to be chosen by the jury. But the jury had to decide on the question of guilt or innocence before it could consider the question of punishment. If the defendant was judged innocent of the charges against him, the court no longer had authority to issue penalties or stipulate conditions for release. Accordingly, Socrates' jurors could not declare him innocent and then order him to refrain from philosophical inquiry. Such an order would have no legal standing.[25]

(B) If an Athenian jury found a defendant guilty as charged, and if punishment was not fixed by law, then the jury had to decide between two penalties; the first was proposed by the prosecutor and the second by the defendant. A jury had no other choice but to decide between these two—it could not invent a third alternative of its own.[26] Accordingly, Socrates' jurors could not have assured him that they would vote him guilty but then release him on easy terms. Had they ignored the proposed penalties of Meletus and Socrates, and voted instead for a ban on philosophy, that ban would have had no legal force.

Armed with these two points, someone might argue that Socrates is not being as defiant as we might have thought. The court is thinking of acquitting him and then restricting his activity, or it is proposing to find him guilty and punish him by banning further inquiry. In either case, the jury's order would be contrary to law. Therefore, when Socrates says that he will obey god rather than the court, he may only mean that he will

---

See *Proceedings and Addresses of the American Philosophical Association* (1981), p. 513. I am grateful to the authors for allowing me to see a copy of their paper. I treat this issue briefly in "Two Recent Studies," pp. 657-658.

[25] For a summary of the legal procedure, see MacDowell, *The Law in Classical Athens*, pp. 247-254.

[26] Ibid., p. 253.

refuse to abide by an illegal order. In that case, he might still subscribe to a doctrine of submission to all *lawful* commands.

But I do not think there is much plausibility to this proposal. Our passage tells us that Socrates "shall not cease from philosophizing" so long as he is alive, and throughout the *Apology* Socrates repeats the point that his practice of cross-examining others is required by god.[27] His commitment to philosophy is therefore so strong that it has to take precedence over any civil command, whether legal or illegal. And we should realize that a legally valid ban on the practice of philosophy would not be an impossibility in democratic Athens. The Assembly would merely have to pass a law, by a simple majority, prohibiting all persons from challenging conventional beliefs in public places. This would be an outrageously vague decree, but Athens had no Supreme Court to strike down broad restrictions on speech. Since Socrates is unconditionally committed to obeying god and practicing philosophy, he would have to violate such a ban on inquiry, despite its legality.

If we need any further assurance on this point, we can find it in a famous passage that occurs later in the *Apology*. Socrates has been found guilty, Meletus has proposed that he be put to death, and now a counter-penalty is in order (36b3-4). Should he propose exile? Socrates says (37c4-e2) that this would have some chance of acceptance. But he nonetheless refuses to recommend it, for if he goes to other cities and continues to ask philosophical questions, he will receive the same treatment Athens is giving him. He can hardly expect other communities to be more tolerant of philosophy than his native city. And so, if he continues to practice philosophy, he will be exiled from one city after another—a life in which he sees no value. But what about proposing exile and then giving up philosophy? Once again, Socrates reminds the jury that this is unacceptable.

> Perhaps someone might say, "Can you not leave us and live in peace and quiet?" On this point it is most difficult of all to persuade some of you. If I say that this is disobeying the god and that for this reason it is impossible to keep

---

[27] See too 28e4-6, 30a5, 30e2-6, 37e5-6.

quiet, you will not be persuaded, but will think I am being ironical. If I go on to say that this happens to be the greatest good for man—to construct arguments every day about virtue and the other things about which you hear me conversing as I examine myself and others—and if I say that an unexamined life is not worth living for man, you will be even less persuaded. (37e3-38a6)

Notice that Socrates would have to give these same arguments were Athens to adopt a legal prohibition on philosophical activity. Obviously, such a decree would be designed to hound Socrates out of the city; and if Athens were to use this legal weapon against him, other cities, which are no more tolerant of criticism, would follow suit. Socrates therefore has no alternative: faced with a law against philosophy, he could not give it up, and he would not leave the city; he is unavoidably committed to disobeying a valid law, if need be.

Still, a sense of puzzlement may remain. Admittedly, Socrates is prepared to disobey even lawful decrees prohibiting philosophy. But why does he express this point by threatening to defy a court order that would in fact be illegal? Doesn't the unlawfulness of that order weaken the force of his statement? I think we can answer this question if we consider a point Socrates makes in the sentence immediately preceding our passage. It reports a statement Anytus had made to the jury: either Socrates should not have been brought to court, or, since he is being tried, there is no alternative to finding him guilty and sentencing him to death (29c1-3). What is important here is the fact that the prosecutors have already announced that they are going to recommend the death penalty, for this must have raised a poignant difficulty for many of the jurors. They are not convinced that Socrates deserves to die; he later says, as we have seen, that exile might be acceptable to them (37c4-5). On the other hand, they really think that Socrates is undesirable, if not downright dangerous, and they wish they could muzzle him in some way. Accordingly, many jurors must have been tempted to vote for acquittal, in the hope that his trial would be enough to scare Socrates into quiescence. But such a strategy would certainly be risky, since nothing could assure the court that the defendant would in fact change his ways. Thus many jurors must have found themselves thinking, "If only we could let Socrates go this time and order him to give up philosophy, on pain of death." Socrates realizes that his audience is ambivalent, but he does not want them to vote for acquittal in the hope that he might stop philosophizing. He wants them to know just what sort of person he is, and so tells them that he is not going to abandon philosophy, no matter what they do. They might as well stop wishing that they had the power to forbid further inquiry, for he would disobey any such order. True, the court's ban on philosophy would be unlawful, but that is not relevant to the point Socrates is making, and he therefore does not even mention the issue of legality.

I suggest that when we read our passage with this background in mind, it makes perfect sense. And I conclude that Socrates was clearheaded enough to see where his uncompromising principles led him. Unwilling to leave Athens, religiously dedicated to a philosophical way of life, he realizes that he would have to disobey any order or decree prohibiting him from examining himself and others.

4

Leon and the Thirty

It will be helpful to take a more careful look at the other case in which Socrates expresses a willingness to disobey a city's orders. In this instance, his defiance is not hypothetical but real. It occurred after the close of the Peloponnesian War, some five years before his trial, when the Spartan general Lysander pressured Athens into adopting a new oligarchic regime.

> . . . When the oligarchy came into being, the Thirty sent for me and four others to come to the Rotunda, and ordered us to bring from Salamis Leon the Salaminian, so that he would be killed. Such orders they gave to many others, since they wanted to spread the blame as widely as possible. However, I then proved, not by talk but by ac-

tion, that—to put it in an uncultivated way—death doesn't mean a thing to me; rather, to do nothing unjust or unholy: that is my whole concern. That government, powerful as it was, didn't scare me into doing anything unjust. When we came out of the Rotunda, the other four went to Salamis and brought in Leon, but I walked away and went home. And perhaps I would have been killed because of this, if the government hadn't been overthrown soon afterwards. (32c4–d8)

The implications of this passage are clear: Socrates was given an order by the government in power, and he disobeyed because he refused to commit an unjust act. Generalizing, we may say that he will not do what is contrary to virtue, even when he has been given a command by the Athenian government. Is there any reasonable objection to drawing this conclusion?

(A) Burnet says: "There is no inconsistency . . . between the attitude of Socrates in the *Crito* and his disobedience to the arbitrary orders of the Thirty some years earlier. . . . The Thirty were a temporary body appointed . . . to revise the laws, and they had no legal authority to do anything except what was necessary to carry out this duty."[28] Evidently, Burnet thinks that according to the *Crito* citizens must obey all laws and all *lawful* commands. Since the order to arrest Leon was *un*lawful, Socrates could consistently disobey it and still subscribe to a highly authoritarian political philosophy.

Whether Burnet is right about the *Crito* is an issue we shall soon discuss at length. Let us see whether he is right about the *Apology*. If we have to decide whether the command to arrest Leon was in fact lawful, we enter a thicket of historical and conceptual questions. Was the authority formally given to the Thirty by the Assembly so broad and vague that they did have some legal basis for arresting and condemning such men as Leon?[29] When a new regime arises through force of arms, is the

---

[28] *Plato's Euthyphro, Apology of Socrates, and Crito*, p. 173.

[29] The facts are summarized in Bury and Meiggs, *A History of Greece*, pp. 318–322; and Sealey, *A History of the Greek City-States*, pp. 379–384. For a list of ancient sources, see Sealey, p. 385 n. 4. For a fuller treatment, see Krentz, *The Thirty at Athens*.

distinction between legal and illegal applicable? If a revolutionary government issues orders that circumvent the legal machinery of the prior constitution, is it in effect creating a new legal system? Fortunately, we need not be led astray by these difficult questions, for what matters to us is the justification Socrates gives in the *Apology* for having disobeyed the Thirty. Did *he* believe that this order was illegal? It would be absurd to answer this question by first deciding whether in fact the order was illegal and then assuming that Socrates would agree with us. We can simply look at the *Apology* and see why he thought disobedience justified in this case. He tells the court that the order of the Thirty was unjust, and says nothing whatever about its legal status.[30] Socrates did not have to worry about the issue of legality, since the injustice of arresting Leon gave him all the reason he needed to disobey. In this passage, the *Apology*, like the *Crito*, upholds the view that one must never commit an unjust act.

If we need any further support for this interpretation, we can find it in the lines that immediately precede our passage. In them (32b1–c4), Socrates reminds his judges that several years before the democracy was overthrown, he had opposed a motion in the Assembly to try ten generals as a group for having failed to pick up the survivors in the battle of Arginusae. Such a collective trial, Socrates says, was unjust and illegal, and that is why he opposed it. The fact that Socrates emphasizes the trial's illegality (he repeats the point twice) makes it all the more significant that he says nothing, in the lines that follow, about the legal status of the Thirty's order to arrest Leon.[31] His silence suggests that he either thinks their order legal, or he does not care to discuss the issue. In either case, the wrongfulness of their command was enough to justify his defiance.[32]

[30] See Santas, *Socrates*, p. 37.

[31] Similarly Woozley, *Law and Obedience*, p. 52; but note the change of direction on pp. 54–55. As Woozley says, p. 52, Xenophon's treatment of this event is significantly different from Plato's: *Mem.* IV iv 3 implies that Socrates disobeyed the Thirty because their order was illegal. Curiously, Burnet cites this passage to support his interpretation of Plato's *Apology*. See his edition, *Plato's Euthyphro, Apology of Socrates, and Crito*, p. 174.

[32] Allen comes to the same conclusion, *Socrates and Legal Obligation*, p. 106.

(B) Woozley says: ". . . while Socrates should have had no difficulty in allowing . . . that . . . an executive order might require a man to do what was unjust, it is perhaps less certain that he would have said the same thing of a *nomos* [law]; and *nomos* is the word used uniformly throughout the *Apology* and the *Crito*. . . . It would have been impossible for Socrates to believe that in disobeying their [the Thirty's] order to bring in a man for summary execution he was disobeying the law."[33]

I agree that the Thirty's order was merely that—an order, and not a law. But Woozley proposes that for Socrates this is a distinction that makes all the difference, and that I cannot accept. We have just seen that Socrates does not challenge the legal authority of the Thirty; he objected to their order because it required an unjust act, not because that government had no right to issue orders. He apparently believed that Leon had done no wrong, and he refused to collaborate in the murder of an innocent person. Now, since Socrates says in the *Apology* that he would never commit an injustice, he surely would have refused to arrest Leon even if such acts had been sanctioned by statute. If what an order calls for is a wrongful killing, then it remains wrongful even if it is required by law. Furthermore, we already know that Socrates is committed to disobeying the law, if need be. As I have argued, he would have violated a law prohibiting philosophical inquiry. Since Socrates believes that lawbreaking is sometimes justified, and since he is committed to avoiding all wrongdoing, he could not have submitted to a law that calls for wrongful killing.

I want to correct one other mistake Woozley makes when he says that ". . . *nomos* [law] is the word used uniformly throughout the *Apology* and the *Crito*. . . ." I take him to be suggesting that the *Crito* is about disobedience to the *law*, rather than obedience to orders, decrees, or any other political decisions that have a lower status than the law.[34] His idea is that although the *Crito* might require blind obedience to the law, it would still leave room for disobeying orders, since it simply does not dis-

---

[33] *Law and Obedience*, p. 54.

[34] For the distinction between a law (*nomos*) and a decree (*psēphisma*), see MacDowell, *The Law in Classical Athens*, pp. 44-45.

cuss this topic; and thus the submissiveness of the *Crito* can be reconciled with defiance of the Thirty. But Woozley is simply wrong to suggest that the *Crito* does not discuss disobedience to orders. Consider the dialogue's statement that the citizen must "either persuade or do what the fatherland commands . . ." (51b3–4). In what way does Athens (or any other city, for that matter) issue commands? Only through its laws? Not at all, since the supreme political power in the city, the Assembly, delegates the right to command to those who occupy various legal offices and fulfill various legal functions. A court, for example, is given the authority to order individuals to submit to certain penalties if they are found guilty of specified offenses. And similarly a general is given the right to issue orders to his subordinates and soldiers. Therefore, when the *Crito* says that citizens must "either persuade or do what the fatherland commands . . . ," it is as much talking about obeying a court or a military officer as it is about obeying a law. This comprehensiveness is explicitly advertised by the text: ". . . one must neither yield nor run away nor leave one's post, but in battle and in court *and everywhere* one must do what the city and fatherland commands, or persuade it as to the nature of justice . . ." (51b7–c1, my emphasis). In this passage, the *Crito* is striving for generality. It wants to say something about every case in which a citizen might disobey the city, and therefore its political philosophy is extended to every situation in which a citizen is given an order by a legal official or body, whether that be the Assembly, a court, a military officer, or a magistrate.[35] So the *Crito* confirms the point I made earlier: for Socrates, the distinction between a law and an order is of little significance. He is interested in the perfectly general question of when a citizen should do that which his city, through its legal institutions and officers, tells him to do.[36]

---

[35] See Santas, *Socrates*, p. 26.

[36] A number of Greek texts suggest or assert that nothing should count as a *nomos* (law) if it conflicts with some higher ethical standard. See *H. Ma.* 284d1–7, and *Minos* 314b8–315a3, 317c1–7. But no such suggestion is made in the *Crito*. Evidently, this dialogue wants to discuss the general question of whether the citizen must do whatever the city commands, and the terminological point that unjust commands cannot be laws would not help decide this matter. Two

(C) When Socrates tells the story of Leon, he calls the Thirty an oligarchy, and he reminds his audience that the regime they replaced was democratic (32c3-4). It might therefore be suggested that he saw nothing wrong with disobeying the Thirty because he thought power should reside in the hands of the many and not the few. But I see no merit in this idea. When Socrates explains why he disobeyed, he only refers to the injustice of the order to arrest Leon. What he objected to in this oligarchy was the way in which it used its power; we have no evidence that he believed thirty to be an unduly small number when it comes to rulers. We saw earlier that according to Socrates the many are unalterably corrupt, and he would therefore have no objection in principle to a sharp reduction in the number of those holding power in Athens. When he disobeys the Thirty, he does so because of the content of their commands, and not because of the oligarchical form of their government.[37]

Later, I will present a more thorough examination of Socrates' attitude toward democracy. For now, I conclude that when he disobeys the Thirty, his reason has nothing to do with the legality of their order; nothing to do with the fact that it was merely an order and not a law; and nothing to do with the fact that they were only thirty in number. Plainly and simply, he disobeyed because their order called upon him to do an unjust act. It is safe to generalize and say that according to the *Apology*

---

further points should be noticed: (A) At 54b8-c1, the *Crito* says that Socrates has not been treated unjustly by any law. It might be suggested that according to this passage no law could possibly do injustice to a citizen (presumably because laws are just by definition). But that interpretation goes well beyond the text: the fact that no law *has* wronged Socrates is compatible with the fact that laws *can* wrong a citizen. (B) It was not a point of general usage, at the time of Socrates, that no law could be unjust. See Ostwald, *Nomos and the Beginnings of the Athenian Democracy*, pp. 37-40; Dover, *Greek Popular Morality*, pp. 306-309.

[37] Contrast Santas, *Socrates*, p. 38. He tentatively suggests that according to Socrates one need obey a ruler only when "ruler" means "properly constituted authority in a democratic regime." As he points out, Socrates says in the *Apology* that he *obeyed* an unpopular law (in the trial of the Arginusae generals) when Athens was *democratically* ruled, but *disobeyed* the rulers after the democracy had been overthrown. See *Ap.* 32c3-4. But this need not be taken to mean that according to Socrates the democratic nature of a government gives us reason to obey it. As we will see in VII.1, there are too many antidemocratic statements in the early dialogues to justify Santas' interpretation.

Socrates will disobey any law or order of any government, if that law or order calls upon him to perform an act he considers unjust.[38] This general principle also stands behind his refusal ever to abandon his role as a moral critic of Athens. To disobey the god's command would have been an act of impiety, according to Socrates, and since impiety is injustice toward the gods

[38] It is sometimes said that according to the *Apology* one must always obey the city unless one has been given a contrary command by a god. Thus Murphy, "Violence and the Socratic Theory of Legal Fidelity," p. 17. However, Socrates never says that his disobedience to the Thirty was divinely sanctioned. I do not think any statement in the *Apology* commits him to the view that political orders can be violated only when divine orders supersede them. However, a philosophy of blind obedience to political orders (in the absence of divine commands to the contrary) might be read into the following two passages:

(A) Wherever someone stations himself, thinking it to be best, or is stationed by a ruler, there he must—as it seems to me—remain and run the danger, taking into account neither death nor anything else, in preference to what is shameful. (28d6-10)

(B) To do an injustice and disobey a superior [*beltion*], whether divine or human: that, I know, is bad and shameful. (29b6-7)

But (A) does not address itself to the crucial issue. What if a ruler orders you to do something that is shameful? Should you obey the authority, even if you believe his orders to be evil? Nothing in (A) or its immediate context answers that question, and we should not press these lines for more than they can deliver. Socrates is merely trying to get across the idea that he will obey the god's command to practice philosophy even if this should result in his death.

What of (B)? These lines seem to assume that a "superior"—whether divine or human—would never require the performance of an unjust act. It is easy to understand why Socrates would say this of a god (see *Ap.* 21b5-7), but how can he say it of a *human* superior? Everything depends on how we take *beltion* ("superior"). If someone is superior merely by being in a position of political power or authority, then Socrates is committing himself to an extremely conservative political doctrine—and he is also contradicting the position he took when he disobeyed the Thirty. After all, they were his "superiors" in the sense that they were his rulers. (See *Ap.* 32d4 and 8: Socrates concedes that the Thirty were the government [*archē*], and so he would have no qualms about calling them his rulers [*archai*].) But a "superior" can mean someone who is more virtuous (*Protag.* 320b3, cf. *ameinon* at *Ap.* 30d1), and surely that is what Socrates means here. He will always obey someone who is at a higher moral stage than the one that he has reached, for he assumes that such a person will never give orders that are contrary to justice. (Woozley, *Law and Obedience*, p. 49, also adopts this interpretation.) I think this doctrine does have authoritarian implications, which will be explored later (VII.4, 8). Socrates is committed to obeying moral experts, if there are any, but that does not in any way commit him to obeying each and every political order of a government in power. For a different treatment of (A) and (B), see Santas, *Socrates*, pp. 33-40. I briefly discuss his interpretation of (B) in "Two Recent Studies," pp. 654-655.

(*Euphr.* 12c10–d4), giving up a philosophical life would have been an act of injustice. Socrates insists upon doing what is just, according to his understanding of justice, and he clearly recognizes that such an attitude can lead to trouble with the law. Our two examples of defiance in the *Apology* show us that Socrates did in fact draw the conclusion we would in any case have expected of him: since he will always do what he believes to be just, and since his city's conception of justice will not always match his own, he will sometimes have to disobey.

If Socrates is clearheaded enough in the *Apology* to recognize that political orders can conflict with virtue, we should expect comparable lucidity in the *Crito*. Since he applauds the speech of the Laws, he presumably interprets it in a way that leaves room for his principle that one must never act unjustly. So we too ought to look for parts of that speech that open the door to justified disobedience. And once we find them, we must see how they can be integrated into the rest of the speech to form a consistent theory.

II

JUSTICE, AGREEMENT, AND DESTRUCTION

1
The principle of justice

WE WILL BEGIN our examination of the *Crito* somewhat before the Laws enter the conversation. Crito has completed his case against submitting to the death penalty, and Socrates is preparing the way for a reply. He criticizes his friend for being too concerned with the opinions of the many: the important question is whether escape would be just or unjust, not what people will think of them if Socrates remains in jail and dies (46b1–49b6). We then find Socrates putting together a series of principles to which Crito quickly assents:

(A) One must never do injustice (*adikein*).[1] (49b8)
Corollary: Even if one is treated unjustly, one must not do injustice in return. (49b10-11)

---

[1] Throughout this study, I follow the common practice of using "to do injustice" for *adikein*, and "just" for *dikaios*. Since "to do injustice" is often a narrower notion than *adikein*, some translators (e.g. Grube and Tredennick) use "to do wrong" instead of "to do injustice." (Translations are included in the Bibliography, under the translator's name.) However, I stick to the more conventional translation for two reasons: (A) At 49e6, Socrates asks, "Should the things one agrees upon with another be done, if they are *dikaia* . . .?" Here there is no better alternative to translating *dikaia* with "just," and every translation I have consulted does so. But then, if we translate *dikaia* at 49e6 with "just," we ought to use "to do injustice" for *adikein* at 49b8, since we thereby mirror the close relationship between the two Greek terms. (B) I want to use "to do wrong" for *kakourgein* at 49c2, for reasons to be explained in the next note. It would be misleading, then, to use "to do wrong" for *adikein* as well.

(B) One must not do wrong (*kakourgein*).[2] (49c2-3)
Corollary: One must not do wrong in return for wrong-doing. (49c4-6)

(C) Treating people wrongly (*kakōs poiein anthrōpous*) does not differ from doing injustice.[3] (49c7-9)

Crito is reminded that (A), (B), and their corollaries are scorned by the many, and though he has frequently accepted them in

---

[2] *Kakourgein* is frequently translated "to injure," "do injury," "work injury," etc. (thus Grube, Tredennick, and Allen), and in certain contexts this is preferable to my "do wrong." For example, at *Rep.* 416a6, Plato says that sheepdogs should not be bred so as *kakourgein* the sheep, as wolves do. Obviously, "to injure" is better here than "to do wrong." But I am convinced that in this part of the *Crito* a great deal of damage has been done by using "to injure" for *kakourgein*. For as Allen, *Socrates and Legal Obligation*, p. 76, points out: "The notion of injury has eroded in English to the point where it is often used very nearly as a synonym for damage or harm. . . ." Now, if we translate *kakourgein* by "do injury" and take "injury" to be equivalent to "damage" or "harm," then Socrates will be taken by many readers to be opposed to any act of damage or harm to a person or city. But it is quite clear that Socrates has no such view, if we take "damage" or "harm" in the common way. He knows as well as we do that wars do physical damage and harm to human beings and cities, but he is not unconditionally opposed to war. Furthermore, Socrates claims in the *Crito* that to do violence against one's parents is always *kakourgein*, whereas to do violence against others is not always *kakourgein*. If we substitute "to injure" or "to harm" for *kakourgein* in this claim, it becomes: "to do violence against one's parents is always to injure (or harm) them, whereas to do violence against others is not always to injure (or harm) them." This is a confusing way of putting Socrates' point into English. But if "to wrong" is substituted for *kakourgein*, the resulting statement is perfectly straightforward. So, when Socrates says at 49c2-3 that one must never *kakourgein*, he is saying something much closer to "one must never do wrong" than to "one must never do harm, injury, or damage." He is willing to do physical harm in order to defend his city, but he will never do anything that he considers wrong, even in defense of his city. See n. 28 for further discussion. The Socratic paradox (*Ap.* 30c9-d1) that a good man cannot be harmed (*blaptesthai*) is discussed in n. 21. Socrates does not hold the absurd view that a good man cannot be the victim of injustice (*adikia*) or wrongdoing (*kakourgia*). So when he says that a good man cannot be harmed (*blaptesthai*), he is using that Greek term in a special way. Elsewhere, as at *H. Mi.* 372d5, *blaptein* and *adikein* are used interchangeably.

[3] *Kakōs* by itself does not mean "wrongly," but in combination with *poiein* and a direct object (*anthrōpous*, *tinas*) it must mean "treat wrongly." See Liddell and Scott, *A Greek-English Lexicon*, s.v. *kakos* (D). "Treat badly" (Woozley), "do ill" (Allen), "do evil" (Church) are acceptable alternatives; Grube has "injure," which I want to avoid, for reasons given in the preceding note. Whenever the *Crito* talks about *kakōs poiein* (49c7, 49c10-11, 50a1), it always assumes that there will be a victim of such behavior (*anthrōpous* at 49c7 and c11, *tinas* at 50a1).

the past, he must reject them now if they do not represent his honest convictions (49c11-e3).[4] But he accepts them once again and the conversation continues. Before we move on, let us make some elementary observations.

First, Socrates is putting us on notice that for the purposes of his argument, three Greek terms are going to be used interchangeably: *adikein, kakourgein,* and *kakōs poiein.* A different sort of philosopher—Prodicus, for example—might have devoted a good deal of attention to the differences between these terms, but Socrates and the Laws are uninterested in such linguistic subtleties.[5] In the text that begins at 49a and stretches to the end of the dialogue, they move back and forth freely among these three expressions. Thus, at 49e9-50a1, Socrates asks Crito whether they would be *treating* anyone *wrongly* (*kakōs poioumen*) by escaping, but his question is never answered precisely in those terms. Rather, it is affirmatively answered several pages later (51e5) when the Laws claim that escape would accomplish a threefold *injustice.* They could equally well have said that escape would *treat* the city *wrongly* in three ways. And at the close of the dialogue (54c2-3), the Laws reaffirm their belief that an escaping Socrates would be returning injustice for injustice (*antidikēsas*) and doing wrong in return for wrongdoing (*antika-*

---

[4] Allen, *Socrates and Legal Obligation*, p. 76, says: "It is easy to read the proposition that one ought never to do injustice or wrong as tautological: one ought to do what one ought to do." He goes on (pp. 76-81) to argue that for Socrates it is no tautology, since for him it is "equivalent to the principle that one ought never so act as to diminish human excellence in oneself or in another . . ." (p. 81). It should be pointed out, however, that *no one* in classical Athens would have treated "one must never do injustice (*adikein*)" as a tautological equivalent of "one ought to do what one ought to do." Otherwise, Socrates could never say, as he does at 49c10-d5, that principle (A) is highly controversial. The Greeks could agree to a large extent about which acts to count as unjust. For example, there would have been widespread agreement that the killings undertaken by Archelaus (see *Grg.* 471a4-d2) were unjust. But as the *Gorgias* and *Republic* Bk. II indicate, many contemporaries of Socrates were inclined to say that it would be reasonable to commit such acts if one could get away with them. Socrates has no such inclination, as principle (A) shows.

[5] Prodicus' interest in shades of meaning is parodied at *Protag.* 337a1-c4. Cf. 358a6-b1. When Socrates describes himself as a pupil of Prodicus (*Protag.* 341a4, *Meno* 96d5-7), I take him to be speaking ironically. So too Bluck, *Plato's Meno,* pp. 400-401; Burnyeat, "Socratic Midwifery, Platonic Inspiration," p. 15 n. 9. By contrast, Guthrie, *History,* Vol. III, p. 276, thinks that Socrates is sincerely acknowledging a debt of gratitude to Prodicus.

kourgēsas). But they have given no separate argument for their claim that Socrates would be doing wrong (*kakourgein*). They simply assume that their argument for the injustice of escape serves equally well to show that to escape is to do wrong.[6] Committing one fault—*adikein, kakourgein, kakōs tinas poiein*—is committing them all.[7]

Second, we should be aware of the direction in which the *Crito*'s argument is heading. The Laws are going to concede that Socrates has been unjustly treated and wronged by Athens (50c1-6, 54c2-3). But if he wants to abide by the corollaries of (A) and (B), he cannot use this as a reason for doing injustice or wrong in return. Once the Laws prove that escape would be unjust, their argument can come to an end; they do not have to consider the objection that Athens deserves injustice from Socrates because of the injustice it has done to him.

Third, we should realize that (A), (B), and (C) are only intended to lay the groundwork for the arguments yet to come. Socrates merely asks Crito whether "we shall *begin* our deliberation with this point: it is never right to do injustice, or to do injustice in return, or to react to wrongful treatment with further wrongful actions . . .?" (49d6-9, my emphasis). It would be a mistake, therefore, to think that after Socrates puts forward (A), (B), and (C), he has already given one argument against escape. We must not take him to be reasoning in the following way:[8]

(i) One must not respond to injustice with further injustice.

(ii) Socrates has been treated unjustly.

(iii) If Socrates escapes, he will be responding to injustice with further injustice.

(iv) Socrates must not escape.

---

[6] *H. Mi.* 375d1-4 is another text in which *adikein* and *kakourgein* are used interchangeably.

[7] As we will see later (n. 31), the Laws are justified in moving back and forth between these terms.

[8] This interpretation is put forward by Murphy, "Violence and the Socratic Theory of Legal Fidelity," pp. 22-23.

Premise (iii) of course is question-begging, since it assumes with no argument that escape would be unjust. But, fortunately, nothing in the text suggests that Socrates is making such an outrageous mistake so early in the game. Statements (A), (B), and (C) are clearly meant to form the beginning of an argument, and they should not be expected to deliver more than they can.

2
The principle of just agreements

After Crito accepts the controversial proposition that injustice must never be done (49e4), Socrates immediately raises a new question: ". . . Should the things one agrees upon with another be done, if they are just, or should one be deceptive?" (49e6-7). Crito replies that one should honor such agreements, and the conversation continues. But we ought to linger over this new idea, since it contains more complexity than might be realized. Changing Socrates' question into a declarative statement, we get:

> *The principle of just agreements*: One must do the things one agrees upon with another, if they are just.

I assume that these last four words are doing some work: Socrates could not mean that one must abide by just and unjust agreements alike. He has just finished saying that we must never do what is unjust, regardless of the circumstances, and so he presumably means that what one has agreed to do must not be done if it involves doing injustice. For example, suppose the other four who were sent to arrest Leon had in fact agreed to follow the orders of the Thirty. The principle of just agreements implies that they are still wrong to collaborate in the murder of Leon, in spite of their agreement. Apparently, then, the principle has to be interpreted as follows:

> (A) If the things one agrees upon with another are *just*, one must do them.

(B) If the things one agrees upon with another are *unjust*, one must *not* do them.

I think (A) and (B) come close to capturing the *Crito*'s meaning, but because of a statement made later by the Laws, they require a slight modification.

To see this, imagine that someone has made an agreement to perform an act that happens to be entirely unobjectionable. Is the *Crito* saying that the act must be performed, regardless of the circumstances in which the agreement was made? Definitely not. For when the Laws later argue that Socrates implicitly agreed to obey the city, they claim that this was not the sort of agreement that can be set aside:

> Are you doing anything . . . but transgressing the compacts [*sunthēkas*] and agreements [*homologias*] that concern us? You did not agree out of compulsion nor were you tricked or forced to decide in a short time. Rather, you had seventy years in which you could have gone away, if we did not satisfy you and the agreements did not seem just to you. (52d8-e5)

This passage tells us that agreements can be broken under three conditions: when the individual is compelled, tricked, or rushed into giving his assent. And it implies that if any of these three conditions holds, then the agreement is unjust; "unfair" or "dishonest" (common alternatives to "unjust" as translations of *adikos*) would come close to the *Crito*'s meaning at this point. If the Laws want to build their case against escape on the principle of just agreements, then they cannot merely argue that Socrates made agreements to obey the city; they also have to show that those agreements were just. And that is precisely what they are trying to do in the above passage.[9] Of course,

[9] If 52d8-e5 is not the passage in which the Laws affirm the justice of Socrates' agreement, then what is?

(A) Santas, *Socrates*, pp. 21-25, claims that the Laws argue as follows: Athens has benefited Socrates as parents benefit their children; it is just that a child obey his parents if he cannot persuade them; therefore, it is just that Socrates obey Athens, if he cannot persuade it; therefore, what Socrates agreed to do—namely, to abide by the verdicts of the courts—is just. The problem with this analysis of the *Crito* is that it commits Socrates to obeying every order he

the Laws are not saying that all agreements fairly made must be honored, even those which require the doing of injustice. Had that been their meaning, Socrates would never have applauded their speech. The Laws are taking it for granted that in condemning Socrates to death, Athens was not calling upon Socrates to do anything unjust.[10] Therefore, in agreeing to obey the city and abide by the judgments of the courts, Socrates was not agreeing to perform an unjust act. If he wants to show that his agreement was unjust and therefore void, he will have to argue that it was made in unfair circumstances. And that is a line of argument the Laws are at this point closing off.

We are now in a position to see why (A) and (B) are not quite adequate:

(A) If the things one agrees upon with another are *just*, one must do them.

---

receives from Athens, whatever that order requires. See my review, "Two Recent Studies," pp. 652-653, for more discussion. As we will see later in this chapter and in Chapter IV, the parent-city analogy is not designed to show that Socrates' agreement with the city was just. Rather, it is meant to show why it is wrong for Socrates to act violently against Athens. The Laws do not get around to supporting their claim that Socrates made an agreement until 51d1; and their argument for that conclusion stretches to 53a7. So it is hardly surprising to find their argument for the justice of Socrates' agreement within these later lines—not in the earlier analogy between offspring and citizens.

(B) Woozley, *Law and Obedience*, p. 104, says: "If the laws are technically begging the question, in that they have not argued for the proposition that what he has agreed to do in agreeing to obey the laws is just, it might be said that, by the persuade-or-obey doctrine, and by the claim that the laws are reasonable rather than despotic in their requirements, they are paying sufficient attention to it and therefore need not actually mention it." The persuade-or-obey doctrine is simply the claim that Socrates must persuade the city or obey it; for further discussion, see Chapter III. For now, we need only observe that there is no obvious and plausible way of going from (i) "Socrates must persuade or obey" to (ii) "The agreement Socrates made to obey the city was just." By contrast, there is an obvious connection between (ii) and (iii) "Socrates was not forced, rushed, or tricked into agreement."

[10] Contrast, Woozley, *Law and Obedience*, pp. 23-25, 57-58. He says, "If the death sentence on Socrates was unjust, and as the method of execution was by self-administration, it is not far-fetched to say that he would be acting unjustly to himself in carrying it out" (p. 58). But surely *Socrates* does not think he would be acting unjustly (to himself or anyone else) by drinking the hemlock. The fact that the verdict against him was unjust does not entail that he is acting unjustly in accepting his punishment.

(B) If the things one agrees upon with another are *unjust*, one must *not* do them.

The trouble with these formulations is that they ignore the fact that "the things one agrees upon" can be unjust in two very different ways. First, the act agreed upon can be unjust; second, the agreement can be unjustly made.[11] In the former case, the act *must* not be done; in the latter, it *need* not be done. To take account of this ambiguity, our interpretation of the principle of just agreements must be set out as follows:

(C) If the act one agrees upon is *unjust*, then, regardless of the circumstances in which the agreement was made, one *must not* honor the agreement.

(D) If the act one agrees upon is *not unjust*, but the circumstances of the agreement are unjust (coercive, dishonest, or rushed), then one *need not* honor the agreement.

(E) If the act one agrees upon is *just*, and if the circumstances of the agreement are *just* (noncoercive, honest, and unrushed), then one *must* honor the agreement.[12]

---

[11] Allen, *Socrates and Legal Obligation*, p. 72, thinks there is no significant ambiguity: "it may be claimed that the premise is ambiguous: is it that one must do what he agreed if the agreement is just? Or that one must do what he agreed if to do so is just? But the two elements in the ambiguity are equivalent, since each implies the other: an agreement cannot be just if, in a given situation, to act according to it is not to act justly." This overlooks the point that an agreement can be unjust (i.e. unfairly made) even when the act agreed upon is just.

[12] There are two ways of reading principle (E):
(i) If the act one agrees upon is *permitted* by justice. . . then one must honor the agreement.
(ii) If the act one agrees upon is *required* by justice . . . then one must honor the agreement.
Young, "Socrates and Obedience," p. 10, opts for (i): "if it meant the latter, there would be no need for the agreement: one should do what is required, whether one has agreed to do it or not." Now, if required acts are a subclass of permitted acts, then in opting for (i), Young has not succeeded in eliminating (ii). What he wants to say is that the principle of just agreements must mean:
(iii) If the act one agrees upon is permitted but not required by justice . . . then one must honor the agreement.
But I find it implausible to think that Socrates means this. Consider an example. Suppose Antigone has voluntarily promised Oedipus that she will be his guide and helper, and suppose that this was in any case what justice required of her. Would Socrates say that Antigone's promise gives her no *additional* reason to help Oedipus? Surely it does, and Socrates has no interest in denying this ob-

This is admittedly more complex than the simple statement we derived from Socrates' question at 49e6–7: one must do the things one agrees upon with another, if they are just. But I am not claiming that (C), (D), and (E) can be derived by staring at the words of this simple statement. Rather, I am saying that this statement must be interpreted both in the light of what Socrates tells us just prior to 49e6–7, and in the light of what the Laws say later, at 52d8–e5. When Socrates says that we must never do what is unjust, he commits himself to (C). When the Laws say that the agreement Socrates made was uncoerced, honest, and unrushed, they imply their belief in (D). But obviously (C) and (D) do not by themselves exhaust the principle of just agreements. To complete the idea implicit in this principle, we have to add (E). These three statements represent an attitude toward agreements that is shared by both Socrates and the Laws.[13]

---

vious point. So we ought to take (E) to mean:

> (iv) If the act one agrees upon is *permitted or required by* justice . . . then one must honor the agreement.

Equipped with (iv), Socrates could argue that if Antigone fails to help Oedipus, then she is to be blamed for two independent reasons: she has failed to do what justice requires of children in their relationship to their parents, and she has failed to abide by a just agreement. The mere fact that he could criticize a delinquent Antigone without (iv) does not make it otiose. Notice that the Antigone example is pertinent to the *Crito*: the Laws (as I shall argue) think that escape is wrong, even apart from any agreement that Socrates made, and in this sense the principle of just agreements is redundant. But they believe that escape would be blameworthy in more ways than one, and so they argue that it violates the principle of just agreements.

[13] Woozley, *Law and Obedience*, pp. 23–27, 57, also finds an ambiguity in the principle of just agreements, but of a different sort. He distinguishes:

> "(1) a man should keep his agreement to do x (where x is what he has agreed to do), provided that doing x is right.
> (2) a man should keep his agreement to do x, provided that what he has agreed to do in agreeing to do x is right." (p. 24)

And he then goes on to explain (2) in a way that makes it equivalent to my (C). But he argues that (1) is the preferable reading, and takes (1) to fit into the pattern of the *Crito*'s argument in the following way: obeying the law is right; Socrates agreed to obey the law; so what Socrates agreed to do is always right; and therefore (by virtue of [1]) he should keep the agreement. As Woozley puts it (p. 25), "in (1), he is incurring his duty of obedience to the law by a blank cheque. . . ." But precisely for that reason, his interpretation of the principle of just agreements should be rejected. As the case of Leon shows, Socrates refuses to obey orders when the act required of him is unjust. The principle of just agreements must be and can be read so as to license such disobedience. That is, agreeing to commit unjust acts would not be a justification for performing them.

3

The testimony of Hyperides

Hyperides, in his speech *Against Athenogenes*, cites four statutes to support the thesis that according to law a contract is binding if and only if it is just (3.13–17). We might infer from this that Socrates' principle of just agreements was at some point embodied in Athenian law. But if we look at the four examples that Hyperides gives, it becomes obvious that nothing so broad as this principle was ever spelled out in so many words by a statute. For example, he cites a law that "allows a man to bequeath his property as he wishes unless he is affected by old age, illness, or insanity, and provided he is not influenced by a woman or imprisonment or otherwise coerced."[14] Evidently, Hyperides is assuming that when property is bequeathed through trickery or force, an unjust agreement has been made; and he moves from this and his three other examples to the conclusion that it is the general intention of the law to invalidate all agreements made in unfair circumstances.[15] His inference is arguable, and we do not know whether he succeeded in persuading the jury. Fortunately we do not have to resolve that question. What is important for our purpose is the ease with which a Greek speaker could go from "the agreement was reached through force or trickery" to "the agreement was unjust." *Against Athenogenes* was composed between 330 and 324, and it therefore postdates the *Crito* by some sixty or seventy years. But it nonetheless gives additional credibility to my claim that the Laws are upholding the justice of Socrates' agreement when they say

[14] See 3.17. This speech is included in *Minor Attic Orators*, Vol. II, trans. J. O. Burtt. (I have used his translation of the passage just cited.) Demosthenes 46.14 refers to the same law.

[15] A different interpretation of the case can be found in MacDowell, *The Law in Classical Athens*, p. 140. He says, "There was a law saying that any agreement made voluntarily by one man with another before witnesses was valid, *provided that the thing agreed was not unjust*" (my emphasis). But the passages he cites (Hyperides 3.13; Demosthenes 42.12, 47.77, 56.2; Dinarchus 3.4; Plato *Symp.* 196c) do not show that any law spelled out the proviso I have emphasized. Hyperides wants the jury to accept the proviso, but he argues in a way that suggests that no such clause was ever spelled out in law. My reading of Hyperides coincides with that of Sorabji, *Necessity, Cause, and Blame*, p. 262 n. 9.

that it was uncoerced, honest, and unrushed. This speech of Hyperides shows us that a speaker in the lawcourts could expect his audience to perceive a connection between the justice of a contract and the conditions under which it was made. It is not implausible to assume that the Laws have this same connection in mind.

4

Agreements and unjust treatment

I now want to skip ahead briefly and discuss an interchange that occurs at 50c1-6. Just prior to this passage, the Laws argue that if Socrates tries to escape, he will have committed a destructive act against Athens. And then, at 50c1-2, Socrates asks Crito to consider a rejoinder to this accusation. "Shall we say to them, 'The city treated us unjustly and wrongly rendered judgment?' " Crito enthusiastically endorses this reply, but Socrates indicates that it will get them nowhere. "What if the Laws say, 'Are these the things that were agreed between you and us—or was it to abide by the judgments that the city decided upon?' " (50c4-6). Now, someone might think that Socrates is too impressed with this point. After all, even if he did, as the Laws say, make an agreement to accept the judgments of the courts, that agreement will cut no ice if in fact it was unjust. And why shouldn't we count an agreement as unjust whenever it calls upon the person who made it to suffer an injustice? It might seem that Socrates and the Laws have no plausible way to resist this suggestion.

But in fact they do. They can say that when someone freely makes an agreement, realizing that it calls upon him to suffer an injustice, then he has no right to go back on his word at a later point, when it comes time to honor his commitment.[16]

---

[16] Suppose a club I belong to is deciding where to hold its meetings next year. Site X is the leading candidate, but I think this an unfair choice, since it makes me travel far more than anyone else. Nonetheless, I voluntarily agree to go along with this, and voice no objections. Having made this agreement, I cannot justifiably break it on the grounds that the rule I agreed to is unfair to me. (Suppose at the time of the meeting I don't believe—though I have full information and plenty of time—that the rule is unfair to me. If I change my

*agreement → must abide by unjust decisions against me
but not decisions requiring me to act unjustly*

Furthermore, we sometimes voluntarily agree to abide by the
unforeseeable results of judicial procedures, with the full understanding that the outcome of those procedures might treat
us unjustly. Socrates has sense enough to realize that if he agrees
to abide by the judgments of the courts, then he is agreeing to
accept those judgments that are unfavorable to him. If he is
unwilling to suffer injustice from the courts, then he should not
have made the agreement in the first place; if he made the agreement with full knowledge of what he was getting himself into,
then he cannot fairly back out of it now. So the Laws are not
stipulating that voluntary agreements remain just even when they
call upon the contracting party to suffer injustice. It is the voluntariness of such agreements that enables them to back up this
thesis.

Someone other than Socrates might want to take this line of
reasoning a step further: it might be said that voluntary agreements are binding even when they call upon someone to *do*
injustice. After all, if you are not willing to act unjustly, then
you ought not to have made the agreement; having freely made
it, you must now deliver. But Socrates cannot go to this extreme. He insists that one must never do injustice under any
circumstances, and he must therefore say that if a contract commits you to acting unjustly, you must break it. The *Crito* is
moderate in the amount of respect it shows for voluntary agreements. It insists that people keep their word, if freely given,
even to the point of suffering injustice, but not to the point of
doing injustice.

It is often said that, according to Socrates and the Laws, citizens must accept every injustice that their city chooses to impose on them.[17] Whether this interpretation is correct is a mat-

mind after the meeting is over, that still does not give me a reason to break the
rule. See too VI.11 below.) Of course, agreements can be broken justifiably
when new information comes to light: if I agree to play three games of chess
with Jones, and he keeps trying to cheat during the first game, I can legitimately
break off the match, rather than continue to be the victim of unjust treatment.
For I didn't consent to play under those conditions.

[17] Of course, this interpretation is accepted by everyone who takes the *Crito*
to be advocating absolute submission to all orders. (See Ch. I n. 3.) But even
those who think that the Laws leave some room for disobedience say that,
according to the *Crito*, disobedience is never justified by the mere fact that an

ter we shall investigate at a later point. The crucial question will be this: does the *Crito* claim that all citizens who continue to reside in a city thereby agree voluntarily to obey all the laws and orders of their government? If they necessarily make such a sweeping commitment, then they cannot disobey a law because of the injustice it makes them suffer. But if citizens can legitimately reside in a city without thereby agreeing to all of its laws, then the grounds for justified disobedience might be wider. The *Crito* might concede that if a citizen has not agreed to a certain law, then he can point to the injustice he suffers from that law as a legitimate ground for disobedience. Of course, it is far too soon to tell whether the Laws give the citizen quite that much latitude; at this point, we do not even know whether their speech leaves room for any disobedience at all. For now, I only make the cautionary remark that although Socrates has agreed to abide by the judgments of the courts, this does not in itself show that he has agreed to abide by every law the city adopts and every order it issues. And even if Socrates did make this sweeping commitment, it does not follow that citizens have no choice but to make such an agreement if they continue to reside in a city. Thus far, we know only that Socrates agreed to abide by the judgments of the courts, and this commits him to accepting unfavorable verdicts. Before we look carefully at the text, we shold refrain from drawing the conclusion that, according to the *Crito*, citizens can never object to or break a law that treats them unjustly.

Nothing in the early dialogues of Plato entails that we should be completely indifferent to unjust treatment. Of course, Socrates says that it is far worse for a person to act unjustly than

order does the citizen an injustice. E. Barker, *Greek Political Theory*, p. 123, says: ". . . the gist of the *Apology* and *Crito* comes to this: 'Obey the law, and obey it cheerfully, where a material interest is at stake: otherwise you are a disobedient son and a faithless partner. Disobey it only, and disobey it even then in anguish, when a supreme spiritual question is at issue.' " I take this to mean that disobedience is justified if and only if the state calls upon the citizen to commit an act of injustice. The same interpretation can be found in Allen, *Socrates and Legal Obligation*, p. 109; Wade, "In Defense of Socrates," p. 324; and Santas, *Socrates*, p. 26. In fact, I have not been able to find a single writer who takes the *Crito* to allow the avoidance of unjust treatment as a legitimate ground for disobedience.

doing harm is always worse

to suffer unjust treatment; doing what is unjust harms one's soul, but the soul is not corrupted if one is the victim of injustice.[18] But none of this implies that a rational person will take no steps to avoid injury. Socrates never suggests, for example, that we should seek no medical advice to ward off disease.[19] Now, if it is rational to resist disease, then it must also be rational to defend oneself in legitimate ways against the unjustified attacks of other human beings.[20] And if evil men happen to have political power and adopt laws that treat the citizens unjustly, why should those citizens agree to those laws? And if they do not agree to them, why should they obey them? The early dialogues, aside from the *Crito*, give Socrates no reason to accept a philosophy of passive submission to injustice.[21] If we recall the case of Leon, we can see how paradoxical such a

[18] See *Grg.* 469b8–c2, 477b1–479a3, 508a8–e6, 509c6–7, 512a2–b2.

[19] On the contrary, he says that life is not worth living if one's body is ruined (*Crito* 47d7–e5, *Grg.* 512a2–5). So it is obviously rational to seek expert medical advice, as Socrates points out at *Crito* 47a13–c7.

[20] See *Grg.* 469b8–c2: although doing injustice is worse than suffering it, it does not follow that Socrates has no objection to the latter. In fact, 469b3–6 suggests that someone who is unjustly killed is to be pitied. At 509c8–d6 and 510a6–e2, Socrates shows interest in the question of how best to avoid becoming the victim of injustice. Notice that at 509c6–7 he calls suffering injustice an evil.

[21] There are, however, several passages that might seem to suggest such a philosophy.

(A) Socrates believes that a good man cannot be harmed (*Ap.* 30c9–d1, 41d1–2), and this might be taken to mean that a good man has no reason to resist unjust treatment. Why should he, if no injustice can harm him? To this there are two replies: (1) The doctrine that a good man cannot be harmed should be interpreted in a way that makes it consistent with the claim that life is not worth living when one's body is ruined (*Crito* 47d7–e5; *Grg.* 512a2–5). Socrates must mean that so long as a person is virtuous he is well off and happy (*Grg.* 470e4–11, 507c3–5; *Crito* 48b8–9; *Rep.* 353e10–354a11; *Euthyd.* 280a6–8, 282c8–d1), but that one can no longer be virtuous if one's body is ruined. Presumably the idea is that virtue requires such activities as discussion and self-examination (*Ap.* 38a1–8) and certain physical afflictions block these activities. If this is what Socrates believes, then he will resist (by virtuous means) those injustices that might prevent him from leading a virtuous life. Notice that in the *Apology* Socrates refuses to suggest permanent imprisonment as a counter-penalty, because he knows that this would be an evil (37b7–c2). Presumably he is assuming that the prison authorities would prevent him from holding moral conversations with his friends. (He explicitly says, at 37c1–2, that he would be a slave to these officials.) So Socrates here seeks to avoid an injustice that would pre-

philosophy would have to be. Socrates refused to arrest Leon because he would not do an injustice. But *Leon* would not have acted unjustly had he voluntarily come forward and appeared before the Thirty. Can the *Crito* mean that since he would merely have been the victim of injustice, he and every citizen similarly summoned were obliged to appear? Can the Laws or anyone else seriously believe that it is both wrong for Socrates to arrest Leon and wrong for Leon to stay away?

I raise such questions only to caution the reader. We should realize how radically authoritarian Socrates is, if he believes that individuals must accept whatever injustice the state does. Before we attribute such a doctrine to the *Crito*, we must take a hard look at the evidence. That is a problem we shall turn to in Chapter VI.

---

vent him from leading the life of a virtuous man. At 38b1-2, he says that a financial penalty would not harm him: supported by his friends, he would still be able to engage in moral discussion. (2) Socrates can plausibly argue that the virtuous have reason to avoid even those injustices and physical injuries that do leave intact their capacity to engage in moral inquiry. Such injustices and injuries would not count as evils, in the sense that a virtuous individual who experiences them would still continue to live happily (*eudaimonein*) and fare well (*eu prattein*). But it does not follow that a good person is rationally required to be indifferent to such injuries. If someone carelessly drops a book and injures his foot, the good person is not thereby deprived of happiness, and in this sense his injury is no evil; but surely he has reason to be more cautious.

(B) Two passages in the *Gorgias* might be taken to counsel indifference to injustice and physical threats: ". . . A true human being should forget about how long he will live, and should not love life, but should entrust these matters to god. . . . He should examine the question how best to live the stretch of life he shall have . . ." (512e1-5). ". . . Forget about someone who despises you as a fool and who slings mud at you, if he so chooses; by Zeus, confidently forget about someone who strikes you with a humiliating blow. You will suffer nothing dreadful [*deinos*] if you really are an admirably fine man [*kalos kagathos*] who practices virtue" (527c7-d2). Socrates might mean that one should let diseases take their course, and never go to a doctor; he might mean that one should never lift a finger in self-defense. But what he says elsewhere speaks strongly against such a reading. The *Crito* (47a13-e4) and the *Gorgias* (467e4-6, 517d6-518a5) show due regard for medical advice and health, and Socrates could hardly have survived in battle had he lived a philosophy of nonresistance to physical threats. When he counsels Callicles to forget about (*eaein*) longevity and injustice, he must be taken to mean that such matters are unimportant in comparison with virtue. Survival and the avoidance of unjust treatment should never become dominant goals; but it is implausible to take Socrates to be saying that we should be utterly indifferent to them. The passages cited in the previous footnote argue decisively against such a reading.

5

Enter the Laws

At 49e8, Crito accepts the principle of just agreements, just as he had earlier agreed to the principles that prohibit injustice and wrongdoing. Then, at 49e9-50a3, Socrates applies these rules to the case at hand. "By going from here, without persuading the city, are we treating others—those whom we least of all should— wrongly, or not? And are we abiding by just things agreed upon, or not?" When Crito admits that he cannot answer these questions, the Laws enter the dialogue and press the case against escape. From this point on, Socrates and Crito are given only a small and passive role to play. When the Laws come to the end of their speech, Socrates endorses their argument without reservation, Crito agrees that his plans must be abandoned, and the dialogue ends. It might be wondered why Plato chose the Laws to carry through the argument begun by Socrates. Why didn't he allow his hero to remain the protagonist of the dia- logue? Certainly, by giving the major speech of the *Crito* to the Laws, Plato is able to write with a tone of rebuke and indig- nation that would not otherwise have been possible. But I sus- pect that there is also a philosophical motive behind Plato's per- sonification of the Laws. By putting the argument against escape in the mouth of the city's imaginary spokesmen, Plato can rep- resent the dialogue's political philosophy as the theory a city ought to propound to its citizens, and not merely as a theory Socrates proposes to Crito. By allowing Socrates to lay down the basic premises of the argument against escape, Plato indi- cates that the argument to come is not only consistent with but founded on Socratic morality, and the harmony between Soc- rates and the Laws is emphasized once again at the end of the dialogue. But Plato also wants to suggest that the political phi- losophy Socrates accepted can serve as a public charter that a city and its citizens can appeal to in dealing with each other. Some theories are incapable of governing the public life of a community: one need only think of the immoralism of Calli- cles, and in modern times this charge has been made against some forms of utilitarianism. But Plato wants to tell his readers

that the political views of Socrates do not have this character;
if everyone believed what Socrates believed, the city would be
well governed. He achieves this effect by permitting the philosophy which Socrates accepted to be presented and defended
by the impersonal representatives of the Athenian legal system.
The fact that what we read in the *Crito* comes straight from the
Laws assures us that the doctrine that led to Socrates' death is
fit to regulate public life.

Of course, this explanation can be easily challenged. Someone might say that by giving the main speech of the *Crito* to
the Laws, Plato is hinting that there is something unsocratic
about the dialogue's legal thought. This idea can be developed
in two opposite ways: (A) Perhaps Plato is suggesting that the
argument is too weak, sloppy, and authoritarian to be put in
the mouth of Socrates; or (B) perhaps he thinks that the argument is fine, but wants the reader to realize that it is really his
own viewpoint, and not that of Socrates.[22] I do not think that
either of these suggestions is correct, but I cannot prove my
point until we have examined the speech of the Laws. Obviously, we cannot decide whether their philosophy is in some
way unsocratic until we have a better idea of its contents. I will
argue that their ideas are worthy of Socrates' endorsement, and
that they are completely consistent with the philosophy he ex-
pounds throughout Plato's early dialogues. In the end, there
will be no reason to deny that what we find in the *Crito* is the
legal philosophy of Socrates, propounded—for dramatic and
philosophical purposes—by his imaginary adversaries. But in
order not to prejudge this issue, I will continue to speak of
Socrates and the Laws as two separate characters.

6

Destroying the city

The Laws begin as follows:

Tell me, Socrates, what do you have in mind to do? With
this attempted act, are you thinking of anything else than

[22] See Ch. I n. 22.

destroying us, the Laws, and the entire city, for your part? Or does it seem to you that a city can exist and not be overturned if its verdicts have no force, but are robbed of authority and destroyed by private persons? (50a8-b5)

To their credit, the Laws do not claim that by escaping Socrates will in fact destroy the city; it would be absurd to think that this single act of jailbreaking will have such dire consequences. The Laws do not even say that if Socrates escapes the city *might* be destroyed. Rather, their idea is that if Socrates tries to escape he is willing to destroy the city *for his part*. And they support this point by asking Socrates to generalize. What would happen if private individual*s* (note the plural) overturned the verdict*s* (again a plural) of the courts? Wouldn't the city's legal system be destroyed? Could the city continue to exist? The *Crito* seems to be the first document in Western philosophy to use a form of reasoning that is now called a "generalization argument."[23] The basic idea underlying all such arguments is this: if the consequences of everyone's doing X would be bad, then no one ought to do X. Whether everyone will in fact do X, or is likely to, is irrelevant; what matters are the hypothetical consequences of everyone's behaving in a certain way.

Strictly speaking, the Laws do not in fact ask, "What would happen if *everyone* were to disobey the courts?" Rather, they

[23] Thus Guthrie, *History*, Vol. IV, p. 101, says of 50a8-b5: "It is the first appearance of a question sometimes discussed by philosophers today, namely whether, as a rule of conduct, one should ask oneself: 'What would happen if everyone behaved like me?' " Allen, *Socrates and Legal Obligation*, p. 85, says that the *Crito*'s "account of judicial authority rests . . . on a universalization argument, found nowhere else in ancient philosophy." But I am not sure what he takes a universalization argument to be. He simply says that such an argument "explains why, if *this* judgment as judicially rendered is not authoritative, then *no* judgment as judicially rendered is authoritative" (ibid., his emphasis). Santas, *Socrates*, pp. 17-18, with some hesitancy, thinks that the argument of the Laws does not rest on what he calls "a version of the generalization principle," which holds that "if everyone's doing something resulted in harm, then no one must do that thing." For further discussion of the *Crito*'s argument at 50a8-b5, see Woozley, *Law and Obedience*, Ch. VI; Martin, "Socrates on Disobedience to Law," pp. 24-27; and Wade, "In Defense of Socrates," pp. 313-317. Wasserstrom, "The Obligation to Obey the Law," pp. 368-374, rejects all attempts to use the question, "What if everyone did that?" as a weapon against disobedience, and accuses the *Crito* of confusion on this score.

ask, "What would happen if *private individuals* disobeyed the courts?" Whether the emphasized phrase (*idiōtōn*) is doing some important work in their argument is a question we shall have to examine at a later point (see Chapter V). We will also want to ask whether the Laws are falling into a trap. For it is often quite all right to perform an act even when it would be disastrous for many others to do the same. If everyone withdrew a substantial sum of money from the bank, there would be a financial disaster; but surely that does not mean that no one may make such a withdrawal.[24] Similarly, one might admit that a city would be destroyed if all the verdicts of its courts were subverted; but does that show that there can be no circumstances in which disobeying a court is justified? For the moment, I want to reserve judgment on the question of whether the Laws are really guilty of this error. For there is a prior question which is much more important: should we assume that in the passage I have just quoted, at 50a8–b5, the Laws have come to the end of their first argument against escape? Or is there more still to come? If the argument is as yet incomplete, then of course we cannot fairly evaluate it. Now, several authors do treat 50b5 as the end of a self-contained argument.[25] It could be set out as follows:

(A) No one should treat the city unjustly.

(B) Whoever, for his part, destroys the city treats it unjustly.

[24] The generalization argument is most fully treated in M. Singer. *Generalization in Ethics*, especially Ch. IV. His method is to protect the argument against obvious counterexamples by narrowing the range of cases to which it can be applied. Thus circumscribed, he thinks the argument plays a central role in ethical thinking. For criticism of his attempt to derive the argument from more abstract principles, see Lyons, *Forms and Limits of Utilitarianism*, Appendix. Further discussion can be found in Strang, "What If Everyone Did That?" and Ullman-Margalit, "The Generalization Argument: Where does the Obligation Lie?"

[25] Such an argument, formulated with greater or less detail, is attributed to the *Crito* by Santas, *Socrates*, pp. 15-19; Woozley, *Law and Obedience*, pp. 20-22, 58-59, 62-63; Murphy, "Violence and the Socratic Theory of Legal Fidelity," pp. 22-23; Frankena, *Ethics*, pp. 2-3; and Young, "Socrates and Obedience," pp. 13-16.

(C) By escaping, Socrates would be, for his part, destroying the city.

(D) So Socrates should not escape.

But it is easy to see that something important is missing from this argument. For precisely how should we interpret the reference to "the city" in sentences (A) and (B)? This might mean:

(E) No one should treat any city unjustly.

(F) Whoever, for his part, destroys any city treats it unjustly.

But in this case, (F) surely needs further defense, for it is not at all obvious—except to the pacifist—that to destroy a city is always to treat it unjustly. Surely Socrates does not assume that destroying *a man*, i.e. killing him, is always wrong, and analogously there is no reason for him to allow the Laws to assume without argument that destroying *a city* is always wrong. We should recall that Socrates was proud of his military service, and others admired his courage in battle;[26] presumably he realized, as would any Greek soldier, that war can result in the destruction of peoples and cities.[27] So it is unlikely that Socrates would have understood the Laws to be adopting (F).

Perhaps then, instead of (F), we should attribute to the Laws one of the following assumptions:

(G) Whoever, for his part, destroys Athens treats it unjustly.

[26] *Ap.* 28d10-29a1, *La.*181a7-b4, *Charm.*153a1-c6, *Symp.*220d5-221c1.

[27] In classical times, many Greek cities were villages of a few thousand or less, and therefore they could easily be destroyed in war: if the men were killed in battle and the women and children taken as slaves, no ongoing community would remain. Of course, if destroying a city involved burning its physical structures, including temples and altars, then the Greeks would have recognized religious and prudential objections to such violence. But that kind of destruction is not at issue in the *Crito*. The Laws think that widespread disobedience of the sort Socrates is contemplating would mean the end of Athens as a functioning social organization. The community would fall apart, though the buildings would still stand. Precisely that kind of destruction could have come about as the result of war; yet no Greek thought that any such war would be wrong in all circumstances.

(H) Whoever, for his part, destroys his own city treats it unjustly.

But either of these statements requires further elaboration and defense. Consider (G): Why should it be wrong for anyone whatever, whether Athenian or Spartan, Greek or barbarian, to take part in the destruction of Athens? What special features does this city have—features missing in certain other cities—that make attacks upon it wrong? Or consider (H): Why should it be wrong for me to act in a violent way toward my own city, but not toward any other? And what makes a city one's own? I do not claim that these are unanswerable questions. Rather, I am only pointing out that the argument thus far given by the Laws is incomplete.[28] And this leads to the question: do they go on to complete the argument somewhere in the following lines?

7
Does the court's verdict justify destructive acts?

If we look at the next few lines (50b5-c6), we find three further developments. (A) Socrates indicates that his attempt to escape would destroy a particular law—one that makes court decisions authoritative (50b7-8). (B) An objection is considered: hasn't the city done an injustice to Socrates by not deciding his case

---

[28] If one translates *kakourgein* or *kakōs poiein* as "to do harm" or "to injure" (see n. 2 above), then one might easily miss the point that 50a8-b5 does not constitute a complete argument against escape. For one might then take the Laws to be arguing:

(i) One must not do harm or injury to anyone.
(ii) To escape would be to commit a destructive act against the city.
(iii) To act in a destructive way toward Athens is to harm or injure it.
(iv) Therefore, Socrates must not escape.

Premise (iii) looks reasonable enough, for destructive acts are obviously harmful and injurious. But once we realize that "harm" and "injure" are misleading translations, premises (i) and (iii) will have to be rewritten; (iii) will then become: "to act in a destructive way toward Athens is to wrong it." And it is clear that *this* premise is no truism, but instead needs further support.

rightly (50c1-2)? (C) The Laws reply to this objection: Socrates did not make an agreement to abide only by those court decisions that do him no injustice. Instead, he agreed to abide by any judgments reached by the courts (50c4-6). Let us now try to determine what (B) and (C) are getting at.

(B) does not deny that escape would be destructive; it only says that Athens has done Socrates an injustice. So the idea underlying this objection is that the destructiveness of escape is not a decisive consideration against it, and that aggression is an appropriate response to injustice. (B) in effect says, "We admit that escape would be a destructive act, but so what? Isn't a person sometimes justified in taking part in the destruction of a city? In particular, isn't Socrates right to do this, since Athens has treated him unjustly by deciding his case wrongly?" It is important to realize that (B) is *not* suggesting that injustice be answered with injustice. Rather, it is proposing that injustice be answered with a destructive act, and as we have already seen Socrates does not assume that all such acts are necessarily wrong.

How does (C) handle this challenge? At first, it might seem that it ducks the issue by changing the topic. Suppose it is true, as the Laws claim in (C), that Socrates agreed to abide by court decisions, and suppose that this was a just agreement. It will obviously follow from these assumptions that Socrates should not evade the court's verdict. But if this is all (C) does, then the Laws have merely changed the argument against escape; they have not advanced or completed the argument initiated at 50a8-b5, but have moved instead to a new one. And it is very peculiar that Plato should have composed the dialogue in this way. For (B) would have no point unless it were challenging the idea that politically destructive acts are never justified. But if Plato was aware that the "argument from destruction" needs to be completed, then why would he simply change the argument he is giving, as he seems to do in (C)?

I think, however, that there is a better way of interpreting (C)—one that makes it a genuine response to (B), rather than a change of strategy. I suggest that (C) tacitly concedes the underlying assumption of (B); it grants, in other words, that if you are the victim of injustice, then aggression is sometimes a justified response. But it points out that there is a special relationship between Socrates and Athens that makes aggression an unwarranted reaction to the particular injustice mentioned in (B). Socrates has agreed to abide by the decision of the court, whether that decision is right or wrong, and he therefore cannot point to the injustice of the court's verdict as his grounds for destructive behavior. If we read (C) in this way, then the Laws are making a perfectly valid response to the objection contained in (B). They are not avoiding the challenge but are responding to the very issue that has been raised. Victims of injustice *are* sometimes entitled to respond with violence, but not when they have agreed in advance to accept that injustice. We can put the point in this way: (C) can be used for two different purposes, but at the moment the Laws are interested in one rather than the other. First, it can form part of a fresh argument against escape, one based on the notion of agreement rather than the notion of aggression: if Socrates made a just agreement to obey the court, and if just agreements must always be honored, then Socrates must not disobey. Second, (C) can work within the "argument from destruction" by replying to a point that has been made about the limits of that argument. It is this second purpose that (C) serves. The "argument from agreement" will come into its own later, as an independent argument against escape; at the moment, we are still in the midst of the "argument from destruction." For (C) implicitly concedes that more work is to be done if the "argument from destruction" is to succeed. Suppose that Athens has mistreated Socrates in many ways that are not mentioned in (B), and suppose that Socrates has not agreed to accept those injustices. Wouldn't that show that aggression is justified after all? To solidify their argument, the Laws can now do one of several things. They can argue that the injustice recently done to Socrates is the only one he has ever suffered from Athens; therefore, since it was a wrong he agreed to accept, he has no legitimate complaint that would justify an attack on his city. Alternatively, they could argue that however many injustices Socrates may have suffered at the hands of his city, he has implicitly agreed to endure them all. Or they might show that there are certain goods Socrates has received from Athens, and that because of these benefits he would be wrong to treat the city violently and destructively, no matter what it may have done to him. As we will see in the next section, this last path is the one the Laws follow.

8
Parents and cities

The Laws now ask a question that confirms the interpretation I have been proposing. They say to Socrates: "Come now, because of what accusation against us and the city are you trying to destroy us?" (50c9–d1). Here, as in (B) above (Section 7), it is recognized that the argument against escape has not yet been completed. For the question is once again being raised whether Socrates' circumstances might justify political violence; the mere fact that he has agreed to abide by court judgments, as pointed out in (C), still leaves open the possibility that he has legitimate complaints that would justify destructive acts against the city. But now the Laws argue that this line of thought will lead Socrates nowhere. For they go on to say, in the lines that follow, that Socrates imputes no fault to the laws that concern conception, marriage, nurture, and education. Furthermore, they claim that, by virtue of those laws, Socrates owes his existence and his upbringing to Athens, and accordingly violence against the city is no more appropriate than violence against his own parents (50d1–51c3). These points are made in a lengthy and passionate passage, the details of which will be examined later. For now, I want to stress a simple point that has far-reaching consequences for any interpretation of the *Crito*: the Laws recognize that although the destruction of cities is not universally wrong, it is wrong in this particular case because of the special debt Socrates owes to Athens. That debt no more arose through voluntary agreement than do the duties of gratitude we owe our parents. Athens is responsible for the birth and education of Socrates, and *that* is why he cannot justifiably try to destroy it. The Laws are relying on the assumption, widespread in ancient Greece, that although there is no general objection to violence and killing, attacks upon one's parents are absolutely forbidden.[29] They seek some rational basis for this ban on parricide, and they find it in the extraordinary benefits conferred. Logically, anything that is no less responsible for these benefits is no less entitled to forbearance from attack; since Socrates owes his existence and upbringing not only to his parents but also to Athens, he must not, for his part, destroy its laws. Others, who are not similarly indebted to Athenian law, might justifiably attack it, just as one's own parents might justifiably be killed by legal authorities. But if one has incurred a large enough moral debt to certain institutions or persons, one cannot willingly take part in their destruction.

Some scholars think that before the Laws even mention the analogy between parents and cities, they have already completed one argument against escape.[30] According to this view, the *Crito* begins with an argument against destructive acts and then it moves on to claim, quite independently, that citizens should treat their city as individuals treat their parents. We can see now that this way of breaking up the text is a mistake. If we begin at the point where the Laws enter the conversation (50a8), we have to continue all the way through the parent–city

---

[29] The special inviolability of parents was built into the legal system. Whereas the normal penalty for assault in Athens was a fine, it was far more serious—disenfranchisement—when the victim was a parent or a grandparent of the accused. See MacDowell, *The Law in Classical Athens*, pp. 92, 123. Self-defense was recognized as a legitimate reason for killing (ibid., p. 114), but Plato's *Laws* does not allow children to kill their parents in self-defense. "In this case alone (where a man is about to be killed by his parents), no law will permit killing to defend oneself against death" (869b7–c2, trans. by Pangle). Contrast the legal situation that existed in the United States until quite recently: a child whose parents died was thereby entitled to receive Social Security payments, even if he deliberately killed them.

[30] See n. 25 above.

analogy before we come to the end of a natural unit. If we reach farther back, and begin with the Socratic premise that injustice must never be done, we can set out the *Crito*'s first argument against escape in the following way:

(i) One must never treat any city or person unjustly. (49b8)

(ii) By escaping, Socrates would be destroying Athens, for his part. (50a8–b5)

(iii) Athens is responsible for the birth and education of Socrates. (50d1–51c1)

(iv) If some person or city X is responsible for the birth or education of Y, then Y treats X unjustly if Y uses violence against X. (51c2–3)

(v) Whoever destroys a city, for his part, uses violence against that city. (supplied)

(vi) If Socrates escapes, he will be treating Athens un-justly.[31]

Of course, this is only a sketch, and many details have to be filled in before we can claim to understand the first argument against escape. But we have nonetheless made some progress. As we see now, the Laws do not think they have come to the end of an argument when they assert (ii); for destructive acts against cities are not always wrong. What makes destruction wrong in this particular case is the special nonvoluntary relationship that exists between Athens and Socrates. He did not ask for the benefits he received from Athens any more than children ask to be born or nurtured; nonetheless, those benefits

[31] Alternatively, one could use *kakourgein* ("do wrong") or *kakōs poiein* ("treat wrongly") instead of *adikein* ("treat unjustly, "do injustice") throughout this argument, i.e. in premises (i), (iv), and (vi). The crucial point is that those who use violence against their parents or their parent-city are guilty of all three charges: they act unjustly, they do wrong, and they treat others wrongly. It is this substantive claim that entitles the *Crito* to move back and forth freely among the three expressions; neither Socrates nor the Laws need assume that these expressions have the same meaning.

engender debts, and one of those debts is paid when we refrain from violent or destructive behavior toward our benefactors.

9
How many arguments against escape?

Once the comparison between cities and parents has been made, the Laws move on to a further point: Socrates, like every other citizen, had the opportunity to leave Athens if he was dissatisfied with its laws. But he chose not to, and therefore he has made an agreement to obey the city's orders. The Laws then interrupt the development of their argument to summarize the points that have now been made against escape:

> . . . We say that the one who disobeys us acts unjustly in three ways: because we begat him and he disobeys, because we nurtured him, and because he agreed to obey us but neither obeys nor persuades us, if we are doing something wrong . . . (51e4–7)

These few lines give us some useful information. To begin with, the Laws are saying that birth and nurture are each such great benefits that either one by itself creates debts to parents and cities. If Socrates escapes, he will be doing something (violence) that should never be done to a city that has given him life; on top of that, he will be doing something (violence) that should never be done to a city that has nurtured him. Evidently, the single argument outlined in the previous section is now being divided into two:

(i) One must never treat any city or person unjustly.

(i') Same.

(ii) By escaping, Socrates would be destroying Athens, for his part.

(ii') Same.

(iii) Athens is responsible for the birth of Socrates.

(iii') Athens is responsible for nurturing Socrates.

(iv) If some person or city X is responsible for the birth of Y, then Y treats X unjustly if Y uses violence against X.

(iv') If some person or city X is responsible for nurturing Y, then Y treats X unjustly if Y uses violence against X.

(v) Whoever destroys a city, for his part, uses violence against that city.

(v') Same.

(vi) If Socrates escapes, he will be treating Athens unjustly.

(vi') Same.

How one enumerates arguments is of course an artificial matter. If we combine (iii) and (iii') into a single proposition, and if we similarly consolidate (iv) and (iv'), we will have one argument; if we keep them separate, we will have two. The Laws want to portray escape as a dastardly deed, and so they double the yield of their parent-city analogy by extracting from it two separate arguments against escape. Whether we should go along with them is an arbitrary decision. In any case, it is fair to say that the analogy with parents provides the Laws with one *type* of argument against escape. It is an argument based on benefits that the citizen never asked for; by contrast, the argument from agreement contends that the citizen extends his commitment to the city through a voluntary decision.

Another point should be noticed. This summary of the case against escape confirms our conclusion that there is no "argument from destruction" that is independent of the parent-city analogy. If we set aside the double debt citizens owe their parent-cities and the obligations they undertake through implicit agreement, no argument against escape will be left. The Laws do not condemn political violence *per se*; they only condemn violence and destructive acts against a parent-city.

We have arrived at the conclusion that the Laws have two types of argument against escape: one stems from the analogy between parents and cities, and the other depends on the notion of implicit agreement. As the Laws deploy each argument, they use or anticipate ideas that are developed in the other. We have already seen that in the argument against destructive acts, the Laws claim that Socrates made a certain agreement with the city. And the argument from agreement will make use of an idea (the persuade-or-obey doctrine) first introduced in the analogy between parents and cities. We shall see (VI.12) that these two arguments depend on and complement each other in important ways. Neither is intended as a complete picture of a city's powers over its citizens.[32]

---

[32] Contrast Allen, *Socrates and Legal Obligation*, p. 112: "The *Crito* does not, as has often been thought, present a series of independent arguments for the conclusion that it is wrong to escape. It presents one argument . . ." Cf. pp. 86–87, 91, 94, 97. But he does not explain how his interpretation can be squared with the statement (51e4–7) that escape does a threefold injustice, two stemming from benefits received, and one from agreement. This entails that if agreement is set aside, an argument against escape can still be made; and similarly if the benefits mentioned (birth and education) are set aside, there is still an argument from agreement. But notice that the Laws are not committed to the view that even those citizens who leave Athens and take up residence elsewhere owe obedience, by virtue of the benefits they have received. By allowing emigration, the city can be said to release the citizen from a debt he would have had, by virtue of benefits received, had he remained. The citizen who decides to remain fails to cancel this debt, and should he be satisfied with the laws, then he establishes a new tie to the city, by making an implicit agreement. The mechanism by which agreement is made will be described in Chapter VI. It will turn out that a citizen can remain in residence and yet avoid agreeing to obey each and every command of the city; but even in this case, he will owe the city obedience, because of benefits he received at an earlier time.

III

PERSUADE OR
OBEY

1
Grote and Green

IN THE MIDST of the passage that compares cities to parents, the Laws say that citizens must "either persuade or do what the fatherland [*patris*] commands . . ." (51b3-4).[1] Several lines later, they return to these two alternatives. The citizen "must everywhere do what the city and fatherland commands, or persuade it as to the nature of justice . . ." (51b9-c1). And then, after the laws claim that Socrates implicitly agreed to obey the city, they state their persuade-or-obey doctrine one more time:

> . . . We say that the one who disobeys us acts unjustly in three ways: because we begat him and he disobeys, because we nurtured him, and because he agreed to obey us but neither obeys nor persuades us, if we are doing something wrong. We do not harshly order [him] to do what we command, but allow either of two [alternatives]—either to persuade us, or to do [what we command], but he does neither of these. (51e4-52a3)

---

[1] Most English translations avoid "fatherland" as a way of rendering *patris*, perhaps because the word is so rarely used in political discourse. But those who rely on such translations should be aware of two facts: (a) the Greek word for "father" (*patēr*) is closely related to *patris*; (b) though the Laws most frequently use *polis* (city) to name the entity to which Socrates is indebted, *patris* is also quite common (occurring at 51a2, a5, a9, 51b3, 51c1, and 54c5). The Laws obviously think that the similarity between *patris* and *patēr* is philosophically suggestive, though their argument against escape is completely independent of this linguistic fact. Even if the Greek language suggested no parent-city analogy, the argument that lies behind this analogy would still stand.

Evidently, the need to persuade or obey arises from two sources: as we learn from the parent-city analogy, the citizen must persuade or obey his city because he has benefited from it as offspring benefit from their parents; and as the above passage tells us, the citizen who makes an agreement with his city is thereby obliged to persuade or obey. Since the Laws state the persuade-or-obey doctrine three times, they obviously think that they are making an important point. They emphasize their leniency in allowing persuasion as an alternative to obedience, but they do not explain precisely what is involved in these two choices. Who should be persuaded? Of what? How much leeway are the Laws giving the citizen? Can one disobey and then persuade, or must one first try to persuade and then obey if persuasion fails? What happens if one both disobeys and also fails to persuade? Until we arrive at satisfactory answers to these questions, we cannot hope to understand the *Crito*'s legal philosophy.

Grote thinks that the *Crito* requires "absolute submission" to the city's commands,[2] and accordingly he finds no room for disobedience in the persuade-or-obey doctrine. "The laws allow to every citizen full liberty of trying to persuade the assembled public: but the citizen who fails in persuading must obey the public when they enact a law adverse to his views."[3] So interpreted, the attitude of the *Crito* toward disobedience is not too distant from the position advocated by T. H. Green. He says:

> Supposing . . . the individual to have decided that some command of a 'political superior' is not for the common good, how ought he to act in regard to it? In a country like ours, with a popular government and settled methods of enacting and repealing laws, the answer of common sense is simple and sufficient. He should do all he can by legal methods to get the command cancelled, but till it is cancelled he should conform to it.[4]

[2] *Plato*, Vol. I, p. 303.
[3] Ibid., p. 300.
[4] *Lectures on the Principles of Political Obligation*, Sec. 100, p. 111. I am indebted to P. Singer, *Democracy and Disobedience*, p. 2, for this reference.

Athens too had a "popular government and settled methods of enacting and repealing laws." Perhaps the *Crito* is also saying that these two features, or at least the second of them, make disobedience inappropriate. One may try to block a proposed law or repeal a statute in the Assembly, and if one succeeds, then of course the offending legislation will not exist and cannot be disobeyed. But so long as a law does exist, one must obey it. If we are looking for a passage in the *Crito* that leaves room for justified disobedience, we will not find it in the persuade-or-obey doctrine, according to Grote.

Grote's interpretation goes well beyond the text, but that in itself is no objection to it. We cannot understand the persuade-or-obey doctrine unless we fill in what the Laws leave out. Nonetheless, to evaluate Grote's reading, we have to be quite aware of what he has added to the text. (A) The Laws do not talk about "the assembled public," i.e. the Assembly, which alone had authority, in the time of Socrates, to pass and repeal a statute. The *Crito* merely tells the citizen to persuade the city and the Laws, but does not make it clear which Athenian political institution is to be addressed. (B) Grote evidently assumes that the point of persuading is to prevent a law from being enacted, or to repeal an already existing law. That is why he takes the Assembly to be the appropriate object of persuasion: it is this body that enacts and repeals a law. Grote's assumption that "persuade or obey" means "change the law or obey" is widely shared. Thus Guthrie says, "The choice before the individual was either to obey the laws or to get them changed by peaceful persuasion, or else to emigrate."[5] According to Woozley, "The . . . *Crito* does allow the limited freedom of persuading (or trying to persuade) authority to change its mind before submitting to it. . . ."[6] And Allen takes the dialogue to mean that ". . . the citizen is under obligation to obey those laws, unless he can alter them by persuasion rather than force. . . ."[7] Nevertheless, we should be aware that there is not a word in the *Crito* about *changing* the law through persuasion. (C) Fi-

---

[5] *History*, Vol. III, pp. 412-413.
[6] *Law and Obedience*, p. 71.
[7] *Socrates and Legal Obligation*, p. 104.

nally, Grote says that, according to the persuade-or-obey doctrine, when efforts to persuade fail, one must obey. Thus too Woozley, as the above quotation shows. Similarly, Morrow writes, "A citizen may try to persuade the laws that they are wrong, as Socrates puts it in the *Crito* (52a), but he may not disobey. . . ."[8] And Santas takes the Laws to be saying that ". . . it is just that citizens either persuade their country where justice lies, or (failing that) do whatever their country commands. . . ."[9] Of course, the text itself does not say, "persuade, or (failing that) obey;" it merely tells the citizen to persuade or obey.[10]

I believe that scholars have been too quick to read these three assumptions into the *Crito*, and I will argue that all three should be rejected. Let me begin by reminding the reader of a point I made in Chapter I. Outside of the *Crito*, Socrates says that a city's commands must sometimes be disobeyed. So our first obligation, when we read the speech of the Laws, is to see whether their political philosophy leaves room for justified lawbreaking. If it does, we can understand why Socrates applauds them at the end of the dialogue. Now, the persuade-or-obey doctrine seems to be a good place to look, if we want to find a loophole for disobedience. After all, the Laws themselves insist that they are being lenient in allowing an alternative to obedience (52a1-3). And surely there is no strain in taking the phrase "persuade or obey" to mean that if one does not obey then one must persuade. Notice that when the Laws state the persuade-or-obey doctrine a second time, they say that the citizen "must everywhere do what his city and fatherland commands, *or persuade it as to the nature of justice* . . ."(51b9-c1). The emphasized words imply that the city might be wrong in its conception of justice, and that in these cases one has an alternative to obedi-

---

[8] *Plato's Cretan City*, p. 569.
[9] *Socrates*, p. 25.
[10] Tredennick wrongly translates 51b3-4: " . . . if you cannot persuade your country you must do whatever it orders. . . ." This differs in a subtle but important way from the *Crito*'s simple command, "persuade or obey." The latter does not say whether one must obey if one tries to persuade but fails; but Tredennick's command does. For further discussion, see III. 3-6.

ence.[11] Can we be blamed for thinking that in such cases, according to Socrates, the alternative to obedience involves disobedience? Several lines later, the Laws complain that a Socrates who escapes "neither obeys nor persuades us, if we are doing something wrong . . ." (51e7). Here, the city's liability to error is explicitly recognized. The Laws are conceding that an alternative to obedience is appropriate when the city's orders are wrong. That is not an explicit admission that disobedience is sometimes justified, but it certainly lends itself to such an interpretation.

One further point. The Laws build their case against escape on premises that were laid down by Socrates, and one of those premises, as we saw, allows agreements to be broken when they are unjust. In particular, an agreement that requires the performance of an unjust act must not be honored: that is how Socrates must interpret the principle of just agreements, and when he endorses the speech of the Laws, he must be assuming that this point has been accepted. Now, notice what the Laws do as soon as they have put together the basic steps in their argument from agreement. They announce that the injustice of escape has been proved in a third way, and they then return to the persuade-or-obey doctrine, emphasizing their leniency in giving the citizen an alternative to obedience. And having made these points, they return to the argument from agreement, and fill in its details. Why have the Laws interrupted the development of their argument at precisely this point? The persuade-or-obey doctrine has already been stated twice, so why bring it up a third time? I suggest that the Laws are thinking back to the principle of just agreements. Someone could say, "Why are you bothering to prove that Socrates made an agreement to

[11] There are two different ways in which the city's command might reveal a defective sense of justice: (A) the command might be unjust to the citizen (i.e. it might make him suffer injustice); or (B) it might require him to do an injustice. A disobedient citizen who defends his behavior by claiming (A) or (B) is persuading his city "as to the nature of justice." Nothing in these last words suggests that disobedience motivated by (A) is out of order. So the parent-city analogy, as I understand it, does not claim that citizens can justifiably disobey laws only under condition (B). Of course, as we saw in II.4, if the citizen has voluntarily agreed to obey a certain law, then the grounds for legitimate disobedience would narrow down to (B). I will come back to this point in IV.6.

obey the city? The principle of just agreements tells us that agreements do not always have to be honored, and therefore the agreement to obey the city can sometimes justifiably be broken." The Laws concede the point, since they build their argument on the Socratic principle that an agreement must not be honored when it requires wrongdoing. But they point out that such a concession will not do the least damage to their case against escape. For if you make an agreement to obey the city and that agreement is unforced, honest, and unrushed, then you must not simply run away even if you think a particular order is unjust. You owe an explanation to those with whom you made a voluntary agreement, if you break your word. That is, if you violate an agreement, then you must persuade the party to whom you have voluntarily obligated yourself; and this is something Socrates refuses to do. The Laws are saying, "Yes, you may break an agreement, and therefore you may violate a city's orders—but not if you refuse to persuade the city that its order was unjust."

No single point I have made shows decisively that the Laws recognize disobedience as a legitimate possibility. But if we put them together, I think they suggest that there is a promising alternative to Grote's authoritarian reading of the persuade-or-obey doctrine. We must now explore that alternative more thoroughly, to see if it can satisfactorily explain the text and survive criticism. If, after careful examination, it remains a plausible reading, then we have no choice but to reject Grote's interpretation. A reading of the *Crito* that makes it consistent with Socratic doctrine must prevail over one that produces inconsistency.

As we saw, Grote's interpretation goes beyond the text in several ways. He takes the persuade-or-obey doctrine to mean that one *cannot* justifiably disobey; according to my proposal, it means that one *can* justifiably disobey, so long as one persuades. He suggests that the Assembly is the appropriate forum for persuasion, and that the object of persuasion is legislative change; my idea, by contrast, is that the law courts are the appropriate forum. If someone has disobeyed a law then he must, when summoned, appear before the court to persuade his fellow cit-

disobedience allow if can
persuade that law was unjust

izens that disobedience was justified.[12] Of course, he is not trying
to get them to change the law, since as a jury they have no
power to do so. Persuasion is required of the disobedient citizen
because he owes the parent-city with which he has made an
agreement some explanation for his behavior. The point of persuasion is to pay a debt and not to change the law. And if the
citizen should fail to persuade the jury? If, in other words, he
neither obeys nor persuades? That is a question that will soon
be tackled.

2
The paradox of permitted disobedience

The Laws tell the citizen that he must obey or persuade, and I
take this to mean that one may disobey, as long as one persuades. But Santas thinks there is a difficulty that should dissuade us from reading the *Crito* in this way.[13] For if the Laws
mean that one may disobey, then they are conceding that disobedience is permitted. But isn't "permitted disobedience" a
self-contradiction? When one disobeys, one does what is not
permitted; and if an act is permitted, then whoever performs it
is not being disobedient. Since the notion of permitted disobe-

[12] I take the Laws to be focusing exclusively on one type of disobedience, in
which the citizen violates an order because of an unwavering belief that the
order is in some way objectionable. These are the cases in which the citizen
believes that his city is in the wrong, and that is why he must persuade the
court "as to the nature of justice." There are other kinds of disobedience which
the persuade-or-obey doctrine ignores. For example, the citizen might disobey
a command without intending to do so; or he may knowingly disobey, but
realize immediately afterwards that his violation of the law was unjustified. In
these cases, the Laws cannot be interpreted to mean that the citizen must defend
his disobedience in court. Though he owes it to his city to appear in court and
explain his behavior, he is not required to *persuade* the jury that he was in the
right. The debt all citizens owe their parent-city accounts for the fact that they
must appear in court whenever they disobey the law; but the most important
cause of disobedience is moral disagreement, and this is what leads to the persuade-or-obey doctrine.
[13] *Socrates*, p. 307 n. 9: "Surely if what Socrates is doing, or rather proposing
to do, is a *permitted* alternative or exception, then it is not disobedience?" (his
emphasis). Woozley, *Law and Obedience*, p. 31, raises the same problem, but
thinks it can be handled. Against his solution, see my review, "Two Recent
Studies," p. 661.

dience is incoherent, we ought not to foist it on to the *Crito* if some alternative is available. And of course we do have an alternative: we can take the persuade-or-obey doctrine to mean that one may try to persuade, but that if persuasion fails, one must obey.

I find echoes of the point Santas is making in some recent discussions of civil disobedience. Marshall Cohen, for example, asks, ". . . What would it mean to extend a general legal or de facto right to civil disobedience? And if there were such a right, in what sense would those who exercised it thereby express dissent . . . ?"[14] Similarly, Joel Feinberg says, ". . . One wonders whether an ideally just constitution will itself make some reference to civil disobedience and the conditions of its permissibility. If not, why not? If so, in what sense is civil disobedience 'illegal'?"[15] Neither Santas nor Cohen nor Feinberg gives this problem more than a sentence or two, and so it is difficult to say precisely how they would elaborate on the point or points they are making. Nonetheless, there evidently is something paradoxical about the notion of permitted disobedience, so we had better take a closer look at it.

There is of course no contradiction in saying that one and the same act is legally permitted and legally forbidden. For it can be permitted by one law and forbidden by another. But merely to state this is not a satisfying way of resolving the paradox; for if one and the same system of laws both prohibits and permits a certain type of act, then the citizen has been given contradictory directives. He has been told that he must refrain from some type of act, and that he may perform it. Surely any legal system that conflicts with itself in this way is irrational. So the issue before us is really this: would the Athenian legal system contain contradictory orders if it were supplemented by the persuade-or-obey doctrine as I interpret it? That is, if the speech of the Laws were officially adopted by Athens as an expression of the city's philosophy of law, and if the persuade-or-obey doctrine means what I think it means, would the result be an inconsistent legal code? I think the answer is no, and perhaps

[14] "Liberalism and Disobedience," p. 313.
[15] "Duty and Obligation in the Non-Ideal World," p. 264.

an analogy will help make this answer plausible. Suppose a father is engaged in dangerous work, and hires his daughter as an assistant. He frequently has occasion to give her orders, and circumstances make it impossible for him to rescind them once they are issued. His daughter therefore asks him what she is to do when she believes that the orders she receives are, for one reason or another, unwise. Is she to follow them no matter what, or does her father think that on occasion she should disobey an order? After careful thought, the father decides that it is more dangerous to have her follow him blindly than to permit her to exercise her independent judgment. So he tells her that she may disobey him only when obedience would be much more dangerous than he had realized. Furthermore, he adds that if she ever does disobey an order, she should let him know, and explain her reasons. He will then decide whether or not her disobedience was blameworthy.

Both the father in this example and the Laws in the *Crito* believe themselves entitled to give orders, and both are telling their subordinates how those orders are to be construed.[16] My interpretation of the persuade-or-obey doctrine takes the Laws to be adopting the same policy regarding their commands that the father in this example adopts toward his. Both admit that they may make mistakes and both therefore admit that disobedience may be justified. Each specifies conditions under which an order may be disobeyed. But each asks that the subordinate individual openly confess and justify any disobedient acts. Because of these parallels, anyone who thinks that the Laws, as I understand them, are being inconsistent ought to believe that the father is being inconsistent. But *that* seems a hard conclusion to swallow. For surely there is nothing irrational in what the father tells his daughter. It is possible, of course, that he may be making an unwise decision; perhaps if she is untrustworthy or unintelligent he should insist that his orders be followed

---

[16] It could be claimed that the father in my example is no longer issuing *orders* to his daughter, but is only giving her *advice*. But I would resist this suggestion. The father is still in a position to punish his daughter if he tells her to do X and she fails to do so for no satisfactory reason. If he has the right to punish her for noncompliance, then he is issuing commands and not merely offering advice—in spite of the fact that he tells her that noncompliance might sometimes be justified.

however wrong they seem. But surely he does not have to insist upon blind obedience as a matter of logic. Giving his daughter some leeway and independence is at least a coherent policy, though it need not always be the best policy. And if this is so, the same must apply to our interpretation of the *Crito*. If the Athenian legal system concedes that disobedience is justifiable, it does not thereby contradict itself. And so we are not committing the Laws to any inconsistency if we interpret the persuade-or-obey doctrine in the way I advocate.

If a legal system contains one law that says, "Citizens are required to do A," and another that says "Citizens are permitted to refrain from A," then of course it contains inconsistent commands. Similarly, if the father in my example were to tell his daughter to do A and not to do A, he would be speaking at cross-purposes. But his policy about legitimate disobedience does not commit him to anything so silly. He is saying that whenever his orders meet certain specified conditions, then they may be disobeyed, so long as his daughter also meets certain specified conditions. So too the Laws. There is nothing incoherent or even unusual about a legal system that contains second-order principles that specify when its first-order rules are void or superseded. And this is the role that the Laws, as I understand them, are trying to play: they are defining the conditions under which political orders might justifiably be disobeyed, and they are also defining the conditions that citizens must satisfy when they disobey. No contradictory directives would arise were the speech of the Laws attached to a codification of Athenian law.

A comparison with contemporary jurisprudence might be helpful at this point. In the American legal system, anyone who engages in constitutionally protected activities is justified in disobeying a Congressional statute or a legal official prohibiting such activities. For example, if Congress were to prohibit the publication of religious material, it would exceed its authority under the Constitution, and anyone who violated the law would be engaging in an act both prohibited (by Congress) and permitted (by the Constitution).[17] Similarly, the Supreme Court

---

[17] It could be argued that in such a case Congress has failed to enact a law,

has held that individual citizens may violate police orders that contravene the Constitution, as when an officer enforces racial segregation by ordering a black person to leave a public park.[18] In effect, acts of disobedience are permitted when statutes or legal commands that prohibit behavior lack validity under the law. Another sort of example is relevant: in many countries, individuals are advised by the legal system that they may justifiably disobey perfectly valid laws, should dire circumstances arise that the law cannot foresee. "Property may be destroyed to prevent the spread of a fire. A speed limit may be violated in pursuing a suspected criminal. An ambulance may pass a traffic light. Mountain climbers lost in a storm may take refuge in a house or may appropriate provisions."[19] Since rules cannot cover all cases, the legal system does not insist on blind obedience; instead, it holds that disobedience may be justified in unforeseen circumstances. By recognizing "the defense of necessity," as it is sometimes called, the law, paradoxically, acknowledges that citizens may sometimes disobey the law.[20]

since an invalid law is no more a law than counterfeit money is legal tender. Thus W. Douglas once wrote, "When a legislature undertakes to proscribe the exercise of a citizen's constitutional right to free speech, it acts lawlessly; and the citizen can take matters in his own hands and proceed on the basis that such a law is no law at all." (Quoted in Kadish and Kadish, *Discretion to Disobey*, p. 105.) I do not need to contest the point, since it does not affect my argument. The citizen who violates an invalid law is still disobeying an act of Congress, and the Constitution as interpreted by the courts allows him to disobey.

[18] *Wright v. Georgia*, 373 U.S. 284 (1963). This case is cited by Kadish and Kadish, *Discretion to Disobey*, p. 106. See too p. 105, where they cite Article 147 of the Constitution of Hesse, in West Germany: "It is the right and duty of every man to resist unconstitutionally exercised public power."

[19] *Model Penal Code* (Tent. draft No. 8, 1959), comment at 8-9. Cited by Kadish and Kadish, *Discretion to Disobey*, p. 121.

[20] Objection: "In such cases, the individual is not really violating the law, since the rules of the legal system are not meant to apply to emergencies." I find this move implausible. Suppose a tree blocks a driver's legal right of way; to bypass it, he crosses a solid line and briefly drives on the lefthand side of the road. Hasn't he violated a rule of the road? Or does the rule really mean that one must not cross a solid line unless one's way is blocked by fallen trees? Do all laws contain an implicit clause that suspends the law in emergencies? Does a fallen tree constitute an emergency? I find it more straightforward and plausible to say that the driver justifiably violated the law. Here I follow Kadish and Kadish, *Discretion to Disobey*, pp. 123-127. They argue that the "lesser-evil principle," as they call it, does not modify the law in the same way as e.g. the plea of self-defense. The latter is "an exception, included in the law, to the

Similarly, according to my interpretation, the Laws are telling Socrates that they will tolerate disobedience when the city has made a mistake about justice and the citizen so persuades a court. Admittedly, this gives the citizen far more discretion than he receives from the doctrine of necessity or the American system of judicial review. Perhaps too much discretion: it could be argued that it is *unwise* for a legal system to acknowledge that citizens are justified in disobeying unjust orders, for justice is too vague and controversial a notion to provide a workable standard for legitimate disobedience. But in any case, a legal system is not being *incoherent* or *inconsistent* if it tells the citizen that he has an alternative to obedience when he receives unjust orders. I conclude, then, that the paradox of permitted disobedience is only an apparent paradox.

3
Unsuccessful attempts at persuasion

Suppose someone disobeys a law and is brought before a court, where he tries to explain and justify his action. However, a majority of the jurors are unpersuaded by his defense and therefore they vote in favor of conviction. Two questions now arise. First, would the Laws blame this individual for having acted wrongly? After all, he has neither obeyed the law nor succeeded in persuading the city that disobedience was justified. Must the Laws therefore condemn him for having violated their persuade-or-obey doctrine? Second, must the citizen who has failed to persuade the jury accept his punishment? I will leave this second question aside for now, and concentrate on the first.

definition of the conduct prohibited" (p. 124). But pleas of "necessity" or "the lesser evil" do not rest on specific exceptions explicitly built into the law. Rather, the "legislature has gone as far as it can (or will) in defining the special circumstances of nonliability appropriate to the ends of its legislation. The task of defining others it remits to the courts on an ad hoc basis as the cases arise. It is in this sense that the lesser-evil defense may be said to be included in the law. The law includes the requirement that the courts assess whether breaching the rule was preferable to complying with it in the circumstances" (p. 124). So, when someone pleads self-defense to a murder charge, he claims that he broke no law; but when I find shelter on someone's property during a winter storm, I justifiably break the law against trespass.

I concede from the start that the citizen who has failed to persuade the jury will be blamed by a majority of its members for having disobeyed the law. (This will be true, at any rate, if their votes reflect their sincere beliefs concerning the merits of the case.) And since the jury represents and speaks on behalf of the city, it would be accurate to say that, in my example, the city of Athens is blaming the citizen for having broken the law. But I do not concede that therefore this disobedient individual is guilty in the eyes of the personified Laws of the *Crito*. In fact, the text tells us that the Laws are able to recognize mistakes that have been made by the city's legal institutions. Though Socrates has been found guilty and is being blamed and punished by the city, the Laws agree with him that he is innocent of the crime with which he was charged. They accept the truth of his statement that he was a victim of injustice (50c1-6, cf. 54c2-3), and this means that in their eyes he was wrongly accused, convicted, and sentenced. So it would be an error to think that the Laws must always have the same opinions as the city and its citizens. Rather, they are ideal observers of the Athenian legal scene, equipped with a philosophy of law which no Athenian, other than Socrates, need ever have held. They may therefore apportion praise and blame by means of standards and perceptions that depart from those of their flesh-and-blood contemporaries. (For example, the Laws accept and build on the Socratic point that injustice does not justify an unjust response.) So the fact that a disobedient individual has been found guilty by a court does not show that, according to the Laws, he has acted wrongly. We have to set aside what an actual court thinks about a disobedient individual, and ask what the Laws would say. Suppose they were to address themselves to every disobedient citizen who has tried but failed to persuade a jury that his disobedience was right. Would they blame the citizen for having neither obeyed nor persuaded? Or would they excuse him, on the grounds that at least he tried to abide by their legal philosophy?

There is of course no passage in the *Crito* that raises or answers these questions, but if we merely leave them hanging, we will have no adequate idea of what the persuade-or-obey doctrine amounts to. Furthermore, there is a natural answer for the Laws to give, if we take seriously the possibility that their persuade-or-obey doctrine tolerates some disobedience. They tell the citizen to obey or persuade the city "as to the nature of justice." If this means that disobedience is justified when the city makes a mistake about justice, then the Laws have to recognize two different ways in which a citizen can disobey and then fail in his attempt to persuade the jury.

First, the citizen might be wrong and the jury right. That is, he disobeys an order because he thinks it unjust, but when he tries to convince the jury of the order's injustice, they see through his argument. In this case, would the Laws blame the citizen for having neither obeyed nor persuaded? The natural answer is yes. After all, by hypothesis, the jury came to the right conclusion when it decided that the citizen should have obeyed, and there is no reason why the Laws should dissent from the city's judgment. The citizen neither obeyed nor persuaded, and he is to be criticized for his refusal to opt for the first alternative. He refused to obey because he had a mistaken conception of justice, and he failed to persuade for this same reason. The Laws have to say, in such a case, that the citizen ought to have obeyed.

Second, the citizen might be right and the jury wrong. In this case, the citizen disobeys an order because he realizes it is unjust; but the jury, either through ill will or ignorance, decides that the order was just. If the Laws were to appear before him as they appear before Socrates and Crito, would they blame him for having neither obeyed nor persuaded the city "as to the nature of justice"? If the persuade-or-obey doctrine is designed to allow some disobedience, then the Laws cannot fairly blame the citizen for his failure to persuade or for his refusal to obey. By hypothesis, this is a case in which the citizen makes the right choice in disobeying; so the Laws cannot fairly blame him for doing so. But it would be equally unfair for them to hold him responsible for failing to persuade the jury. After all, he did everything he could to persuade them, and it was only through their ignorance or ill will that he did not succeed. He tried to live in accordance with the requirement of the Laws that he pursue one of two alternatives—either to persuade or obey—and through no fault of his own he failed at the former. Surely it is open to the Laws to hold him blameless, just as it is open to a flesh-and-blood jury to hold citizens blameless for their involuntary failures. After all, the Laws do not criticize Socrates for having acted impiously. Though this is the verdict the city arrived at, the Laws do not think he was at fault for having failed to persuade the jury of his innocence. If the Laws do not have to rubber-stamp the verdicts of an Athenian court, then they can side with a citizen who has disobeyed an unjust law and made every effort to persuade the city that he was in the right.

It might be helpful at this point to recall the third charge made by the Laws against escape: they say that if Socrates flees, he will have done an injustice, because, having agreed to obey the city, he neither obeys nor persuades. I take the Laws to mean that contracts can justifiably be broken, but that you must persuade the person to whom you gave your word that you are right to break your agreement. But what if that person refuses to be persuaded? The Laws cannot mean that in this case the agreement must be honored no matter what it requires. For if this is what they mean, then they are violating the principle of just agreements. That principle says that agreements must be broken if *in fact* they require injustice. It does not say: you may break an agreement only if you succeed in persuading the person to whom you gave your word. Now, the person who justifiably breaks an agreement need not be at fault for his failure to convince the other party that he is right to do so. Although the Laws say that whoever makes an agreement must honor it or persuade, they must admit that a person who breaks an agreement and fails to persuade might be blameless. Similarly, they must be willing to excuse a citizen who breaks an unjust law but fails, through no fault of his own, to show the jury that he was in the right.

So my interpretation comes to this. A citizen will be justified in violating an order issued to him by his parent-city only if that order is in fact unjust. If the order does him an injustice he agreed to accept or risk, then he cannot rightly disobey it. The citizen who disobeys his city must, when summoned, persuade a jury that he was right to disobey. But if he was right yet fails in his efforts to show this to the jury, he has done no wrong. All of this is an elaboration of the simple doctrine that the citizen must obey or persuade the city as to the nature of justice. It is the only elaboration of that doctrine that Socrates and the Laws can agree upon.[21]

4

First objection: Involuntary unpersuasiveness

The reader may suspect that some sleight-of-hand lies behind my interpretation. For I am saying that a citizen might refuse to obey and fail in his attempt to persuade, yet still be blameless in the eyes of the Laws. But how can they require the citizen either to obey or persuade, and then excuse the behavior of someone who has done neither?

To see what is wrong with this objection, let us imagine for a moment that the Laws had said something quite different from what we actually find in the *Crito*. Instead of telling the citizen to persuade or obey, suppose they had said, far more simply: "Obey!" Now, consider a citizen who tries as best he can to live in accordance with this severe legal philosophy. Whenever his city orders him to do something, he tries to comply, but

[21] A difficult problem should be mentioned here, though I cannot defend a solution to it until the next chapter. In which of two ways do the Laws want to exploit the parent-city analogy? (A) They think that, by virtue of the analogy, the city is owed obedience, persuasion being the proper course of action when the debt ought not to be paid. (B) They think that the analogy leads to the conclusion that the citizen owes it to his city to take one of two alternatives: persuasion or obedience; but obedience is not owed, by virtue of the analogy. The issue can be clarified if we consider promises. If I promise to do X, I might justifiably break the promise, but even so it remains true that I had an obligation to do X; it is not as though my obligation was merely to do X or to explain why I won't do it. Therefore, if a citizen agrees to abide by a certain law, then he owes it to his city to do what the law requires. He owes obedience, and not merely persuasion or obedience. But do the Laws think that the parent-city analogy, no less than the argument from agreement, leads to the conclusion that the citizen owes obedience? Or do they think that, by virtue of this analogy, the citizen merely owes it to the city to take one of two alternatives: obedience or persuasion? The former alternative is correct, I think. The citizen owes obedience, though he may be right not to pay his debt. See Ch. IV n. 9.

now and then an official gives him a command that he fails to carry out, despite his best efforts. We look to our revised copies of the *Crito* to see whether the Laws say anything about this type of case, but they do not. They merely say, "The citizen must always obey his city's commands"; but they do not discuss the citizen who tries to obey but fails. Must we conclude that according to this revised *Crito*, the Laws are committed to condemning those who fail to obey the city through no fault of their own? Surely not. The mere fact that they say, "Obey the city," does not mean that they will blame anyone who fails to obey. After all, Athenian courts were accustomed to the idea that a defendant might be blameless if he acted involuntarily. That is why Socrates tells Crito that "one must never *voluntarily* do an injustice, whatever the circumstances . . . (49a4, emphasis added). Similarly, in the *Apology* he tells the jury, ". . . either I do not corrupt (the young) or, if I do, it is involuntary; so what you say in either case is false. And if I corrupt involuntarily, it is not the law to bring me here for such offenses, but to take me aside privately and to teach and admonish me . . ." (25e6-26a4).[22] If a real jury composed of flesh-and-blood judges may excuse a person because he involuntarily committed an offense, then the personified Laws of our hypothetical *Crito* will also be willing to excuse those who try but fail, through no fault of their own, to live up to their strict legal philosophy.

This lesson should now be applied to the real *Crito*. The Laws say that citizens must do one of two things: persuade or obey. Someone who takes this legal philosophy to heart will always try to achieve one alternative or the other, but there may be times when he fails in his attempt to obey, and other times when he fails in his efforts to persuade the jury that his disobedience was justified. Neither failure will necessarily move the Laws to condemn him. If the citizen ought to have obeyed, but failed to do so through no fault of his own, then the Laws will excuse him. And if he was justified in disobeying, but despite every effort was unable to persuade the jury that he was in the right, the Laws again will find him faultless. But if someone

---

[22] Similarly *H. Mi.* 372a4-5.

both disobeys an order and rejects an opportunity to persuade a jury that he is right to disobey, then he is in flagrant violation of the persuade-or-obey doctrine. At a later point in this chapter, I will explain why the Laws make precisely this accusation against an escaping Socrates.

5
Second objection: Trying to persuade

Suppose the Laws had said, "Obey or *try* to persuade the city as to the nature of justice." In that case, there would be little doubt about their meaning: they would be saying that a citizen can be right to violate an order, provided that he appears before a court to argue that his disobedience was justified. Actually persuading the jury would not be a necessary condition of legitimate disobedience. Now, someone might claim that the Laws are undeniably saying "persuade or obey," rather than "try to persuade or obey." And from this it might be inferred that they are not going to tolerate a mere attempt to persuade the city; rather, the citizen has to obey the law or *succeed* at persuasion. If this is correct, then the Laws cannot approve of someone who first disobeys a law and then tries to persuade a jury that he was in the right. The Laws are demanding success at persuasion, and the disobedient citizen has no way of knowing in advance that he can achieve such success. Therefore, the citizen must play it safe: he may try to get a law repealed, but until he actually persuades the Assembly to do so, he must obey that law.

There are two mistakes in this argument. First, it is simply not true that whoever says "persuade so-and-so" will tolerate no failures. Imagine a government official telling his subordinate, "You must persuade Mr. Jones to vote for our bill." Nothing in this command suggests that the subordinate will be blamed for anything less than success. There is only the smallest of differences between "you must persuade" and "you must try to persuade." The latter expresses the speaker's awareness that persuasion is not entirely in the hearer's power, and it signals a willingness to tolerate honest failure. But someone who says

"you must persuade" may be equally tolerant. We do not have
to say "try to do X" every time we realize that the hearer may
not be able to do X through no fault of his own. Therefore,
even if the Laws say "persuade or obey" rather than "try to
persuade or obey," that fact does no damage to my interpretation. They are not thereby making successful persuasion a necessary condition of justified disobedience.

To see the second mistake, we must take note of a gram-
matical point. In the present and imperfect tenses, Greek verbs
can have what is called a "conative" force; that is, a word that
means "to do X" can in the right context mean "to try to do
X."[23] For example, in the *Apology*, Socrates says, ". . . I go
about doing nothing other than persuading [*peithōn*] you, young
and old, not to care for your body and possessions in preference
to or as strongly as the best possible state of your soul . . ."
(30a7-b2). Somewhat later, he compares himself to a gadfly that
alights upon a sluggish horse; he tells his judges that wherever
he settles down, he "never ceases to rouse you and persuade
[*peithōn*] you and blame each of you, the whole day long . . ."
(30e7-31a1). Of course, Socrates realizes that he has not actually
succeeded in persuading his fellow citizens that his moral opinions are correct: he admits that on some of the most important
points, he remains practically a minority of one. Thus, when
he says that he does nothing other than persuade the citizens,
or that he never ceases to rouse and persuade them, he must
strictly mean "try to persuade." Now, wherever the Laws tell
the citizen that he must persuade or obey, the tense of *peithein*
(persuade) is present, and so the Greek is more ambiguous than
we may have realized. That is where the second mistake occurs:
the Laws do not necessarily mean "persuade or obey" rather
than "try to persuade or obey." But how can we tell which is
the right reading? Are we dealing with a persuade-or-obey doctrine or a try-to-persuade-or-obey doctrine? The right reading
will be the one that makes the best sense of the speech of the
Laws, and this means that whichever interpretation makes the
Crito consistent with the *Apology* should be chosen. In my own

[23] See Smyth, *Greek Grammar*, pp. 421 (present conative) and 424 (imperfect
conative).

opinion, both readings of *peithein* allow for consistency. For reasons I have just given, even if the Laws mean "persuade or obey" rather than "try to persuade or obey," their doctrine makes room for disobedience. So I think it is an arbitrary matter whether we translate *peithein* by "persuade" or by "try to persuade." For the sake of brevity, I will continue to refer to their doctrine as the persuade-or-obey doctrine. But someone might disagree with my argument. It might be said that the Laws allow disobedience only if *peithein* has conative force. Those who take this position ought to come to the conclusion that "try to persuade" is the proper translation, since it is the one that makes best philosophical sense of the dialogue.[24] They will therefore agree with me that when the *Crito* tells the citizen to obey or *peithein*, it allows for justified disobedience.

6
Third objection: Woozley and civil disobedience

As we saw earlier, Woozley believes that the Laws allow the citizen "the limited freedom of persuading (or trying to persuade) authority to change its mind before submitting to it. . . ."[25] But at the same time, he takes the persuade-or-obey doctrine to permit disobedience: it "says that a man is *either* to persuade *or* to obey, not that he must go on obeying until he can persuade the law that right is on his side."[26] According to this interpretation, the Laws concede that a citizen may violate a law as part of a campaign of protest and civil disobedience. By acting unlawfully, he might persuade his fellow citizens to repeal the offensive statute. But if the city does not change its mind, and the law remains in force, then the citizen must in the end obey.

[24] If the Laws mean "obey or *try* to persuade," they do not have to concede that a citizen who tries but fails to persuade cannot be criticized or punished. For he may have made the wrong decision when he chose to disobey. The fact that an alternative to obedience (namely, an attempt at persuasion) may be justified does not mean that it is always the right alternative. See III.7 for further discussion.
[25] *Law and Obedience*, p. 71.
[26] Ibid., p. 30, his emphasis.

Although I applaud Woozley's idea that the persuade-or-obey doctrine leaves room for disobedience,[27] I reject his claim that an unsuccessful persuader must submit to his city's orders. But it might be thought that logic is on his side: if someone is told to do A or B but fails at one, isn't he required as a matter of logic to do the other? If the citizen decides not to obey, then he must persuade the city that he is in the right; but if this attempt to persuade fails, he has to pursue the other alternative, however reluctantly.

But logic requires nothing of the sort. Someone who is told to do A or B does not necessarily have to do B if he fails at A. Consider an example. Suppose a father tells his son to clean either the kitchen or the dining room floor. He chooses the former task, but after much effort, fails to get the spots out. Is he now required by "the logic of commands" to clean the other floor? If so, then "Do A or B" means the same as "Either do A (and failing that, do B) or do B (and failing that, do A)." But obviously these are different commands. "Do A or B" simply does not say what someone is to do if he tries one of the alternatives and fails; it is therefore a far more indefinite command than the ludicrously precise order, "Either do A (and failing that, do B) or do B (and failing that, do A)."[28] The father in our example has simply failed to say what is expected of his son should the floor prove uncleanable; and similarly, we have to admit that the Laws do not tell the citizen what to do if he tries to persuade but the jury proves unpersuadable. But surely there is a reasonable way to fill out their idea. They must mean that if the citizen has violated an unjust order, and if he has failed to persuade the jury only because it is unpersuadable, then he has already done enough; he need not turn to the other alternative, and obey the law. At any rate, this is what Socrates must take the Laws to mean. As we can see from the *Apology*, he is not going to disobey the god and commit an injustice

---

[27] Woozley first put forward this interpretation in "Socrates on Disobeying the Law." See esp. pp. 306-308.

[28] And for the same reason, "persuade or obey" is different from Tredennick's "if you cannot persuade your country you must do whatever it orders."

merely because he is unable to persuade the city to rescind its order.

One further point. We must be careful not to confuse the contemporary tactic known as "civil disobedience" with the kind of illegal behavior that the Laws are willing to approve. A person engages in civil disobedience when he publicly breaks a law as a way of demonstrating his sincere belief that legal change is necessary. Typically, those who act in this way are eager to influence the law-making branch of the government, and it is common to view their illegal protest as a form of speech or persuasion.[29] Woozley evidently believes that this is the sort of disobedience the Laws have in mind: "The *Crito* view is that he [the citizen] may disobey, but not unless he is engaged in publicly *protesting*, or trying to persuade the authorities of, the injustice."[30] But surely this is an anachronism; Woozley is reading a contemporary form of political action back into the *Crito*, where it does not belong. The Greeks did not go on protest marches; Socrates never staged a sit-in. When the Laws tell the citizen to persuade or obey, they merely mean that a citizen who does not obey must persuade in the good old-fashioned sense of the word: he must speak before a court and justify his disobedience. No Greek ever thought that illegal behavior might itself be a form of speech or persuasion. Contrast the way Woozley uses "persuade" in the following sentence: "Gestures such as blacks daring to sit at the front of the bus, or to drink from whites-only water-fountains, may have been less effective *persuaders* than their economic boycott of white-owned businesses, but they were carried out as part of a campaign of *persuasion*."[31] These uses of "persuade" have no parallel in ancient Greek politics, for the Greeks had no tradition or notion of protesting against a law by violating it.[32] When Antigone and Socrates disobey an order, they do not think of their illegal acts as "persuaders" or as parts of a "campaign of persuasion." Therefore, when the *Crito* tells the citizen to persuade or obey,

[29] Thus Rawls, *A Theory of Justice*, p. 366.
[30] *Law and Obedience*, p. 41, emphasis added.
[31] Ibid., p. 31, emphasis added.
[32] Here I am repeating a point I made in "Two Recent Studies," pp. 661-662.

it is not proposing an attention-getting tactic for changing the law. Rather, it is saying that whoever disobeys owes the city an explanation. It is therefore best to avoid the term "civil disobedience" when we talk about this dialogue. That phrase denotes a modern form of political protest, and should not be used to describe every act of principled law-breaking.[33]

7
Fourth objection: Are the Laws too lax?

In my opinion, the Laws can be taken to mean either "persuade or obey" or "try to persuade or obey," since these injunctions come to the same thing. But Woozley says that the try-to-persuade reading is unsatisfactory: ". . . the trouble with that solution . . . is that it is too easy, too permissive; it makes any disobedience at all to a law legitimate, only so long as it is a sincere and principled attempt to change the minds of those who have the authority to alter or repeal the law."[34] Similarly, Santas protests against the obey-or-try-to-persuade interpretation: ". . . anyone could get out of having to obey any law or order simply by attempting to persuade."[35] Evidently, Woozley and Santas think that the Laws are laying down necessary and sufficient conditions for justified political behavior. On their interpretation, whoever has either persuaded or obeyed has done enough, and therefore if "try to persuade" were to replace "persuade," the *Crito* would emerge with an absurdly lenient legal philosophy.

But why should we assume that the persuade-or-obey doctrine gives us necessary and sufficient conditions for justified political behavior? The text merely says, ". . . in battle and in court and everywhere one must do what the city and fatherland commands, or persuade it as to the nature of justice . . ." (51b8-c1). And this can easily be taken as a necessary but not a sufficient condition for right action. The citizen must choose one or

---

[33] Here I follow Rawls, *A Theory of Justice*, pp. 363-368; and Cohen, "Liberalism and Disobedience," pp. 283-285.

[34] *Law and Obedience*, p. 32.

[35] *Socrates*, p. 308.

the other of these alternatives, but that does not mean that by merely choosing one or the other he will be beyond criticism. After all, Socrates could hardly endorse the idea that so long as you obey the law you will be in the right. *That* would be too lax. When the Laws tell the citizen to persuade or obey, they must mean that anyone who refuses both alternatives is doing the city an injustice. That is all they need to say, since they think that an escaping Socrates will be such a person.

So, if the Laws mean, "one must obey or try to persuade," they are not making life ridiculously easy for the citizen. Whoever disobeys must "persuade as to the nature of justice," and obviously if someone disobeys out of a faulty conception of justice, then he has acted in error. Similarly, those who break their word must try to persuade the person to whom they are obligated (51e6-7), but this does not mean that breaking an agreement is justified whenever one tries to persuade. The Laws build on the principle of just agreements: they must therefore realize that the only agreements that can be broken, and the only orders that can be disobeyed, are the ones that are unjust. Persuasion is the procedure to be followed when one disobeys or breaks one's word, but we have no reason to accuse the *Crito* of confusing procedural and substantive questions. Whoever disobeys the law because he thinks it unjust will be subject to criticism if in fact it is just.

8
Fifth objection: Athenian law and opportunities for persuasion

There is a final, lingering doubt the reader may have about my interpretation of the persuade-or-obey doctrine: "You seem to be ignoring the fact that there has to be some intimate connection between what the Laws are saying and the legal institutions of Athens. When the Laws say that they allow the citizen two alternatives—to obey or persuade—they must mean that the actual laws or legal practices of the Athenians did allow for these two alternatives. To see this, consider another point they make: they tell Socrates that every Athenian citizen had the opportunity to take his belongings and leave the city if the laws were not satisfactory to him (51d2-e1). Obviously, the Laws would not say such a thing unless Athens actually did grant this freedom to its citizens; they are not inventing things about the legal system to suit the purposes of their argument. Similarly, when they say that the citizen can either persuade or obey, they must be referring to some actual alternative that was built into the legal system at that time. But doesn't this fact count heavily against your interpretation? For you are saying that the persuade-or-obey doctrine concedes that under certain conditions disobedience is justified. But what Athenian law granted this? Was there really a custom or practice in fifth-century Athens which allowed citizens to disobey orders? Did some second-order law or some common understanding specify the conditions under which disobedience could be carried out? There is not a shred of evidence for such a law or practice. But we do know that Athens built opportunities for persuasion into its institutions in certain ways: the full-fledged Athenian citizen could participate in the creation and repeal of the law; furthermore, anyone who was tried for a crime could not only speak in his defense, but could even propose an alternative form of punishment. But in all these cases, it was the common understanding that if one did not succeed in persuading others, then one had to go along with the majority. Surely that is what the Laws must mean by their persuade-or-obey doctrine. Although your proposal is a theoretical possibility and does reconcile the *Crito* with Plato's other early works, it cannot be accepted, since it does not fit the historical facts."

But this objection insists on too close a fit between the *Crito*'s legal philosophy and the actual customs of Athens. The speech of the Laws is a complicated mixture of Socratic philosophy and Athenian legal practice, and thus certain features of the speech will be straightforward reportage of facts, and other parts will be controversial philosophical doctrine which few Athenians other than Socrates would have accepted. The Laws agree with Socrates that injustice must never be done; though this unconditional principle had few adherents in ancient Greece, it is the foundation on which the Laws build their case against escape.

Furthermore, the Laws agree that Socrates was innocent of the charges against him, in spite of the fact that he has just been found guilty by a large, popular jury. So we must not think that every presupposition and claim made by the Laws would have been widely accepted. They are putting forward the sort of jurisprudence that Socrates can applaud, and we should not assume that this will also be the jurisprudence of the average citizen, if there was such a thing. In any case, there was no common understanding in Athens that one ought always to abide by the decisions of a lawful majority. To see this, we need only recall the complaint Crito makes at the beginning of the dialogue: if Socrates fails to escape, the many will think of him and his friends as cowards (45d8-46a4). Evidently, by remaining in jail, Socrates is doing something that many do not expect of him. It should be no surprise, then, if the philosophy that led him to die was not part of the common understanding either.

When the Laws say that citizens must persuade or obey, they are not uttering a phrase that was on the lips of every Athenian citizen actively engaged in politics. Nor should we hold our breath waiting for the day when we find an inscription of an Athenian law telling the citizen to persuade or obey. Books on Greek law do not and should not use the *Crito* as evidence that there was in fifth-century Athens a law, perhaps unwritten, according to which each citizen had to obey the city's orders or persuade it "as to the nature of justice." Obviously, what the persuade-or-obey doctrine gives us is a philosophical doctrine about how the citizen should treat the law; it is not an actual part of the legal system. Of course, if the Laws are making any sense at all, there has to be some correspondence between their persuade-or-obey doctrine and Athenian law. Certain legal institutions had to provide the citizen with opportunities to persuade, if he did not want to obey. More specifically, my interpretation will be correct only if there were in late fifth-century Athens courts before which a citizen could explain why justice prevented him from carrying out an order. But of course this presents no problem for my view, for whenever citizens violated a law or an order, it was not the customary practice in Athens to condemn and punish them without a trial. Even those who had violated a military officer's command—for example by running away in battle—were given an opportunity to defend themselves before a jury and to seek acquittal.[36] So, I happily accept the point that there is an intimate connection between the speech of the Laws and the legal institutions of Athens. But I insist that my interpretation satisfies this condition.

One further point about Athenian legal practices should be made. Athenian juries had far more latitude and were far less bound by rules of procedure than their contemporary counterparts in the democratic world. No legally trained officer instructed them on points of law or controlled their decision making. Rather, the five hundred[37] amateur jurors formed a small-scale popular assembly, with full power to acquit even when the defendant admitted that he had in fact violated the law or order in question. As Dover says:

> Since the Athenian people was the source of the law, the people, as sovereign, could forgive its breach. Thus the question before a jury, as representing the people, was not exactly, "Has this man, or has he not, committed the act with which he is charged?" but rather, "What should be done about this man, who has been charged with this offence?"[38]

Therefore, the courtroom was the appropriate place for a citizen to defend his disobedience by impugning the justice of the law or order he violated. No one had the legal authority to silence such a defense. No one would have instructed the jury: "we are not here to decide the justice or injustice of the order that was violated; all that matters is whether the accused did in fact voluntarily disobey the city." So the persuade-or-obey doctrine, as I understand it, had a natural setting in the Athenian legal system. The courts could be used by those who disobeyed, and could be persuaded "as to the nature of justice."[39]

---

[36] See MacDowell, *The Law in Classical Athens*, pp. 160-161.

[37] A common number in the fourth century, though the size of juries varied. About the size of fifth-century juries we know far less. See MacDowell, ibid., pp. 36-38.

[38] *Greek Popular Morality*, p. 292.

[39] I know of no case in which an Athenian actually admitted to a court that

9

The Laws and the laws

When we ask what the *Laws* of Athens say—I stress the capital "L"—we are concerned with the legal philosophy of Plato's *Crito*. But if we ask what the *laws* of Athens say, we are concerned with statutes that were actually in force at the time of Socrates. The *Crito* does not make this distinction, and the Laws do not refer to themselves with a capital "N" (for *nomoi*). They thus blend together what we ought to keep apart, for the sake of clarity. For example, they say, "With this attempted act, are you thinking of anything else than destroying us, the Laws, and the entire city, for your part?" (50a9-b2). As the text soon tells us (50b7-8), if Socrates escapes he will be destroying a particular law that was in force in Athens—the law that gave authority to the democratic courts. Of course, escape will not destroy the hypothetical figures that appear in the *Crito*, since they are merely characters in a dialogue and do not exist. Nonetheless, those personified Laws think of themselves as continuous with laws that really do exist, and they therefore describe an attack on the actual laws of Athens as an attack upon *themselves*. Similarly, they say that whoever remains in the city and is satisfied with it "has agreed with us to carry out whatever we command . . ." (51e3-4). Socrates "neither obeys nor persuades us if we are doing something wrong . . ." (51e7). Here and in many other

---

he had disobeyed an order but argued that nonetheless he was blameless because the order in question was unjust. But I am not claiming that such a defense was ever used. Rather, my claim is that according to the speech of the Laws such a defense would be perfectly legitimate. Suppose Socrates had been brought to trial by the Thirty for having disobeyed them in the case of Leon. Undoubtedly, he would have said, "It is true that I disobeyed you, but the order you gave me required wrongdoing, and therefore I was right to disobey; and since I am blameless, I deserve no punishment." This is not a defense that would have saved his life, the Thirty being what they were. In general, the persuade-or-obey doctrine might not have given Athenian citizens a good chance to win acquittal, even when they were democratically governed. Nonetheless, "I disobeyed because the order was unjust" is the sort of defense that Socrates thinks one should be willing to give when one deliberately refuses to comply with the city's commands. And it is the sort of plea one could have presented in an Athenian court. Socrates would not have been moved by the complaint that such a defense might be unlikely to win acquittal.

cases, the Laws identify themselves with the city and its legal apparatus. Socrates did not make an agreement with the hypothetical Laws; rather, he committed himself to obeying a real city. If he disobeys, he is not to hold an imaginary conversation with imaginary Laws in order to persuade *them* that *they* are wrong. He is to address the city in the appropriate public forum, and convince his fellow citizens that the city they represent is wrong.

This blending of the Laws and the laws into a unitary being has an obvious danger: we might come to think that whatever the city's legal apparatus condemns is also condemned by the Laws. After all, if Socrates is destroying "us"—i.e. the Laws— by destroying a law, then he will be disobeying "us"—i.e. the Laws—whenever he violates a law. This sounds perfectly logical, and it leads immediately to Grote's reading of the *Crito*, but as we have seen, it turns out to be wrong. What the Laws say in the *Crito* includes much that no law of Athens ever said, and the Laws can see through the city's errors. In the same way, to disobey a law is not necessarily to disobey the Laws; in other words, someone who violates the city's orders is not necessarily departing from the philosophy of the Laws. The laws and the Laws of the *Crito* are an artful mixture of the real and the ideal: the dialogue's main speakers identify themselves with the laws that actually exist, but they also describe the jurisprudence that Athens ought to have. Fortunately, once we recognize these two sides of their personality, they are easy enough to disentangle.

10
Accepting the punishment

Thus far, I have been assuming that when a citizen violates a law or an order, the appropriate time for persuasion comes after he has acted illegally. That is, I have been imagining that first a citizen is called upon by the Assembly or a legal official to perform some act; then the citizen refuses to obey; and finally he is called before the court, where he tries to justify his illegal behavior. Now I want to point out that this need not always be the pattern of disobedience. Consider the following kind of case. A citizen is being tried for having committed a crime (it doesn't matter which), and has just been found guilty. The prosecutor recommends that the guilty party be punished by being made to perform act X, an act that the guilty party correctly believes to be one that a just man must never do. Now, the persuade-or-obey doctrine, as I interpret it, allows a citizen to violate an order that requires unjust behavior, so long as he justifies his conduct before the city. In this particular case, therefore, the citizen must explain to the court that the impending order, which is being recommended by the prosecutor, is one that he will do his best to evade. After all, this would be the open and honest thing to do: better for the citizen in this situation to explain then and there that he cannot go along with that form of punishment, than to evade his punishment with no prior warning.[40] So in this case, persuasion (or an attempt at persuasion) comes before disobedience, rather than afterwards. But that is something which the text allows, for the Laws do not always present the alternatives—persuade or obey—in the same order, and so their doctrine can as much be called the obey-or-persuade doctrine as the persuade-or-obey doctrine. At 51b3-4 we are told to persuade or to do what the city commands; several lines later (b9-c1) the order is reversed. Then,

[40] Recall our discussion in I.3: Socrates tells the jurors that if they were going to propose a ban on philosophy, he would disobey it. Suppose the historical facts had been different, and Meletus really had told the jury that he was going to recommend a ban on philosophy as the appropriate punishment for Socrates. Surely Socrates would have told the jury that he would violate such a ban. I take him to believe that this sort of honesty is what every citizen owes his city: faced with a penalty that requires wrongdoing, anyone ought to give prior warning that he will not cooperate. If this is what Socrates believes, and if the Laws are a vehicle for the expression of Socratic thought, then they would hold that attempts to persuade must sometimes precede disobedience. A further line of thought supports this same conclusion. Any interpretation of the persuade-or-obey doctrine must explain the complaint, made at *Crito* 52a2-3, that an escaping Socrates has neither persuaded nor obeyed. When was the appropriate time for Socrates to persuade? Whom should he have persuaded? Of what? I shall argue in III.11 that the Laws are alluding to the way Socrates conducted his defense. He did not even try to persuade the jury that cooperating with the death penalty would be an unjust act. If this is the right reading of 52a2-3, then we have a further reason for thinking that, according to the Laws, the appropriate time for persuasion is sometimes prior to the time one disobeys.

when the Laws come back to the doctrine at 51e7–52a3, they again pay no attention to the order of the alternatives: they complain that Socrates neither obeys nor persuades (51e7), and point out that they are being very lenient in allowing the citizen either to persuade or obey (52a2–3). Evidently, the text gives no indication that the attempt to persuade must precede or that it must follow the failure to obey. And this is as it should be, for surely the appropriate temporal sequence depends on the circumstances. When one is about to be issued an order by a court, it is appropriate to announce one's reasons for not co-operating then and there, for the court is the proper body before which such explanations must be given. But when the Assembly passes a law that one cannot obey, and one is brought before a court for disobedience, then one will be defending one's illegal behavior after it has taken place.

It is important to remember that in many legal cases, including the trial of Socrates, no fixed penalty was attached to a guilty verdict. The prosecutor could recommend any penalty he wished, though death, exile, disenfranchisement, and fines were the most common forms of punishment; in turn, the defendant could propose any alternative punishment; and the jury was forced to choose between these two alternatives—it could not select a third. So, in many cases the legal system left open the possibility that a jury would require some unusual punishment to which the defendant might object on moral grounds. Perhaps it will be thought that the possibility of such a form of punishment was remote, and that it would have occurred to no one. But that suggestion seems doubtful to me. Meletus might have proposed that Socrates be forbidden to conduct philosophical conversations with young people in public places. And that is certainly a form of punishment with which Socrates could not cooperate: given his conception of his philosophical mission, he would have had to consider himself an unjust man had he continued to live in Athens while abiding by such restrictions. We should also recall the point that Socrates makes in the *Apology*: if the court were to release him on condition that he refrain from philosophical inquiry, he would disobey (29b9–d5). Socrates is quite capable of thinking of unreal or unlikely possibilities and saying that he would not obey an order in those fanciful situations. So I see nothing strained about attributing to him the position that, had Meletus recommended a ban on Socratic inquiry and had the jury voted in favor of that, he would disobey. But certainly his disobedience could satisfy the conditions for legitimate law-breaking established by the persuade-or-obey doctrine. The whole of the *Apology* is an attempt to explain the idea that Socrates must engage in philosophy in order to be a virtuous man. It is, in other words, an attempt to persuade the jury that he could never give up the philosophical life, no matter what he were commanded to do. So, had the court ordered him to give up philosophy, he would have disobeyed, but he would also have tried to persuade the jurors that he could not obey such an order, since it required him to act unjustly.

The interpretation I am supporting goes contrary to the views of a number of scholars, who hold that according to the *Crito* one must always accept one's punishment.[41] I see no reason for attributing such a doctrine to the Laws or to Socrates.[42] Of course, it is true that Socrates thinks he should accept the punishment of death, even though he has committed no crime. But that does not show that he thinks one must always accept the punishment, no matter what it is. It is crucial here to observe the usual distinction between doing injustice and suffering injustice. The Laws are arguing that Socrates must accept his punishment even though he thereby suffers an injustice. That hardly

---

[41] Santas, *Socrates*, pp. 50, 53; Allen, *Socrates and Legal Obligation*, p. 86; Cohen, "Liberalism and Disobedience," pp. 288, 292.

[42] Here again, (cf. nn. 10, 28) the reader should be warned against Tredennick's translation. He renders 51b3-5, ". . . if you cannot persuade your country you must do whatever it orders, and patiently submit to any punishment that it imposes, whether it be flogging or imprisonment. . . ." It is closer to the Greek if we say, ". . . you must persuade it or do what it commands, and endure in silence what it orders you to endure, whether you are beaten or bound. . . ." As I interpret these lines, they mean that one must either (A) persuade, or (B) do whatever the city commands, and endure in silence what it orders you to endure, whether you are beaten or bound. That is, persuading is an alternative to silently accepting the city's punishment. On Tredennick's interpretation, however, one must always accept one's punishment if one fails to persuade. I think this a misinterpretation; more important, his translation misleads the reader, since it prejudges the issue.

commits them to the view that citizens must accept punishment even when it requires them to *do* injustice or to lead an unjust life. There is no evidence that they advocate such a thesis, and of course Socrates could never have endorsed it.[43]

If my view is correct, then the *Crito*'s legal theory treats court orders, military orders, and all other political orders in just the same way: none is to be obeyed blindly and unconditionally. To determine whether any order can be obeyed, one must always examine its content; the fact that it comes from a legislative body or a court or a general does not settle the matter. Notice that the text of the *Crito* makes a court's orders no less and no more important than a military officer's: ". . . in battle and in court and everywhere, one must do what the city and fatherland commands, or persuade it as to the nature of justice . . ." (51b8–c1). This shows that the Laws do not think there is a greater need to obey a court than there is to obey a military officer: both cases are governed by the persuade-or-obey doctrine. Whenever one voluntarily agrees to obey the unjust orders of an officer or legal body, one must honor one's agreement, except when that agreement requires the doing of injustice. It is this general principle—not some unconditional acceptance of punishment—that leads Socrates to his death.

In Section 3 of this chapter, I separated two questions that might be asked about a disobedient person who tried but failed to persuade a jury that his illegal behavior was right. First, would the Laws find fault with him? To that, I replied that the Laws would find fault if and only if the citizen was wrong to violate the order in the first place. Second, must the citizen who has failed to persuade the jury accept his punishment? To this too, as we now see, a conditional answer must be given. If the citizen has agreed to abide by court decisions, then he may refuse to accept the court's punishment if and only if that punishment

---

[43] Recall that we still have not answered this question: can one legitimately reside in a city and refuse to agree to certain laws, on the grounds that they are unjust to the citizens? If so, there will be wider scope for refusing to accept one's punishment. For there can be penalties, fixed by law, that are unjust to the convicted individual, and if the citizen has justifiably refused to agree to such laws, then he might also be justified in resisting those penalties. I return to this issue in Ch. VI n. 13.

requires the doing of injustice or the leading of an unjust life. Thus, a citizen who is not in fact guilty of the crime for which he is being punished must accept certain forms of punishment, though he need not accept others. To die, according to Socrates, is to do no one an injustice, and it certainly does not involve leading an unjust life. So his agreement to abide by the court's decision must be respected.

Another loose end can now be secured. In Section 2 of this chapter, we looked at a question raised by Cohen: ". . . What would it mean to extend a general legal or de facto right to civil disobedience? And if there were such a right, in what sense would those who exercised it thereby express dissent . . .?"[44] Since we have seen the dangers of using the term "civil disobedience" in discussions of the *Crito*, let us transform this question so that it reads: "What would it mean to extend a general right to disobey the law?" But surely this question does not have to be answered by the *Crito*, since this dialogue extends no such *right*. If someone has a right to do something, then it is wrong for the government to punish him for doing it. But as we have just seen, the Laws do not argue that all those who disobey the city should go unpunished. What the dialogue recognizes is that disobedience can be *justified* in certain circumstances; we should not speak loosely and turn this into a "right to disobey."[45] Morrow is therefore technically correct when he says, "There is no hint in any of the dialogues that Plato recognizes the *right* of civil disobedience" (emphasis added). But the spirit of his remark becomes apparent when he next says, "A citizen may try to persuade the laws that they are wrong, . . . but he may not disobey. . . ."[46] On the contrary: the citizen

---

[44] "Liberalism and Democracy," p. 313.

[45] If "permitted" is used in such a way that "A is permitted by B to do X" entails "B gives A a right to do X, " then I would also deny that the Laws are permitting the citizen to disobey the law. But "permitted" is often used more loosely. If a moral theory permits a certain kind of act, this means that such acts can be justified, not that we have a right to perform them. In this sense, utilitarianism permits lying: it doesn't give people a right to lie, but it insists that lies are justified in certain circumstances. It is only in this looser sense that the Laws permit disobedience.

[46] *Plato's Cretan City*, p. 569.

may be right to break the law, even though no one has a general
right to disobey.

11
Why do the Laws say that Socrates neither persuades nor obeys?

At 51e7-52a3, the Laws complain that Socrates neither obeys
nor persuades. Precisely what are they getting at? Which order
is he disobeying? For which proposition has he given no effective argument?

One reply to these questions is as follows. "The city has ordered its citizens not to introduce new gods, and not to corrupt
the young. For these prohibitions are included in its law against
impiety. Now, Socrates has been charged with disobeying this
law, and he has not persuaded the jury of his innocence. Anyone who voted to find him guilty would agree that he neither
obeyed nor persuaded." The trouble with this reply is that it is
the Laws who are charging Socrates with neither obeying nor
persuading, and the opinion of the Laws does not coincide with
the opinion of the court's majority. The Laws think that in fact
Socrates did *not* violate the law that Meletus accused him of
violating; for they admit that the jury came to the wrong verdict (50c1-6, 54c2-3). So, in the eyes of the Laws, he did fail to
persuade the jury of his innocence, but nonetheless he obeyed
the law. In this respect, he successfully fulfilled one of the alternatives in the persuade-or-obey doctrine, and so the Laws
must have something else in mind when they accuse him of
violating that doctrine.

Surely what they have in mind is this. After a court decides
that someone is guilty as charged, the prosecutor recommends
that a certain form of punishment be inflicted. The defendant is
thereby put on notice that he is about to receive a certain order
from his city, and it is now his job to propose an alternative. If
the prosecutor's order requires him to do something wrong,
shameful, or unjust, then he must persuade the court of this
fact, and he must show that the act of disobedience he would

attempt is justified.[47] Applied to Socrates, this means that if he thought that a good man ought not to cooperate with his own death penalty, then he should have argued as much in the courtroom; he should have announced that he would escape from jail, and he should have shown the jury that this act would be justified. But obviously he did no such thing. He did not even attempt to persuade the court that he would justifiably resist the death penalty, nor did he try to show that escape from jail would be a legitimate act of disobedience.[48] Since he made no such attempts at persuasion, he obviously would be flouting the persuade-or-obey doctrine were he to escape from jail. He passed up his chance to persuade at the time of his trial, and that means that he must now accept the other alternative: to obey. He did, of course, try to persuade the court of his innocence, and he halfheartedly proposed a counter-penalty;[49] but in neither case

[47] Of course, if the defendant is innocent of the charges against him, then the proposed penalty will require him to *suffer* injustice; but as we saw earlier (II.4), that will not provide him with a reason for disobedience, if he agreed to abide by the court's decision. That agreement can be justifiably broken only when it calls for unjust behavior, and in all such cases the violator must persuade the other party that the act by which he breaks faith is legitimate.

[48] The injustice of escape is made all the more obvious by the fact that Socrates refused to propose exile as a counter-penalty. As the Laws say, ". . . At the trial you could have proposed exile as a penalty, if you had wanted to, and what you are now attempting, against the will of the city, you could then have done, with the city willing" (52c4-6). This should not be taken to mean that if Socrates *had* proposed exile, then he would be justified in escaping. But this remark of the Laws does show that, in their opinion, the wrongfulness of escape is connected with the way Socrates conducted himself at his trial. Escape is legitimate only if exile was the appropriate form of punishment for Socrates, and if it was appropriate, then he should have said so to the jury. Socrates refused to propose exile for the same reason that he refused to announce, at his trial, that he would attempt to escape from jail: he thinks death preferable to the life of a homeless and rejected wanderer, since as a wanderer he could not carry out his philosophical mission.

[49] Socrates does offer thirty minae (*Ap.* 38b6-9; contrast Xenophon, *Ap.* 23; Diogenes Laertius 2.41-42) as a counter-penalty, and it has been argued that this was a substantial sum. See Brickhouse and Smith, "Socrates' Proposed Penalty in Plato's *Apology*." But even so, I think it fair to say that his counterproposal is half-hearted. His first idea—that he deserves free meals in the Prytaneum (*Ap.* 36d4-37a1)—assures the jury that he is entirely unrepentant; so the court knows, when he supersedes his first proposal with another, that even if Socrates pays a hefty fine, he is nonetheless going to be back in the marketplace, committing philosophical acts once again. And surely, in that case, he would

was that the sort of persuasion or attempt at persuasion that would have satisfied the persuade-or-obey doctrine. According to that doctrine, someone who disobeys an order must at least try to persuade a jury that his act of disobedience was or will be justified. To meet this demand, Socrates ought to have argued at his trial that escape would be just. Once we understand what the Laws are getting at when they accuse an escaping Socrates of neither persuading nor obeying, it becomes obvious that they are right.

---

be tried and convicted a second time. In effect, by first proposing free meals, Socrates sabotages the attempt made by his friends to extend his life a bit longer. That is why thirty minae, whatever its value in the Athenian economy, represents a half-hearted counter-proposal.

IV

CITIZENS AND
OFFSPRING

1
Review

WE HAVE BEEN looking at a few important lines in the speech of the Laws, so perhaps it will be useful if we briefly step back and remind ourselves of the larger picture. The Laws begin with the accusation that if Socrates escapes, he will be trying to destroy the city, for his part. They then point out that there is no excuse for such violent behavior: the laws that concern marriage and nurture have played an important role in his birth and education,[1] and so violence against his fatherland is no more justified than violence against his father. In all matters, he must do what his city commands or persuade it as to the nature of justice. Moreover, Socrates has remained in Athens even though he was free to leave, and by showing his satisfaction in this way he has agreed to obey the city. But he neither obeys nor persuades. Though he is indebted to Athens for his life and edu-

---

[1] More specifically, they refer to a law that called upon Socrates' father to educate him in music and gymnastics (50d8-e1). Harrison, *The Law of Athens*, Vol. I, pp. 78-79 n. 3, speculates that this is Plato's "free interpretation" of a law (attributed to Solon by Plutarch) requiring fathers to teach their sons a craft (*technē*). But I see no reason not to take the *Crito* at its word: some law urged parents to spend what they could on music and gymnastics lessons for their children. It is apparent from Aeschines 1.9-12 that the city regulated the conduct of music and gymnastics teachers, but this does not mean that Athens *required* all children to attend. We know from *Protag.* 326c3-6 that the amount of training the child received depended on the wealth of his parents. In any case, even those children whose parents could not afford to train them in music and gymnastics were indebted to the law Plutarch attributes to Solon: it was because of the city that they received a useful trade.

cation, and though he voluntarily agreed to obey, he nonetheless plans to violate the city's command without defending his behavior. Thus he does the city a threefold injustice.

There is still a good deal in this argument that requires explanation. For example, we saw in Chapter II that the opening move of the Laws—their attempt to implicate Socrates in the destruction of the city—is suspicious. ". . . Does it seem to you that a city can exist and not be overturned if its verdicts have no force, but are robbed of authority and destroyed by private individuals?" (50b2-5). What is meant by a private individual? Are the Laws fallaciously moving from "not everyone should do that" to "no one should do that"? Furthermore, there are more questions to be raised about the persuade-or-obey doctrine. What presuppositions about parental authority are they relying on? What is implied by their statement that the citizen is not only the offspring of the city, but also its slave (50e4)? In this chapter, we will take a closer look at the analogy by which the Laws defend the persuade-or-obey doctrine. Then, in Chapter V, we will finally return to the puzzling claim that an escaping Socrates destroys the city, for his part.

2
Honor and independence

The Laws claim that a citizen of Athens is the city's offspring (*ekgonos*, 50e3). Because of the way the city regulates marriage and early training, the individual is as much a product of his community as he is a product of his parents. Soon afterwards, they draw some conclusions from this analogy between offspring and citizens:

> Are you too wise to realize that your fatherland is more to be honored, more revered, more holy, and held in higher esteem, both among gods and among sensible men, than your mother, father, and other ancestors? It is more necessary to honor, yield to, and soothe an angered fatherland than an angered father. *You must persuade it or do what it commands*, and endure in silence what it orders you to en-

dure, whether you are beaten or bound, whether you are led into war to be wounded or killed; these things must be done, and there justice lies. You must neither yield nor run away nor leave your post, but in battle and in court and everywhere *you must do what your city and fatherland commands, or persuade it as to the nature of justice.* Violence against your mother or father is unholy, and still more so against your fatherland.[2] (51a7–c3, emphasis added)

This passage is noteworthy for its passionate tone, but amidst the rhetoric and emotion there is a perfectly coherent argument. The persuade-or-obey doctrine is stated twice. When first introduced, it is treated as a consequence of the fact that one must respect one's parent-city as well as one's parents. When it is repeated, it leads to the point that one must never do violence to a parent or to a parent-city. Here, as a first approximation, is the bare structure of the argument:

(A) An Athenian citizen is indebted both to his parents and to Athens for his life and his upbringing.

(B) Because he has received these benefits from his parents, he must honor them and he must never treat them with violence.

(C) Because he has received these benefits from his city, he must also honor it and he must never treat it with violence.

(D) To honor a city, a citizen must either obey the orders it gives him, or he must persuade it as to the nature of justice.

(E) If a citizen refuses to persuade or obey his parent-city, he is treating it with violence.

Each time the Laws state the persuade-or-obey doctrine—in (D) and in (E)—they leave something out. Consider (D). Why do they say that honoring a city requires either obedience or per-

---

[2] In Burnet's edition of the Greek text, 51a7–c3 is a single sentence, 51c2–3 ("violence against your mother . . .") being separated from the rest by a semicolon. To make the passage more readable, I have divided it into several sentences. So far as I am aware, this does not beg any interpretive questions.

suasion? Why must honor, or respect, or reverence take that
particular form? A similar question applies to (E). Why is a
citizen doing violence to his city when he neither obeys nor
persuades it? But let us leave (E) aside temporarily, and concentrate on the transition from (C) to (D).

I suggest that there is a missing step between (C) and (D):

(F) Offspring honor their parents either by obeying them
or by persuading them as to the nature of justice.

This is nowhere in the text, but it is a detail the Laws need if
their analogy between cities and offspring is to work.[3] For why
should citizens have to show respect to their parent-city by persuading or obeying, if that is not the manner in which offspring
honor their parents? Evidently, the Laws are assuming that when
parents make demands on their sons and daughters, the latter
cannot merely ignore those demands—or if they do, they thereby
show great disrespect. Offspring must either persuade their parents that the parental demands are unjust, or they must obey;
and since Athenian citizens are the offspring of Athens, they
must treat the city with this same form of respect.

As I argued in Chapter III, the persuade-or-obey doctrine
allows citizens to disobey the city under certain circumstances.
In other words, (D) must mean that a citizen can continue to
respect his parent-city even when he disobeys it. Now, if the
Laws arrive at (D) by implicitly assuming (F), then the latter
must be equally permissive. It must mean that a child may disobey his parents' commands whenever those commands are unjust; so long as he tries to persuade them that he is in the right,
he does them no disrespect. After all, if the relationship between city and citizen is based on that between parent and child,
then the parent can exercise no more authority over the child
than the city exercises over the citizen. The Laws concede that
a citizen's conception of justice may be superior to his city's,
and when it is he may disobey;[4] similarly, they must be assum-

---

[3] This point is made by Santas, *Socrates*, p. 25.

[4] Recall that the parent-city analogy, as I interpret it, does not confine legitimate disobedience to those cases in which a citizen is motivated by a desire to
avoid acting unjustly. He may also disobey in order to avoid suffering injustice—unless he has made some agreement that disqualifies this objection.

ing that a child can be wiser than his parents and that he can justifiably disobey them. Now, it might be objected that the *Crito* cannot be making such outrageous assumptions about the child-parent relationship. How can the Laws assume without argument that a ten-year-old might be wiser than his parents? Surely they are making the conventional assumption that parents have a right to their children's obedience. A child might try to persuade his parents to change their minds, but if they refuse to do so, he must obey. And therefore, the interpretation I defended in Chapter III is wrong: the persuade-or-obey doctrine must mean that until a citizen gets the Assembly to change the law, he must obey it, no matter what it requires. That doctrine cannot mean one thing for children and another for citizens. The Laws take it for granted that a ten-year-old cannot disobey his parents, and they infer from this that the citizen is equally subordinate to his parent-city.

I think this objection rests on a careless reading of the *Crito*. The Laws do indeed say that the citizen is an offspring (*ekgonos*, 50e3) of the city, but this does not mean that the citizen is a little boy in his relation to the state. *Ekgonos*, like "offspring," merely signifies descent, and carries no suggestion of youth. A fifty-year-old man is as much an *ekgonos* of his parents as a newborn baby. Therefore, when the Laws say that a citizen must treat the city as offspring are expected to treat their parents, they do not necessarily mean that the city ought to exercise as much authority over its citizens as a father exercises over his ten-year-old child. They could mean instead that grown-up children have duties of respect to their parents, and that this includes the duty to persuade when one disobeys. Let us examine these alternative interpretations more fully. I can think of three possible readings.

First, the Laws might mean that throughout their lives, children must obey their parents, if they fail to persuade them to change their minds. A ten-year-old child and a fifty-year-old man are equally subordinate to their parents: they must never disobey, no matter what they are told to do. However, all offspring—even a very young child—are given the opportunity to persuade their parents that their demands are unjust.

Second, the Laws might mean that the persuade-or-obey

doctrine, interpreted conservatively, applies only to children who are old enough and rational enough to engage in argument. A five-year-old must simply obey, since his reason is too poorly developed for him to merit the opportunity to persuade. But when he reaches a certain age, he is capable of reasoning and might persuade his parents that their commands are unjust. He should therefore be given that opportunity. Nonetheless, if he fails to persuade, he must obey, no matter how old he is.

Third, the Laws might mean that the persuade-or-obey doctrine, interpreted liberally, applies to a child only when he becomes, at the age of seventeen, legally independent of his parents. From then on, he might be justified in disobeying them, but he must continue to show his respect by telling them why he thinks their commands are unjust. Of course, a mature adult might be wrong to disobey this or that order of his parents; but he need not always be wrong.

Corresponding to each of these alternatives, there is a different argument from analogy:

First alternative

(A1) Throughout his life, a child must honor and show respect to his parents.

(A2) Therefore, at every point in his life, a child must either persuade his parents or, failing that, obey them.

(A3) Therefore, a citizen must either persuade his parent-city or, failing that, obey it.

Second alternative

(B1) Throughout his life, a child must honor and show respect to his parents.

(B2) When a child reaches the age of reason, this respect is shown either by persuading his parents or, failing that, obeying them.

(B3) Therefore, citizens, all of whom have reached the age of reason, must either persuade their parent-city or, failing that, obey it.

Third alternative

(C1) Throughout his life, a child must honor and show respect to his parents.

(C2) When a child becomes legally independent at the age of seventeen, this respect is shown either by obeying his parents or, if he disobeys them, by persuading them.

(C3) Therefore, citizens, all of whom have reached the age of legal independence, must either obey their city or, if they disobey, persuade it.

We should immediately notice that there is something fishy about the first alternative. If an Athenian has the opportunity to persuade his parents at every point in his life, and if political authority is modeled after parental authority, then the citizen should also have the opportunity throughout his life to persuade his parent–city. But in fact he did not. An Athenian had to wait until he was seventeen (perhaps eighteen) before he could attend the Assembly and try to persuade the city to adopt or repeal a law.[5] If the first alternative were a proper account of the *Crito*'s argument, then five-year-olds could legitimately demand the vote. But surely the Laws are not advocating political rights for young children. They only mean that an adult citizen must manifest his respect for the city in the same way he shows his respect toward his parents. In both cases, he must persuade or obey. It would be silly to take this to mean that even a five-year-old child is given the right to persuade his parents.

But how should we decide between alternatives two and three? As I argued in Chapter III, the liberal reading of the persuade-or-obey doctrine is to be preferred, and so we already have good reason to choose the third alternative over the second. But we can now supplement the argument of Chapter III with fur-

[5] At the age of seventeen, or perhaps eighteen, the son of Athenian citizens was enrolled on an official register of citizens, and he then became legally independent. See Harrison, *The Law of Athens*, Vol. I, p. 74; MacDowell, *The Law in Classical Athens*, pp. 68–70. But, then as now, a young man who had recently received his legal independence would not have been taken seriously by his elders as a public speaker. See Xenophon, *Mem.* III vi 1. The *Crito* explicitly refers to the registration process (the *dokimasia*) by which a young man became a citizen: see 51d3. More on this later.

ther evidence. The Laws must be assuming that their conception of the child–parent relationship will meet with widespread
approval. They think it so obvious that a child must persuade
or obey his parents that they don't bother mentioning this step
in their argument. But how do they expect their audience in
fourth-century Athens to interpret the assumption that children
must persuade or obey? Did Plato's compatriots assume that
even an adult male must always obey his parents if he cannot
persuade them to change their minds? In that case, our third
alternative would have to be rejected. On the other hand, if the
Athenians took it for granted that male citizens in their majority
could, in certain circumstances, justifiably resist parental control, then our third alternative would be vindicated. To see which
interpretation is correct, consider these legal facts.

> An Athenian male child seems to have been almost wholly
> free from parental control as soon as he reached the end of
> his seventeenth (conceivably eighteenth) year. At that point
> he was presented by his father or guardian to his demes-
> men, and after passing an examination into his qualifica-
> tions to be a citizen . . . he was enrolled among the demes-
> men. . . . It is reasonably certain that [this coming of age]
> meant release from all legal control except in one impor-
> tant respect. . . . The exception is the father's continuing
> right, as head of his house, to remove the son from the
> house. . . . [This] would exclude the son from his share in
> the inheritance of his father's property. . . .[6]

> Once he had reached that age [seventeen or possibly eight-
> een] it seems that a man could marry (or for that matter
> refrain from marrying) without the consent of his father.[7]

> Until a son came of age his father represented him in every
> kind of legal transaction, whether procedurally before a court
> or in matters of contract, since a minor was incapacitated
> from entering into any contract.[8]

[6] Harrison, *The Law of Athens*, Vol. I, pp. 74–75.
[7] Ibid., p. 18.
[8] Ibid., p. 73.

Now, if an adult male Athenian citizen was beyond the legal control of his parents, then that surely tells us something about social attitudes. The legal system would not have given its full-fledged citizens such a high degree of independence from parental control had there been a general belief that even adult males should obey their parents in all circumstances. The city of Athens had the legal power to require its citizens always to obey their parents; yet there was no such law, nor was there ever an attempt to enact such a law. This shows that in Athenian society, as in our own, the age of majority was regarded as the time when a boy could finally begin to exercise some independent judgment, even to the point of disobeying his parents.

But did the Athenians think that an adult male should simply ignore the demands of his parents? Would they have said that if his parents tell him what to do, they are stepping beyond the limits of their role? I very much doubt it. I suggest that the authority of parents over a male child diminished when he reached his majority, but did not end. To be more precise, I suggest that the following two propositions capture the general attitude of the Athenians toward parental authority over adult male children.

(i) Even after a male child has become an adult, his parents still have *some* claim to his obedience. They are still acting within their rights if they make demands on him.

(ii) But parental demands can be excessive or misguided, and when they are, adult males might justifiably disobey.

If (i) and (ii) are correct, then the relationship of adult children to their parents was in a way similar to the relationship that holds between promisor and promisee. If X makes a promise to Y, then Y has a claim to some act or forbearance on the part of X; yet X can be justified in breaking that promise, as Y himself ought to recognize. Similarly, in classical Athens parents had some claim to the obedience of their adult children, though they would have been expected to realize that disobedience might be justified in certain circumstances. In either case— whether a claim rests on agreement or on parental benefits—an explanation is owed when the claim is not honored. That is the intuition that underlies the persuade-or-obey doctrine.[9]

But what reason do we have to accept (i)? One strong piece of evidence comes from the *Crito* itself. The Laws think it too obvious to need mentioning that making demands on one's adult children is among the prerogatives of parenthood. If parents were not entitled to such authority by virtue of the benefits they have bestowed, the city would also lack title to give commands. And if parents are within their rights to give orders to their children, then they must also have some claim to obedience. For there can be no right to command unless those over whom this right is exercised have some obligation to obey. Nonetheless, the contemporaries of Socrates and Plato must have believed that parents can sometimes go wrong in the way they treat their children, and that adult males, at least, can sometimes be justified in disobeying. Had this concession to autonomy not been made, the right of parents to blind obedience would have found its way into the legal system.

If further evidence for (i) and (ii) is needed, we can find it in Aristotle's brief discussion of parental authority in the *Nicomachean Ethics*. He opens IX 2 with this remark: "A further problem is set by such questions as whether one should in all things give the preference to one's father and obey him, or whether when one is ill one should trust a doctor, and when one has to elect a general should elect a man of military skill . . ." (1164b22-25).[10] The question is left unanswered, for Aristotle thinks that the solution varies according to the details of each particular situation. As he puts it, "All such questions are hard, are they not, to decide with precision? For they admit of many variations . . ." (1164b27-29). This refusal to discuss the matter further is highly significant for our purposes: Aristotle evidently

---

[9] When A promises B to do X, then what A owes B is to do X; it would be a mistake to say that he only owes it to B either to do X or to explain to B why he won't or hasn't done X. Similarly, if (i) is true, then it is incorrect to say that citizens merely owe obedience or persuasion to their parents and their parent-city. Rather, what they owe is obedience, though they might be justified in refusing to pay this debt. Thus (i) is crucial to the defense of a claim I made in Ch. III n. 21.

[10] Translated by Ross; so too the next two passages.

believes that it is quite in order for a father to give commands to his adult children even about medical and political matters. If he thought that fathers had no claim to obedience in these areas, then he would not have said that children are placed in a ticklish situation by such demands. But at the same time, Aristotle obviously believes that children need not bow to authority in all such cases. As he says later in the chapter, "That we should not make the same return to everyone, nor give a father the preference in everything, as one does not sacrifice everything to Zeus, is plain enough . . ." (1165a14-16). Aristotle thinks that sometimes an adult male ought to say no to his father's demands, and here he is surely expressing the attitude of many fourth-century Greeks. For his discussion of conflicting loyalties stays within the moral framework of his community, and we can safely assume that the perplexities he discusses in this chapter were widely felt.

We can return now to our choice between alternatives two and three. The second alternative takes the Laws to be assuming that an adult who cannot persuade his parents to withdraw their demands must accede to them; the third holds that adults might justifiably disobey their parents, but that when they do so they must persuade. I conclude from our discussion that this last alternative is the correct one. The *Crito* cannot be advocating or presupposing the perpetual subordination of free citizens to their parents. The Laws could not afford to rest their case against escape on a tacit premise no Athenian would have accepted. Rather, they must be saying that honor is owed to parents throughout their lives, but when children come of age, honor is paid by obeying or by persuading that disobedience is justified. Once this tacit premise is conceded, the Laws can infer that when a parent-city issues orders to its citizens, they must comply or explain in court why disobedience is justified. So, a widely shared assumption about what children owe their parents leads to the surprising conclusion that an escaping Socrates would be wronging Athens.

Does any passage or line from the *Crito* cast doubt on this interpretation of the parent-city analogy? The reader might recall that according to the Laws the Athenian citizen is not only the offspring of his city, but also its slave (50e4); and this certainly suggests a relationship of total subordination. We will soon look more carefully at this analogy, and we will see how mild a point the Laws are making. For now, let us look once again at the passage that introduces the persuade-or-obey doctrine. Does anything here suggest that parents have an unconditional and perpetual right to obedience?

> Are you too wise to realize that your fatherland is more to be honored, more revered, more holy, and held higher in esteem, both among gods and sensible men, than your mother, father, and other ancestors? It is more necessary to honor, yield to, and soothe an angered fatherland than an angered father. You must persuade it or do what it commands, and endure in silence what it orders you to endure, whether you are beaten or bound, whether you are led into war to be wounded or killed; these things must be done, and there justice lies. . . . (51a7–b7)

It is easy to feel some frustration with the *Crito* as one reads these lines, because of their vagueness. One is justified in asking: How reverent, yielding, and mollifying should one be to one's angry father? Exactly what actions are the Laws expecting of offspring—that they do anything and everything that their angered parents order? Does one mollify one's parents by reasoning with them, soothing their passion, and trying to justify one's acts, or by letting them have their way? Are the Laws thinking of a situation in which one has already gone against one's parents wishes, thus arousing their anger, and are they saying that one ought to respond to this anger with persuasion? Or are they thinking of a situation in which one's parents express anger at one's intention to disobey them, and are they saying that one should abandon one's defiance in all such cases?

The only strategy for answering these questions is to focus on the persuade-or-obey doctrine, and then interpret the rest of the passage in the light of this doctrine. For surely it is the central point made by the passage; that is why the Laws come back to it two more times. Of course, the persuade-or-obey doctrine is itself in need of interpretation, but in this case we have two guidelines to help us. When applied to the child-parent relationship, the doctrine must reflect contemporary Athenian practices; and when applied to the political realm, it must be acceptable to Socrates. As we have seen, both of these tests lead to the same result: the persuade-or-obey doctrine means that one may disobey, if one persuades. Therefore, when the Laws urge the citizen to "honor, yield to, and soothe an angered fatherland," they must mean that he should either obey Athens or assuage the city's anger at his disobedience. Just as an adult who disobeys his parents must yield to their angry demand for an explanation, so the citizen must either "endure in silence" the demands of his city or he must persuade a court that his disobedience is justified. Nothing in the passage that introduces the persuade-or-obey doctrine contradicts the way we have interpreted it. On the contrary, our interpretation helps us understand the whole passage.

3
Violence and persuasion

At the end of the passage that compares citizens to offspring, the Laws say:

> . . . You must do what your city and fatherland commands, or persuade it as to the nature of justice. Violence against your mother or father is unholy, and still more so against your fatherland. (51b9–c3)

The juxtaposition of these two statements suggests that there is a logical relationship between them. But what is it? I think there are two possibilities, and will present one of them in this section, but unfortunately the second cannot be set out until we get to V.6. In any case, the choice between them is not momentous.

One way of reading the above passage is to construe the second sentence as lending further support to the first: one must persuade or obey *because* a refusal to do either is, in the light of the enormous benefits one has received, a form of ingratitude that amounts to violence. To see what the Laws may be getting at, let us go back to an earlier point in the text. After claiming that an Athenian citizen is the offspring and slave of the state, the Laws infer that the relationship between citizen and city is as one-sided as the relationship between offspring and their parents: if a father insults his children, they are not thereby permitted to reply in kind; if he strikes them, they may not strike back; even if he tries to destroy them, they are not allowed to kill him (50e2–51a5). Now, which of these acts do the Laws characterize as acts of violence? Assault and attempted destruction, certainly; but perhaps they are operating with a wide conception of violence that includes insults as well. After all, violence does not require physical force, for us or for the Greeks.[11] And if this is correct, then it is possible that the Laws would also characterize the refusal to persuade or obey such great benefactors as one's parents as a kind of violence. They might say that whenever honor and gratitude are owed but not paid, violence of an nonphysical sort is done. So interpreted, their full argument would be this.

(A) An Athenian citizen is indebted both to his parents and to Athens for his life and his upbringing.

(B) Because he has received these benefits from his parents, he must honor them, and he must never treat them with violence.

(C) Because he has also received these benefits from his city, he must also honor it, and he must never treat it with violence.

(D) Offspring honor their parents either by obeying them or by persuading them as to the nature of justice.

(E) Therefore, citizens honor their city either by obeying it or by persuading it as to the nature of justice.

---

[11] The notion of nonphysical violence I take to be unobjectionable, though it is far from obvious that violence is done whenever honor is owed but not paid. For further discussion, see Audi, "On the Meaning and Justification of Violence," pp. 54–59; and Holmes, "Violence and Non-Violence," pp. 110–111. At *Antigone* 1073, Teiresias says that the gods are receiving violent treatment (*biazontai*) from Creon: by forbidding the burial of Polyneices, he is dishonoring the gods.

(F) Whenever honor is owed but not paid, violence is done.

(G) Therefore, if offspring refuse to persuade or obey their parents, or if citizens refuse to persuade or obey their city, they are wrongfully using violence.

If this analysis is right, the Laws do not need to characterize escape as a violent act in order to show that it is wrong. Once they reach (E), their case has already been made. So when they go on to characterize the refusal to persuade or obey as a form of violence, they are merely icing the cake.[12]

One further point. The opposition between persuasion and violence was a familiar thought pattern among Socrates' contemporaries,[13] and it is tempting to suppose that it had an effect on the argument of the *Crito*. For the disobedient citizen has a choice between precisely these two alternatives: persuasion or violence. So the Laws may be inclined to characterize escape as a violent act not only because it shows disrespect, but also because of the Greek tendency to think in terms of the opposition between persuasion and violence.

4
Slavery and asymmetry

It might be thought that the *Crito*'s comparison between an Athenian citizen and a slave (50e4) creates a grave difficulty for me. For a slave was expected to obey his master and not to exercise any independent judgment about the propriety of his

---

[12] The alternative interpretation, to be considered in V.6, holds that escape does violence because Socrates is thereby trying to destroy Athens, for his part. Destruction is a paradigm of violence, and so it might seem that this interpretation is obviously preferable to the one embodied in (F). But there is a difficulty for this alternative reading: why do the laws condemn violence against parents and city (51c2-3) *immediately after* they call upon the citizen to persuade or obey (51b9-c1)? If these two thoughts are not merely juxtaposed, but have some logical relationship, what is that relationship? Granted, violent acts are destructive; but why does the refusal to persuade or obey convict one of violence? I think these questions can be answered, and the alternative interpretation vindicated, after we examine the claim (50b4) that escape is a *private* act. We will see that the privacy of escape is essential to its destructiveness, and that the refusal to persuade or obey makes escape private.

[13] See Lloyd, *Magic, Reason and Experience*, pp. 251-252, esp. p. 251 n. 109.

orders. The opposite of a slave is a *free* man, that is, a man that is free to lead the life he chooses. So when the Laws say that citizens are slaves of the city, they are perhaps implying that citizens should have no more freedom in their relationship to the state than slaves have in their relation to their masters. They must do whatever the city says.

However, a moment's reflection shows that they mean no such thing. The Laws remind Socrates that, like any other Athenian citizen, he has always been free to leave the city and take his property with him (51d2-5). No such opportunity existed for slaves, of course: since they were the property of their masters, they had no freedom of movement whatever. Furthermore, the Laws say that citizens can either persuade the city or obey it, and even on Grote's conservative interpretation, this alternative to obedience existed only for citizens and not for slaves. Recall his gloss of the persuade-or-obey doctrine: "The Laws allow to every citizen full liberty of trying to persuade the assembled public. . . ."[14] There was no such liberty for slaves, since they had no vote in the Assembly. And so even the reader who prefers Grote's interpretation to mine will have to admit that the Laws are not advocating any diminution of a citizen's freedom. All of the legal rights that come with citizenship are left intact.

But then what *do* the Laws mean by comparing citizens to slaves? Let us look at the use they make of this analogy.

> Since you were born, nurtured, and educated [because of us], can you deny first of all that you are our offspring and slave, both for yourself and your forefathers? And if that is so, do you think that justice between you and us is on an equal basis, and that whatever we try to do to you, you can with justice do back to us? Justice in your relationship with your father was not on an equal basis, or with your master if you happened to have one. Whatever you suffer, you cannot do those things back: if you were insulted [*kakōs akouonta*], you cannot respond in kind; if you were struck, you cannot strike back; and so on for many examples. As

---

[14] *Plato*, Vol. I, p. 300.

for your relationship with the fatherland and the laws: if we try to destroy you on the supposition that this is just, do you have the freedom to try to destroy us, the Laws, and the fatherland, so far as you are able? Are you claiming that doing this is doing justice—you, who really care about justice? (50e2–51a7)

Notice that there is not a single word in this entire passage about obedience. The Laws are pointing to only one similarity in the relationships between offspring and parents, slaves and masters, citizens and city. In all three cases, violence can justifiably be undertaken by the superior party against the inferior, though it can never be justified when done by the inferior against the superior. The Laws do not claim that the violence of cities, masters, and parents is *always* justified. Their point is that it can, in certain circumstances, be justified, and this is enough to establish an asymmetry—or, as they say, an inequality—in these relationships. For violence in the reverse direction is *never* justified.

Because the Laws point to this one similarity between slaves, offspring, and citizens, we should not infer that they deny that there are important differences as well. In particular, they never assert or even suggest that the authority of masters over slaves is a fitting model for the authority cities ought to have over citizens. Rather, when the Laws move on to the question of how much obedience citizens owe their city, their model is the relationship between offspring and parents. The master-slave relationship is dropped as soon as it has served its limited purpose, which is to illustrate a point about violence. It has nothing to do with authority.

One further confusion should be avoided. It might be wondered why the Laws bother making the point that children and slaves should never return violence for the violence of their superiors. Hasn't Socrates already said that one must never return injustice for injustice, no matter what the relationship between the two individuals is? And doesn't that entail that violence is always wrong? Why are the Laws ignoring this Socratic premise?

The mistake embodied in these questions should be apparent. The Socratic prohibition of injustice is not a prohibition of violence. On the contrary, both Socrates and the Laws imply that violence can be justified, since they rule it out only in a limited range of cases: offspring may not kill their own parents, but they may kill anyone else if the circumstances are right; citizens may not destroy their parent-city, but war between cities is not wrong in itself. So the Laws have understood the Socratic prohibition of injustice rather well. They realize that it is not a point about destruction or violence. And they see that they cannot condemn Socrates simply on the grounds that escape is a destructive act. To show that escape is wrong, they must argue that in his early life Athens was as great a benefactor to him as were his parents.

5
The illusion of authoritarianism

We can now see how many factors conspire together to create the false impression that the *Crito* advocates an authoritarian philosophy of law. The benefits Athens gives to its citizens are received at the earliest stage of their lives, and so we quickly assume that according to the Laws citizens are little children in their relationship to the city. Our attention is first focused on the young child, and then when the Laws go on to say that the relationship between offspring and parent is unequal, our original impression is reinforced. We tend to forget that the Laws have merely called the citizen a product or offspring of the state, not a child. And in any case, since "offspring" strikes us as an artificial word, it is difficult to stick to it in our discussion of the *Crito*. We quickly move from "offspring" to "child," a word much more likely to suggest a person's relative age than his status as a descendant. Since the Laws compare a citizen to a slave, we are all the more certain that they are saying something outrageously authoritarian. And then, when we read that ". . . it is more necessary to honor, yield to, and soothe an angered fatherland than an angered father . . ." (51b2-3), and that the citizen must "endure in silence" what the city orders him to endure, even if that means death (51b4–6), we become utterly convinced that the Laws are advocating blind obedience. True, they never say quite that: they do give the citizen an alternative, since he can persuade or obey. But the accumulated weight of our first impressions inclines us to belittle this choice. Since the Laws have already made so many seemingly authoritarian remarks, we fail to take persuasion seriously as an alternative to obedience. What the *Crito* must mean is that we can try to persuade the Assembly to change the law, but until we succeed, we must obey.[15] And in any case, how can the Laws permit disobedience? It wouldn't be disobedience anymore, if they were to allow it. Surely the Laws cannot mean that citizens have a right to disobey any order, so long as they try to persuade the city.

So it is no mystery that a conservative reading of the *Crito* has enjoyed widespread support. But I hope the reader now sees that there really are no reasonable grounds for such an interpretation. Recall the various arguments I have given for an alternative approach: (A) When the Laws say that citizens have a choice between obedience and persuasion, it is entirely natural to take them to mean that disobedience is sometimes the right choice. (B) If we interpret the Laws in this way, it is much easier to reconcile the *Apology* and the *Crito*. (C) The Laws accept the principle of just agreements, and so they concede that agreements can be broken when unjust. It is significant that they repeat the persuade-or-obey doctrine immediately after arguing that Socrates has agreed to obey the city: the implication is that if Socrates wants to break his agreement and disobey the city, he must persuade. (D) When the Laws say that citizens must honor their city in the way that offspring honor their parents, they are thinking of the relationship between an adult male and his parents. In Athens, only adult males were citizens, and they were no more required to obey their parents uncon-

---

[15] Those who rely exclusively on Tredennick's translation have no choice but to adopt this interpretation. As we saw in Ch. III n. 10, he has 51b3–4 read, ". . . if you cannot persuade your country you must do whatever it orders. . . ."

ditionally than are their contemporary counterparts.[16] There-fore, the city is no more entitled to require blind obedience of the citizen than are parents of their adult sons.

Inevitably, someone will ask, "But if the Laws think that disobedience is justifiable, why don't they say so?" There are two replies to this question. First, interpretations of a historical work must go beyond bare repetition. There are always questions about an author's meaning that the author does not explicitly answer, and so if we refuse to attribute to a philosopher anything that is not written in his text, we will have to stop writing about the dead. Second, the question can be equally directed against the usual authoritarian reading of the *Crito*. "If the Laws really think that disobedience is always wrong, why don't they say so? All they actually say is that the citizen must persuade or obey."Obviously, if one is going to press this sort of question, it will count against any interpretation at all. The only real issue is whether we have reason to choose one alternative over another. That of course is a matter of judgment, but I submit that the case for a liberal reading of the dialogue is rather strong.

6

Some consequences

I now want to draw some conclusions from my preceding argument. First of all, we should notice that the Laws need say nothing at all about agreement in order to show that escape is wrong. They say that Socrates neither persuades nor obeys; that is, he is disobeying the court's command that he die, and he has not even attempted to persuade them that escape would be justified. Therefore, any argument for the persuade-or-obey doctrine will be an argument that Socrates is doing something

---

[16] Of course, if I am right, there is a major difference between the authority of parents in classical Athens and that of parents in contemporary industrial societies. They thought parents were entitled to give adult male children orders on any subject whatever, whereas we do not. On the other hand, they believed that such children could be justified in disobeying their parents; the authority of parents over male children significantly diminished when the latter came of age. In this respect, we are like them.

wrong. And the parent-city analogy provides such an argument, without making any use of the premise that Socrates agreed to obey the city. If the parents of an adult issue him an order, he must persuade or obey, whether or not he has agreed to do so; similarly for city and citizen. So our earlier conclusion—that the *Crito* contains two types of argument against escape—has been sustained. Whoever receives the two benefits Athens has given Socrates—life and education—and whoever makes the sort of agreement he has made with the city, must persuade or obey; but since he does neither, he commits a threefold injustice.

Second, we can now add something to our earlier discussion of the persuade-or-obey doctrine. I argued (III.7) that this doctrine lays down a necessary but not a sufficient condition for justified political behavior. Faced with an order from his city, an Athenian citizen must try either to obey or to persuade, but the mere fact that he tries to persuade a jury does not show that he was right to disobey. If a citizen falsely believes that the order in question was unjust, the Laws can condemn him for his moral ignorance. What I would like to add to these points is simply the following: the Laws can concede that whoever tries but fails to persuade the city has paid it the honor it deserves, and is not guilty of violence. At any rate, that would be the reasonable position for them to adopt. After all, if someone disobeys his parents but explains to them why he has done so, he is showing them respect and he is treating them in a nonviolent way, even if he was wrong to disobey them. And similarly for the citizen in his relation to his city. So there are two questions to be asked about any act of disobedience: (A) Is it the right choice? (B) Does the citizen thereby dishonor the city? The Laws of course do not make this distinction, but it is a plausible elaboration of their position.

Third, we should realize that the persuade-or-obey doctrine gives the citizen wide scope for disobedience. The Laws say that if he disobeys he must persuade as to the nature of justice, and this means that he must show the city that its order was unjust. But there are two ways for commands to be unjust: the city might be doing the citizen an injustice, or it might be requiring the citizen to commit an injustice. And so far as the analogy between parent and city goes, either fault is sufficient reason for disobedience. That is, the mere fact that the city has benefited its citizens as parents benefit their children does not by itself require citizens to suffer any injustice the city might impose. Only voluntary agreements commit people to suffering injustice, and therefore the only argument in the *Crito* for accepting the city's injustice is the argument from agreement. This point can be seen most clearly when we consider the relationship between an adult and his parents. The Laws say nothing to suggest that adult Athenian citizens should disobey their parents only in order to avoid wrongdoing. Assuming that they have made no agreements to abide by the decisions of their parents, they can disobey whenever the demands of their parents treat them unjustly. Therefore, the citizen who has agreed to abide by his city's orders is more tightly bound to it than an adult male is bound to his parents. He can disobey his father and mother whenever their order does him injustice or requires wrongdoing; but whoever has voluntarily agreed to obey his city is more restricted in the reasons he can give for disobedience. On the other hand, if the *Crito* concedes that a citizen can somehow reside in the city and avoid agreeing to obey certain laws, then the citizen will have wider grounds for breaking them. He will still need to persuade, if he breaks those laws, but he will be able to disobey them merely because they treat him unjustly. Of course, this is still an unresolved problem. We do not yet know whether it is possible, according to the Laws, to remain a resident of Athens without agreeing to all of its orders.

Fourth, the analogy between city and parents does not show, and is not meant to show, that the city has a right to punish its citizens in whatever way it chooses whenever they violate the law. That analogy does show that a city is entitled to make demands on its citizens and to require an explanation when those demands are not satisfied. For these are precisely the privileges that parents enjoy in their relationship with their adult children. But no Athenian parent could punish his grown children in the way that the city often punishes law-breakers; Athenian law did not allow parents to kill, exile, fine, or disenfranchise their adult children for having failed to meet their demands.[17] Now, how can the Laws show that Athens has these punitive powers, even though Athenian parents lack them? Obviously, the mere fact that citizens are indebted to Athens for their lives and their upbringing does not establish its right to kill law-breakers; for otherwise parents would have the right to kill their disobedient children. To show that Athens is entitled to use certain forms of punishment, the Laws must go beyond the parent-city analogy and develop their argument from agreement. Socrates has to submit to his punishment not because Athens is his parent-city but because he agreed to abide by the verdicts of the courts. In other words, certain punitive powers of the state are voluntarily given to it by the adult citizen, though he does not give any such power to his parents. This explains why the Laws appeal to agreement at such an early stage in their speech. As soon as Socrates points out that he has been unjustly punished, the Laws reply that he agreed to accept even those verdicts that are unfavorable to him. It might seem puzzling that the Laws reply in this way; they haven't yet begun to show that Socrates made a just agreement with his city, and so their claim is entirely unsubstantiated. Why don't they postpone this point about agreement, move immediately into the parent-city analogy, and show that Socrates must accept his punishment in the same way that a child must accept a beating from his father? The answer is that the Laws do not attribute such punitive rights to parents in relation to their grown children, and so they must derive that punitive power from a different source. The premature claim about agreement makes the speech of the Laws seem disorganized, but in fact they know what they are doing. They realize how limited the analogy between parent and city is, and there-

---

[17] Athenian parents had *some* power to punish their adult children. For example, as we saw in Sec. 2, a father could "exclude the son from his share in the inheritance of his father's property . . ." (Harrison, *The Law of Athens*, Vol. I, p. 75). More generally, a parent could punish his adult children by withholding benefits that would ordinarily have been expected. But if a city has no more punitive power than this, it can hardly survive. It must be entitled to inflict far graver evils, and the right to inflict such evils cannot be justified by the parent-city analogy.

fore they make no use of it when they claim that Socrates must accept unjust punishment.

The point can be put in this way: Only the argument from agreement gives the city the full punitive power that a sovereign political organization needs. And that argument is therefore essential to the *Crito*'s political theory, although as a point against Socrates it is superfluous. We saw earlier in this section that the parent-city analogy by itself suffices to show that escape would wrong the city. So, for the purpose of condemning an escaping Socrates, the argument from agreement merely puts another nail in the coffin. But for the purpose of building a political theory—that is, a theory of why the city is entitled to the full powers it has—the argument from agreement is indispensable.

My fifth and final point brings us back to the initial remarks of the Laws. They tell Socrates that if the judgments of the courts were robbed of their authority by private individuals, the city could no longer exist. And so by escaping he would be doing his part to destroy Athens. I argued in Chapter II that these lines do not form a self-contained argument, but merely the beginning of the *Crito*'s first argument against escape. What the Laws oppose is destructive acts against a parent-city, not political destruction *per se*. But now it may seem that these opening remarks about destruction are entirely unnecessary, for the parent-city analogy shows by itself that Socrates is wrong to escape. Evidently, to condemn Socrates, the Laws do not need to ask, "What would happen if private individuals set aside the verdicts of the courts?" They need only observe that if Socrates escapes, he neither persuades nor obeys. But then why do the Laws bother with an attempt to implicate him in the destruction of the city? What does this add to the argument of the *Crito*? We should also recall the questions we raised earlier (II.6): Are the Laws falling into a trap by going from "not everyone should do that" to "no one should do that"? And what do they mean by "private individuals"? At long last, we must face up to these difficulties.

V

PRIVATE PERSONS AND GENERALIZATION

⌘

1
Private persons

WE MUST NOW try to understand the questions with which the Laws open their attack on Socrates:

> Tell me, Socrates, what do you have in mind to do? With this attempted act, are you thinking of anything else than destroying us, the Laws, and the entire city, for your part? Or does it seem to you that a city can exist and not be overturned if its verdicts have no force, but are robbed of authority and destroyed by private persons? (50a8–b5)

Evidently, they are assuming that if Socrates escapes, he does so as a private person. And then they imagine a general pattern of similar disobedience: what would happen if private persons treated the verdicts of the courts in the way that this private person, Socrates, is treating this particular judgment? If we want to see what the Laws are getting at, we have to pay attention to the Greek noun, *idiōtēs*, which I have translated "private person."

An *idiōtēs* is an individual who in some way or other lacks an official connection with his city; as the dictionary puts it, he is "one in a private station, opp. to one holding public office or taking part in public affairs. . . ."[1] We can get a better grasp on

---

[1] Liddell and Scott, *A Greek-English Lexicon*, s.v. *idiōtēs* II.

the noun if we look at its cognate verb, *idiōteuein*, "to occupy a private station." A physician appointed by the Assembly in Athens is engaged in public practice, whereas a doctor who does not work for the city practices privately, i.e. *idiōteuei*.[2] And in the *Apology* Socrates explains why he has decided to live in a private rather than a public way (*idiōteuein* rather than *dēmosieuein*, 32a1-3). His divine sign has warned him against a conventional political career (31d2-6), i.e. a career in which one votes and speaks in the Assembly, aspires to political office, forms political alliances in the clubs (36b5-9), etc. Instead of speaking before a large group in the political forum, he addresses himself to each individual separately. *Idiōteuein* is the appropriate verb whenever someone acts in a way that is unconnected with public office or public life, and the person who does this is an *idiōtēs*.

So much for the meaning of *idiōtēs*. Now we must ask what justification the Laws have for assuming that if Socrates escapes from jail, he does so as an *idiōtēs*. In what way would he be separated from public life? One way of elaborating on their accusation would be this: "Socrates, you are a private person, insofar as you have rejected a conventional political life. As you yourself admit, you have generally stayed away from meetings of the Assembly, and you have no interest in holding office. Now, what would happen if the judgments of the courts were robbed of their authority by all those Athenians who are private persons in this sense? Wouldn't the city be destroyed?" But if this is what the Laws mean, then they are implying that those who do lead a normal political life are exempt from their criticism. And that would be absurd. After all, a great many people do attend the Assembly and do take part in conventional politics: surely the city would be destroyed if they were to ignore the verdicts of the courts. So this interpretation of *idiōtēs* does not fit the context; although the term does sometimes refer to someone who is uninterested in normal politics, that is not what the Laws are getting at here.

An analogy may help at this point. Suppose I am walking in

---

[2] See *Grg.* 455b2 and Dodds' note ad loc.

the park and notice that a man wearing combat boots is about
to litter. In protest I say, "Think of how the park would look
if everyone wearing combat boots were to litter." Obviously,
I am ruining my case against him by generalizing in this peculiar way. The fact that the man is dressed as he is has nothing
to do with the wrongness of his act. Similarly, the fact that
Socrates has kept away from the Assembly has nothing to do
with the wrongfulness of escape. The Laws must recognize this
obvious point, and so we must look for a different way of interpreting their assumption that if Socrates escapes, he does so
as a private person.

Perhaps the *Crito* means that whoever disobeys an order is
thereby cutting himself off from his city and is in this way a
private person. In other words, the Laws are not calling Socrates an *idiōtēs* because he has for many years led an apolitical
life, but because he is at the moment proposing to disobey the
court's command that he die. According to this interpretation,
anyone who violates any law or order is thereby an *idiōtēs*, a
person who stands apart from the community. The Laws are
asking, "Does it seem to you that a city can exist and not be
overturned if its verdicts have no force, but are robbed of authority and destroyed by individuals who violate the city's orders?" But the trouble with this interpretation is that it makes
the Laws opposed to the violation of *any* court order whatsoever. Anyone who disobeys a court—even Socrates defying a
judicial ban on philosophy—would be overturning the decision
of a court as a private person, and would therefore be impli-
cated in the destruction of the city. Yet, as we have seen, the
Laws are not opposed to the violation of all court orders whatever. Rather, they concede that the citizen may justifiably disobey and persuade, and they insist that this option is as available
in the courtroom as elsewhere (51b8–9). Certainly Socrates could
not accept a legal philosophy that required him to obey a court's
order to give up philosophy. So, when the Laws seek to implicate an escaping Socrates in the destruction of the city, they
cannot mean that whoever disobeys a court order is acting in a
destructive manner. They do not distinguish good ways of destroying a parent-city from bad: all destructive acts against such

cities are wrong. Therefore, if Socrates is to accept the philosophy of the Laws, he must take them to mean that only certain acts that defy a court are destructive. It is only when the judgments of the courts are violated *by private persons* that the laws and the city are destroyed.

Another analogy may help here. Suppose I think that the state should protect the survival of certain species, and therefore I favor the regulation of hunting. Only those who have been licensed to hunt for a certain period of time should be allowed to do so. Now, if I see someone about to shoot a deer, I should not automatically protest; I should not ask, "Wouldn't this species be destroyed if everyone were to shoot a deer?" For my question implies that I am opposed to all deerslaying, and I am not. However, I might ask to see this hunter's license, and if he has none I could legitimately ask, "Wouldn't this species be destroyed if the state's restrictions on shooting deer were generally ignored?" It is the *private* hunting of deer that I oppose, not state-licensed hunting, and therefore my "What if everyone . . . ?" question should reflect this distinction. Similarly, the Laws are not opposed to every violation of a court order, and the question they put to Socrates reflects their willingness to tolerate some disobedience. As they say, it is a general pattern of disobedience by *private* persons that will rob the courts of their force and authority and thereby destroy the city. Whom they are referring to by "private persons" is not immediately apparent on a first reading, but as often happens in philosophy, a crucial term is clarified by what comes later. The Laws go on to explain the distinction they have in mind: a citizen who violates an order can either appeal to his city and defend his disobedience, or (like Socrates) he can run away and refuse to persuade. Anyone who pursues the latter alternative is disobeying as a private person, since by shunning the court and the city, he refuses to take part in public life as he should. *Idiōtēs* of course does not mean "someone who refuses to persuade or obey." As we have seen, it is a vague term that can refer to anyone—a private doctor or an apolitical Socrates—who does not act in an official, public capacity. My claim is that here in the *Crito*, when the Laws call Socrates an *idiōtēs*, they are thinking of a particular way in which he would be avoiding public affairs, if he escapes. They are talking about someone who disobeys an order but refuses to address the court as he should. This is what *idiōtēs* can refer to, and given the context, this is what it must refer to here.

Evidently, the Laws believe that the city is not destroyed, and the courts are not robbed of their authority, when they are disobeyed by public persons, i.e. those who attempt to persuade. We will soon ask whether this is a defensible position for them to take. But before we pursue this matter, I want to discuss a different sense of "public" and "private." Sometimes we say that a person acts *privately* when his activities are disclosed to only a few, *publicly* when they can be observed by all. A private conversation, for example, is sequestered from general observation; analogously, by "private disobedience"—or "disobedience by private persons"—we might mean secret violations of the law. Does this sense of "private" have anything to do with the *Crito*? Does it matter to Socrates or to the Laws if an act of disobedience is deliberately kept from public view?

2
Secret disobedience

Several scholars have claimed that according to Socrates disobedience is justified only if it is unconcealed.[3] That is, if a citizen secretly violates the law, or if he makes sure that only a few are aware of his disobedience, then he is acting wrongly. As evidence for this interpretation, they contrast the secrecy of escape with the openness with which Socrates would violate a hypothetical ban on philosophy. In the *Apology*, he announces to his jurors that he would disobey them if they were to order him to give up philosophy. As Woozley says, ". . . there is no suggestion of concealment, of trying to evade the law by clandestine philosophical meetings."[4] By contrast, he has given the court no warning that he will flee from jail, and if his escape

---

[3] Santas, *Socrates*, p. 50; Vlastos, "Socrates on Political Obedience and Disobedience," pp. 531-532; Woozley, "Socrates on Disobeying the Law," p. 307.
[4] "Socrates on Disobeying the Law," p. 307.

plans are to succeed, they must be carried out secretly. So, in the *Apology* Socrates is willing to undertake open and public disobedience, whereas in the *Crito* the disobedience he refuses to engage in is covert. Can we infer that he is in principle opposed to all clandestine disobedience? I think it would be unwise to rely too heavily on this single contrast. After all, Socrates says in the *Apology* that he has been ordered by god to practice philosophy; but we cannot infer from this one example that he favors disobedience *only* when god commands it. Similarly, the mere fact that his philosophical defiance would be overt does not show that all legitimate disobedience must have this quality. What we need is further evidence from the *Crito*. The Laws advocate a Socratic jurisprudence, and if Socrates is opposed to all clandestine disobedience, then we should find some signs of this opposition in their speech. So we must ask: Are the Laws bothered by the secrecy of escape? Do they imply that it is always wrong to conceal one's violation of a parent-city's order? And if they are opposed to covert disobedience, do they give any argument against it?

Clearly, the Laws are quite conscious of the fact that escape is a clandestine form of disobedience, and they think that Socrates should be troubled by this fact. As they say, Crito's friends in Thessaly "might hear with pleasure how laughable you were when you ran away [*apedidraskes*] from prison, put on a disguise—a leather coat or some other such thing that those who run away [*apodidraskontes*] usually wear—and altered your appearance . . ." (53d4–7). The term used here for flight (*apodidraskein*, to run away) by itself suggests stealth, since it was commonly applied to slaves when they ran away. And the comparison between Socrates and a runaway slave had been made explicit at an earlier point: ". . . you are doing what the lowest kind of slave might do—trying to run away [*apodidraskein*] . . ." (52c9–d2). If we go even farther back and look at the last line uttered by Socrates before the Laws enter the conversation, we see that the slavish stealth of escape is already on his mind. "Suppose as we intend—either to run away [*apodidraskein*] or whatever it should be called—the Laws and commonwealth stood beside us and said . . ." (50a6–8). Here we see that *apodidraskein* is not a flat and neutral word; otherwise Socrates would make no bones about using it. Somewhat like our "running away," it suggests blameworthy evasion, though in Greek the pejorative flavor is enhanced by the fact that slaves are typically the ones who run away.

These several allusions to stealth show that Socrates and the Laws are disturbed by the secrecy that must accompany escape. But do they give us the evidence we need? Do the Laws think that the secrecy of escape is one of the features that make it wrong, or are they merely trying to embarrass Socrates when they point out the need for a disguise and compare him to a runaway slave? I am inclined to think that embarrassment is beside the point. The Laws are assuming that when slaves run away they are acting wrongly; that of course would have been the automatic assumption of Plato's readers. And so when they compare a disguised Socrates to an escaping slave, they imply that the need for secrecy shows that he is no more justified than the worst kind of slave. Furthermore, I don't see why Socrates and the Laws would be so concerned with secrecy if they thought that this feature of escape was merely an embarrassment and had no connection with injustice. After all, Socrates does not care how he will look in the eyes of others. His whole concern is with avoiding injustice, not with avoiding embarrassment. Surely then, the secrecy of escape is meant as a serious objection to it.

One further piece of evidence points to this same conclusion: there is a connection between the persuade-or-obey doctrine and the need for openness in one's dealings with the state. I take that principle to mean that whoever disobeys an order must appear before a court, *when summoned*, to persuade the jury as to the nature of justice. But a person cannot be summoned if his disobedience is kept a secret. And so the openness of legitimate disobedience is a natural presupposition of the persuade-or-obey doctrine. Whoever disobeys must give his fellow citizens a fair chance to bring him to court, and he gives them this chance if he takes no steps to conceal his disobedience. If no one brings him to court, even though he disobeyed openly, then the city has in effect decided that his disobedience was justified. But in fact, in a city as litigious as fifth-century Athens, the overwhelming likelihood was that whoever disobeyed a law or order would be summoned to court to face the charges against him. And just think how absurdly lenient the persuade-or-obey doctrine would be, if citizens were merely required to reveal and defend their disobedience at some time or other. A law banning philosophical activity could be violated in secret for a whole lifetime, so long as, in the end, one confessed and faced the charges. Obviously, the persuade-or-obey doctrine has teeth only when it is combined with a prohibition against concealed disobedience. And by linking persuasion and open disobedience in this way, we can understand *why* the Laws are bothered by the secrecy of escape. They have an argument for openness, and do not merely insist upon it for no reason at all. Open disobedience is the citizen's sign that he honors and respects the city, in spite of the fact that he violates its orders. Though he disobeys, he virtually assures the city that he will be brought to court, and he thereby demonstrates his willingness to persuade.

We have seen that the Laws are not opposed to all violations of a court's orders; rather, they think that the city will be destroyed if *private persons* rob the courts of their authority. Now, it is important not to pack into *idiōtēs* more than is really there. The word always refers to someone "in a private station, opp. to one holding public office or taking part in public affairs. . . ." To call someone an *idiōtēs*, or to say that he *idiōteuei*, never entails, by the very meaning of these terms, that he acts in secret. In fact, Socrates is a perfect example of an *idiōtēs* who carries out his characteristic activity—asking philosophical questions—in public. As he insists in the *Apology*, ". . . if someone says that he has at some time been taught something by me or that he heard something privately [*idiai*] that all others did not, be assured that he is not telling the truth." (33b6–8).[5] So, there is no semantic transformation that will take us from:

[5] Cf. 26a1–4, *Protag.* 343b5–7.

(A) He overturns the court's judgment as a private person (*idiōtēs*),

to:

(B) He overturns the court's judgment privately (secretly, *idiai*).

And my argument relies on no such linguistic shortcut. If Socrates escapes, he does so as an *idiōtēs* because he refuses to defend his disobedience in the appropriate public forum. The mere fact that he acts covertly does not by itself make him an *idiōtēs*. Yet it is a point about human psychology that whoever rejects the persuade-or-obey doctrine will be tempted to disobey secretly. For if someone wants to violate a city's commands without being brought to court, he will take steps, where possible, to act in secret. The Laws oppose such concealment not because they think that secret disobedience is wrong *per se*, but because they assume that such stealth will be motivated by the desire to disobey without persuading. That is why the *Crito* contains so many allusions (50a6–8, 52d1–2, 53d4–7) to secrecy. The fact that this point is made so frequently suggests that the covertness and the injustice of escape are in some way bound up together, and the persuade-or-obey doctrine is the link that connects them: to be just to one's parent-city, one must persuade or obey; and whoever disobeys but refuses to persuade will try to conceal his illegal act. Therefore, if you see someone secretly disobeying the law, you already know that he is acting wrongly.

We should distinguish two different ways in which the requirement of openness might be formulated. First, the Laws might mean that the citizen who disobeys must take no steps to conceal his illegal act. Second, they might mean that the citizen must take positive steps to publicize his illegal behavior before it occurs; that is, he must give the appropriate official or public body prior warning of his intention to act unlawfully. I think that the first and less demanding of these two alternatives is the more likely interpretation, for in certain cases prior warning might be impossible to give. A soldier might be ordered by his superior officer to kill some innocent person immediately. If he says no, he thereby commits an act of disobedience, but he has given no prior warning. Similarly, circumstances might prevent a citizen from telling the Assembly that he could not in good conscience obey a proposal that is under consideration. If it is adopted and calls for wrongdoing, the citizen must disobey, even though he has had no chance to announce his intentions. We should also recall the way Socrates reacted when he was ordered to arrest Leon: he walked away, and expected to die for his disobedience. Obviously, he made no attempt to conceal his violation of the Thirty's order; that is why he thought he would be punished. But can we say with any assurance that he warned the Thirty ahead of time that he would disobey them? If we want to reconcile the philosophy of the Laws with the disobedience of Socrates, we had better attribute to the *Crito* a relatively modest requirement of openness: the citizen must take no steps to conceal his unlawful behavior. That, after all, is the principle that Socrates would be flouting were he to flee from prison. Of course, the persuade-or-obey doctrine sometimes calls upon a citizen to tell the city in advance of his opposition to an impending order. If a court is considering a punishment that calls upon the defendant to act unjustly, he must persuade the jury that it is something a good man cannot do; in effect, then, he is giving prior warning. But we cannot generalize and say that prior warning is always required, for it is not always possible.

A cautious reader might wonder whether the requirement of openness really applies, as I have assumed, to the citizen who lived under the Thirty. The Athens that gave Socrates his life and upbringing was governed in a democratic way, but during the brief reign of the Thirty the city was under tyrannical rule. Wasn't Socrates therefore released from the requirement that he persuade or obey? I have four brief remarks to make in response to this question: (A) Nothing in the *Crito* suggests that a citizen is indebted to a parent-city only when its constitution remains unchanged. And it is unlikely that Socrates took himself to be indebted to Athens for only such time as it remained a democracy. For he definitely rejects the idea that democracies are the only legitimate forms of government. (B) The Laws do not say what a citizen's duties are when the government punishes citizens without trial, or when trials are perfunctory. (Such things occurred when the Thirty were in power.)[6] In these cases, the citizen has no real opportunity to persuade the city that disobedience is justified. But the Laws might still maintain that even in these extreme situations, the citizen must show, by his openness, that he would be willing to persuade. (C) Socrates remained in Athens while the Thirty were in power, though some democrats—including his friend Chaerephon—went into exile (*Ap.* 20e8–21a2). And this raises an important question: would the Laws say that, by virtue of his continued residence, he implicitly agreed to accept the dictates of the Thirty? This question has to be temporarily shelved, for we have not yet considered the *Crito*'s notion of implicit agreement. But we will return to it in Chapter VI. (D) In spite of these uncertainties, one thing remains clear: Socrates made no effort to conceal his defiance of the Thirty. Thus, he did as a matter of fact conform to the *Crito*'s requirement of openness, as I interpret that requirement. We do not know whether Socrates thought that he had to persuade or obey the government of the Thirty, but in any case, he acted in precisely the way the persuade-or-obey doctrine demands.

One further point. We should recognize an important difference between the *Crito*'s principle that legitimate disobedience should always be overt and the point, made in more recent political works, that civil disobedience is a public act. As I have said, the Laws have an argument for their assumption that secret violations of a city's orders are wrong: they claim that a citizen must always honor his parent-city, and this means that when he disobeys he must demonstrate his willingness to persuade. By contrast, some recent discussions of civil disobedience treat openness as part of its definition. Thus, Rawls says:

> I shall begin by defining civil disobedience as a public, nonviolent, conscientious yet political act contrary to law usu-

---

[6] Leon was put to death without trial. See Andocides 1.94 in *Minor Attic Orators*, Vol. I (trans. Maidment). Isocrates tells us that 1,500 met this fate. See 7.67, 20.11

ally done with the aim of bringing about a change in the law or the policies of the government.[7]

A further point is that civil disobedience is a public act. Not only is it addressed to public principles, it is done in public. It is engaged in openly with fair notice; it is not covert or secretive. One may compare it to public speech, and being a form of address, . . . it takes place in the public forum.[8]

Here, openness is part of the definition of civil disobedience because it is a necessary means to the end that such acts are supposed to serve. Since the disobedient act is itself a "form of address," and since it is an appeal to the public sense of justice, it must of course take place in public. It cannot have the desired effect if it is clandestine. But the speech of the Laws refers to something quite different: it is not characterizing one form of protest, and it does not regard the disobedient act as itself a form of speech. Openness is required not because it is a means to the citizen's end, but because it enables the city to prosecute him.

3
Three problems

Several questions still remain.

(A) To show that Socrates is acting unjustly, the Laws do not need to implicate him in the destruction of Athens. They argue that a citizen must persuade or obey his parent-city; since Socrates refuses to do either, he is already wrong. Why then do the Laws bother with the point that Athens will be destroyed if private individuals rob the judgments of the courts of their authority?

(B) One cannot automatically move from:

(i) It would be bad if everyone of a certain type did A,

to:

(ii) No one of that type should do A.

---

[7] *A Theory of Justice*, p. 364.
[8] Ibid., p. 366.

For example, it would be disastrous if all American farmers planted nothing but corn, but that does not show that no single American farmer should grow this crop exclusively. Similarly, it might be true, as the Laws allege, that Athens would be destroyed if citizens, acting as private persons, disobeyed the orders of the courts. But they cannot legitimately infer from this that no private person should disobey the court. Are the Laws falling into an obvious trap?[9]

(C) Suppose every *public* (as opposed to *private*) person were to violate court orders. That is, suppose every Athenian citizen who received an order from a court refused to obey, but tried instead to persuade. Wouldn't such widespread public disobedience destroy the city, no less than widespread private disobedience? If so, Socrates is committed, like it or not, to condemning all violations of civic orders whatever—including public violations. What city could survive, if its citizens were always to disobey the laws? The fact that they disobey openly and are willing to persuade in court does not help matters: a city simply cannot continue to exist if its citizens regularly disobey the laws. So it seems that the generalization argument used by the Laws against Socrates inevitably forces them into an extremely authoritarian position. Either they must renounce their attempt to implicate him in the destruction of the city, or they must condemn all disobedience whatever. Is there any way to save them from this dilemma?

We can begin with (A), the easiest of our problems. It is quite true that the Laws can condemn Socrates without trying to implicate him in the destruction of Athens. But nonetheless, there is no reason why they should not try. After all, killing is a more serious matter than mere violence and disrespect. If a child kills his father, his act is more despicable than a mere slap in the face, and similarly, if an escaping Socrates is doing something akin to murder, then the Laws have every reason to point this out. In fact, we can easily understand why they begin their case against escape with a question about destruction. If their claim— that Socrates is destroying Athens, for his part—can be made to stick, then escape is no minor offense, as Crito might have

---

[9] See Ch. II, nn. 23 and 24 for some of the literature on this subject.

destruction is particularly severe form of disobeying parents

conceded, but one of the most serious crimes a citizen can commit against a city. Thus, by bringing out their most serious accusation first, they intend to heighten the reader's interest in what is to come. Generalization is not needed to show the wrongfulness of escape, but it does demonstrate the gravity of this undertaking. Compare someone who is particularly indignant that an attorney has lied under oath at a trial: he might say that the courts and the country would be destroyed if lawyers generally did that sort of thing. He does not have to generalize in this way to show that the lawyer was wrong to perjure himself; still, he may be right that this is a particularly destructive form of perjury. Similarly, the Laws do not have to generalize to show that Socrates does wrong, but that does not mean they are confused when they try to depict escape as a destructive act.

4

Generalization

I now want to show that the Laws commit no obvious fallacy when they seek to implicate an escaping Socrates in the destruction of Athens. Their aim is to show that if Socrates escapes, he does so from a certain motive—one it would be wrong for him to have. Note how often the Laws state their objection to escape in conative terms:[10]

(A) If Socrates escapes, he has it in mind to destroy Athens and its laws, for his part. He is thinking of nothing else. (50a8–b2)

(B) If Socrates escapes, he is trying to destroy the laws. (50d1, 52c9)

(C) If Socrates escapes, he is trying to destroy the laws, so far as he is able. (51a5)

(D) If Socrates escapes, he is trying to destroy the laws, for his part. (54c8)

---

[10] Adkins, *Merit and Responsibility*, pp. 262-264, takes the *Crito* to condemn any act, regardless of its motive, that weakens civic stability. But this overlooks the fact that the Laws constantly complain about what Socrates is *trying* to do.

I take their strategy to be as follows: they assume that it is wrong to destroy a parent or a parent-city; and they also assume that if it is wrong to commit some type of act X, then it is wrong to *try* to do X. So, once they reach any of the conclusions listed above, their case against escape is made. The trick is to understand how they arrive at these conclusions. More specifically, we have to see how these propositions are connected with the following generalization:

(E) If enough private persons do what Socrates is doing— i.e. if they privately overturn the verdicts of the courts— the city will be destroyed. (50b3-5).

My claim is that there is a perfectly reasonable way of moving from (E) back to propositions (A) through (D), once certain plausible psychological assumptions are made about Socrates. But before I explain my interpretation more fully, it will be helpful to consider the following example.

Suppose a man is ill, and to survive he must drink large quantities of very pure water. He has ten sons, and asks them to take turns visiting him daily and chemically treating his drinking water, so that all impurities are removed. One son, out of secret hatred, would like to kill his father, and so he decides to deceive him: he tells his father, as he visits him every tenth day, that he is giving him treated water, though in fact it comes straight from the tap. The son also does research on his father's condition, and learns that his health will not be impaired, even over the long run, if he drinks tap water one day in ten. But the son also learns that his father will die if three other sons are equally deceptive, and the father drinks purified water on only six days out of ten. Nonetheless, the murderous son decides that it would be too risky to conspire with any of his brothers. He doesn't know whether any of them hate their father as he does, and so he doesn't know whether his constant deception will kill him. But he thinks it possible that several other brothers have murderous intentions, and he certainly hopes they do.

What I find illuminating about this example is the fact that someone could reproach the deceptive son in terms that are similar to the ones that the Laws use against Socrates:

> Tell me, what do you have in mind to do? By deceiving your father, are you thinking of anything else than destroying him, for your part? Or does it seem to you that your father can survive, if his sons deceive him and deprive him of the means with which to live?

Of course, one could argue that the son is acting wrongly simply because he deceived his father; but it is important to realize that this is no minor form of deception, since the son is trying to kill his father, so far as he is able. Now, what entitles us to accuse the son of this more serious crime? How can we go from:

> (i) If enough sons do what the deceptive son is doing, their father will die,

to:

> (ii) The son is trying to destroy his father, for his part?

The obvious answer is that a good deal of psychological material has to be filled in. First of all, we already know that the son hates his father, and this gives him a motive for murder. Second, the son is aware of the truth of (i). Third, he believes there is some possibility that some of his brothers will be equally deceptive. From these three facts, it is plausible to infer that the son is hoping to make a causal contribution to the death of his father. And that means that he is trying, so far as he can, to kill him; alternatively put, he is trying to destroy his father, for his part.

My suggestion, then, is that the Laws are making certain assumptions about Socrates' state of mind, and if these are taken into account, the path from (E) to (A) and its ilk is fairly smooth. First, they assume that Socrates has a motive for murder: he has just been unfairly sentenced to death, and so it would not be surprising if he were to have a desire to respond in kind. Second, he can be credited with enough sense to realize that if many others privately disobey the orders of the courts, the legal system will lose its authority and viability. Third, Socrates is in no position to know how the Athenian legal system will fare in the future. Athens, unlike Sparta, was no paradigm of a law-and-order town; and in the time of crisis through which Socrates lived, no one could have been certain that the general level of disobedience would not gradually increase to the breaking point. So Socrates cannot discount the possibility of anarchy, nor can he know that his escape will play no causal role on the road to anarchy. And this means that he is disposed toward Athens in just the way the deceptive son is disposed toward his father: driven by a desire for vengeance, aware of the consequences of widespread and deceptive disobedience, unable to eliminate the possibility that his own piece of deception might contribute to the downfall of his greatest benefactor, Socrates is vulnerable to the charge that he is trying to destroy Athens, for his part. And certainly the Laws think that if he decides to escape, his decision will arise from the desire to do some damage to his native city. For otherwise they would not describe him as *trying* to destroy Athens. When we describe agents as making attempts, we necessarily take those agents to believe it possible for their actions to increase the probability, to some slight extent at least, that their goals will be achieved.

Perhaps the reader will object that the Laws are still making an obvious mistake: to defend himself, Socrates need only reply that he has just one purpose in mind, as he tries to escape—to stay alive. The fact that fleeing from jail might contribute in some way to the downfall of Athens is only a possible side-effect of his action; it is not the purpose with which he acts. But I don't think this provides Socrates with the reply he needs. If the aim of escape is self-preservation, then why didn't Socrates propose exile as his proper punishment? That would have saved his skin. The Laws can plausibly argue that if Socrates is trying to flee to other cities now, having rejected this alternative at his trial, then he must be moved by a desire for vengeance. By refusing exile when it was a legal option, he maneuvered himself into a position from which he could both save his life and defy the legal system. And why would he want to do that, if he were not trying, for his part, to destroy the city? In any case, even if the Laws were to give up their claim that Socrates is trying to destroy the city, they could retreat to another plausible thesis: given what Socrates knows, he is recklessly exposing the life of the city to danger, if he escapes. Consider the deceptive son once again. Even if he were not trying to kill his father, his failure to treat the water would be inexcusable, since he knowingly puts the health of his father at risk. And his deception is equally blameworthy, whether his father dies or remains in good health. Similarly, the Laws have a strong case against Socrates, even if he is not trying to destroy the city, and even if his actions have no causal consequences whatsoever. If one's attempt to do evil fails, or if one's recklessness has no ill effects, one is none the less to blame.

How can escape increase the probability of destruction? It is important to distinguish two scenarios that the Laws might have in mind. According to the first, they think that escape might by itself lead to many other acts of defiance, each of which in turn leads to many others, and so on. If each "X" represents an act of disobedience and each arrow a causal connection, then the first idea can be pictured in Figure 1. But there is good reason to doubt that this is what the Laws have in mind. Even if one concedes (as one should) that a general breakdown in the habit of obedience was a real possibility in Athens, it would be

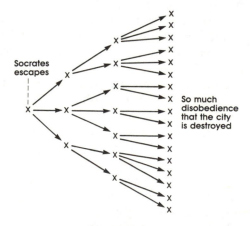

Figure 1

farfetched in the extreme to suppose that every act constituting such a breakdown, should it occur, would be inspired, directly or indirectly, by the single act of Socrates' escaping from jail. Perhaps some figures have had so much influence that one defiant act on their part might have brought down the state, but it would be ludicrous to put Socrates into that category, and we should not attribute this extreme position to the Laws unless we have better textual evidence. Futhermore, if the Laws seriously thought that escape might start the kind of chain reaction depicted in Figure 1, they would have denounced him in more damning terms than the ones they use. They would have said that Socrates is trying to be the *chief* cause, or the *ultimate* case, of the destruction of his city. Certainly, according to Figure 1, Socrates is far more responsible for the destruction of Athens than any other citizen. With his picture in mind, the Laws would not have limited themselves to the point that he is trying to destroy the city, *for his part*; rather, they would have said that Socrates is trying to play the *leading part* in the destruction of his city.

A second scenario is one that the Laws are more likely to have had in mind (Figure 2). Here, escape plays a far more modest role in leading to a decline in the level of obedience.

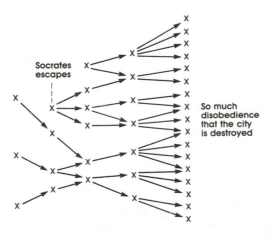

Figure 2

And in fact, we could give it a still more limited role than the one depicted, and the Laws could nonetheless make their point: all they need is one arrow that leads, directly or indirectly, from escape to the final column.[11] In other words, if Socrates escapes in the hope that his act will play some small causal role in the eventual breakdown of the social order, then he is trying, for his part, to destroy Athens. And surely there is nothing absurd about such a wish: more likely than not, escape from jail would eventually inspire at least one other act of defiance; and more likely than not, that would inspire some further act of disobedience. And so, if there is a future decline in the level of obedience, and it reaches the point of anarchy, then Socrates' wish to do what he can to get even with Athens will have been fulfilled. Perhaps the probability of such a decline is quite low, but that does not affect the argument of the Laws. They accuse Socrates of trying to bring about an effect, and he can hardly defend himself against this charge by pointing out how unlikely it is that he will succeed.

There is another way of interpreting the Laws. We could take them to be moving from:

(i) If every private person were to disobey the courts, the city would be destroyed,

to:

(ii) No private person may disobey the courts,

by means of this Generalization Principle:

(GA) If terrible consequences would be produced by everyone of type A doing X, then no one of type A should do X.

[11] There is also this possibility: the laws think that if Socrates escapes, there might be so much disobedience going on *at the same time* that the legal system would, on that very day, collapse. In this case, the example Socrates sets is irrelevant; he is condemned because he is trying to participate in a sudden breakdown in the social order. Now although I think the Laws would condemn anyone who privately disobeys in the hope that, by coincidence, others will privately disobey on that same day, I doubt that this is the scenario they are really worried about. The habit of obedience does not suddenly come to an end, without some extraordinary cause; the more likely danger—the one the Laws are probably thinking of—is that the level of obedience might gradually decline, because of people like Socrates.

One problem for this interpretation, as I have mentioned several times, is that it saddles the *Crito* with an assumption that is vulnerable to obvious and endless counter-examples. No one believes (GA) as it stands,[12] and it is reasonable to assume that the Laws could have seen the objections that everyone else quickly recognizes. As I have argued, there is an alternative interpretation that gives the Laws a much stronger argument, and so charity alone requires us to refrain from foisting (GA) onto the *Crito*. Furthermore, there are sound textual reasons for rejecting the interpretation that invokes (GA), and for preferring mine instead. This can best be seen if we alter the case of the deceptive son.

Suppose the son takes special care, before he deceives his father, to determine whether his brothers are doing what their father asks. And suppose he goes ahead with his deception only after he has made certain that they are all treating the water. In that case, no one could accuse the deceitful son of trying to kill his father; he does not have it in mind to take his father's life, for his part. Nonetheless, anyone who believes or implicitly assumes that (GA) is correct will continue to accuse the deceitful son of acting wrongly, since terrible consequences would flow from everyone's doing likewise. That is, the upholder of (GA) doesn't care if the deceitful son knows that his action will have no destructive effects; he doesn't express his objection by saying that the son is *trying* to kill his father. What bothers the upholder of (GA) is that the son isn't willing to act on general principles: he makes an exception in his own case, even though he doesn't want his brothers to do likewise.[13] The real objection that (GA) makes against the deceitful son is that he is being unfair to his brothers. Though he is making sure that no harm

---

[12] For example, M. Singer takes (GA) to be the popular expression of a much more complicated idea. See *Generalization in Ethics*, p. 73, where (GA) becomes: "If the consequences of every member of K's doing x in certain circumstances would be undesirable, while the consequences of no member of K's doing x (in those circumstances) would not be undesirable, then no member of K has the right to do x (in such circumstances) without a special reason." The principle becomes still more complex in the following pages.

[13] See M. Singer, ibid. pp. 90–91.

comes to his father, he is not sharing in a reasonable cooperative scheme.[14]

The general lesson to be learned from this example is that someone who relies on (GA) will not express his objections to particular acts in conative terms. He will ask, "What if others did the same?" but not, "What are you trying to do?" Now, if we return to the *Crito* with this in mind, we see that the Laws give every sign that they are not upholders of (GA). In (A), (B), (C), and (D), above, they accuse Socrates of trying to bring about a certain consequence, and this is a charge they ought not to make, if their complaint is based on (GA). Furthermore, they never suggest that Socrates is being unfair to his fellow citizens by doing what would, if generally done, destroy the city. The intended victim of his wrongdoing is the city, not the citizen; and this shows that the Laws are not accusing Socrates of failing to share the burdens of cooperation.[15]

I conclude that the Laws do not tacitly invoke an argument that now goes by the name of "the generalization argument." Yet it is easy to see why this interpretation, though mistaken, is tempting. For the Laws do generalize: they ask what would happen if private citizens disobeyed the judicial orders of the city. And they aren't predicting that escape will in fact have bad consequences. According to the Laws, escape would be a destructive act even if Athens were never destroyed, and even if it did not inspire a single other act of disobedience. But that does not show that they are relying on (GA), for an individual can be guilty of wrongful attempts and malicious risk-taking whether his actions have damaging effects or not. (GA) is not the only moral principle that condemns actions because of what could happen, rather than what does in fact happen. The reason (GA) does not apply to the *Crito* is because it is indifferent between real and unreal possibilities: it considers what would happen if others did likewise, even when the agent knows that

---

[14] The connection between the generalization argument and fairness is pointed out by Strang, "What if Everyone Did That?" pp. 157-162. See too Aune, *Kant's Theory of Morals*, pp. 125-126.

[15] This point is made by Woozley, *Law and Obedience*, p. 135.

others will not do so. It is therefore a more blunt and implausible weapon against escape than the Laws want or need.[16]

5
Private *versus* public

We can now turn to the third problem raised in Section 3. The Laws claim that *privately* disobeying the courts is somehow destructive of the city, and this implies that *public* disobedience is not vulnerable to this same criticism. But can this distinction be justified? Doesn't disobedience always destroy the social order when it is sufficiently widespread, whether it is public or private in the *Crito*'s sense? After all, if everyone publicly disobeyed the courts, the community would no longer have a functioning legal system. And so it might seem that if the Laws

---

[16] Two alternatives to my interpretation should be mentioned:

(A) Allen, *Socrates and Legal Obligation*, pp. 84–85, takes the argument in the following way: to escape is "to deny . . . the authority of the verdict and sentence," which is "to deny authority to any sentence so rendered," which is "to deny authority to law itself," which is "by so much . . . destructive of all law." But this differs significantly from what we find in the text. The Laws never speak as though (i) a single act can deny the authority of a sentence, verdict, or law. Rather, they say that (ii) if the verdicts of the courts lose their authority (*akuroi . . . gignōntai*), the city can no longer exist. The move from (ii) to (i) is difficult, and attributing (i) to the *Crito* needs further defense. Allen gives no answer to the main question about 50a8–b5: how does the generalization in (ii) contribute to the conclusion that Socrates is trying to destroy the city, for his part? There are similar problems in the interpretation advocated by Wade, "In Defense of Socrates," pp. 313–317.

(B) Woozley, *Law and Obedience*, p. 126, has this to say: "Their argument against him is of a non-consequential kind. They are not protesting that his conduct will actually do the laws any harm at all, let alone destroy them, nor even that there is any risk that it will. But they are protesting at his showing, by his attempt to destroy them, the sort of man that he is, a man whose attitude to the law is that of a destroyer, even whose aim is that of a destroyer. That such an aim does not have the slightest chance of success is irrelevant; what is significant is what it reveals—the character of a man who would destroy the laws, if only he could." But if the Laws know that Socrates' attempt to destroy them cannot succeed, then why shouldn't Socrates know this as well? If he knows that he cannot destroy the city, then he cannot be trying to do so. Yet he is trying, according to the Laws. Woozley sees that escape cannot *by itself* destroy the city; and he rightly assumes that the Laws see this too. But he fails to realize that we can try to bring about a certain effect even when we realize that we cannot succeed unless others do likewise.

want to implicate Socrates in the destruction of Athens, they have to oppose all disobedience toward the courts. In fact, to put it more generally, they apparently must condemn the violation of any law, regulation, or public command. For if everyone violated such orders, the city would be destroyed.

But the reader should now realize that the *Crito*'s distinction between public and private disobedience cannot be collapsed or dismissed so easily as this. The previous paragraph creates trouble for the Laws by assuming that they rely on (GA) to implicate an escaping Socrates in the destruction of Athens. And it also assumes—quite correctly—that (GA) can be used to condemn public and private disobedience alike. But if the argument of Section 4 is correct, the Laws do not rely on (GA), and so our question is still open: can their case that escape is destructive also be made against someone who accepts the persuade-or-obey principle and *publicly* disobeys a court's command? To answer this question, let us imagine that Socrates had acted publicly, in the relevant sense, and then let us see whether in this case he can still be described as trying to destroy Athens, for his part. Suppose he had told the court, at his trial, that he could not cooperate with the death penalty, should the jury vote for it, and that he would therefore try to escape from jail before drinking the hemlock. The Laws can plausibly claim that if Socrates had acted in this way, then he should not be accused of *trying* to destroy Athens, so far as he is able. By publicly announcing his intention to disobey, he would have shown his respect for the city, and at the same time greatly diminished his chances of avoiding the death penalty. It would therefore be absurd to portray him as trying his best to destroy the city, for if that had been his motive, he would have disobeyed privately. A disobedient act is more likely to contribute to a breakdown in the social order if it actually succeeds, and if the public later learns of its success. But whoever is moved by the persuade-or-obey doctrine to announce his intention to disobey is undermining his chances of success in order to show his respect for the state. The motive for disobedience, in this case, cannot be to contribute in a small way to the destruction of the state.

There is a different way in which public acts of disobedience can occur: one can disobey first (for example, by refusing to carry out an order given by a public official) and try to justify one's act afterwards, in the courtroom. In this case, the act of disobedience is not announced ahead of time, but it is public because the individual makes no attempt to avoid giving a courtroom defense. Can the Laws plausibly argue that someone who acts in this way should not be accused of trying to do his part in the destruction of the city? Again, the answer is yes, for the same reason. A citizen who disobeys openly, in order to provide the city with an opportunity to bring him to court to hear his defense, is obviously increasing his chances of being punished, and this shows that he is not aiming at the destruction of the social order. A disobedient act is most likely to weaken the fabric of public order if it is widely known that someone violated the law without having been later brought to trial. By making oneself available for trial and punishment, one shows that destroying the legal system was not the motive behind one's act.

There is one difficulty, however, with this attempt to show that private disobedience is destructive and that public disobedience is not. Admittedly, the Laws can show that no one who accepts their philosophy and publicly disobeys is *trying* to do his part to destroy the state. But as we saw earlier, even if the claim that someone is trying to destroy a parent or a city turns out to be false, it may still be true that he is recklessly *endangering* the life of that parent or city. The Laws would surely want to condemn any act of disobedience that puts the life of a parent–city at risk. But can they show that if someone disobeys a law *publicly,* then he is not guilty of this charge? If both public and private acts of disobedience show reckless disregard for the city's survival, then it hardly matters that acts of public disobedience cannot be characterized as *attempts* to destroy the state.

Once again, however, I think that the Laws can be defended. For it can be argued that someone who disobeys publicly is taking reasonable precautions so that his act will have no ill effects on the city. Consider an analogy. A parent who drives with a child in his lap is showing reckless disregard for the life of the child (though of course it is quite a different matter to say that he is trying to kill it). By contrast, someone who straps the child into a car-seat is taking reasonable precautions, and even if the child is injured in an accident, the parent cannot for that reason alone be accused of wrongdoing. Admittedly, if the parent had adopted the policy of never allowing his child in a car, the injury would not have occurred. But we do not accuse people of recklessness or wrongdoing merely because an alternative that imposed fewer risks was open to them. Rather, we use some vague but unavoidable standard of proper precaution. Similarly, the Laws can say that whoever disobeys publicly is taking sufficient care to protect the city from eventual destruction. Perhaps those who adopt a policy of never disobeying the city create less danger for it than those who on occasion publicly violate the law. But that shows nothing. We cannot be expected to arrange our lives so that the least possible danger is posed to others. And if public disobedience is an expression of respect for the state, as the Laws concede, then those who publicly disobey cannot be accused of having insufficient concern for the well-being of the state. It would be too great an infringement on the moral life of the citizen to expect him never to disobey orders, no matter what. The state must therefore concede that disobedience is sometimes justified, and accordingly it must put public and private disobedience into different moral categories: it can condemn private disobedience as a form of recklessness, but it must grant that whatever risk is created by public disobedience is something we have to live with. Once this is conceded, then even if a public act of disobedience does (contrary to all expectations) cause a growth in the amount of lawlessness, and even if the state is eventually destroyed as a result, the citizen who publicly disobeyed is nonetheless not morally responsible—not even partially responsible—for the breakdown in social order. He is of course *causally* responsible, in that his act contributed to the downfall of the city. In the same way, if I invite a passing stranger to seek refuge from the storm on my front porch, and he is there struck by lightning, then I am causally but not morally responsible for his death. For I had no reason to expect this result, and violated no reasonable standard of precaution. The Laws can defend public disobedience in this same way.

6
Violence and persuasion revisited

We can now return to a passage that puzzled us in IV.3:

> . . . You must do what your city and fatherland commands, or persuade it as to the nature of justice. Violence against your mother or father is unholy, and still more so against your fatherland. (51b9-c3)

I said that the relationship between these two sentences is problematic: what does refusing to persuade or obey have to do with violence? The suggestion of IV.3 was that according to the Laws nonphysical violence is done whenever disrespect is extreme and unwarranted. By escaping, Socrates would be—as we might put it—"violating" his parent-city. But now we can see that there is a different way of understanding our passage. The Laws might be relying on the obvious assumption that if an act can be characterized as an attempt at destruction, then it is rightly regarded as a form of violence. And they think that escape is destructive in the following sense: by refusing to persuade or obey, Socrates is violating the law as a private person, and he hopes that the verdicts of the courts will be disobeyed by so many private persons that the city will be destroyed. Escape is violent because destructive, destructive because private, and private because it represents a refusal to address the city openly and publicly. One advantage of this interpretation is that it does not require the Laws to use *biazesthai* ("to do violence") at 51c2 in an extended or metaphorical sense. They do not have to rely on the questionable assumption that one uses violence whenever one refuses to persuade or obey a parent or a parent-city. Nonetheless, I do not think that this second interpretation is obviously correct or greatly superior to the first; and in any case, as I said in IV.3, the choice between the two readings is less than momentous. On either interpretation, the Laws do not have to characterize escape as an act of violence in order to reach the conclusion that it is wrong.

One further point should be mentioned. Although the Laws implicate Socrates in the destruction of Athens, they do not say or suggest that this same argument can be used in a wide vari-

ety of circumstances. They nowhere claim that whoever violates an order without trying to persuade is doing his part to
destroy the city. On the contrary, they stress the fact that the
law Socrates would be disobeying—the law that gives the courts
their authority (50b7-8)—is particularly important (53e1-2). They
say that the city will be destroyed if private persons disobey the
courts, but this does not commit them to the view that widespread disobedience of any law at all will have the same effect.
And such a position would be highly questionable. Surely there
are many statutes of such small importance that the city could
easily survive their covert destruction. By contrast, the law
Socrates would disobey, if he escapes, *is* essential to the survival
of the city. Which other laws have this same status, the *Crito*
does not say. Presumably there will be some: for example, since
a Greek city in the fifth century is in constant danger of attack,
the authority of military officers is no less crucial for the survival of the city than the authority of courts. So in this case too
we might expect the Laws to say that whoever refuses to persuade or obey is doing his part to destroy his parent-city. But
the *Crito* does not propose a way of distinguishing vital from
peripheral laws. It simply claims that the particular law that
Socrates disobeys is vital, and on this basis it characterizes escape as a destructive act.[17]

7
Recounting the arguments

This completes my analysis of the long passage that runs from
50a8 to 51c3. It opens with the accusation that Socrates is thinking of destroying Athens for his part, moves to the parent-city
analogy, and returns in the end to the charge of violence. The
intended conclusion of this passage is complex: (A) it is unjust
for Socrates to escape; (B) so unjust, in fact, that it is akin to
and worse than an attack on the lives of his parents. The parent-

---

[17] Do the Laws think that privately disobeying even a minor command is an
act of *violence* (even though it would not be an act of *destruction*)? Yes, if they
think that every refusal to persuade or obey is an act of violence. (This is the
interpretation put forward in IV.3.) No, if they need to show that a disobedient
act is an attempt at destruction, before they can characterize it as violent.

city analogy, with its persuade-or-obey doctrine, would by it-self enable the Laws to reach (A), but had they stopped at that, they would have seriously understated the case they want to make against Socrates. His crime, they think, is no ordinary act of disrespect, and so they go beyond (A) and implicate him in the destruction of Athens. But we should not think that the Laws are presenting an "argument from destruction" that is independent of the parent-city analogy and the persuade-or-obey doctrine. For they do not claim that destroying a city is always wrong; rather, they only condemn the destruction of one's par-ent-city. Furthermore, it is only *private* disobedience that is con-sidered destructive, and as we have seen, the notion of privacy is tied up with the persuade-or-obey doctrine.

So we were right to say at the end of Chapter II that the Laws use two types of argument against Socrates. One relies on the parent-city analogy to show that escape is an extreme form of injustice; and the Laws divide this argument into two, when they say (51e5-6) that birth and education provide two separate reasons against escape. The other type of argument relies on the idea that Socrates made an agreement with Athens to obey its commands. To this argument—the one the Laws take to be their third (51e6-7)—we shall soon turn. But before we leave the parent-city analogy, I would like to make some final remarks about its philosophical faults and merits.

8
How good is the parent-city analogy?

There is much in this argument that I reject. To begin with, the Laws hold that even if parents merely give their child one benefit—life—the child thereby incurs a significant debt of grat-itude: he must honor them and never treat them with violence. (See II.9.) But is bringing someone into existence a way of ben-efiting him? How can that be, if he is not better off than he was before? And even if it is true that to be born is to receive a benefit, it is not *by itself* so great a benefit as to give rise to duties of honor and respect. If X gives birth to Y, abandons him, and then reappears many years later, does Y have to show special respect for X, merely because X is his biological parent?

The Laws are on safer ground when they claim that parental care engenders a debt of gratitude that continues into adulthood. But even here, I would amend their position. If parents do a good job of bringing up their child, it does not follow that the child must never intentionally use violence against them. If they attack him, he still has a right to self-defense. Furthermore, even if they have taken proper care of their child, they may severely mistreat him when he is an adult. In this case, it could be argued that on balance they have been poor parents, and it is not clear that they are still owed a debt of gratitude. And even if parents have done a good job on balance, there are certain demands they have no right to make. A mother who tells her adult son what to wear fails to respect his independence, and is not entitled to an explanation of why he didn't wear this particular tie, or that particular shirt. The Laws assume that parents are entitled to give commands to their adult children, though they concede that these commands might justifiably be disobeyed. (See IV.2). What we must say, instead, is that although parents have a right to tell their young children how to behave, they lose this right when their children become adults.

Nonetheless, I think that adult children owe their parents something significant, and that there is a political analogue to this debt. The principle I advocate is this:

(A) If X has been and continues to be a good parent to Y, and if X asks Y to contribute to his well-being, Y must comply or explain to X why he will not.

For example, if a parent is ill and asks his child to help him recover, the child cannot simply refuse without an explanation. It may be that the parent's request is unreasonable, or that the child is unable to meet it; but in either case, simply ignoring the parent's appeal is an unjustifiable form of dishonor and disrespect. If a perfect stranger asks you to come to the hospital to visit him, you can refuse without explanation or apology; but good parents should not be treated like perfect strangers. Although they cannot give us commands and cannot meddle in our personal lives, they have, by virtue of the benefits they have conferred, a moral standing that makes it appropriate for them to ask for help.[18]

I suggest that there is a political analogue to (A):

(B) If state X has given person Y, during his childhood, at least as many benefits as a good parent should give Y, and if Y has, as an adult, no serious and legitimate complaint against X, then when X asks Y to contribute to its well-being, Y must comply or explain to X why he will not.

I do not see how (A) can be true unless (B) is true as well.[19] For if we owe debts of gratitude to our parents, that is because of certain benefits we have received from them; and if equivalent benefits, or more, have been given to us by some other moral agent, then we must owe that other agent at least what we owe our parents. If my country seriously abridges my rights as an adult, or in some other way treats me with disdain, then it loses or at least compromises any claim it might otherwise

---

[18] Objection: "Parents have a duty to care for their children. And if the benefit A gives B is one A had a duty to provide, then B incurs no duty of gratitude to A." I reject the second statement. Friends owe each other aid, yet such support deserves gratitude and repayment. Of course, fulfilling a duty does not always deserve gratitude. If someone refrains from interfering with my rights, I do not owe him anything in return. Similarly, benefits received as part of a contractual agreement do not give rise to debts of gratitude. For further discussion, see Simmons, *Moral Principles and Political Obligations*, pp. 179-182.

[19] Locke accepts a principle at least as strong as (A), but his notion that political obligation is contractual in nature prevents him from adopting anything like (B). See the *Second Treatise*, Secs. 66-68: though adult children do not have to obey their parents, they owe them "defense, relief, assistance, and comfort" (Sec. 66). Why wouldn't the state similarly be entitled to defense and assistance, if it had benefited the citizen when he was a child? Is Locke assuming that the state has no right to nourish and educate the child, or is he simply assuming that it does not in fact provide such benefits? I do not claim that (A) logically entails (B), but only that a political theory that accepts (A) and rejects (B) will be implausible. Someone could say that (A) is true because parents give life to their children and develop intimate relationships with them; one could then reject (B), on the grounds that states do neither of these things for their citizens. But I do not see why birth and intimacy should make so great a difference between the two cases. If a mother benefits her children in a way their father cannot, but he benefits them equally in other ways, the children will owe both parents equal regard. Similarly, if the state benefits its citizens as much as their parents do, and they owe their parents special consideration because of those benefits, then they also owe special consideration to the state.

have had to my loyalty.[20] But if a country has given me great benefits when I was a child—benefits comparable to those I received from my parents—and if it respects my rights when I am an adult, then it has a moral standing that entitles it to an explanation if I turn down the appeals it makes in the pursuit of its legitimate concerns. Although the state must respect our privacy and independence, it has a legitimate concern in its own survival and in justice for its citizens. And when it asks those it has greatly benefited to contribute to these legitimate projects, they ought to comply or else give the state some explanation for noncompliance. So principle (B) does not say that the citizen has an obligation—even a *prima facie* obligation—to obey the law, but even so it has serious moral consequences. If a state meets the conditions spelled out in (B), its citizen-beneficiaries cannot engage in secret disobedience of legitimate state demands. They must show the state that they have a special respect for it, and a special concern for its well-being. As defenders of civil disobedience have argued, disobeying the law is compatible with this special respect and concern;[21] but disrespect is shown if we try to conceal our failure to comply with the legitimate demands of those who have benefited us.[22]

The position I advocate is denied by the philosophical anarchist, whom Wolff describes as follows:

> In a sense, we might characterize the anarchist as a man without a country, for despite the ties which bind him to the land of his childhood, he stands in precisely the same moral relationship to "his" government as he does to the government of any other country in which he might hap-

[20] What if the state respects my rights, but not those of other citizens? Does it compromise or lose its claim to my loyalty and respect? If my parents treat me well but mistreat my sister, can I cease to give them the respect they would otherwise deserve? I am unsure what to say.

[21] See for example Rawls, *A Theory of Justice*, pp. 366–368.

[22] Raz, *The Authority of Law*, p. 258, says: "Nobody does any wrong in not respecting the law even in a good state." But by "respect for law" he means (p. 251) "a disposition to obey the law (i.e. to do that which it requires because it so requires . . .)." Why should respect be so closely tied to obedience? I can respect my parents without obeying them in all matters—indeed, without conceding that they have a right to tell me what to do. Similarly, I can respect a country and its legal system even when I have no disposition to obey its laws merely because they are laws.

pen to be staying for a time. When I take a vacation in Great Britain, I obey its laws, both because of prudential self-interest and because of the obvious moral considerations concerning the value of order, the general good consequences of preserving a system of property, and so forth. . . . My obedience to American laws, if I am to be morally autonomous, must proceed from the same considerations which determine me abroad.[23]

I have said nothing to contest Wolff's claim that I do not owe my country obedience. But even if I have no such debt, even if I have no general obligation to obey the law, it does not follow that my moral relationship to my country is the same as my moral relationship to any other state. For if a country has treated its citizens well, they must give its appeals for aid far more weight than the equally urgent appeals of other nations. Consider two hypothetical lands, Narnia and Oz, and suppose that although they have equally good governments, I happen to have been born in Narnia, and received many benefits from it when I was a child. Even if I have no obligation to obey its laws, it is absurd to say that I owe no more to it than I owe to Oz. This would be as ludicrous as the claim that I owe no more to my parents, if they have been good to me, than I owe to any other equally good people.[24] Our parents give us benefits that we have no hand in choosing, and because of those benefits, we have an ongoing duty to show special respect for their legitimate concerns; just so, if a state treats us in a certain way, then even if we did not choose the benefits it conferred, we owe it a degree of respect that we owe no other state.[25]

---

[23] *In Defense of Anarchism*, pp. 18-19. This passage is cited with approval by Simmons, *Moral Principles and Political Obligations*, p. 195.

[24] There may be a highly general duty to promote just institutions wherever they occur or might develop; and it may be that, as a practical matter, I can best fulfill this duty by focusing on the country of which I am a citizen. But a political theory that admitted only future-looking political duties would leave out something important: just as I am morally tied to particular individuals because of the good they have done me in the past, so I can be tied to my country because of benefits I received even before I acquired the right to participate fully in the country's political affairs.

[25] This is why Simmons, *Moral Principles and Political Obligations*, p. 162, is

Principle (B) tells us what a citizen owes, not to his fellow citizens, but to a certain institution—the state. It might be wondered whether we really can be indebted to things that are not persons. I see no serious grounds for skepticism, however. When I owe the telephone company $40, my debt is owed precisely to the company and to no particular person within it. If I write a check to Mr. X, who is the head of the billing department, I still owe the telephone company $40. If we can owe money to institutions, I see no reason why we cannot owe them debts of gratitude.[26] Institutions, though they are not persons, are nonetheless moral agents: they can act for reasons, and they can intentionally try to help others. If states deliberately aim at the well-being of their citizens, debts of gratitude can arise, though these may fall short of obligations to obey the law.[27] Of course, which states, if any, deserve such gratitude is a different matter.[28]

---

wrong to dismiss the *Crito*'s comparison between parents and the state. The parent-city analogy frees us from the assumption that the benefits of political life have to be freely accepted before they can bind citizens to their country.

[26] Contrast Simmons, ibid., pp. 187-188. He rightly insists that gratitude is owed only when benefits are conferred for certain kinds of reasons. But I do not accept the further point that therefore gratitude cannot be owed to institutions. Why should we believe that it is only legislators and judges—not legislatures and courts—that can act for reasons? If we admit that legislatures and courts (not just legislators and judges) exist, we must also admit that they act; and if we go this far, how can we stop short of saying that they have motives and intentions? Of course, nations and political organizations are dependent entities: they cannot exist unless people do, and they have motives by virtue of the fact that people acting in their names have motives. But none of this shows that gratitude can never be the appropriate response to the actions of political bodies.

[27] Objection: "The benefits I received as a child from the state have already been paid for. For example, my parents paid the state to educate me. Therefore, gratitude would be out of place." But it wasn't just my parents who paid for such benefits as education (if this was in fact a benefit): it was all taxpayers. Do I owe a debt of gratitude to them, but not the state? Why should we eliminate all talk about debts to institutions in favor of talk about debts to individuals?

[28] The practical upshot of my discussion depends a great deal on the way we answer the questions raised above in n. 20. For most nations are vulnerable to the charge that they mistreat many of their citizens, and frequently others besides. If this is so, do those who have greatly benefited from political institutions still owe their countries respect and support?

VI

DOKIMASIA, SATISFACTION, AND AGREEMENT

1
Agreement: Some unsolved problems

ALTHOUGH the Laws assert at an early point in their speech (50c5-6) that Socrates agreed to abide by the judgments of the courts, they do not immediately defend their claim. They say only as much as is needed to discourage Socrates and Crito from pursuing a line of reasoning that will get them nowhere. Admittedly, Socrates has recently suffered an injustice at the hands of his city, but if, as the Laws allege, it is an injustice he agreed to risk, then his unfortunate trial will give him no legitimate reason to try to destroy the city. But to defend immediately their claim that Socrates made such an agreement would take the Laws too far away from their present task. They first need to complete their "argument from destruction" by showing that Socrates would be unjustified in acting violently or destructively against Athens, regardless of the injustices inflicted on him by the city. And, as we have seen, that brings them to the analogy between offspring and citizens. But once this business is taken care of, the Laws can return to the point they left hanging. What makes them say that Socrates agreed to abide by the judgments of the courts? By which acts, undertaken or omitted, did he make this agreement? Furthermore, what reason do they have for saying that it was a just agreement? The Laws now

parent argument
agreement argument

devote sixty lines (51d1–53a7) to these questions. They proceed as follows.

(A) 51d1–e4: They first explain the process by which all citizens make an agreement with the city. When an Athenian comes of legal age and observes the political practices of his city, he is, if dissatisfied, allowed to expatriate, and he may even take his property with him. But whoever is aware of the city's institutions and decides to stay has agreed, through what he does, to abide by its commands.

(B) 51e4–52a3: They next assert that this creates a third argument against escape, and they repeat their earlier point that everyone is given two choices: to persuade or obey. But Socrates refuses to do either.

(C) 52a3–d7: The argument now turns more specifically to the relationship between Socrates and Athens. By escaping, he would be more guilty than anyone else, for he especially has agreed to live as a citizen, and he has been especially satisfied with the city. Unlike others, he has rarely left Athens; furthermore, he has had children there; and most recently, when he could have proposed exile as a punishment, he claimed instead that he would rather die.

(D) 52d8–53a7: Finally, the Laws add some further facts about the agreement Socrates has made. He was not forced, rushed, or tricked into this agreement, but in fact had seventy years during which he could have left, if he was dissatisfied or thought his agreements unjust. But he did not prefer even Sparta or Crete, cities he has always thought to be well governed. This satisfaction with his native city shows that he has been satisfied with its laws, for no one can be satisfied with a city apart from its laws.

I have already made some use of the material presented in (B) and (D). In (B), the Laws are saying that even when someone breaks an agreement and disobeys the city, he must persuade. (See III.1.) In (D), they are arguing that the agreement Socrates made was just. (See II.2–3.) But several questions were previously shelved, and now they must be answered. First, we want to know whether it is ever permissible for a citizen to violate an order on the grounds that it does him an injustice. (See II.4.)

Obviously, if the citizen voluntarily agrees to every order Athens gives, then he is agreeing to risk such suffering. But can a citizen remain in Athens and legitimately refuse to agree to certain laws or orders? Can he refuse to agree to a law because it does him an injustice? Or must he leave the city and go into exile if he is dissatisfied with any laws? Second, we want to know whether the argument from agreement compensates for the weakness of the parent-city analogy. (See IV.6.) As I argued earlier, that analogy gives the city the right to issue orders to and to demand explanations from its citizens. But it does not give the city the right to kill or imprison its citizens for disobedience, since this is not a right that parents have in relation to their adult offspring. If the city has this right, it must be given to it by the agreement of its citizens. But what if the citizens refuse to give it? In that case, the city will have too little power. On the other hand, if a citizen who continues to reside in Athens has no choice but to agree to the judicial system, in what sense is his agreement voluntary and therefore just? Is it voluntary only in the sense that he can leave Athens if he wants to? In that case, the Laws are adopting the highly authoritarian doctrine that departure is the only way to avoid making an agreement to obey one's city. It seems that the Laws are caught between two equally unappealing extremes: either agreement is too easy to avoid, in which case the city has too little power; or agreement is too difficult to avoid, in which case the citizen has too little freedom. Must the Laws fall into one or the other of these two traps?

To answer these questions, it will be necessary to look carefully at the mechanics by which an agreement is made. What is the precise role of residence in the argument of the Laws? Does residence constitute an agreement to obey, or is it merely a sign of satisfaction? Do they think that being satisfied with a law is the same thing as agreeing to it? Are there any other factors besides residence and satisfaction in the mechanics of making an agreement? We are forced to tackle these questions if we want to determine whether permanent departure from Athens is the only way to avoid making an agreement to obey the city.

Is leaving only way to avoid agreeing according to Socrates?

2

Implied agreement

The Laws say that an Athenian who conducts himself in a certain way "has agreed with us, by what he does (*ergōi*), to carry out what we command . . ." (51e3–4). Later, at 52d5, they expand on this *ergōi*: Socrates has agreed to be a citizen "by what he does and not by what he says" (*ergōi all'ou logōi*). So they do not claim that Socrates ever said, in so many words, "I agree to do whatever the city commands," or "I agree to be a citizen."[1] Rather, their point is that his nonverbal behavior gave rise to such an agreement; as we might put it, his agreement was tacit or implied, though it was not expressed in words. Now, I take it to be quite uncontroversial that agreements can be made by what we do, and not merely by what we say or write. A nod of the head, to take a trivial example, can express assent as easily as "yes." Or a speaker at a meeting can ask his listeners to rise if they agree to the conditions he has just described. We can fix upon any convention we like to serve as a signal of agreement: a green tie can mean "I agree to join the club" and a red tie can mean "I refuse."

But in addition to these obvious examples, there are others that are less straightforward and more interesting. Suppose someone agrees to play a game of chess with me. While the game is in progress, I am out of the room, and he alters the positions of some of the pieces. No doubt, this is a case of cheating, but can we also describe it as the breaking of an agreement? True, my opponent never explicitly said, "I will play by the rules," but that hardly seems to matter. He did agree to play chess, and what does that agreement come to if it is un-

[1] In the second half of the fourth century, military recruits took an oath to "obey those who for the time being exercise sway reasonably and the established laws and those which they will establish reasonably in the future." In "The Ephebic Oath in Fifth-Century Athens," Siewert (whose translation I have just used) argues that fifth-century citizens also took the oath. But the silence of the *Crito* is significant: though it would suit their purpose, the Laws never say that Socrates or others verbally agreed to obey them. So even if the oath is as early as Siewert thinks, it may have been taken by only some of the citizens. It is reasonably certain, at any rate, that Socrates never took it; for otherwise the Laws would have said so.

accompanied by the understanding that certain rules will guide our conduct? Of course, players can agree to change the rules if they want to, but in the absence of such an arrangement, the agreement to play chess is an agreement to pursue a certain goal by means of certain rules.

Consider a second example. A man enters a restaurant, looks at a menu, and orders a certain dish, which, as the menu indicates, costs $10. When the waiter brings the bill at the end of the meal, the customer refuses to pay, and claims in his defense that he never agreed to pay $10 or any other amount; he merely requested a certain dish, and the waiter was nice enough to bring it to him. Now, if this man understands the conventions by which restaurants operate, then he is obviously guilty of sophistry. He knows that the restaurant requires payment for his meal, and by ordering that particular meal he created the legitimate expectation that he would pay for it. Any court of law would hold that he had made an agreement to pay $10, even though he merely said, "I'll have that dish."[2] And surely the courts are right that valid agreements do not always have to be spelled out in so many words.

One final example. The rules of a certain club are prominently displayed on the walls of its admissions office, and membership is granted to anyone who pays a certain fee and submits some information about himself. Does an individual who joins thereby agree to abide by the rules posted on the walls? The application form does not include a statement of allegiance to the club's rules, and so the act of joining does not involve an *explicit* agreement to obey. But does it *imply* an agreement? Of course, we are not asking whether the new member *ought* to abide by the rules of the club. Perhaps, if the organization is evil or its rules absurd, he should not. What we want to know is whether someone who violates those rules is also violating— justifiably or not—an agreement implied in the act of joining.

---

[2] Such agreements are called "implied-in-fact" contracts. See Kessler and Gilmore, *Contracts*, pp. 116-117. For further discussion, see the references in Fried, *Contract as Promise*, pp. 142-143 n. 4. He says, ". . . offeree acceptance of a proferred benefit for which he knows payment is expected is the paradigm case" of the "tacit acceptance" of a contract.

Surely our previous two examples suggest that an implicit agreement has been made. Neither the chess player nor the restaurant customer explicitly agreed to abide by any rules or conventions. If they implied an agreement when they accepted a match or ordered a meal, then our club member has also implicitly agreed to the rules of the organization. He knows what will be expected of him when he joins, for the club has gone out of its way to make sure that new members are aware of its regulations. So, by joining, he gives the others to understand that he will abide by those rules. And this understanding is appropriately called an agreement.

3
The club of Athens

I have dwelled on these examples because I think the last of them is relevant to the *Crito*. During the late fifth century, becoming an Athenian citizen was not something that happened automatically either at birth or at any other time. Male children born of citizen parents had to take positive steps to enroll themselves as citizens at the age of seventeen, and unless their names appeared on the official lists of citizens, they could not legally exercise the judicial and legislative privileges of adult Athenians. The process of registration was carefully regulated. The candidate for citizenship had to provide evidence of his age and citizen parentage at the year's first official meeting of his deme. If the deme members were not satisfied with his credentials, the case could be appealed to a court, but if the case went against the candidate, he was enslaved. If the deme was satisfied with his credentials, his name was registered on the official lists, but the deme's decision to do so was reviewed by the Council, which could fine deme members for inaccurate judgments. If anyone tried to exercise the rights of a citizen without having gone through this process, he was imprisoned, and if found guilty, sold by the city to the highest bidder. The whole process was called a *dokimasia*, which literally means a "testing."[3]

---

[3] See MacDowell, *The Law in Classical Athens*, p. 69.

So, becoming a full-fledged Athenian citizen was very much like joining a club. Not only did one need certain qualifications (that is true of the citizens of every state), but one also had to take positive steps to enroll as a member. Merely reaching a certain age, merely being eligible for citizenship, was not enough: one actually had to apply for membership. Now, this fact about Athens provides the Laws with a sounder basis for argument than we might have thought available to them. If citizenship had merely been a matter of reaching a certain age, then it would surely have been absurd for an Athenian philosopher to say, "You are now seventeen, and therefore you have agreed to obey the city." If citizenship is conferred on you whether you like it or not, then becoming a citizen cannot involve a voluntary agreement. But what if you actively apply for citizenship status: won't you be committed thereby to the laws of the city? At any rate, won't you be committed to the laws if you show that you understand them? Might the *Crito* be relying on this idea when it argues that the Athenian citizens have agreed to obey the city?

Let us now look at the passage which describes the mechanics by which citizens make an agreement to obey the city.

> . . . We make this proclamation, by giving freedom to any Athenian that wants it: When he has passed the test for citizenship [*dokimasthēi*] and has observed the affairs of the city and us the Laws, if we do not satisfy him he is free to take his belongings and go wherever he wants. No law prevents or forbids you, if one of you wants to settle in a colony [*apoikia*], should we and the city not satisfy you. Or if you want to go somewhere else and be a resident alien [*metoikein*], you can go wherever you want and take your belongings. But whichever of you remains, seeing the manner in which we decide court cases and the other ways in which we manage the city, we say that by this time he has, by what he does, agreed with us to carry out whatever we command. . . . (51d1–e4)

The verb, *dokimasthēi*, that appears at the beginning of this passage is cognate to the noun, *dokimasia*. So the Laws are definitely referring to the testing procedure by which Athenians applied for admission to the citizenry.[4] But they do not say that this act of enrollment is the sole act by which one makes an agreement to obey the city, nor do they claim that this agreement is made at the very moment one is accepted as a full-fledged citizen. In addition to the *dokimasia*, they talk about the citizen's grasp of legal institutions, his freedom to leave, his satisfaction with the city, and his decision to remain. Any interpretation of the argument from agreement must explain how these various factors are supposed to combine to constitute an agreement to obey the city. What I propose is that the process by which one makes this agreement takes a good deal of time, and that the initial step is going through the *dokimasia*. It is no accident that, in the above quotation, the *dokimasia* is mentioned first, and the activity of observing the city's affairs comes second. The idea is that at the time someone enrolls as a citizen, he does not yet understand the way his city works. The new citizen, in other words, is now being given an opportunity to observe the legal machinery of Athens, and he cannot be taken to have agreed to the city's laws until he has had sufficient time to understand them. This same point is implied when the Laws say, in the above passage, ". . . whichever of you remains, seeing the manner in which we decide court cases . . . by this time . . . has agreed with us. . . ." Until one was seventeen and had passed one's *dokimasia*, one was not allowed to take part in legal proceedings; one could not bring a case to court, and in all legal matters one was represented by one's father or guardian. Furthermore, the temporal adverb, "by this time" (*ēdē*) reinforces the idea that some time elapses between the *dokimasia* and the completion of the agreement to obey the city. Finally, at a later point in their argument, the Laws explicitly say that the agreement made by Socrates was not the result of deception or lack of time for reflection (52e2-4). The implication is that one is justified in breaking agreements if one is tricked into them, or

[4] To my knowledge, no English translation of the *Crito* properly alerts the reader to the institutional meaning of *dokimasthēi*. Grube, for example, has: "after he has reached manhood;" Tredennick "on attaining to manhood;" Woozley "when he comes of age." Allen's "when he has been admitted to the rights of manhood" is better.

if one had to make a snap decision. It is unlikely that the Laws would claim that a citizen who has just emerged from his *dokimasia* has already agreed to obey the city. Were they to take this line, they would be vulnerable to the charge that the citizen has had too little time to understand and evaluate the organization he has just entered.

None of this shows that enrolling as a citizen is not *one* of the steps by which one agrees to obey the city; rather, it shows that this act is not by itself sufficient to constitute agreement.[5] The Laws must therefore mean that undergoing the *dokimasia* for citizenship is the act that initiates the process of committing oneself to the city's orders. That process goes on for some time longer, and there is no fixed time at which it terminates. But at some point or other, the new citizen has gathered enough understanding of the club he has entered; from then on, if he is satisfied with the city and does not quit, he has in effect agreed to its rules. The act of making this agreement therefore consists of three stages: the *dokimasia*, the period of increasing political awareness, and the point at which one has stayed so long that one can fairly be said to have agreed. No agreement has taken place until stage three has been reached, and the boundary between stages two and three is indeterminate. Evidently, the Laws have a complex theory of implied consent, but it is intelligible and even appealing. Some clubs are so simply organized that their rules can be explained to any prospective member, and in these cases, those who join with full information have thereby agreed to obey the rules. This was my thesis in the preceding section, and the Laws are relying on a variant of that thesis. Some clubs are so complex that they can be understood and evaluated only by those who have had some first-hand experience as members. In these cases, anyone who has voluntarily joined and has remained a satisfied member for a certain period of time has in effect agreed to abide by the rules.[6]

---

[5] Contrast Allen, *Socrates and Legal Obligation*, pp. 111-112: ". . . Socrates by voluntarily assuming the status of citizenship has thereby entered into an implied agreement to abide by the decisions of courts. . . ." Allen recognizes the institutional background of the *dokimasia* (pp. 90-91), but he seems to think that according to the Laws becoming a full-fledged citizen is sufficient for making an agreement to obey the city's orders.

[6] Objection: "But the Athenian citizen did not think of himself as having

4

Socrates and Locke

As we have seen, the agreement made by the citizens is an agreement "to carry out whatever we [the Laws] command" (51e4). But the next three times the *Crito* specifies the content of their agreement, it uses different words: it is an agreement "to live as a citizen in accordance with us" (*kath' hēmas politeusesthai*: 52c2, 52d2-3, 52d5). Surely this is merely a change in verbal formulation; the Laws say nothing to suggest that a single pattern of behavior gives rise to two different implicit agreements.[7] An agreement "to live as a citizen in accordance with us" is the same thing as an agreement to do what is commanded by the laws that govern the behavior of citizens.

Nonetheless, an important fact is brought out by the words, "to live as a citizen in accordance with us." The Laws are obviously confining their attention to the way in which *citizens* have become committed to the city through their voluntary acts. Only such individuals could be described as having agreed "to live as citizens." Contrast a resident alien who has lived in Athens for a good deal of time: he may understand the way the city works, he may be satisfied with its laws, and he has decided to stay in Athens rather than reside elsewhere. In other words, he differs from the citizen who has agreed to obey the

---

made an agreement to obey the laws; he never formed the intention to do such a thing. And without an intention to agree, there can be no agreement. So the Laws are wrong." (Cf. the claim of Simmons, *Moral Principles and Political Obligations*, p. 83, that there is no consent in the absence of a "*deliberate* undertaking" (his emphasis) to consent. See too p. 77: ". . . consent must be given intentionally and . . . knowingly.") Reply: One can discover that one's previous actions constituted an agreement, even though one did not at the time think of them in that light. For example, when we order food in a restaurant, we agree to pay the price on the menu, even though few realize that in ordering they are making an agreement to pay. Socrates is claiming to have discovered that his previous actions constituted an agreement, and it is irrelevant that neither he nor his fellow citizens realized, at the time, that their actions had this effect.

[7] Contrast Woozley, *Law and Obedience*, pp. 97-98. He ignores the *kath'hēmas* and takes *politeuesthai* to mean not only obeying the law but making some fuller contribution to the political life of the city. I see no reason for such an interpretation.

city in only one respect: he has not passed the *dokimasia* for citizenship. And because of this single difference, the Laws would never say that the resident alien has agreed "to live as a citizen." Furthermore, there is no way of telling whether the Laws take such resident aliens to have implicitly agreed to obey the city, for they simply do not address this issue. Of course, the Laws are not hinting that individuals who are not citizens of Athens but who nonetheless reside there (resident aliens, women, slaves) ought to dishonor the city and covertly violate its laws. Rather, they simply ignore the problem of why these groups should feel any commitment to the city. Notice that their analogy between cities and parents is similarly restricted in scope. The laws that concern marriage and education apply to citizens only, and therefore citizens are the only ones who have been shown to owe a debt of gratitude to Athens. The Laws are quite aware of this limitation. They say, "We begat, nurtured, and educated you, and gave all the fine things we could to you and all the other citizens . . ." (51c8–d1). Those who have not received these benefits have been given no reason to obey or persuade, even though they live on Athenian soil.

It might be suggested, however, that the argument from agreement can easily be extended to cover a great many resident aliens. Suppose we simply drop the *Crito*'s reference to the *dokimasia* and retain everything else. According to this new theory, anyone has agreed to obey the city if he has fulfilled these three conditions:

(A) He understands and is satisfied with the laws.

(B) He is legally free to leave the city.

(C) He chooses to remain a resident.

Adult citizens and many resident aliens satisfy these conditions, and so this revised theory has greater scope than the one we actually find in the *Crito*. But the trouble with this new theory is that (A), (B), and (C) do not constitute jointly sufficient conditions for implied consent. We can grant that if someone resides in a city and is satisfied with its laws, then he has probably benefited from them. And it might be argued that whoever has willingly benefited from an organization owes some debt of gratitude to it. But even if we concede these points, they do not show that the individual made an agreement to obey the organization from which he benefited. Consider an example. A man may think that his community's rescue squad is doing a good job, but he may refuse to join it or help it financially. If he later voluntarily accepts its help, that does not show that he thereby agreed to join it, obey it, or contribute to it. No doubt, he owes the squad some gratitude for its help, but we should not automatically treat such debts as implicit agreements. Similarly, a man who lives in Athens and who has benefited from the city does not agree to obey it merely because he voluntarily chooses to remain there. When we drop the *Crito*'s reference to the *dokimasia*, what remains is not enough to constitute an implied agreement.

It is Locke, not Socrates, who wants to show that visitors and resident aliens, no less than citizens, have agreed to obey the laws. In a well-known passage from the *Second Treatise of Government*, he says:

> . . . Every man that has any possessions or enjoyment of any part of the dominions of any government does thereby give his tacit consent, and is as far forth obliged to obedience to the laws of that government, during such enjoyment, as any one under it; whether this his possession be of land to him and his heirs for ever, or a lodging only for a week, or whether it be barely travelling freely on the highway; and, in effect, it reaches as far as the very being of anyone within the territories of that government. (Sec. 119)

We can sympathize with Locke's desire to show that citizens are not the only ones who ought to obey the laws of the state in which they reside.[8] The failure of the Laws to tackle this

---

[8] See Bennett, "A Note on Locke's Theory of Tacit Consent," for a recent interpretation. According to Bennett, Locke's argument, though unsuccessful, does not depend on the notion that whoever resides within or visits a state thereby benefits from it and in fairness must repay those benefits in the coin of obedience.

question is one of the limitations of their theory. Nonetheless, the *Crito*'s conception of implied agreement has more intuitive appeal than Locke's, for those who enroll as citizens of a state are more plausibly held to have agreed to obey its laws than are those who merely travel on its highways. Suppose the state bans all abortions: could we say that those who walk down the street thereby tacitly agree to obey this law? We cannot easily avoid the use of public property, and for this reason, if no other, "travelling freely on the highway" is not an act of tacit consent to a nation's laws. By contrast, there are many states in which one can live comfortably without becoming a citizen. And if a country does offer someone citizenship and he accepts that of-fer, doesn't he agree to abide by its terms, as he eventually comes to understand them? This suggestion, I will argue (VI.13), does not quite work, but nonetheless it is based on a perfectly reasonable assumption: when an offer of membership is made and its terms are understood by the eligible candidates, then those who voluntarily accept the offer are also accepting those terms, even if they say nothing to this effect.

5
Completing the agreement: An authoritarian reading

We come now to a serious difficulty. According to the *Crito*, what is the precise relationship between agreement and satisfac-tion? Does remaining in the city complete one's agreement to obey its laws, regardless of one's attitude toward those laws? Or does remaining complete one's agreement only because it demonstrates one's satisfaction with the city? May a person who is dissatisfied with certain laws continue to reside in Athens, or is he required to leave? Is leaving the only way to avoid com-pleting one's agreement? The remainder of this chapter will be devoted to these questions.

Let us begin with the observation that the parties to an agree-ment often accept a certain voluntary act as the sole vehicle by which their agreement is ratified. Suppose I tell you, for ex-ample, to shine your lights three times at midnight if you agree to join the club. If you fail to signal but tell me the next day how much you want to join, your expression of enthusiasm has no contractual effect, for you have failed to perform the only act designated as the vehicle of agreement. Conversely, if you tell me, while you shine your lights three times at midnight, that you object to some of our rules, you are nonetheless agreeing to join; disclosing your dissatisfaction does not diminish your commitment. And there are many other examples in which a single, mutually understood, voluntary act bears the entire burden of conveying one's agreement. If you write up a contract and I tell you how happy I am about it but refuse to sign, then I am as uncommitted to its terms as I would be had I said nothing; and if grumblings of dissatisfaction accompany my voluntary signature, I am nonetheless as bound to the document as would be the happiest of signatories. Until and so long as the act of assent is voluntarily performed, public signs of satisfaction or dissatisfaction are just so much noise.

It is a worthwhile experiment to apply this model to the *Crito*. Let us assume then that freely remaining in Athens is the sole act by which a citizen completes his agreement to abide by the laws, and self-exile is the sole act by which he can break off that agreement. On this interpretation, voluntarily remaining in Athens is understood by the Laws and the public to be a fairly reliable sign of one's satisfaction with the political system, but even if one is dissatisfied, remaining nonetheless commits one to obedience. Satisfaction, in other words, is the normally expected concomitant of the act by which one completes one's agreement, but after one's *dokimasia*, the sole vehicle of agreement is one's continued residence in Athens for a certain length of time. Accordingly, if one has become a full member of this club, then publicly disclosing one's dissatisfaction with some of its rules in no way cancels one's agreement. Others may be surprised that one remains a member, if one is dissatisfied, and they may even think that the dissatisfied citizen should quit. But in any case, they will insist that so long as one remains, the rules of the club must be observed.

If we look again at the *Crito*'s initial discussion of consent (51d1-e4), it seems to fit this interpretation nicely.

(A) . . . We make this proclamation, by giving freedom to any Athenian that wants it: When he has passed the test for citizenship and has observed the affairs of the city and us the Laws, if we do not satisfy him he is free to take his belongings and go wherever he wants.

(B) No law prevents or forbids you, if one of you wants to settle in a colony, should we and the city not satisfy you. Or if you want to go somewhere else and be a resident alien, you can go wherever you want and take your belongings.

(C) But whichever of you remains, seeing the manner in which we decide court cases and the other ways in which we manage the city, we say that by this time he has, by what he does, agreed with us to carry out whatever we command. . . .

The first two sections, (A) and (B), portray the developing citizen as someone who is in the process of making a decision. He is studying the political system to determine whether he should be satisfied with it. Their implication is that departure is a sign of dissatisfaction with the laws, and conversely, remaining is a sign of satisfaction. But then, in sentence (C), satisfaction is no longer in the picture: the sole act that is mentioned is remaining. It is as though the Laws are saying that although remaining is a sign of satisfaction, the really important thing is the remaining, and not the satisfaction. Freely remaining is the act that solely constitutes one's finally assenting to the city's orders, and accordingly departure at the right time is the only way to prevent one's agreement from being completed.

After the Laws describe the mechanics of agreement in (A), (B), and (C) above, they state the persuade-or-obey doctrine for a third time (51e4–52a3), and having done that, they return to the topic of agreement. But now they do not rest content with the claim that Socrates agreed to obey the city. Rather, they insist that he is among the Athenians who made this agreement most of all (52a6–8). To justify this claim, they point out that there is a great deal of evidence that they and the city satisfied him (52b1-2). Since he stayed at home more than any other Athenian, he must have been especially satisfied with the city (52b2-c1), and in this way he emphatically (*sphodra*: very much, exceedingly, strongly) chose the city and agreed to live in accordance with its laws (52c1-2). Furthermore, Socrates had children in the city, again indicating that it satisfied him (52c2-3). And at his trial, he chose death rather than exile, so great was his unwillingness to live outside of Athens (52c3-8).

In their attempt to show that Socrates "most of all agreed," the Laws are evidently not confining themselves to actions he performed in the earliest stage of his political life; he had children and spoke at his trial long after his enrollment as a citizen at the *dokimasia*. And the later remark (52e2-3) that Socrates had seventy years of opportunities to leave Athens again indicates that the Laws are searching for signs of agreement within the whole range of his political career. Their assumption is that there never comes a point when the behavior of a citizen residing in Athens can no longer be taken as giving assent to the laws. If remaining for three years after one's *dokimasia* is enough to show that one agrees to obey the city, then remaining for ten years or twenty shows this all the more. The more one stays, the more one agrees, and accordingly the less one travels outside the city, the more one agrees. All of this attention to the length of a citizen's presence in Athens seems to fit nicely with the interpretation we are exploring, for that reading makes voluntary presence the sole vehicle of agreement. If freely remaining constitutes the completion of one's agreement, what better way to show that someone "very much agreed" (52a6-8, 52c1-2) than to point out how very much he remained?

It is important to realize how authoritarian the *Crito* becomes if we read it this way. Consider a young citizen who has recently passed his *dokimasia* and is examining the city's laws. He sees that there are many good ones, but also finds that a few are unjust, and he decides that he would never obey those few. What is he to do? He would like to agree to most of the laws without agreeing to a few others—but there is no way to do that. There is no such thing as remaining-with-respect-to-law-A and leaving-with-respect-to-law-B. So if this citizen remains for a sufficient length of time, he will have agreed to obey all the laws that exist, including the ones that he considers unjust. If he can never bring himself to obey those unjust laws, then remaining in Athens will be agreeing to do what he has no intention of doing. But surely the Laws could not countenance such dishonest agreements: assenting to an order that one intends to disobey is hardly a way of showing respect for the laws. Accordingly, the *Crito* must mean that if a person knows of a law that he would refuse to obey, his only permissible course of action is self-exile. That is, if quitting the club of Athens is the only way to avoid completing one's agreement to obey its rules, then the virtuous citizen of an imperfect city must leave—a harsh legal doctrine, if ever there was one.

Now, the Laws never quite say in so many words that a disgruntled citizen should pack up and leave Athens. The closest they come to this idea is 52e3-5: ". . . you had seventy years in which you could have gone away, if we did not satisfy you and the agreements did not seem just to you." They do not say that he *should* have left if he was dissatisfied—only that he was *free* to leave. Nonetheless, it has to be admitted that the *Crito* mentions only one way to avoid completing one's agreement to obey the city: taking up residence elsewhere. Their silence about any other way of preventing one's agreement from being completed suggests that there simply is no other way.

When we put all of these considerations together, they create an argument that deserves serious consideration. To summarize:

(i) Whether someone is satisfied with an agreement is never relevant to the question of whether he made it. The Laws must surely realize this.

(ii) The sentence that claims that Socrates agreed to obey the city makes no mention of satisfaction.

(iii) If continued residence in Athens is what constitutes the completion of an agreement, we can understand why the Laws say that Socrates agreed more than anyone else.

(iv) The Laws mention only one way in which a citizen

can prevent his agreement from coming to completion: taking up residence in another city.

But as I will show, the authoritarian interpretation that is based on these four points is faced with grave difficulties. The text is better explained by a reading that gives satisfaction a significant role to play in the *Crito*'s theory of consent. When we later reconsider points (i) through (iv), we will see how unconvincing they are.

6
Problems for the authoritarian reading

On the authoritarian reading, the *Crito* is saying that a citizen should not agree to a law that he knows he will not obey; and the only way to avoid completing one's agreement to such a law is to leave the city. It should be obvious that this interpretation is completely at odds with the persuade-or-obey doctrine no matter which way that doctrine is understood. Suppose my argument in Chapters III and IV was correct, and the doctrine means that disobedience can be justified, so long as one persuades. Socrates, for example, may disobey an order to give up philosophy, so long as he is willing to persuade a jury that his conduct is justified. Obviously, if this is what the *Crito* means, then the Laws cannot also be insisting that Socrates must leave if he is dissatisfied with any Athenian command. But suppose my interpretation of the persuade-or-obey doctrine is wrong, and Grote's is correct. Then that doctrine means that anyone may try to persuade the Assembly to change the law, but that until he succeeds he must obey. Even this conservative reading of the persuade-or-obey doctrine cannot be reconciled with a love-it-or-leave-it political philosophy. For the Laws cannot both welcome dissent and tell the dissatisfied citizen to get out. Athens allowed any citizen to try, for as long as he wished, to have a statute repealed and the Laws cannot pretend to represent the city if they insist that dissidents must leave.

Furthermore, the authoritarian reading does not explain why the Laws are interested in showing that Socrates demonstrated his satisfaction with the city frequently, and in several ways. Recall that, according to this interpretation, to show that someone agreed to obey the city it is neither necessary nor sufficient to prove that he was satisfied with it. Correspondingly, the fact that he was *very* satisfied should be irrelevant to the conclusion that he *very much* agreed. But if this is so, then much of what the Laws say to Socrates is pointless:

> We say, Socrates, that if you do what you have in mind, then you are among those who are not the least but the most guilty of these accusations. If I should then ask why, they might justly upbraid me by pointing out that I have been among those Athenians who most of all made that agreement. They could say: Socrates, there were many indications [*tekmēria*] that we and the city satisfied you. You would not have stayed in the city so much, compared with other Athenians, if it had not satisfied you so much. . . . (52a3–b4)

As we can see, they use (A) his almost constant presence in Athens as evidence that (B) he was especially satisfied with the city, and from this they infer that (C) he has very much agreed to obey the laws. Why not skip the middle step, and say that since he was present so often he agreed very much? And why go on to say (52c2–8) that having children in Athens and refusing exile also demonstrate satisfaction with the city? By citing these acts as evidence of satisfaction, the Laws are implying that *any* act by which a citizen displays satisfaction with the city is an expression of his agreement to obey its laws. At any rate, the Laws clearly believe that a citizen's voluntary presence in a city is not the only sign by which he completes his agreement.

7
From residence to satisfaction

To reinforce the conclusion we have reached, let us look at another portion of the text. After the Laws have referred to the trial of Socrates and have pointed out that he then refused exile but now seeks it, they make these fundamental points:

(A) Are you doing anything . . . but transgressing the compacts [*sunthēkas*] and agreements [*homologias*] that concern us? You did not agree out of compulsion nor were you tricked or forced to decide in a short time. Rather, you had seventy years in which you could have gone away, if we did not satisfy you and the agreements did not seem just to you. (52d8-e5)

(B) But you preferred neither Sparta nor Crete, which you frequently say are well governed, nor any other Greek or foreign city, and you made fewer visits outside the city than do the lame, the blind, or others who are crippled. In this way, it is clear that the city and we, the Laws, have especially satisfied you, of all Athenians. For whom could the city satisfy, apart from its laws? (52e5-53a5)

Part of (B) is mere repetition, for we have already been told that Socrates wins the award for most days spent in Athens by a single citizen. But part of this section gives us important, new information: Socrates thinks that there are well-governed cities outside of Athens, yet he prefers his native city. And the Laws rely on this when they infer (53a3-4) that he has been satisfied with Athens. We will examine this inference more carefully in Section 9, but for now let me suggest that the Laws are making the following concession. If someone believes that there are no well-governed cities, then the fact that he stays in his own city does not show that he is satisfied with its laws. Continued residence may reflect the belief that one's city is merely the best of a bad lot; and if that were the attitude of Socrates toward Athens, then none of the alleged signs of agreement—residence, children, trial—would show his satisfaction with the city's laws. So, the statement about Sparta and Crete is not incidental, but rather fills an important gap in the argument of the *Crito*. Socrates is indeed satisfied with Athens, since he prefers it even to well-governed cities elsewhere. The important point is that the Laws are moving beyond residence to satisfaction. That Socrates remained in Athens by itself shows nothing; what counts is the satisfaction displayed by his residence.

Turning back now to (A), we can begin with a point that

everyone would admit. Although the Laws do not explicitly say so, they clearly mean that if an agreement is coerced or rushed or arises through deception, then it is not valid. They would hardly bother mentioning the unforced nature of the agreement Socrates made unless they were willing to concede that, had it been forced, their criticism of him for breaking an agreement would fail. But the next point I want to make is less obvious. It seems to me that (A) initiates a line of thought that is continued in (B). Throughout the whole paragraph, the Laws are concerned to show that Socrates' residence in Athens expressed his satisfaction with the city. They want to prove this because they admit that, had residence not reflected satisfaction, it would not have conveyed any agreement to obey the city. So what we have, when we put sentences (A) and (B) together, is a list of four factors that can block the inference from residence to satisfaction: force, deceit, insufficient time, and the belief that there are no well-governed cities. The role of the paragraph is to point out that since Socrates was bothered by none of these problems, the inference from residence to satisfaction is legitimate.

Now, this reading is obviously in direct conflict with the authoritarian interpretation we have been examining. For that interpretation holds that, according to the Laws, the agreement Socrates made is to be respected whether the acts constituting agreement express satisfaction or not. A person signing a mortgage contract cannot justify the violation of its terms by pleading that his signature did not express any enthusiasm; the fact that he signed the contract only because it was the best of a bad lot does not diminish his obligation. Similarly, the Laws are saying, according to the interpretation under scrutiny, that Socrates would be bound to his commitment whether there were worthwhile alternatives to Athens or not. The presence or absence of such alternatives is relevant to the question of whether satisfaction can be inferred from residence; but residence constitutes agreement so long as it is voluntary, i.e. unforced, unrushed, and open. And if the agreement is voluntary, then Socrates must abide by it, whether he was satisfied with it or not.

If we adopt this interpretation, then we will have to say that passages (A) and (B) serve different purposes. The first tries to show that the agreement was voluntary, the second that Socrates was satisfied with the laws. The first is crucial, for without it the agreement Socrates made would not be one he must respect; but the second is peripheral, serving only to show that the laws Socrates agreed to are ones with which he is satisfied. By contrast, the interpretation I propose unifies the paragraph, since each sentence is designed to help show that Socrates was indeed satisfied with the city and its laws. Now, surely it is *ad hoc* to hold that (A) and (B) serve such different purposes: such a view is justified by nothing in the text, and it is designed only to salvage the theory that agreement requires no evidence of satisfaction. In fact, the text suggests that *both* segments are equally designed to show that residence reflected satisfaction. (A) points out that Socrates had a great deal of time to leave if the laws did not satisfy him. That is, to the question, "Did he have enough time?" the Laws reply, "Yes—seventy years, if he was dissatisfied." This suggests that the full question being asked is, "Did Socrates have so little time to make up his mind that we can't tell whether he was satisfied?" In other words, both (A) and (B) are concerned with the question whether Socrates' residence expressed his satisfaction. The idea that (A) is concerned solely with the voluntary nature of his agreement, and (B) with his satisfaction, has no support from the text. The word for voluntary (*hekōn*) does not occur in (A); but both segments explicitly refer to satisfaction.[9]

[9] At 52d6-7, Socrates and Crito concede that an agreement has been made, and this might suggest that the argument of the Laws can be neatly divided into two parts: prior to 52d6-7, they merely try to show that Socrates made an agreement; after that, they claim that it is an agreement he should honor. If this is the right way to break up the text, then it could be claimed that 52d8-53a7 has a certain unity, in that the Laws here give two reasons for keeping the agreement: it was just (52d8-e5), and Socrates was satisfied with the city (52e5-53a5). I reject this interpretation for several reasons. First, if Socrates' satisfaction with Athens is (as alleged) a reason for honoring his agreement, then the Laws have been putting forward this reason far before 52e5-53a5. Second, after Socrates and Crito concede at 52d6-7 that an agreement has been made, the Laws assert that Socrates has been free for seventy years to leave Athens. Now, if he had not been free to leave, remaining would hardly constitute or provide evidence for an agreement. Evidently, even after 52d6-7, the Laws continue to support their claim that Socrates made an agreement. The fact that he was free

I conclude that the authoritarian reading does a poor job of explaining the text. As we saw in the preceding section, and as we have now seen again, the Laws point to various and frequent signs of satisfaction as evidence that Socrates agreed to obey the city. Remaining in Athens, when one is legally free to leave, does not by itself constitute the completion of one's agreement. Rather, one's presence in the city completes one's agreement only when it provides evidence of one's satisfaction with the laws. And there are other ways of demonstrating satisfaction besides continued residence: e.g. having children and statements one makes about the relative merits of cities. The authoritarian interpretation goes wrong by underemphasizing the role of satisfaction in the *Crito*'s argument, and by failing to recognize the variety of ways in which satisfaction can be shown.

8
Implicit agreement revisited

If the interpretation we have been examining is flawed, what should we put in its place? It might seem that only one alternative is available to us: the Laws are saying that the citizen completes his agreement by being satisfied with the city. In other words, what completes the agreement is the fact that the citizen is in a certain mental state. His behavior—remaining in the city, having children, refusing to propose exile—gives us

---

to leave supports two points simultaneously: he made an agreement; and the agreement, being just, should be kept. Third and most important, it is hard to see why satisfaction with the city or its laws should be a reason for honoring an agreement to obey its commands. As the Laws know, Socrates will honor all just agreements, and this means that he will keep them even when he doesn't like the people or cities to whom he has given his word. It is far more plausible to regard satisfaction as a way of expressing agreement, rather than a reason for honoring an agreement already made in some other way. I conclude that the interpretation under consideration is inadequate. Though Socrates and Crito concede at 52d6-7 that an agreement has been made (in fact, they offer no resistance at 50c4-6 either), the Laws have not at that point completed their argument for that conclusion. After 52d6-7, they claim that the agreement was just, but in addition they add further support for their claim that Socrates was satisfied with the city and that he therefore completed his agreement to obey it.

evidence that he has completed the agreement, but his actions do not themselves constitute its completion.

Yet surely this is an interpretation that we should be reluctant to attribute to the *Crito*. For any reasonable thinker ought to realize that what counts in the making of agreements is observable behavior rather than a person's inner satisfaction. If I ask someone whether he will do me a favor and he nods, then he has made an agreement even if he was not satisfied with my request. After all, a person who explicitly says, "I agree to do it," cannot void the effect of his words by saying to himself, "But I don't really agree to do it." Someone who voluntarily undertakes certain observable acts, knowing that others will regard these acts as the making of an agreement, *has* in fact agreed, whatever his inner mental state. Can the Laws have been too stupid to realize this? And yet, if we credit them with the realization that it is external behavior and not satisfaction that counts, we will be making the same mistake that was made in the authoritarian reading. The text simply does not allow us to eliminate satisfaction as a crucial element in the *Crito*'s conception of implicit agreement. We seem forced to choose between an interpretation (satisfaction alone completes the agreement) that is silly and an interpretation (residence alone completes the agreement) that is refuted by the text. We might try to avoid the defects of these two extremes by saying: what is essential is *both* remaining *and* being satisfied; and the Laws simply assume that the two go along with each other. But that cannot be right, for as we saw in the preceding section, the Laws mention four factors (compulsion, deceit, lack of time, lack of alternatives) that can explain why a citizen who remains might nonetheless be dissatisfied. So we seem to have reached an impasse.

I think we can solve this problem if we deepen our understanding of the variety of ways in which people can make agreements. Consider the following example. John asks Anne whether she would like to take a trip with him tomorrow to the mountains; he tells her to decide quickly, because if they are to go, he has to cancel his earlier plans, rent a car, and make other preparations. Anne has laryngitis, but to indicate her reaction to John's proposal, she smiles, gives him a hug and a kiss, and begins to pack her bags. John takes these actions as expressions of agreement, and prepares to leave. The question I want to ask is this: has Anne in fact agreed to take this trip? I believe that there is a strong case for saying that she did. To begin with, the fact that she has *said* nothing does not show that she failed to agree. Had she nodded, for example, that would certainly have indicated agreement. But if a nod would have sufficed, then why shouldn't the actions she performed also suffice? It might be said, in reply to this question, that a nod is a generally recognized sign of agreement, whereas hugs, kisses, and the packing of bags are not. And, the argument might go, whenever someone tacitly agrees to do something, that person must use either a generally recognized sign of agreement (e.g. nodding), or an *ad hoc* signal accepted by the parties to the agreement (e.g. the flashing of lights). But Anne has not used either kind of signal. She has merely acted in a way from which it can be inferred that she plans on going. If she has no such intention, then she is misleading John and acting wrongly, but her wrong should not be described as the breaking of an agreement.

I see no good reason, however, for using the word "agreement" in such a restricted way. Suppose Anne did not have laryngitis, and had said to John, after hearing this proposal, "Thanks so much—I'll run and pack my bags right away." Obviously, these words, uttered in the proper tone of voice, would have constituted an agreement, even though they are not a promise, nor a generally recognized sign of agreement (like a nod or a handshake), nor an *ad hoc* signaling device (like the flashing of lights). What matters is that Anne's verbal and non-verbal behavior are intended to show that she is delighted with John's offer, and in these circumstances the communication of this fact is all that is needed for an agreement to be made. She does not have to say, "I hereby accept your offer," if she wants to agree to go; in fact, had she made such a stiff remark, it would have been reasonable for John to wonder whether she really was accepting. We cannot make a list of words and phrases (e.g. "I hereby agree," "yes," "okay") that have to be used to ratify agreements, and similarly it is wrong to insist that a nod can ratify an agreement (since it is a conventional signal) but that a hug and a kiss cannot. People can convey assent and register agreement in both conventional and unconventional ways, and it is overly rigid to stipulate that implicit agreements must rely on standardized signals.[10]

My suggestion, then, is that there is a kind of agreement that is expressed by nonverbal signs of satisfaction, and that the agreement to obey the laws is of this sort. The *Crito* is saying that after an individual has enrolled as a citizen, and has had sufficient time to evaluate the city's legal processes, it is fair to count his public signs of satisfaction as the completion of his agreement to obey the laws. But which actions will indicate agreement and which will not? It would be unreasonable to demand an abstract criterion from the Laws. No one can delimit the class of words that signal assent, and similarly the Laws need no definitive list of actions that will count as signs of agreement. *Any* actions that publicly express satisfaction with the laws will complete one's agreement to obey them. Remaining a resident can express satisfaction, given the right background conditions. So can the infrequency of one's trips abroad, one's decision to raise children in the city, and what one says about the relative merits of cities. Thus, on my interpretation, remaining is merely one of many possible signs of agreement; it is not, as the conservative interpretation holds, the unique act by which one's agreement is completed. Here, my interpretation fits the text better: for although the Laws emphasize the citizen's presence more than any other signal of agreement, they do point to other signs as well. Furthermore, it is central, on my interpretation, that the acts that complete one's agreement be acts from which one's satisfaction with the city can be inferred. Here too it has an advantage over the authoritarian reading, which treated satisfaction as the expected but inessential concomitant of the act by which one ratifies one's agreement. As we have seen, satisfaction plays a larger role in the *Crito* than that.

Notice that, on my interpretation, the Laws are not adopting

---

[10] Cf. Fried, *Contract as Promise*, p. 43.

the absurd position that agreements to obey the city are completed only if the citizen actually *feels* satisfied. Rather, what count are the visible actions that express satisfaction, together with the background conditions that allow us to interpret that behavior. If a citizen is not in fact satisfied, but has only tried to create that impression, he has nonetheless agreed to obey the city. So too in the case of John and Anne: perhaps all of her actions were simply an act, and she had no intention of going with him. Even so, she did express satisfaction, and therefore she did agree to go. John had every reason to interpret her behavior as a signal of agreement, and Anne was responsible for leading him to that interpretation. Similarly, in the *Crito*, it is not the feeling of satisfaction, but the public signs of satisfaction, that complete the process of agreement.

A further point should be noticed. Whenever an agreement can be ratified by only one type of act, that is because the parties are relying on some mutually recognized signaling device. Without some such convention, many different types of act would convey agreement, and sometimes it is useful to reduce this variety and thereby lessen the possibility of misunderstanding. So, in certain cases, agreements must be written and notarized; in other cases, we introduce a signal to suit the occasion. Now, if residence is the sole act by which the citizen can complete his agreement to obey the laws, then that would have to be a convention generally recognized in Athenian society. Surely the *Crito* cannot *stipulate* that residence constitutes agreement; rather, Socrates and every other citizen would have to be aware that remaining is generally recognized as the sole act by which one gives one's assent. But as a matter of historical fact, there is no evidence that there was any such convention. By contrast, the interpretation I favor has no need to presuppose the existence of such a convention. For it says that agreement is ratified not by the performance of certain designated acts, but by anything that expresses satisfaction with the laws. The case of John and Anne is helpful here: he did not have to say, "If you agree to go, give me a hug and a kiss, and start getting ready." She conveyed her agreement by expressing her satisfaction, rather than by relying on some longstanding or *ad hoc* convention. Similarly, the Laws can infer an agreement from the citizen's behavior, even though the citizen did not learn ahead of time that acting in certain ways would constitute an agreement.

In Section 5 of this chapter, I said that the authoritarian interpretation is supported by four points. But now we have seen how hollow three of them are:

(i) No one can seriously believe that agreements are ratified by feelings of satisfaction rather than by behavior. And so we originally took the Laws to mean that satisfaction can be expected to accompany residence, but that it is residence and not satisfaction that constitutes the agreement. But now we see that we were using a misleading model of agreement. In certain cases—as when someone signs a contract—satisfaction is indeed peripheral; but as the case of John and Anne shows, signs of satisfaction can sometimes constitute agreement. And even in such cases as these, what counts is the behavior that expresses satisfaction, and not the mental state itself.

(ii) The sentence that claims that Socrates agreed to obey the city makes no mention of satisfaction. Out of charity, we originally took this to mean that what completes an agreement is residence, and not satisfaction. But since then we have seen how great an effort the Laws make to show that Socrates was satisfied with the city. To understand the Laws, we must take account of everything they say about agreement, and not concentrate entirely on the first sentence in which they claim that an agreement was made.

(iii) There is one point that the Laws emphasize more than any other in their effort to show that Socrates agreed to obey the city: military campaigns aside, he has practically never left Athens. But we were wrong to infer from this that residence alone constitutes agreement. For one thing, the Laws point to other signs of agreement as well. For another, they realize that residence does not count as a sign of agreement unless it is also a sign of satisfaction.

We are now left with one remaining argument on behalf of the authoritarian reading. The Laws mention only one way in which a citizen who has passed his *dokimasia* can avoid making an agreement to obey the city: he can take up residence elsewhere. Now, we must not infer from this that residence in Athens is the sole act that constitutes agreement, for we have seen how much evidence there is against this hypothesis. Nonetheless, there is still a possibility that part of the authoritarian reading can be salvaged. The Laws might mean that there are many ways of showing one's satisfaction with the city, but only one way of showing dissatisfaction, namely, by self-exile. But as I will argue in Section 10, this hypothesis has little to recommend it.

9
The preference for Athens

I would like to backtrack for a moment and consider some important details that were passed over in Section 7. There we saw the Laws making the following points:

(A) Socrates has said many times that Sparta and Crete are well governed.

(B) But he has always preferred Athens to these and all other cities.

(C) He has made very few visits to cities outside of Athens.

(D) Therefore, it is clear that the city has especially satisfied him.

(E) No one could be satisfied with a city apart from its laws.

(F) Therefore, it is clear that the laws of the city have especially satisfied him.

(E) presents one possible way of rendering 53a4–5; essentially the same reading can be found in Grube (". . . for what city can please if its laws do not?") and Croiset (". . . car comment une ville plairait-elle à qui n'aimerait pas ses lois?"). But there is an alternative in Tredennick, Woozley, and Allen: "Who would care for a city without laws?" as Tredennick puts it. On philological grounds, there is no reason to choose one translation rather than another. But which makes the best sense of the argument? Our choice is between (E) and

(G) No one could be satisfied with a city without laws.

Surely (E) is preferable, since it justifies the move from (D) to (F), whereas (G) does not. An analogy may help. It would be a mistake to argue that whoever likes Chicago also likes its police force since no one can like a city without a police force. We ought to give the *Crito* the benefit of the doubt, and acquit it of such a fallacy. By contrast, (E) is precisely the premise needed to smooth the way from (D) to (F). The basic idea is that a person's attitude toward the laws of a city determines his attitude toward the city itself. And so if we are satisfied with a city, that is because its laws please us; if the laws do not please us, then neither will the city itself. Thus, from (D) and (E), the *Crito* validly moves to (F).

Now let us look at a consequence that is suggested by (A), (B), and (E). Socrates prefers Athens to Sparta and Crete, though he thinks the latter two well governed. What can be the basis for this preference? (B) and (E), considered together, suggest that he thinks more highly of the laws of Athens than the laws of any other city. For if a person's attitude toward the laws of a city determines his attitude toward the city itself, then we can expect his preference between cities to be determined by his ranking of their legal systems. So Socrates must think that the laws of Athens are more satisfactory than the laws of Sparta, Crete, or any other city.[11] And this is no empty compliment, for he takes Sparta and Crete to be well governed. *Why* Socrates has such a high opinion of the Athenian legal system is a mys-

[11] Though the Greek tells us (52e5-6) that Socrates merely said, on many occasions, that Sparta and Crete were "well governed" (*eunomeisthai*), Tredennick's translation inflates the compliment: Sparta and Crete become Socrates' "favorite models of good government." The sense of the passage, if I am right, is just the opposite: it is, among existing cities, Athens that provides Socrates with his "favorite model of good government."

tery that will exercise us in Chapter VII. For now, I take it to be an undeniable and significant fact that Socrates gives the laws of Athens high marks.

One further point. The Laws do not say what evidence they have for statement (B). Perhaps they think that Socrates has verbally expressed his preference for Athens over Sparta and Crete. Or perhaps they infer (B) from his utter lack of interest in visiting these foreign places; whoever praises the legal system of another city but shows no interest in visiting that city or attending its festivals must think even more highly of his own city. Or perhaps the Laws are relying on both the verbal statements of Socrates and his habit of staying within the walls of Athens. In any case, there is no need for them to assume that Socrates could have taken up permanent residence in Sparta or Crete. The Laws do say, at an earlier point, that Socrates was legally free to live in a colony, or to be a resident alien somewhere outside of Athens (51d7-8). I take them to mean that certain cities would have allowed Socrates to enter and to settle permanently. But the *Crito* never says that Sparta and Crete are among such cities, and its argument has no need for such an assumption. When the Laws talk about possible destinations for an escaping Socrates, they mention Thebes and Megara (53b4). It is understandable that Sparta and Crete are not considered, since they are closed, exclusive societies in which Socrates could not have expected to settle down.[12] Sparta and Crete are benchmarks in the evaluation of Athens, but they are not real alternatives as permanent residences. They are used to make the point that Socrates is satisfied with the laws of his native city; but the *Crito* has other cities in mind when it says that Socrates can permanently leave Athens if he so chooses.

The Laws show that Socrates was satisfied with Athens by pointing out that he preferred it to two other cities that he considers well governed. Naturally, this same argument cannot be applied word-for-word to every citizen of Athens, for surely

---

[12] See Plutarch, *Life of Lycurgus*, 9, 27; Plato *H. Ma.* 283b4-286c2, *Laws* 634d7-e4. Aristotle (*Pol.* 1272b17-18) says that the distance of Crete from the rest of Greece had the same effect as the Spartan explusion of strangers. For further discussion of Socrates' attitude toward Sparta and Crete, see VII.5-6.

there were many ardent democrats who considered Sparta and Crete poorly governed. But so long as these individuals publicly indicate their preference for Athens over *some* well-governed city or other, they are expressing their satisfaction with its laws. Of course, someone who publicly indicates that Athens is, in his opinion, the *only* well-governed city there is, also shows his satisfaction with the city. But what if an individual thinks that there are no well-governed cities at all? Or suppose someone thinks Athens poorly governed, but is barred from whichever cities he does consider well governed? The *Crito* has to admit that in these cases continued residence in Athens does not signal any agreement to obey its laws, since it does not reflect satisfaction with those laws. I suspect that the Laws simply do not think that these cases will occur very often, or at all. They assume that everyone, or nearly everyone, will think that some existing city or other is well governed. They themselves think that Athens has good laws; after all, those laws have done as much for the citizens as laws can (51c8–d1). They also consider Thebes and Megara to be well governed. And these (unlike Sparta) were cities in which any Athenian could take up residence; that is why they are mentioned as possible destinations for an escaping Socrates (53b3–c4). A citizen of Athens who continues to reside there, when he could live in some other city that he takes to be well governed, is thereby indicating that in his opinion Athens is well governed. Why would he stay, if he could live under a better legal system?

Residence, then, is a sign of satisfaction only when certain background conditions are presupposed. The citizen must be legally free to leave, and his decision to remain must not arise from deception or lack of time. Furthermore, it must be assumed that a citizen's decision about where to reside will be based primarily on his evaluation of various legal systems. He must also believe that some cities are well governed, and that he is living in or can move to one of them. The Laws make all of these points explicit. Obviously, they are aware that if the inference from residence to agreement is to be justified, several important assumptions must be made.

10
Dissent and dissatisfaction

When Socrates says that Sparta and Crete are well governed, he does not mean that their legal systems are entirely without fault. After all, as we have just seen, he thinks that Athens is preferable, because of its laws; so he probably believes that Sparta and Crete are politically defective in some way or other. Similarly, when the *Crito* says that Socrates is satisfied with the laws of Athens, it can hardly mean that the city is faultless in his eyes. We know that Socrates was a critic of democracy, since he did not think the many competent to decide matters of right and wrong. The Laws must mean that, all things considered, Socrates was greatly satisfied with his city. With certain institutions and statutes he was no doubt dissatisfied. We should also recall that the persuade-or-obey doctrine, on either a liberal or a conservative reading, invites dissent. The Laws are thus quite aware that a citizen who remains in Athens may nonetheless be dissatisfied with certain statutes and commands.

Now, suppose a new citizen has become acquainted with the legal practices of his city, and is generally pleased by its laws. He plans on remaining in residence, but there are a few statutes to which he is vigorously opposed. He tries to persuade others to repeal them, but does not succeed. Would the *Crito* say that if this citizen remains in Athens, then he will have agreed to obey even those laws he vigorously opposes? Two textual points seem to suggest an affirmative answer. First, the Laws mention only one way to avoid completing one's agreement to obey a city's commands: permanent departure. So they must think that there is no other way to do so. Second, the Laws explicitly say that by remaining, Socrates agreed to carry out whatever the city commands (51e1-4). That means that he agreed to obey every law and every order of the city, without exception. Apparently, the *Crito* is saying that he agreed to obey even those statutes with which he is dissatisfied.

But neither of these arguments is convincing, once we examine them. Consider the first. It is quite true that the Laws mention only one way to express dissatisfaction with a city's laws, namely, through permanent departure. But the *Crito* would be an absurd document if it were to hold that sincerely expressed objections to a statute do not express dissatisfaction with it. After all, to show that Socrates is satisfied with the city, the Laws refer to statements he has made: he spoke against exile at his trial, and he has often said that Sparta and Crete are well governed. Surely, if a man's public statements can be used to build a case that he is satisfied with a city, then they can also be used to show that he is dissatisfied with some of its laws. As we saw before in Section 8, the Laws are not stipulating that such-and-such will count as a sign of satisfaction or dissatisfaction. Rather, they are saying that from certain behavior and background conditions we can reasonably infer that a person is satisfied. Obviously, if agreement is shown through natural expressions of satisfaction, then the Laws must concede that dissatisfaction can be manifested in the same way. And what more natural way to express dissatisfaction than through verbal dissent? It is of course not surprising that the Laws do not explicitly mention dissent as a way of expressing dissatisfaction. They are not concerned to make a definitive list of ways in which satisfaction and its opposite can be expressed—in fact, there can be no such fixed list. The Laws bring out only those points that are needed to support the conclusion that Socrates was satisfied with the city; the fact that dissatisfaction can be expressed through dissent is too obvious and too peripheral to be included in their economical argument. We should also recall a point made earlier, in Sections 5 and 6: The *Crito* cannot be counseling us to make an agreement that we have no intention of honoring, and therefore, if departure is the only way to avoid making an agreement, a conscientious dissenter must go into exile. But that severe position is obviously at odds with the persuade-or-obey doctrine. Surely then, there must be ways to remain a resident and avoid making unconscionable agreements. Sincere and public dissent from offensive laws is the obvious way.

But what of the second point? It is quite true that, according to the *Crito*, Socrates made a sweeping commitment: he agreed to "carry out whatever we command" (51e4). But this is far less significant than we may have realized, for the Laws equate making an agreement with giving indications of one's satisfaction. In the right conditions, residence is a sign of satisfaction with all the laws, but that does not mean that it is decisive evidence in each and every case. Rather, if someone is generally satisfied with a city's laws, then that merely creates a presumption in favor of agreement. Though there may be many statutes that such a citizen has not explicitly endorsed, it can be assumed that he agrees to all the ones he has not opposed. The burden of proof is on him to show that he is not satisfied, and so long as he remains silent, it is fair to infer that he is satisfied with a given law. So, for every Athenian law in force, Socrates has shown signs of his satisfaction with it, unless he indicates otherwise. The analogy with games is helpful here: a person who agrees to play chess thereby agrees to every rule of the game, unless he speaks up and proposes a variant. But notice that the proviso, "unless he proposes a variant," can be dropped and the preceding statement remains true. To state the conditions for *making* agreements, neither we nor the Laws have to refer to a method for *blocking* agreements as well. The *Crito* is saying that through a certain pattern of behavior the citizen undertakes a general commitment, from which he may make particular exceptions if he gives public notice. And this is all the Laws need to say to defend their assertion that Socrates agreed to the law that gives the courts authority. They know that he said nothing for or against that particular statute. But since he never criticized it, his general satisfaction with Athens commits him to it.

Why do the Laws think it so important to show that Socrates has been satisfied with his city? Surely they must be assuming that if Socrates was *not* satisfied, then he did *not* make an agreement to obey. Merely enrolling as a citizen, after all, does not constitute an agreement. But the Laws believe that if certain things happen after that enrollment, then the whole process will amount to an implicit agreement. One of the elements that must be added, beyond merely passing one's *dokimasia*, is understanding: the citizen who has not yet learned the laws and procedures of his city cannot be said to have agreed to them. And satisfaction, as we have seen, is a further ingredient. So it must have occurred to the Laws that if a citizen is dissatisfied with a statute and publicly expresses that dissatisfaction, then the claim that he has tacitly agreed to obey it is put in serious jeopardy. That is why they are so concerned to show that Socrates was satisfied with the legal system, considered as a whole. For that allows them to argue that he did agree to obey each and every law, barring evidence to the contrary. That is, every Athenian law which the citizen has not sincerely and publicly criticized is a law with which he has shown signs of satisfaction.

I am not attributing to the Laws the naive view that if a citizen merely says, "I am dissatisfied with this law," then that by itself prevents his agreement from being completed. For a citizen might be insincere in his expressions of dissatisfaction, and sometimes others can have good reason to believe that he is being insincere. To see whether a person is really dissatisfied with a law, we must look to all available evidence, including verbal reports, and we must search for the best explanation of that behavioral evidence. If a person says he is dissatisfied with a law, then we can expect him to state his reasons, and in appropriate circumstances he ought to support its repeal; his failure to do such things would suggest insincerity. Furthermore, if a law is obviously essential to the existence of the state, we would find it difficult to take at face value any expressions of dissatisfaction with it. Consider, for example, the Athenian statute that gave authority to the courts. That law orders the citizens to accept any lawful verdict brought by a jury, whether that verdict is favorable or unfavorable to the defendant. If someone objects to this, and says that he would like to live in a city where verdicts are enforced only when they are favorable to the accused, we would strongly suspect him of insincerity. For his proposal would in effect destroy the legal system and the city, and any sane person can be expected to see this.[13] So the Laws

[13] But suppose we consider a far more specific law, e.g. one that requires the payment of a large fine as the penalty for a minor offense. And imagine a citizen who campaigns for the repeal of this law, on the grounds that the punishment is too severe; he argues that citizens convicted of such a crime would be justified in refusing to pay so large a fine. If my interpretation of the *Crito* is correct,

can assume that there is a core of legislation that will satisfy every adult in his right mind. A citizen cannot simply announce, "I am dissatisfied with all the laws of the state" and expect to be taken seriously. The only way he can, with a single act, prevent his agreement from being completed is to take up residence in a different city. That is why the Laws emphasize the fact that this option has always been open to Socrates. He can cancel all his agreements at once by leaving; but if he fails to leave, he must express his dissatisfaction in piecemeal fashion. The Laws would admit that many statutes are controversial, and in these cases expressions of dissatisfaction that are backed by argument and action will block agreement.[14]

---

the Laws are not committed to saying that this citizen agreed that, should he ever be convicted of the crime in question, he would pay the full penalty fixed by law. Presumably, Socrates never campaigned in this way against particular penalties, and given his general satisfaction with the legal system, the Laws infer that he has tacitly agreed to abide by all the judgments of the courts, both favorable and unfavorable (50c5-6). But a citizen who sincerely and publicly objected to certain penalties cannot be said to be satisfied with or to have agreed to the very law he fought against. Nor does the parent-city analogy require him to accept the penalty: if a father tells his adult children that if they do not listen to him he will shut them up in a closet, they are not required by the speech of the Laws to submit to that punishment. Of course, the parent-city analogy requires the citizen in question to tell the jurors that he will not pay the fine required by law, and he must argue in court that the penalty is unjust in view of how small the offense is. Since his disobedience must be open, the city may find ways to exact the penalty from him, in spite of his noncompliance. Even so, it is important to realize that nothing in the *Crito* entails that such a citizen cannot be justified in refusing to pay the fine.

[14] If my interpretation is correct, then one of Hume's points against contractual theories of political obligation does not apply to the *Crito*. He considers the view that tacit consent is conveyed by continued residence, and objects that not everyone can afford to leave: "Can we seriously say, that a poor peasant or artizan has a free choice to leave his country, when he knows no foreign language or manners, and lives from day to day, by the small wages which he acquires? We may as well assert, that a man, by remaining in a vessel, freely consents to the dominion of the master; though he was carried on board while asleep, and must leap into the ocean, and perish, the moment he leaves her." "Of the Original Contract," p. 451. Hume indicates, on the last page of this essay (p. 460), that the *Crito* is one of his targets. But as we have seen, that dialogue does not require the citizen to leave the city if he wants to withhold his consent from particular laws. Contrast Woozley, *Law and Obedience*, pp. 106-109, who presses Hume's point against the *Crito*. Like Simmons, *Moral Principles and Political Obligations*, p. 99, he takes this to be a fatal flaw in any attempt to base political obligation on agreement or consent.

11
Later agreements and reversals

I have argued that the *Crito* takes the *dokimasia* to be the initial step in the process of making an agreement, and that after a certain period of time has elapsed and one has shown one's satisfaction with the laws, one has agreed to obey them. But precisely which laws does the citizen agree to—only those that have already been passed, or all future laws as well? At some point, does the citizen who is generally satisfied with his city's legal system give it a blank check to do whatever it likes in the future? Or does he agree only to those laws that have been in force for a certain length of time? Surely the latter, if my preceding argument is correct. Since the Laws give the new citizen some time to evaluate the city before they claim that he has made an agreement, they must believe that a statute one has not yet been able to assess is not a statute one has agreed to obey. And of course that principle applies to future laws as well. The citizen has no way of knowing what sort of orders his city is going to issue in ten or twenty years; revolutions and deep-seated constitutional changes were not merely theoretical possibilities in fifth-century Athens. The Laws say nothing to suggest that at some point or other the citizens agree to obey the orders of any rulers that happen to acquire power in the future. Now, precisely how does an older citizen—suppose he is seventy—go about making an agreement to obey a law that has just been adopted? I assume that the *Crito* will answer this question in the familiar way: the citizen has become a member of the club of Athens, and therefore, if he is generally satisfied with its rules and does not quit, he agrees to obey all those laws that he has had time enough to understand. The older man, in other words, has the same relationship to new laws that a recently enrolled citizen has to all the laws with which he has not yet gained familiarity. He has not agreed to them yet, but he will have agreed if enough time goes by and he voices no dissent. We should notice, at this point, a small textual detail: at 52e3-5, the Laws tell Socrates that he has had seventy years in which to leave, if he did not think the agreement*s* (I stress the plural) just. Evidently, they have no objection to thinking of the citizen's agreement to obey the city as a large multiplicity of agreements, each corresponding to one law or decree. Some of these agreements are made *en bloc*, as the citizen matures and becomes satisfied with the political system. As new laws are added, new agreements are made.

These points help us see that Socrates made no agreement to obey the tyrannical regime of the Thirty.[15] Elected in 404, through the pressure of a Spartan general, they were charged with the task of revising the laws and were given power to control the city in the meantime. They executed many, seized a great deal of property, and repealed a few laws; but the positive task of designing a new and permanent form of government seems never to have begun. Thebes and Megara harbored Athenian fugitives, who organized themselves into a fighting force; within about a year the Thirty were overthrown, and a Spartan king, Pausanias, allowed democracy to be restored. Socrates remained in Athens during this period of civil war, and that raises the question whether he was sympathetic to the regime of the Thirty. Since he did not become a refugee, did he tacitly show that he was satisfied with that government? Not at all. For Socrates accepts a legal philosophy according to which mere residence is not by itself a sign of satisfaction. The citizen never makes an agreement to obey all future laws and rulers, whoever and whatever they may be. Rather, he must always be given an opportunity to see what the laws of his city are, and the Thirty never did carry out this job of revising the laws. Either Socrates was waiting to see what they would produce, or he was waiting for them to be overthrown; in the meantime, he would obey no order that he considered unjust, and he would be willing to persuade them that his disobedience was necessary. (See V.2 on open disobedience.) We might think that, for strategic or moral reasons, Socrates should have joined the exiles, but at any rate we cannot take his decision to remain as a sign of satisfaction. The *Crito* shows that he did not view residence in this way.

One further point. A citizen's attitude toward his city may change not only because its laws change, but because *he* changes.

---

[15] For background, see the works cited in Ch. I n. 29.

Suppose a law has been in existence for some time, and by showing his satisfaction with it, the citizen has agreed to obey it. But then he gradually comes to realize that it is an unjust law, and he publicly expresses his dissent. Presumably he will try to have the law repealed, but whether he succeeds or not, an important conceptual question is raised by his change of attitude. Does his agreement to obey the law terminate when he publicly and sincerely expresses his dissatisfaction with it? We are not asking whether he did at an earlier time have an agreement; rather, we are asking whether that agreement continues to exist even when satisfaction is replaced by dissatisfaction. Is the *Crito* saying that a tacit agreement is made when satisfaction is shown during a certain *limited* period of time, come what may? In that case, signs of dissatisfaction that come too late cannot terminate an agreement. Or is the *Crito* saying that one has made a binding agreement only for those periods of time during which one exhibits satisfaction? In this case, a change of mind will destroy an agreement. I know which answer *I* would favor: it seems to me that an agreement cannot be unmade by a unilateral change of heart. It is essential to agreements that they are commitments to future behavior, and so if a contracting party can terminate his agreement merely by changing his mind, then there really was no commitment to begin with. Since I think the Laws have a reasonable view about agreements, I am inclined to believe that they would give the same answer. But of course there is no textual evidence on this matter, one way or the other. And in many cases the question is not critical, since the Laws concede that agreements can justifiably be broken. If a statute requires the doing of injustice, then the citizen must not obey it, even though he only recently came to the realization that it is unjust. He must not let his earlier attitude bind him to wrongdoing. On the other hand, suppose the issue is whether to *suffer* injustice: a citizen decides that a statute he once liked is in fact unjust to him, and he therefore becomes dissatisfied with it. In this case, the question of whether he still has an agreement is not academic, for if he has none, there is no reason why he should obey the law. Surely the Laws would say that his past satisfaction does bind him and that he must obey, even though he now regrets his earlier naiveté. At any rate, that is what they must say, if they do not want to be absurdly lenient.

12
A conclusion drawn

At the beginning of this chapter, I posed two questions. First, does the *Crito* allow a citizen to violate a law on the grounds that it does him an injustice? We see now that it does. The Laws merely insist that when a citizen agrees to obey a law, he cannot break his agreement merely because it calls on him to suffer injustice. But since agreement is a matter of satisfaction and not mere residence, it is possible for a citizen to remain in the city and avoid making an agreement to obey a law that he thinks does him an injustice. If he publicly and sincerely objects to a particular statute soon enough after it has been adopted, or soon enough after he has passed his *dokimasia*, then he has not agreed to obey it. Of course, if he disobeys, he must do so openly, and when summoned to court he must try to persuade the jury that he was right to disobey. But if the law he disobeyed is in fact unjust to him, then the *Crito* contains not a word to the effect that he has violated the law for insufficient reason. It is therefore a far less authoritarian dialogue than we might have supposed.

Second, we wanted to know whether the Laws avoid falling into one or the other of two extremes: do they make it too difficult or too easy to avoid making an agreement? If a citizen can avoid giving his consent simply by taking no positive steps to make an agreement, then the state will have too little power— it will not even have the right to imprison wrongdoers. But if a citizen cannot avoid agreeing to obey the laws, short of going into exile, then he must leave the state whenever it gives orders that require the doing of injustice. Now, if the argument of this chapter has been correct, then the *Crito* cannot easily be accused of falling into either of these two traps. A citizen cannot avoid making an agreement merely by saying, "I refuse to agree to that law." Unless he publicly shows that he is dissatisfied with a law, he has agreed. And certain laws are so crucial to the existence of the city that it will be difficult, if not impossible, to demonstrate one's sincere dissatisfaction with them. But in many other cases, it will be easy for the citizen to show that he is genuinely opposed to a law, and in these cases he can avoid agreement.

We should notice how the parent-city analogy and the argument from agreement compensate for each other's weaknesses. Though each provides an independent argument against escape, neither by itself presents a complete picture of the state's powers. The parent-city analogy fails to provide the city with the right to use certain forms of punishment, and the argument from agreement tries to fill this gap. Conversely, the Laws would leave the city with too little authority, if, like Locke, they were to claim that all political authority must be based on consent. If one has reason to obey the law only when one has agreed to do so, then the citizen who sincerely dissents will have no reason to obey—even if his objection to the law is groundless. The *Crito* avoids this consequence, not by making agreement unavoidable for residents, but by recognizing a source of political authority that has nothing to do with consent. Both the parent-city analogy and the argument from agreement allow the citizen a fair degree of freedom, but when they are combined, they produce a powerful conclusion: Socrates has to accept his death, in spite of the fact that he is a victim of injustice.

13
How good is the argument from agreement?

Did Socrates and his fellow citizens really agree to obey the laws? Does the *Crito* succeed in establishing this conclusion? I think not, for there is at least one devastating defect in the argument of the Laws: they adopt the false assumption that if citizens are satisfied with their country, they must be satisfied with its laws (VI.9). In fact, there are innumerable reasons for being satisfied with and remaining in a country that have nothing to do with its legal system. A farmer, for example, can love his country for its rich topsoil. I suspect that Socrates overlooks this point because he generalizes from his own case: *he* sees no reason to like a city apart from its laws, for he thinks that the legal system shapes the moral outlook of the citizen (more on this in VII.6), and nothing is more important to him than one's attitude toward virtue. He preferred Athens to all other cities because of the legal system's effect on moral development, and he too quickly inferred that the comparative merits of legal systems must always be the determining factor in our civic preferences.

But suppose we set aside this error. Consider an Athenian citizen who has passed his *dokimasia*, has understood his city's legal system, and has shown by his behavior (including verbal behavior) that he is on balance satisfied with the laws. Did he thereby agree to obey the city's commands—excepting those he sincerely criticized? Our question is both historical and philosophical: we are asking whether a certain kind of person in fifth- or fourth-century Athens did in fact make a certain agreement; but we must also decide what counts as an agreement. It is plausible to assume that when an organization makes an offer of membership, and makes its rules known to prospective recruits, then those who accept the offer implicitly agree to obey the rules. The Laws realize, however, that the Athenian legal system is not well known to its newest members, and they claim therefore that an implicit agreement is completed only when the new citizen understands and shows his satisfaction with the way the city conducts its legal business. I doubt that this move, clever as it is, really works. Agreements exist only when offers are made and accepted, but after the citizen has passed his *dokimasia*, it is no longer true to say that his city is still making him an offer. If no offer is outstanding once the *dokimasia* has been passed, then the new citizen is not really in the business of evaluating the terms of an offer. And since there is no longer an offer for him to accept, there are no terms to which he gives his agreement, should he show his satisfaction with the laws.

For the sake of a philosophical experiment, let us change the historical facts. Suppose Athens had not only had a *dokimasia* for seventeen-year-olds, but had also required its citizens to take an oath when they were thirty and therefore politically experienced. In this oath, they promise to obey the city or persuade it as to the nature of justice, and those who refuse to swear allegiance are stripped of their citizenship, though they may remain indefinitely as resident aliens. If Athens had had this institution, and if Socrates had taken this oath, then of course he would have broken an agreement had he escaped from jail without persuading the city. But would it have been a just agreement? The Laws, I suspect, would say yes, for the citizen is not being forced, tricked, or rushed into agreement, nor does his oath require him to commit unjust acts. My own view, however, is that the adult children of citizens have certain rights—e.g. the right to vote—that cannot be taken away from them merely because they refuse to swear an oath of allegiance. When a child becomes a full-fledged participant in the political process of his native state, he is only getting his due, and if he must first make an agreement before he acquires his rights, then that agreement is unjust. By insisting upon such an agreement, the state is offering to the new citizen something that ought in any case to be his. The state is not a private club which may limit membership in any way it chooses and extend membership on any terms it likes. The state can require naturalized citizens to take an oath of allegiance; it can require its public officials to swear that they will uphold the laws; it can strip citizens of some important rights if they commit serious crimes; and it can make residents who engage in certain activities agree to abide by the relevant laws (for example, those who receive drivers' licenses can be required to agree that they will obey the traffic laws). But even when the state deserves the gratitude of its citizens, it cannot establish an oath of allegiance as a condition that native citizens must fulfill before they exercise such rights as the rights to vote.[16] For if it were appropriate for the state to require such an oath, then in effect there would be no *right* to

[16] Can the state justifiably impose some lesser penalty on native citizens who refuse to agree to take some oath of allegiance? I can't think of anything that would be appropriate. Consider a fine, for example. If it were large, it would be an unfair burden, especially on the poor. If it were small, it would trivialize the oath and thus defeat its purpose, which is to increase the citizen's sense of allegiance to the state.

vote: voting would be a privilege, like driving, which the state extends to citizens on reasonable terms. Once we start thinking in terms of natural rights, we part company with the whole political outlook of the Laws. The central idea behind their argument from agreement is that when someone joins an organization, he agrees to those rules with which he later shows his satisfaction. But there is something profoundly wrong here: the state is not just any organization, but one to which certain individuals have rights of membership. So even if the Laws had succeeded in showing that Socrates had implicitly agreed to obey the laws—even if Athens had required its citizens to make an explicit agreement—the contract in question would nonetheless have been unconscionable, because the state would have been offering a citizen what in any case ought to have been his.

We saw in Chapter V that something in the first type of argument against escape can be salvaged: there can be a significant debt of gratitude that citizens owe their state, just as they owe a debt of gratitude to their parents. But the second type of argument against escape, it now appears, is misconceived at its core.

VII

SOCRATES AND DEMOCRACY

1
The one and the many

I TURN NOW to the second task of this study. In this chapter and the next, I shall discuss Socrates' views about politics in general and Athens in particular. I think he had a more complex and interesting attitude toward democracy than scholars have realized, for although he was highly critical of rule by the many, he also appreciated certain democratic features of his native city. Furthermore, the great value he saw in critical inquiry was combined with, and is consistent with, a highly authoritarian streak, which he passed along to Plato. Socrates thought that moral experts should rule, and he urged withdrawal from everyday politics only because he realized that he and his followers were far from being experts.

Socrates' political orientation cannot be understood apart from his whole moral program, and I shall therefore discuss (in Chapter VIII) some topics long familiar to students of the early dialogues: the search for definitions, the disclaimers of knowledge, and the Socratic conception of virtue and education. I hope to show that we have a better understanding of these central features of the early dialogues when we connect them to Socrates' ideas about politics. On my interpretation, he emerges as a less deceptive and more pessimistic philosopher than he is often thought to be. His disclaimers of knowledge are to be taken at face value, and so are his doubts about the teachability of virtue. Those doubts, as we shall see, are intimately connected with his attitude toward democracy.

It is especially important to remember, at this point, that my subject is the Socrates that *Plato* presents to us in the early dialogues and the *Apology*.[1] Xenophon, whatever the merits or deficiencies of his Socratic works, will be almost entirely ignored.[2] Even if his historical value is higher than I think—even if he is someday shown to be more reliable than Plato—that would not eliminate the need to understand the latter's portrait of Socrates in his early works. For these early Platonic dialogues have a philosophical fascination that is independent of their value as historical sources. Yet I also believe that as we achieve a better understanding of what Plato says about Socrates, his portrait becomes more convincing as a historical representation.[3] So although my main purpose in what follows is to interpret the political ideas of a certain character in a group of Platonic writings, I also take this character to be a credible rendering of Socrates the historical figure.

The first question I now want to ask is this. What did Socrates—the Socrates of Plato's early dialogues—think of democracy? Was he hostile toward it, as many have claimed?[4] Or was he a "champion of the open society, and a friend of democ-

---

[1] See Ch. I n. 1 for further details.

[2] For differences between Xenophon's and Plato's depiction of Socratic politics, see nn. 15, 20, and 48 below; also see Ch. I n. 31. In the *Memorabilia*, Socrates' hostility toward democracy is unmitigated (II vi 26, III i 4, III vii 5-9, and esp. III ix 10); by contrast, in the early dialogues, he is greatly satisfied with the laws of Athens, though he criticizes rule by the many. It is not surprising that such a thinker won the admiration of democrats (e.g. Chaerephon: see *Ap.* 20e8-21a2) and oligarchs (e.g. Charmides) alike.

[3] See nn. 7, 15, and 16 below.

[4] Thus E. Barker, *Greek Political Theory*, p. 97: "Monarchical, and even absolutist, philosophies might . . . draw their inspiration from Socrates; and in this sense he was the enemy of democracy"; A. E. Taylor, *Socrates*, p. 141: "It was out of the question that . . . he should approve of the principle of democracy, the sovereignty of the multitude who have no knowledge of the good . . ."; Winspear and Silverberg, *Who Was Socrates?* p. 84: Socrates was engaged in "a conspiracy against the democratic constitution of Athens . . ."; Wood and Wood, *Class Ideology*, p. 97: he shared "with his conservative friends at least one over-riding interest: the replacement of the . . . democracy by the rule of an aristocratic-oligarchic elite." Guthrie, *History*, Vol. III, pp. 415-416, quotes Barker and Taylor with approval, but thinks that Winspear and Silverberg go too far in one direction and Popper too far in the other. That is, he rejects the idea that Socrates was a "political intriguer" (p. 415), but agrees that he was opposed to the principle of popular election.

racy," as Popper thought?[5] It is best to begin by looking at several passages in which Socrates attacks "the many."[6]

(A) In the *Apology* (31c4–32a3), he reminds the jury that he has not participated in the everyday political life of Athens. His divine sign has warned against it, and rightly so: for he would have died long ago, had he taken part in politics. Then Socrates makes a general point about how corrupt the majority—any majority—is: "Do not be angry at me for telling the truth: no man will be spared if he genuinely opposes you or any other great number [*plēthos*] and prevents many unjust and illegal things from happening in the city . . ." (31e1–4).

(B) Earlier in the *Apology*, Socrates cross-examines Meletus, and it emerges that, according to this prosecutor (24c9–25a11), a great many Athenian citizens know how to improve the young: in fact only Socrates corrupts them. To this, Socrates replies: ". . . Does that hold true of horses too, in your opinion? Do all men make them better, with the exception of one, who ruins them? Or is it just the reverse: only one can make them better, or very few, namely, the horse-trainer, whereas the many, if they own and use horses, ruin them? Isn't that the way it is, Meletus, both for horses *and all other animals?*" (25a13–b6, my emphasis). Most human beings are unable to give the young the moral education they need.[7]

(C) In the *Laches*, Lysimachus asks two generals—Laches and Nicias—whether his sons should be trained to fight with armor. Nicias says yes, Laches no, and so Socrates is asked (184c9–d4) to cast the deciding vote. But he protests: one should not decide such questions by numbers, but should consult an expert in-

---

[5] *The Open Society*, esp. pp. 128–133, 189–196. The quotation is from p. 191. Gulley, *The Philosophy of Socrates*, pp. 168–179, sides with Popper.

[6] I postpone until Sec. 2 the question whether these passages about the many are attacking a specific social class (i.e. craftsmen, farmers, merchants, etc.) or whether they are simply criticizing most people without regard to class.

[7] The presence of (A) and (B) in the *Apology* makes it hard to believe that this work is a sanitized version of what Socrates actually said. Plato makes no attempt to downplay Socrates' hostility to democracy. The story of Leon (32c4–e1) cannot have been invented merely to make Socrates look like an opponent of the Thirty and therefore a friend of the democracy. For if that is the strategy Plato used in writing the *Apology*, why was he so stupid as to retain the anti-democratic remarks found in (A) and (B)?

stead. "It is by knowledge that I think one must make decisions, not by the greater number [plēthos], if one intends to decide well" (184e8–9).

(D) In the *Crito* (47a2–48a7), Socrates tells his friend not to care so much about what the many will think of them if they make no attempt to escape. We should value the opinions only of those who are wise, i.e. those who have attained a high level of expertise in a particular subject. For example, if we want to develop our bodies, we should seek the advice of a doctor or a trainer, and should disregard the views of the many. For if we slavishly follow the advice of the many, our bodies will be harmed. And similarly for moral questions: ". . . With actions just and unjust, shameful and fine, good and bad, [we should not]. . . follow and fear the opinion of the many, [but] that of the one—if there is someone who knows [these things]. . ." (47c9–d2).

(E) Socrates then goes on, in this same dialogue, to lay down the principle (48b8–49e3) that injustice must never be done, even in return for injustice. He warns Crito not to accept this controversial point unless he really believes it: "Crito, make sure that you don't agree to what is contrary to your own belief. For I know that there are few who do believe or will believe these things. Among those who are convinced of these points and those who are not, there is no common counsel [boulē]. Rather, they must think the worse of each other when they consider each other's decisions" (49c11–d5).

In the passages cited above, Socrates says that the many have three flaws: a large number of their moral beliefs are false;[8] on many occasions they act immorally; and they lack the ability to give their children a proper moral education. Does he think that

---

[8] I say "large number" because that seems to be the natural reading of *Crito* 47c9–d2 (cited above in [D]) and 48a7–10. Socrates cannot mean that the many are *always* wrong about moral matters, but he would not be so contemptuous of them if they merely had one false moral belief. I suppose he might have thought that all of their mistaken moral beliefs could be traced back to one central error. Perhaps that central error was the conviction that virtue is only sometimes worthwhile. But I find no evidence in the early dialogues that Socrates was particularly interested in reducing the false beliefs of the many to one basic mistake.

these flaws can be, or someday might be, eliminated? Clearly not. For in (E) he says that few will *ever* agree with him that injustice must never be done; in fact, he is so convinced of this that he claims to know it. Now, if the many will always believe that injustice should be returned for injustice, then they will always act unjustly if they are provoked and have a chance to respond in kind. In any case, (A) is most naturally read as a statement about the permanent corruption of the many: whoever opposes a great number and tries to prevent unjust and illegal behavior shall not survive for long. Socrates is not merely saying that whoever opposed the democracy in the past did not last long; he is making a sweeping statement about what inevitably happens whenever the many are opposed. Similarly, Socrates is saying that the many *will never* be able to give their children a proper moral education. If parents believe that injustice is sometimes justified, and if they will never change their minds about this, then they will naturally teach this to their children, who will in turn teach their children the same thing, and so on. Perhaps now and then an individual will overcome the effects of his early training; after all, Socrates has converted Crito to the view that injustice must never be done. But nonetheless, Socrates has become convinced that most people will learn false moral beliefs from their parents, will retain those errors throughout their lives, and will teach them to their children. That is what he means when he says in (B) that the many corrupt the young.

Now, someone could accept Socrates' low estimate of the many and still remain a proponent of democracy. One could argue that all adult human beings, regardless of their moral faults, have a right to participate equally in the making of political decisions. Or one might claim that participating fully in the political process of a country is a necessary ingredient of the good life, and that no one should be denied such a good merely because he has false moral beliefs. Alternatively, one might claim that false moral beliefs and immoral conduct are a universal and inevitable part of the human situation: since everyone has these flaws, they cannot be used to disqualify anyone from sharing political power. But even though it is possible, in these and other ways, to denigrate the many and still remain an advocate of democracy, there is no evidence that Socrates availed himself of this possibility. Nothing he says in Plato's early works—or in Xenophon's *Memorabilia*, for that matter—even remotely suggests that anyone has a *right* to vote or rule. Nor does Socrates ever say that ruling is a good that every adult deserves to experience. On the contrary, he holds in Book I of the *Republic* that wielding political power is in itself unattractive: the only consideration that could lead a good man to rule is the fear of being ruled by those who are worse (347b9-d2). Furthermore, Socrates nowhere adopts the extreme position that the faults of the many are so widespread as to be universal. He and a few others have managed to free themselves from the common misconception that injustice is sometimes appropriate. At least to this extent, they are better than the many.

I think it is fair to conclude, then, that Socrates is a critic of democracy—rule by the many—for the simple reason that he has a low opinion of the many. Their false moral beliefs and willingness to engage in injustice will inevitably lead to bad laws, bad decisions, and official misconduct. There is never any question in the early dialogues that the democratic process—the vote or the lot[9]—is a fair procedure that we ought to value apart from its results. Instead, Socrates is evidently assuming that a way of making decisions is only as good as the quality of the decisions that usually result from that procedure. Decisions made by majority rule have all of the defects of the majority.[10] And Socrates believes that these defects cannot be remedied.

2
Class bias?

Why did Socrates have such a low opinion of the many? One answer, given by Guthrie, is that ". . . in Socrates' view . . . the mind and the way of life of a good artisan were inevitably

[9] According to Xenophon, *Mem.* I ii 9, (cf. Aristotle, *Rhet.* 1393b3-8), Socrates was accused of having criticized election by lot. No doubt, Xenophon is right here: as (B), (C), and (D) indicate, Socrates is opposed to any decision procedure that takes no account of expertise.

[10] Cf. Nelson, *The Justification of Democracy*, p. 101: "The mechanics of democracy are such . . . that, given certain assumptions about human nature, democracy will automatically tend to produce morally acceptable results."

such as to preclude him from acquiring the knowledge . . . which would make him an adequate guide in political affairs."[11] Similarly Wood and Wood: "The common man, whose labours . . . weaken and taint his soul, is excluded by Socrates from any knowledge of politics. . . ."[12] Now, if these scholars were merely trying to describe the attitude of a typical Athenian aristocrat toward a working man, they would be perfectly correct. Xenophon, Plato, and Aristotle, for example, explicitly say that if someone works with his hands, then what mental powers he has will atrophy.[13] And of course class bias of this sort flourishes in the modern age. (Guthrie cites Hume's statement that "poverty and hard labour debase the minds of the common people, and render them unfit for any science or ingenious profession.")[14] But if we ask the question, "Is there any evidence in Plato's early dialogues that Socrates held the physical-labor-destroys-the-mind thesis?" the answer is no.[15] He admits in the *Apology* that those who spent their days enjoying the spectacle of a Socratic cross-examination were rich (23c2-5). But he also says that he is no more interested in persuading the rich than the poor (33a6-b3), and he made it his business to test the virtue of the craftsmen, as well as of the poets and politicians (22c9-e5).[16] His aim is to change the attitudes of everyone in

[11] *History*, Vol. III, p. 410.

[12] *Class Ideology*, p. 101. They seem to assume that whenever Socrates criticizes "the many," he is confining his attack to the working class. See for example their treatment of *Grg.* 474a5-b1 on p. 98. I will soon be challenging this assumption.

[13] Xenophon *Oec.* IV 2-3; Plato *Rep.* 495d4-e2, *Laws* 919c3-d2; Aristotle *Pol.* 1328b39-1329a2, 1337b5-15.

[14] *History*, Vol. III, pp. 410-411. He cites *Essays and Treatises* (Edinburgh, 1825), p. 195.

[15] I do not deny that if we were to rely on Xenophon's testimony, we could plausibly attribute an aristocratic class bias to Socrates. See *Mem.* II vi 26, III vii 5-7. Since the labor-destroys-the-mind thesis seems to be a favorite dogma of the aristocrats, we would have some reason to attribute it to Socrates. But it is striking that Plato—who himself adopts this thesis—never attributes it to Socrates, even though he frequently has Socrates denounce the many. This is good evidence that Plato never heard Socrates espouse the thesis. (Those who think that the early dialogues are free creations with no historical accuracy will have to say that it is a sheer accident that Plato didn't put this thesis into the mouth of Socrates.)

[16] This remark might be dismissed as Plato's attempt to cover up Socrates'

the city (29d1-30b4, 30e7-31a1), not just a few members of the upper class.[17] Why would Socrates try to goad the craftsmen into examining their lives, if he had already decided that physical labor had made them intellectually hopeless? No doubt, he would have to admit that since the poor have less leisure than the rich, they have less time to participate in moral discussion. But Socrates never suggests that craftsmen have no time at all for moral inquiry; on the contrary, since he cross-examined them, they must have had enough leisure for this activity. He thinks that it is as important for a craftsman to live an examined life as it is for an idle aristocrat,[18] and he never says that the former has a mind so debased by hard labor that he cannot profit from discussions about the virtues.[19]

So our question remains. Why did Socrates—the Socrates of the early dialogues—have such a low opinion of the many? I suggest a simple answer: he has spent a large part of his adult

---

love affair with the wealthy, but I would be skeptical of any such attempt to read the *Apology* as a whitewash: the remaining antidemocratic dirt defies this hypothesis. See n. 7 above.

[17] What of Socrates' statement at *Grg.* 474a5-b1 that he will not enter into discussion with the many? Wood and Wood, *Class Ideology*, p. 98, cite this as evidence of Socrates' contempt for the working class, but they ignore the context of his remark. Polus is trying to cast doubt on Socrates' unorthodox moral convictions by appealing to the opinions of those who are listening to the conversation. Socrates replies that he does not decide questions by taking a poll of listeners, but instead cross-examines one man—the one he is talking with, whoever that may be. This hardly suggests that Socrates will not talk with workers—an interpretation that is decisively refuted by the *Apology*. He merely means that he will not carry on a conversation with a group, whatever its social class. In the *Gorgias*, as in the other early dialogues, the audience is aristocratic.

[18] That is why Socrates says (*Ap.* 38a5-6) that the "unexamined life is not worth living *for man*. . . ." The last phrase stresses the fact that all human beings could profit from engaging in moral inquiry. Notice that Socrates leaves room for the possibility that a woman (*Grg.* 470e9-11) or a slave (*La.* 186b3-5, *Grg.* 515a5-7) has the capacity to be virtuous. Though he thinks that at most a few have the ability to acquire moral knowledge, he never suggests that this capacity will occur only in certain social groups.

[19] In fact, Socrates, ridicules the class bias of an aristocrat like Callicles (*Grg.* 512b3-d6), and would apply *kalos kagathos*, a term often reserved for members of the nobility (it literally means "noble and good," though "gentleman" captures its tone), to anyone who meets his high standards of virtue. See *Grg.* 470e9-11, and Dodds' note (*Plato Gorgias*, ad loc.). If Socrates had thought that labor dulls the mind, would he have ridiculed Callicles for the way he looks down on craftsmen? Would he have sought to free *kalos kagathos* from its affiliation with the upper class?

life talking with people, and he realizes that few have come to accept his unorthodox moral principles (*Crito* 49c11-d5). Much of that time was spent with people who could afford to spend all day, every day, engaged in moral debate, but even in these cases his rate of conversion was extremely low.[20] And so Socrates became a pessimist of sorts and formulated a sweeping law of large numbers: even when time is unlimited, the number of people, of any class, who can be persuaded to give up certain false moral beliefs is and always will be quite low. This law is no *a priori* prejudice, since it is based (however justifiably or foolishly) on personal experience. And it applies to aristocrats no less than workers. Talk to one hundred aristocrats, and perhaps two will be persuaded to see things as Socrates does; talk to one hundred workers, and, by virtue of the law of large numbers (rather than some notion that labor dulls the mind), the chances of success will be no greater. In fact, it is simple common sense to think that the chances of success will be smaller, since one is more likely to convert others to one's own way of thinking, the more time for discussion one has. (This is an idea expressed by Socrates himself: see *Ap.* 18e5-19a5, 24a1-4). It is reasonable to suppose that Socrates expected to have few if any converts among the craftsmen. He could expect more converts among the leisured class, though they would still constitute a small percentage of this group. It is also reasonable to suppose that Socrates' pessimistic law of large numbers was based primarily on his frequent failure to change the minds of wealthy aristocrats. They were the ones who had the most time to spend with him, and therefore they should have been more easily persuaded; yet few had adopted his principles. Socrates could reasonably infer that even if the craftsmen had had more time for discussion, his rate of success in changing *their* minds would have been no greater.

One further point. The Greek terms, *hoi polloi* ("the many") and *to plēthos* ("the greater number"), could be used quite generally to designate any large number of people, whatever its class composition; or they could be used more specifically to

[20] Contrast *Mem.* IV vi 14-15: Socrates persuaded his audience far more successfully than any other man Xenophon ever knew.

refer to the "common people," i.e. the commercial and laboring class that was more numerous in Athens than any other group of citizens.[21] For Socrates' purposes, it does not matter which sense these terms have when he criticizes the many.[22] Few aristocrats and few artisans are ever going to give up their moral prejudices: that is the proper way to interpret Socrates when he says that few will ever believe that injustice must never be done (*Crito* 49d2). Take any sizable group of people, and regardless of their social status and financial condition, Socrates is sure that most of them will be riddled with moral error. Take any democracy, and whether you think of it as rule by the poor (who happen to be many) or rule by a great number (most of whom happen to be poor), Socrates is sure that it is a highly defective form of government.[23]

3
Popper's Socrates

Popper admits that Socrates was "a critic of Athens and of her democratic institutions."[24] He "always criticized the anonymous multitude as well as its leaders for their lack of wisdom."[25] "He criticized them rightly for their lack of intellectual

[21] Liddell and Scott, *A Greek-English Lexicon*, s. vv. *plēthos, polus* II. *Plēthos* can also mean "the majority," whatever its absolute size. Thus *La.* 184d5-e9, cited in (C), Sec. 1.

[22] In (A) and (B), Sec. 1, Socrates could be using these terms in either their wider or narrower sense; it is difficult to tell. In (C), as the context shows, he is saying that majority rule is never a reasonable procedure, whether it is used by a small group of prominent men (the situation in the *Laches*) or by the Assembly. So *plēthos* has no class connotation here. In (D), the context suggests that *hoi polloi* is being used in its broader sense. Surely Crito is worried about what most people—aristocrats and plebes—will think of him, not merely what ordinary people will think.

[23] Like *hoi polloi* and *to plēthos, hoi dēmoi* could refer quite generally to all the free citizens of a given city, nobility and poor alike, or it could refer more narrowly to the "common" people. See Liddell and Scott, *A Greek-English Lexicon*, s.v. *dēmos* II, III. Therefore, some defined democracy as rule by the poor and others as rule by all free citizens. Aristotle seems to have conflicting views. *Pol.* 1279b20-1280a6 favors the former definition, 1290a30-b20 the latter.

[24] *The Open Society*, p. 189.

[25] Ibid., pp. 195-196.

honesty, and for their obsession with power-politics."[26] Nonetheless, Popper believes that these frequent attacks on the many
arose out of Socrates' allegiance to democratic values. He exposed their deficiencies because he wanted to educate them, not
because he was opposed in principle to the widespread sharing
of political power. "He felt that the way to improve the political life of the city was to educate the citizens to self-criti-
cism."[27] In other words, Popper's Socrates prefigured the democratic liberalism of J. S. Mill:[28] human beings are by and large
equal in their capacities, and though the masses are now too
fond of material success and the lower pleasures, this is a condition that can be remedied through universal education. Thus
Popper refers to Socrates' "theory that moral excellence can be
taught, and that it does not require any particular moral facul-
ties, apart from the universal human intelligence."[29] ". . . Socratic intellectualism is decidedly equalitarian. Socrates believed
that everyone can be taught; in the *Meno*, we see him teaching
a young slave . . . in an attempt to prove that any uneducated
slave has the capacity to grasp even abstract matters."[30] Now,
even though Socrates has good reason to believe that virtue is
teachable (since it is knowledge), that hardly shows that he considered everyone or even a large majority capable of learning
it. After all, the skill of playing the flute can be taught—for
there are expert teachers of it—but that does not mean that
everyone can learn it, and in fact this ability may be quite rare.
So Socrates can easily believe that if virtue is teachable, it will
be learnable by only a few. (We will later see how seriously he
took the possibility that virtue may not be teachable at all, a
point Popper overlooks.) Furthermore, nothing of moral significance is proved by the fact that in the *Meno* a slave is shown
to have "the capacity to grasp . . . abstract matters." True, a
slave can learn geometry, but that hardly shows that he can
acquire a knowledge of virtue, justice, the good, etc. None of

[26] Ibid., p. 191.
[27] Ibid., p. 130.
[28] Here I follow Gutmann's interpretation of Mill. See *Liberal Equality*, pp.
51-55. Her contrast between Mill and Comte, p. 241 n. 14, parallels the contrast
Popper wants to draw between Socrates and Plato.
[29] *The Open Society*, p. 128.
[30] Ibid., p. 129.

the passages we looked at in Section 1 casts the slightest doubt on the capacity of the many to learn certain skills and certain subjects. Socrates assures us in the *Apology* that in their special spheres, the craftsmen do have the knowledge they claim (22c9-e5). It is knowledge of the most important matters—virtue and the good—that they lack, and as our earlier passages tell us, they will never acquire that knowledge. If egalitarianism means the belief in roughly equal human capacities to know the good and do what is right, then Socrates was no egalitarian. On the contrary, he believed that at most a few people will ever reach that level. And since most will never have knowledge of justice, they will never be deserving of political power. Popper makes an important concession when he says, "It is not unlikely that he [Socrates] demanded . . . that the best should rule, which would have meant, in his view, the wisest, or those who knew something about justice."[31] But since most people will never have knowledge of justice, they will never merit political office. So Popper ought to have conceded that according to Socrates democracy—the rule of the many—is a highly defective political form.[32]

At one point, Popper tries to find a democratic Socrates lurk-

[31] Ibid., p. 128. Popper goes on to say, "The wisdom he meant was . . . simply the realization: how little do I know!" (p. 128). "Readiness to learn in itself proves the possession of wisdom . . ." (p. 129). If this were correct, then Socrates would have said that the slave is already wise when, realizing that he cannot double the area of a given square, he becomes eager to learn (*Meno* 84a3-c2). But even when the slave finally sees the solution, Socrates says that he still lacks mathematical knowledge (85b8-e7). Guthrie, *History*, Vol. III, p. 410 n. 1, is correct when he dissents from "Popper's statement . . . that the wisdom needed for ruling was only the peculiarly Socratic wisdom of knowing one's own ignorance. This would be like saying that a doctor would be *sophos* [wise] if he confessed his ignorance of medicine but continued to treat patients." I will have more to say about this "peculiarly Socratic wisdom" in Chapter VIII.

[32] Popper, *The Open Society*, pp. 91, 117, 128, 254 n. 14, uses one other passage in his attempt to show that Socrates was an egalitarian: *Grg.* 488b8-489c7. Here, Socrates leads Callicles into the following trap. (A) According to Callicles, whatever the stronger lay down is just; (B) the many are numerically stronger, and they lay it down that justice is equality; (C) but Callicles denies that justice is equality. Popper assumes without argument that in (B) Socrates is endorsing the idea that justice is equality. But it is more likely that he is simply using (B) to create a difficulty for Callicles. In view of the passages cited in Sec. 1, we cannot take Socrates to be endorsing a proposition whenever he attributes it to the many. Irwin, *Plato Gorgias*, p. 186, opposes Popper's interpretation of the *Gorgias* passages in this same way.

ing in the *Crito*. Here is his explanation of why Socrates did not seize the opportunity to escape: "Had he seized it, and become an exile, everyone would have thought him an opponent of democracy. So he stayed and stated his reasons."[33] It is curious that Socrates has suddenly become so concerned with what "everybody would have thought." Popper goes on: "Such an act [escape] would put me in opposition to the laws, and prove my disloyalty. It would do harm to the state. Only if I stay can I put beyond doubt my loyalty to the state, with its democratic laws, and prove that I have never been its enemy." But why does Popper think that in the *Crito* it makes a difference to Socrates that Athens has *democratic* laws? In a footnote, he refers to *Crito* 51d-e, "where the democratic character of the laws is stressed, i.e. the possibility that the citizen might change the laws without violence, by rational argument (as Socrates puts it, he may try to convince the laws). . . ."[34] Evidently, Popper is relying on Grote's interpretation of the persuade-or-obey doctrine: since the citizen has the opportunity to persuade the Assembly to change the law, he has no right to disobey it. In other words, strict obedience is owed to Athens *because it is a democracy*. One is reminded here of T. H. Green's statement (cited in III.1) that "in a country like ours, with a popular government and settled methods of enacting and repealing laws," the citizens must never disobey.[35] That is the view Popper is attributing to the *Crito*. Now, I agree with Popper that the persuade-or-obey doctrine is an important part of the *Crito*'s philosophy, but as we saw in Chapters III and IV, it is unlikely that Grote's understanding of that doctrine is correct. When the Laws say that the citizen must persuade or obey, they mean that whoever disobeys must persuade a court that he was right to do so. The city provides every disobedient citizen with a fair opportunity to explain himself in court, and anyone who is bound to the city through benefits received (birth or education) or through a voluntary agreement must appear in court when summoned. Obviously, democracies are not the only cities that

---

[33] *The Open Society*, p. 194.
[34] Ibid., p. 305 n. 53.
[35] *Lectures on the Principles of Political Obligation*, Sec. 100, p. 111.

can hold fair judicial proceedings; kingships, aristocracies or oli-
garchies could do as much. The philosophy that we find in the
Crito can require loyalty to many different political forms, not
merely to democracies.[36]

4
Politics and expertise

Once it is conceded that according to Socrates democracy is
inevitably a bad form of government, an important question
still remains: did he think it possible to do significantly better?
The question is simple, but answering it correctly is no easy
matter, for it requires an overall interpretation of the early dialogues, and for such a project to succeed a number of difficult
texts must be carefully examined. Perhaps it will be best if I
first lay out my interpretation in a brief but dogmatic way. The

[36] Even if the conservative reading of the persuade-or-obey doctrine were
correct, one could still say that undemocratic forms of government are able to
give their citizens the opportunity to change the law through persuasion. A
king, for example, can listen with an open mind to pleas that his edicts be
reconsidered; in this sense, his subjects have an alternative to obedience. Thus
Guthrie, *History*, Vol. III, pp. 412-413, says: "The choice before the individual
was either to obey the laws, or to get them changed by peaceful persuasion or
else to emigrate. . . . It is not necessarily a democratic view, for both constitutional monarchy and aristocracy, as defined by Socrates, would fulfill his
conditions. . . ." Cf. Irwin, *Plato Gorgias*, p. 186. Popper could reply that when
the Laws tell Socrates that he could have persuaded, rather than obeyed, they
are thinking of the Assembly as the proper forum for persuasion. This is a
claim Guthrie has to accept, since he thinks that the point of persuasion is "to
change the law," and the Assembly is where laws are changed. Popper then
could go on to suggest that Socrates is being influenced by an idea that was
later articulated by such philosophers as Green and P. Singer: if one has an
opportunity to share in the making of laws, then it is only fair that one obey.
I do not think this would be a very promising suggestion; I would want to see
some textual evidence that Socrates has some inkling of this idea. But my real
reason for opposing Popper stems from my rejection of the conservative reading of the persuade-or-obey doctrine.
   There is another way of challenging Popper's treatment of the persuade-or-
obey doctrine. How do we know that, according to the Laws, loyalty is owed
the city only on condition that citizens have the opportunity to persuade? The
Laws might require the citizen to be open in his dealings with a beneficent
state, even when it leaves no room for persuasion (see V.2). Of course, this
does not mean that if a beneficent city insists on strict obedience, and leaves no
room for persuasion, then the citizens must obey every order.

reader will thus be able to see the direction in which I am heading. Then, as we proceed, I will try to provide more and more textual support for my approach. The bulk of this project will be carried out in Chapter VIII.

In my opinion, Socrates is quite pessimistic about the chances of there ever being a better form of government than democracy. He does conceive of the theoretical possibility that a city might be ruled by a few moral experts, and he is sure that such a city—if ever it could exist—would be better governed by far than any democracy. But this is merely a theoretical possibility for him. He has serious doubts about whether it is humanly possible to acquire the level of moral knowledge that would be needed to rule a city well. Socrates does not consider himself to be a moral expert, nor is he aware of any others who are.[37] Furthermore, he doubts that human beings have the capacity to acquire the kind of knowledge that would be needed to rule well. And he thinks that if moral expertise is unattainable, then the state will always be badly run, whether it is governed by the poor or the rich, the many or the few. The defects of democracy will not be remedied merely by disenfranchising the many and installing a few wealthy aristocrats in office. What is needed to rule well is a high level of moral knowledge, and if the sort of knowledge Socrates is talking about is beyond our powers to acquire, then there would be no point in replacing a democracy with some other form of government.

When I speak of a "moral expert" or of someone who has a

---

[37] Similarly Irwin, *Plato's Moral Theory*, p. 71: "The expert in a particular craft offers authoritative guidance, supported by a rational account. . . . In the *Laches* [Socrates] demands an expert craftsman in moral training. . . . However, he does not claim to be the craftsman himself. . . ." But I depart from Irwin when he goes on to say (p. 71) that since Socrates is always willing to reopen any moral question, he cannot consider himself to be an expert, since ". . . this is no expert's procedure." I don't see why willingness to consider new or old objections is incompatible with being an expert. Perhaps Irwin means that according to Socrates an expert's confidence in the truth of his beliefs cannot depend on discussions with others. But there is no reason to attribute this view to Socrates. He refuses to call himself an expert, not because he finds fault with his method of question and answer, but because that method has not yet produced the results that an expert should achieve: "authoritative guidance, supported by a rational account," in Irwin's words. See VIII.12 for further discussion.

"high level of moral knowledge," I mean someone who can satisfactorily defend an answer to the sorts of questions that are typically asked in the early dialogues: "What is courage?" "What is justice?" etc. Socrates thinks that an adequate answer to these questions will provide us with the standard we need in order to answer difficult and important practical questions.[38] Anyone who lacks such a standard—if he has any insight into himself—will be perplexed about a large number of urgent moral issues. Thus our inability to define the virtues is a major moral deficiency. According to Socrates, since most people will never free themselves from false moral beliefs, they obviously will never become moral experts. True belief about certain matters—not to mention knowledge—is beyond them. If moral expertise is ever attained it will be only by a few, but as yet Socrates did not think that anyone had reached that high level, and he was doubtful that anyone ever would.

If Socrates takes the inability to define the virtues to be a major moral deficiency, and if he finds this fault in himself, then he must concede that he is far from being a fully virtuous person. As I will try to show, there is good textual evidence

[38] *Euphr.* 6e3-6, 9a1-b3. I take Socrates to be saying that if one is going to pose as a religious expert (as Euthyphro does) and depart from common sense by prosecuting one's father, then one had better be equipped with a precise standard for resolving religious difficulties. In other words, one important test of a definition is its ability, when combined with other statements (see VIII.9), to give advice in such hard cases as the one Euthyphro faces. This aspect of Socratic definition is properly emphasized by Irwin, *Plato's Moral Theory*, pp. 42-43, 65, 68-69. See too Allen, *Plato's 'Euthyphro' and the Earlier Theory of Forms* (hereafter cited as *Plato's 'Euthyphro'*), pp. 22-23. But I depart from Irwin's view, *Plato's Moral Theory*, pp. 72-73, that according to Socrates definitions should contain no "disputed terms." See Ch. VIII n. 55. Nor do I take Socrates to be consciously committed to standards, if these are construed as abstract entities. But I do take him to be seeking a standard in this sense: he thinks that a satisfactory definition, backed up by a complete ethical theory, will enable anyone who understands that definition and theory to determine which persons and acts are virtuous and which are not. It is obvious and uncontroversial that Socrates is not after dictionary definitions, i.e. pithy descriptions of how words are in fact used. He does not use any word that corresponds, even in a rough way, to our word, "definition." He asks, "What is piety?" "What is courage?" etc., rather than "What is the definition of 'piety'?" "What is the definition of 'courage'?" etc. So, when I talk about Socrates' search for definitions, this is just a shorthand way of referring to his search for answers to such questions as "What is piety?" "What is courage?" etc.

for understanding him in this way. But for now, I ask the reader to construe the interpretation I have just outlined as a working hypothesis. Let us see what sense we can make of Socrates' politics if we adopt it.

To begin with, consider my claim that according to Socrates a move away from democracy would be worthwhile only on condition that moral experts take control. At first sight, this seems to be an irrational form of perfectionism. After all, if there are people who have freed themselves from *some* of the defects of the many—and Socrates thinks there are—then why shouldn't *they* rule, rather than the many? Why wouldn't Socrates have urged some of his followers to establish a new form of government, an oligarchy of Socratic believers? They would not be moral experts, since they lack definitions of the virtues, but they would all believe that injustice must never be done, under any circumstances. Wouldn't they therefore be better rulers than the many?

Let us recast this problem in the following terms. Suppose some friends and admirers of Socrates had asked him whether they should try to overthrow the democracy, and install themselves in power. They want him to say whether such a plan of action would be in their own best interest. I suggest that Socrates would give the following reply: "If you want to pursue your own best interest, then you must try to become as virtuous as possible. And to do this, you must try to acquire knowledge of the virtues. But the only way to acquire moral knowledge—though of course this is not a method that guarantees success or even progress—is to discuss moral questions every day, as I do. Now, if you enter a political career you will have too little time, or none at all, to care for your own souls. If your revolutionary scheme succeeds you will be responsible for ruling the state—a full-time job that will surely interfere with the more urgent task of acquiring moral knowledge. Admittedly, as things now stand, we are being governed by men worse than ourselves. But the worst that can happen to us, as a result, is that we may become victims of injustice. And that is not a great evil: far worse to abandon our moral investigations, which give us the only chance we have to become fully virtuous men.[39] So give up your political ambitions, turn your-selves into moral experts, and then, if you so choose, you can occupy yourselves with politics. Having completed the project of becoming a virtuous person, you can turn to the far less important task of protecting yourself from injustice. But until you become a moral expert, stay away from politics."

I do not take myself to have shown, as yet, that this is the advice Socrates would have given his followers. For I am re-lying on one of my working hypotheses: Socrates took himself and his followers to be quite distant from the ultimate goal of moral development, which is to possess a satisfactory definition of the virtues. No argument has yet been given for this hy-pothesis. But if it proves to be correct, then surely Socrates would have spoken to his admirers in the manner I have de-scribed. He would have advised them to pursue their own good;[40] he thinks that moral development is the only good, or at least a good that outweighs all others;[41] and he believes that ruling

[39] For the claim that doing injustice is worse than suffering injustice, see *Grg.* 469b8–c2, 477b1–479a3, 508a8–c3, 509c6–7, 512a2–b2. Similarly, becoming a more virtuous person is a more important task than protecting oneself against the wrongdoing of others: 512e1–5.

[40] For evidence of Socrates' psychological egoism, see *Grg.* 468b4–6, 468d1–4; *Meno* 77b6–c8. Ethical egoism is assumed when Socrates says (*Rep.* 346e7–347d8) that since ruling the state is aiming at the well-being of others, a good man will not want to rule for its own sake. I take Socrates to endorse "moral egocentrism" in Irwin's sense: "all virtue must contribute to some end valued by the agent as part of his own good." See *Plato's Moral Theory*, p. 255. As Irwin notes, this doctrine must be distinguished from the more pernicious po-sition he calls "moral solipsism" (p. 255), which holds that "all virtue must contribute instrumentally either to some intrinsically valued condition of the agent, or to some state of affairs he values for its own sake apart from any benefit or harm to other people." If Socrates identifies the good with pleasure, as some (including Irwin) think he does in the *Protagoras*, then he is a moral solipsist. However, I side with those who acquit this dialogue of hedonism. See Ch. VIII nn. 36, 37.

[41] *Euthyd.* 281d2–e5 holds that wisdom is the only thing that is good in itself; all others "goods" are good only in the right conditions, i.e. when they are guided by wisdom. Since Socrates thinks that the virtues, properly understood, are forms of wisdom (*Protag.* 361b1–2), they too will be good in themselves. This is the position adopted in the *Meno* (87d2–88d3). Notice that at *Euthyd.* 279c9–d7, Socrates identifies wisdom with good fortune (*eutuchia*); and wisdom bears the same relation to good fortune as to good action (*eupragia*) and hap-piness (*eudaimonia*). See 281b2–4, 282c8–d1. So, wisdom, virtue, good fortune,

over others is not an activity that contributes to one's moral development.[42] The consequence is that, in Socrates' opinion, political involvement is a misuse of one's energies, if one falls short of moral expertise.[43]

Now, suppose we asked Socrates to consider not only the best interests of his followers but the best interests of Athens as well. After all, in the *Crito* (51a7–b4) he agrees that a citizen should treat his parent-city better than he treats his mother and father; and if a child should care for his elderly parents when they are ill,[44] then similarly a citizen ought to show some measure of concern for his city if its affairs are badly conducted. So Socrates cannot afford to say that the welfare of his city is of no concern to him. But doesn't this lead him to a difficulty? Won't he have to admit that Athens would be better governed by his followers than by the many? Were his admirers in power, the city would be governed by men who believe that injustice must never be done. And surely that would be a significant improvement over democracy? Apparently, Socrates is committed to conflicting policies: when he considers the well-being of his friends, he cannot advise them to pursue political careers; but this is the advice he must give them, if he considers the best interests of his city.

good action, and happiness are identical. Similarly, *Crito* 48b8–9 identifies living well and living justly. For the view that according to Socrates virtue is good only as a means, see Irwin, *Plato's Moral Theory*, pp. 71–86, esp. 84–85. Part of his case depends on *Lysis* 219c1–220b5, where Socrates says that whatever is good for the sake of something *different* (my emphasis on *heteron*: 220b1) is not good in itself. This would not commit Socrates to the view that virtue is merely an instrumental good, even if he thinks that virtue is for the sake of happiness. For virtue is not, in his opinion, something *other than* happiness.

[42] If ruling made the ruler more virtuous, then Socrates could not say (*Rep.* 347b9–d2) that a good man will not want to rule for its own sake. A good man, as Socrates conceives him, should want to do anything that makes himself better.

[43] This conclusion is explicitly drawn at *Grg.* 514a5–515b4. Socrates says here that one should not put oneself forward as a public servant until one has perfected one's abilities in private life. He returns to this point at the close of the dialogue (527d2–5). In *Alc.* I, Socrates tries to dissuade his favorite from entering a political career before he has been properly educated in virtue. See esp. 118b4–c2, 132b1–3. However, this is not a dialogue whose status as a genuine work of Plato's is assured.

[44] Athenian law allowed adult children to be prosecuted by their parents for neglect. See MacDowell, *The Law in Classical Athens*, p. 92; Harrison, *The Law of Athens*, Vol. I, pp. 77–78.

I think that Socrates' moral philosophy provides him with a way out of this apparent dilemma. He believes that he and his admirers lack a satisfactory definition of the virtues, and this means that they have no standard for deciding how to act in difficult cases. Now, in many situations one will not need such a standard, for the right way to behave will be obvious to any sane adult. For example, though Socrates has no definition of the virtues, he thinks there is good reason to believe that violence against one's parents is always wrong.[45] And in many cases, normal adults will have no trouble identifying violent acts. But sometimes common sense does not give adequate guidance: the problem facing Euthyphro, for example, is of this sort, and Socrates thinks that in these cases it would be enormously helpful to know what virtue is. Perhaps in private life the number of hard cases is not very large.[46] But in public life the decisions that must be made are far more complex,[47] and unless one is a moral expert one will often go wrong, even if

[45] He has good reason to *believe* this, but the Socrates of the *Meno* (71b3–4), Book I of the *Republic* (354a12–c3), and the *Gorgias* (509a4–5) would not claim that he *knows* this. For in these works Socrates believes that, since he lacks a definition of the virtues, he cannot *know* propositions about them. These passages will be discussed more fully in VIII.8. Cf. Irwin, *Plato's Moral Theory*, pp. 40–41, 294 n. 4.

[46] Socrates implies that his withdrawal from conventional politics has not protected him from the possibility that he might commit unjust acts. For he says that he has never *voluntarily* committed an injustice (*Ap.* 25e5–26a4, 37a5–6; *Grg.* 488a2–4), and this "voluntarily" is pointless if he is not entertaining the possibility that in difficult cases he has sometimes committed unjust acts, because of his moral inexpertise. Socrates does claim to be a good man (*Ap.* 30c8–d1, *Grg.* 521b4–6), but this does not mean that he is perfect; a good man can do the wrong thing in hard cases, in spite of his good intentions. It would be far more difficult for Socrates to justify his claim that he is virtuous, if he conceded that, for all he can tell, he may have frequently committed wrongful acts. And there is no reason why he has to make such a concession. He can plausibly claim that those who lead apolitical lives only occasionally encounter cases in which they simply cannot tell, one way or the other, what is the right thing to do.

[47] I take this to be so obvious that we could plausibly attribute it to Socrates even if it had no textual support. But notice that at *Euthyd.* 281b4–d1, Socrates says that if one lacks wisdom, it is better to have fewer rather than more of the other so-called goods. For one will go wrong on fewer occasions if one is less able to act, and to have fewer "goods" is to be capable of fewer acts. Whatever we think of this reasoning, it commits Socrates to the highly plausible view that those who have political power without wisdom will commit more injustice than private persons who lack wisdom.

one has the best of intentions. A state ruled by well-meaning people who lack the moral standards provided by definitions would enact many bad laws and pursue many unjust policies. Granted, since these rulers would always want to act justly, they might commit fewer injustices than the many. For in some situations, the many will do what they recognize to be unjust, whereas Socrates' followers would go wrong only because of their lack of an adequate moral standard. But the difference between a democracy and an oligarchy of Socratic admirers would not be a great one. Both would be bad governments, and it would not be worth the effort to replace one by the other. Were Socrates' followers to seek political power, they would have no time for moral inquiry—a great loss; yet they would do Athens little good—a small gain. So, the balance of reasons favors a private life. If Socrates advocates such a withdrawal from politics, it is not because he gives no weight at all to the well-being of Athens—he obviously cares for his city—but because he thinks that those who fall short of moral expertise can do the city so little good by holding public office.[48]

If my working hypothesis is correct, then Socrates was no active opponent of democracy, nor was he a partisan of the aristocratic political faction that existed in Athens.[49] He was a critic of democracy, and he thought that under the right conditions the democratic government of Athens should be replaced by something better. But he thought that those conditions would not exist until a few individuals had become moral experts. He advocated withdrawal from politics, but not be-

[48] Xenophon gives the opposite picture: he portrays Socrates as someone who advises his followers to pursue political careers. At *Mem.* II vi 26, Socrates urges Critobulus to join forces with other aristocrats (*kaloi kagathoi*); at III vi 1-18, he chastises Glaucon for his lack of familiarity with the factual details needed by the politically powerful; and at III vii 1-9, he criticizes Charmides for holding back from a political career and leaving the field to mere craftsmen.

[49] Here I depart from Wood and Wood, *Class Ideology*. They claim (p. 97) that Socrates was trying "to regenerate morally the affluent and aristocratic youth who one day might hold the reins of power in a reconstituted Athenian order." Though this statement is supported by Xenophon's portrait of Socrates, it conflicts with Plato's. Wood and Wood fail to realize that to support their interpretation of Socrates, they have to show that Xenophon is more reliable as a historical source than Plato. My interpretation is close to that of Maier, *Sokrates*, pp. 421-424.

cause he was indifferent to the welfare of the city nor because he thought that politics is a waste of effort in all circumstances. If a few individuals ever became moral experts, then the city would benefit enormously from their holding office, for they would have a standard by which to make difficult decisions. And such individuals would profit from ruling the state, for in doing so they would no longer have to risk suffering injustice at the hands of ordinary rulers.

5
Sparta, Crete, and Athens

I would now like to return to a passage that we examined in Chapter VI. The Laws say to Socrates:

> . . . You had seventy years in which you could have gone away if we did not satisfy you. . . . But you preferred neither Sparta nor Crete, which you frequently say are well governed, nor any other Greek or foreign city, and you made fewer visits outside the city than do the lame, blind, or others who are crippled. In this way, it is clear that the city and we, the Laws, have especially satisfied you, of all Athenians. For whom could the city satisfy, apart from its laws? (*Crito* 52e3–53a5)

But unfortunately, they do not say *why* Socrates so frequently referred to Sparta and Crete as well-governed cities. What was it about them that he so admired? The question is especially perplexing because these cities did not allow their citizens to be exposed to the moral questioning that Socrates thought essential to a well-lived life. They were, in Popper's phrase, "closed societies."[50] Spartan citizens, for example, were not allowed to live abroad, lest they be corrupted by foreign ideas;[51] for the same reasons, visitors to Sparta were tightly controlled[52] and periodically expelled.[53] A Spartan boy, from the age of seven

---

[50] *The Open Society*, pp. 173, 182.
[51] Plutarch, *Life of Lycurgus* 27; Xenophon, *Lac. Pol.* 14.
[52] Plato, *H. Ma.* 283b4–286a2; Plutarch, *Life of Lycurgus* 9.
[53] Plutarch, *Life of Lycurgus* 27.

onwards, would have been exposed to no ideas other than those sanctioned by the ministers of public education and others who were assigned to watch over him.[54] They couldn't even enter the marketplace until they were thirty.[55] How could Socrates, the great marketplace iconoclast and advocate of the examined life, have called such a society well governed?

Popper's response to this problem is to throw out the line that creates our difficulty.[56] He suggests that the reference to Socrates' kind words for Sparta and Crete was not a genuine part of the original dialogue. Rather, it was added at some later time by an admirer of these cities—perhaps by Plato himself. But no editor has ever suspected this line on philological grounds, and it is of course a dangerous policy simply to throw out lines that conflict with one's preferred interpretation. Furthermore, as we saw in the preceding chapter (VI.7), the lines in question fit their context perfectly. The Laws need to justify the inference from residence to satisfaction, and therefore they point out that Socrates was not forced, tricked, or rushed into a decision to remain in Athens. They realize, however, that someone might remain in his native city merely because he thinks all other cities are poorly governed, and so they point out that Socrates has frequently called Sparta and Crete well governed. If we throw out this remark, as Popper suggests, we diminish the quality of the Crito's argument. Rather than dismiss 52e5-6 as an interpolation, the cautious and responsible policy is to see whether we can explain Socrates' admiration for Sparta and Crete.

There are other questions, equally perplexing, that we must face. Socrates concedes that he prefers Athens to all other cities; in fact, he is more satisfied with it than is any other Athenian. Yet the laws of Athens give power to the majority, and therefore the orders given by the city to its citizens are in effect

---

[54] Plutarch, ibid. 16-17, 24-25; Xenophon, Lac. Pol. 3-6. Demosthenes 20.106 says that the Spartans were prohibited from praising the laws of Athens and other powerful cities. Similarly, the Athenian stranger in Plato's Laws (634d7-e4) says that in Crete no young person was allowed to criticize the legal system.

[55] Plutarch, Life of Lycurgus 25.

[56] The Open Society, pp. 304-305 n. 53.

commands of the many.[57] As we have seen, Socrates has no respect for the moral integrity or wisdom of the many, and he abides by a theory of political loyalty that justifies disobedience to the city. Why then does he count himself one of the great admirers of Athenian law? Why was such a critic of democracy so pleased with so radical a democracy? Which features of the Athenian legal system attracted him so much? Are they features characteristic of democracy, or can they be found in many different political systems, democratic or not? When we answer these questions, we will see that Popper is in a way on the right track: Socrates is a democrat of sorts, though he is far from being the sort of democrat Popper thinks he is.

Before we move on, I want to emphasize the fact that my discussion will be relying on a number of assumptions that were defended earlier: (A) When the *Crito* says at 53a4–5 that no one can be satisfied with a city apart from its laws, it means that no one can be satisfied with a city unless he is satisfied with its laws. (See VI.9.) (B) The dialogue must also be assuming that if Socrates is more satisfied with city X than with city Y, that is because he is more satisfied with the laws of X than with the laws of Y. Accordingly, he must have been more satisfied with the laws of Athens than he was with the laws of any other city. (See VI.9.) (C) When the *Crito* alludes to the laws concerning marriage and childrearing, it is not trying to back up its later claim that Socrates has been satisfied with the city. Rather, the Laws are putting forward an argument for loyalty that has nothing to do with satisfaction or agreement. (See II.8.) When they go on to claim that Socrates was satisfied with the city, they cite behavioral signs of satisfaction (VI.8), but they do not state his reasons for being so pleased. No doubt, Socrates believed that the statutes regulating marriage and education were good ones, but the *Crito* does not cite them when it argues that he was satisfied with Athens. And we should notice that the Laws are not making the modest claim that Socrates found something or other to like in Athens. Rather, they believe that like every other citizen he has looked at the way the city con-

---

[57] The point is emphasized by Callicles (*Grg.* 483b4–6) and accepted by Socrates (488d5–489a1).

ducts its legal business, and that on balance he has a highly favorable attitude to its legal system. We cannot hope—and the Laws do not try—to explain that attitude merely by appealing to his appreciation for the laws regarding marriage and education. Some other important feature or features of Athenian laws must have deeply pleased Socrates, and to investigate this possibility we must look beyond the *Crito*, to other early dialogues.

6
Conventional virtue and Socratic criticism

According to the *Crito*, a citizen who has passed his *dokimasia* goes through a stage during which he evaluates the laws and institutions of his native city. He asks himself whether the city is satisfactorily governed, and he is free to go elsewhere if he is dissatisfied. Socrates went through this period of evaluation, and for the remainder of his life he never changed his mind: he has been greatly satisfied with the laws of Athens. Now, what criterion would we expect Socrates to use when he asks himself whether the laws of his city are doing a good job? Surely, as he pondered the merits of the Athenian legal system, the question uppermost in his mind must have been this: do these laws, so far as they can, foster the virtue of the citizens? If he had thought that the institutions of Athenian democracy performed badly in this area, then he would have condemned his native city and declared himself dissatisfied with its laws. No matter how wealthy, powerful, or renowned Athens was, Socrates would not have admired it merely for these qualities. He condemns powerful and reputable people for their lack of wisdom, and he thinks that the proper role of a city is to promote the wisdom and virtue of its citizens. Thus he says in the *Euthydemus* that the craft whose job it is to rule over the city (the "royal craft," *basilikē technē*) must make the citizens wise; its aim is not wealth or freedom or harmony—for these goals might be bad or good—but wisdom (292b4-c1). And in the *Gorgias*, he condemns the outstanding leaders of fifth-century Athens—Pericles, Cimon, Miltiades, and Themistocles—because they pandered to the desires of the people but failed to make them more

virtuous (515b6–517c4). Evidently, Socrates uses a single, narrow test to evaluate politicians, private individuals, and cities:
how much virtue do they have or promote?[58]

Is there any evidence that according to Socrates the laws of
Athens make its citizens more virtuous? We do have excellent
evidence that he thinks the young are improved by Athenian
law. At *Apology* 24d3–10, he challenges one of his prosecutors,
Meletus, to say who it is that improves the young men of the
city. Meletus at first replies, "the laws" (24d11), but Socrates
does not allow this as an answer to his question; he wants to
know which particular citizens make the young better (24e1–2).
As it turns out, Meletus is willing to say that everyone in public
life—everyone but Socrates—improves the young (24e3–25a11),
and he is therefore quickly discredited. Now, notice that Socrates has made no objection whatever to Meletus' initial reply:
he agrees that the laws of the city do make the young better.
Why does he accept this point? The speech of the Laws in the
Crito tells us what he has in mind. By urging parents to educate
their children in music and gymnastics, the laws do as much as
they possibly can for the well-being of the citizens (50d8–e1,
51c8–d1). As the Great Speech of Protagoras makes clear, the
traditional Greek training in music and gymnastics is intended
to serve an ethical purpose: through songs and physical exercises, the children develop a sense of right and wrong (*Protag.*
325d7–326c3; cf. *Rep.* 398c1–402a7). Evidently, Socrates has no
quarrel with the Protagorean view that a valuable training in
virtue begins at the earliest stages of life, and that a young adult

---

[58] At *Euphr.* 2c2–3a5, Socrates praises Meletus for concerning himself with
the virtue of the citizens: that is the proper task of a politician, and it is a good
strategy to start with the young, and to turn to the older citizens at a later time.
Of course, Socrates is hiding his contempt for Meletus behind a mask of praise.
But he is perfectly sincere when he says that politicians should concern themselves with the moral development of their fellow citizens. This is precisely the
point he is making in the *Gorgias* and the *Euthydemus* (passages cited above). At
Protag. 319a3–5, Socrates calls the task of making men good citizens "the political craft," and he equates this with teaching virtue. Evidently, he assumes
throughout the early dialogues that the proper use of political power is to make
the citizens as virtuous as possible. In the *Apology*, he never says a bad word
about the law against corrupting the young. For he sees no reason why a city
should not have such a law.

who has received a conventional moral education is far better off than he was before. That is why Socrates agrees with Meletus that the laws improve the young, and that is why he applauds the speech of the Laws in the *Crito*. He agrees with the Laws that a young person ought to be grateful to his parents and his city for the great good he has received in the form of a conventional moral education. Such an education has not, of course, made the young person completely virtuous—far from it. But it has brought him through the elementary stages of a training in virtue.[59]

We should not be surprised or puzzled by the fact that according to Socrates conventional moral training is something worthwhile. For although this low-level inculcation of the virtues is unsystematic and contains many important falsehoods, it also contains a large stock of truths. Certainly someone who has acquired this conventional bundle of attitudes is better off than he would be if he were devoid of moral ideas, or if the vast majority of his beliefs about the good were false. Of course, Socrates insists that someone who has received this traditional training and nothing more is still at a very low stage of moral development. Against Protagoras, he insists that a virtuous adult should examine and systematize his moral beliefs, a process that requires the rejection of false ideas acquired in one's early training. Protagoras argues that unreflective habit and conventional behavior are all there is to virtue; in the dialogue that bears his name, he unsuccessfully tries to defeat the Socratic doctrine that since virtue is knowledge it requires a systematic study that surpasses and corrects our ordinary moral intuitions. Socrates wants to transform a conventional moral training into something better, but he does not urge us to reject all conventional virtue and start from scratch.

So Socrates definitely believes that Athenian law improves the young. But does he also believe that the laws foster the

[59] When Socrates says that the many corrupt their children (*Ap*. 25a13-b6: the passage cited in [B], Sec. 1), he must be thinking of the false beliefs they inculcate; when he agrees, in the *Crito*, that citizens owe their parents and their city a great debt for the education they have received, he must be thinking of the true beliefs they have acquired. There is no real conflict between these passages.

virtue of those who are beyond childhood? I suggest that this would be a natural position for him to take. After all, he thinks that a person is benefited if he adds to his stock of true beliefs about good and bad; and surely an Athenian citizen will continue to acquire many correct moral beliefs as he passes beyond his childhood and comes to understand the law. As we saw earlier, the citizen first begins to learn about the city's laws when he passes his *dokimasia* and enters into adulthood. A new set of rules is now addressed to him—rules that govern marriage, the family, property, religion, and daily life in the adult world. Assuming that many of these norms are unobjectionable, and assuming that the citizen genuinely accepts them, he will be adding to his stock of true moral beliefs as he learns the law. Here too, Protagoras makes the point explicit:

> When [the young] are finished with their teachers, the city in its turn requires them to learn the laws and to live according to the pattern they provide, so that they don't recklessly go off on their own. This is the way writing instructors treat children who don't yet know how to write. They draw lines with a style and then give them the tablet and make them write, using the lines as a guide. So too the city draws up the laws, which were devised by the good men of long ago. It requires us to rule and be ruled in accordance with them, and it punishes whoever steps outside them . . . (326c6–d8)

I see no reason why Socrates should not accept this. Since he believes that music and gymnastics improve the young by inculcating a large number of true beliefs, he presumably accepts the further point that the laws, in many cases, provide the citizens with correct standards of behavior. Here, as before, Socrates has no wish to reject all conventional moral beliefs. As he is reminded in the *Crito*, he has always upheld the belief that ". . . virtue and justice are worth most of all among men, along with what is lawful and the laws" (53c7–8). This does not mean, of course, that Socrates will blindly accept the orders or the laws of his city; we have seen in the preceding chapters that he has a more sophisticated position than that. Nonetheless, it is

entirely accurate for Socrates to think of himself as an upholder
of the laws. He thinks that in Athens the law is in many cases
a correct guide to behavior. So the law continues to play a role
in the education of the citizens, even beyond childhood.

I think we can now see why Socrates so often says that Sparta
and Crete are well governed. He is not, in my opinion, claiming that their political institutions (e.g. kings, ephors, elders,
etc. in Sparta) are admirable, but he is saying that they do a
good job of inculcating a system of moral beliefs, and that many
(not all) of those beliefs are correct. In these societies more than
any others, the life of the individual, both in childhood and
adulthood, was regulated by law. In other words, Sparta and
Crete went to greater lengths than other Greek cities to mold
the individual's conception of right and wrong; and since Socrates believes that conventional morality contains a great many
truths, he has a good reason to use Sparta and Crete as models
of well-governed communities. The main job of the city is to
arrange for the teaching of virtue, and the first stage of that job
is to inculcate a large stock of true moral beliefs. That low-level
process of education is precisely where Sparta and Crete excel.[60]

---

[60] Cf. Aristotle's remark (*N.E.* 1102a8-11) that ". . . the real political expert
seems to be trained best of all in this area [i.e. virtue]. For he wants to make
the citizens good and obedient to the laws. We have, as examples of this, the
lawgivers of Crete and Sparta. . . ." At *N.E.* 1180a24-28 he says, "Only in the
city of the Spartans, along with a few others, does the lawgiver seem to have
made a study of education (*trophē*) and proper pursuits (*epitēdeumata*). In most
cities, no care is taken on these matters, and each lives however he wants. . . ."
Presumably, the cities of Crete are among these few others. Notice that elsewhere (*E.E.* 1248b37-1249a16, *Pol.* 1271b7-10) Aristotle criticizes the Spartans
because they pursue virtue only for the sake of other goods. So he praises their
laws because they *attempt* to mold a virtuous character; but since a virtuous
person, according to Aristotle, must choose virtue for itself and not as a means
to other goods (*N.E.* 1105a31-32), he cannot believe that the Spartan lawgiver
has *succeeded* in molding a virtuous character. Similarly, Socrates is praising
Sparta and Crete for paying serious attention to the most important political
problem: how to make men good. But obviously he cannot believe that these
cities solved the problem. See too *H. Ma.* 283e9-284a2: Socrates says that Sparta
is well governed (*eunomos*) and that in well-governed cities virtue is most highly
regarded. One further remark of Aristotle should be noticed: "There is no
eunomia if the laws are established well, but are not obeyed. Therefore, one
form of *eunomia* must be assumed to be obedience to the laws that have been
established; another form consists in well-established laws that are obeyed; for
there is such a thing as obedience to badly-established laws" (*Pol.* 1294a3-7).

There is no need, as Popper thought, to regard Socrates' kind words for Sparta and Crete as an interpolation.

We should notice, incidentally, that the Laws of the *Crito* say (53b4–5) that two other cities are well governed: Thebes and Megara. (These were the cities to which many Athenian democrats escaped when the Thirty were in power.)[61] And they mention one part of Greece that was definitely not well governed: Thessaly, the place to which Crito had urged Socrates to flee. "Great disorder [*ataxia*] and lack of discipline [*akolasia*] are there . . ." (53d3–4), the Laws remind Socrates. These terms of disapproval indicate that in Thessaly you had a good chance of doing what you liked and getting away with it; *ataxia* and *akolasia* here serve as opposites of *eunomia*. So it is likely that the Laws and Socrates are using the same standard of judgment: Sparta, Crete, Thebes, and Megara are all law-abiding communities, and that is why they are said to be well governed. Though they have different political institutions, they all exert a strong influence on the moral beliefs of their citizens.

What of Athens? We know that Socrates criticizes his fellow citizens for unjustifiably disobeying the law on many occasions. Recall the statement he makes to his jurors: ". . . No man will be spared if he opposes you or any other multitude [*plēthos*] and prevents many unjust and illegal things from happening in the city . . ." (31e2–4). He then goes on to illustrate his point: the generals at the battle of Arginusae were tried by the Assembly as a group, even though the law required a separate trial for each. Evidently, the Athenian majority is too willing to disregard the procedural rules that restrict its power. And we need look no further than Crito's escape plan to see another example of Athenian willingness to break the law. When they had to decide between the conflicting claims of the city on the one hand, and friends and family on the other, many Athenians felt

---

(Cf. the pseudo-Platonic definition of *eunomia* as "obedience to good laws," at *Def.* 413e1.) It is easy to see why Socrates might take Sparta to be *eunomos* in both ways. For its citizens were extremely law-abiding, as Aristotle himself attests in 1102a8–11, cited above (cf. Xenophon, *Lac. Pol.* 8; Herodotus VII 104). And Socrates must have believed that the laws were *well* established, since they encouraged the citizens to hold the virtues in great honor.

[61] See Sealey, *A History of the Greek City-States*, p. 382.

torn, and some decided to break the law.[62] It is therefore understandable that Socrates looks outside of Athens, to Sparta
and Crete, for paradigms of law-abiding communities. In those
cities, there is a tighter connection than in Athens between what
the law requires and what the citizens decide, collectively and
individually. But we should not exaggerate the point: although
Socrates does think that there is a significant amount of unjustified lawlessness in Athens, he never characterizes it in the way
the Laws of the *Crito* characterize Thessaly. He never says that
Athens is a land of disorder and license. After all, Athenian law
did see to it that the children of citizens were given a proper
moral training. In addition, as I have suggested, there must
have been many areas—religion, family relations, property, injury, and assault—in which Athenian adults got their moral ideas
from the law, and took the law as a correct guide to behavior.
So my guess is that, in the mind of Socrates, Athens occupied
a middle ground: the law did not have as much power over its
citizens' ideas and behavior as it did elsewhere, but nonetheless
its influence was far from negligible. It was not a lawless land,
like Thessaly, nor was it a paradigm of law and order, like
Sparta.

Even though Socrates uses Sparta and Crete, rather than Athens, as his common examples of well-regulated communities—
i.e. as paradigms of *eunomia*—he nonetheless prefers Athens.
And as we saw in Chapter VI, he prefers it precisely because of
its legal system. To understand why, he should remind ourselves once again of the narrow test by which Socrates must
evaluate cities and citizens: how much virtue do they have or
promote? If the Athenian legal system is more satisfactory to
Socrates than any other, that must be because Athens does a
better job of promoting the virtue of its citizens than does any
other city. And Athens excels at this task in spite of the fact
that it is not as law-abiding a city as several others. How is this
possible?

I think that what Socrates has in mind is this: what Sparta
and Crete do very well, and Athens less well, is to get their

---

[62] Connor, *The New Politicians of Fifth-Century Athens*, pp. 47-53.

citizens through the elementary stages of moral education. They acquire a large and unsystematic stock of moral beliefs, many of them true and many false. If a city is to do more for its citizens than that, it must in some way get them beyond that elementary stage, or it must foster the conditions under which further moral progress can be made. But what is the next stage of moral development? It is important to recall at this point that according to Socrates a person will never make progress in a subject unless he is shocked into recognizing his ignorance. This idea is presented most clearly and explicitly in the *Meno*: the slave is far better off once he realizes that his common-sense intuitions about geometry have misled him. ". . . Now he would be glad to inquire, being someone who does not know, but before he thought that he could easily and frequently speak well to the many about the square of double size . . ." (84b10-c1). Socrates is obviously alluding to the ethical implications of his geometrical experiment. The way to go beyond conventional *paideia* is to recognize its inconsistencies, and in the *Apology* Socrates credits himself with having forced many of his fellow citizens to make this painful discovery. He does not present himself as someone who tried to help the city but failed; rather, he thinks he is the city's greatest benefactor—a gift from the god (30a5-7, 30d5-31a7)—and he says that he deserves free meals in the Prytaneum because of what he has accomplished (36d1-37a1). Why does he congratulate himself in this way, if he realizes that he has converted very few to the basic principles of Socratic morality? How has he benefited the city, if most of its citizens do not and never will see the light? Socrates would reply that a person who is bothered by difficulties in his moral views has, by this very fact, acquired more wisdom than someone who is satisfied with merely conventional *paideia*. Just as ordinary moral education, with all its limitations, is a great gift we receive from our parents and the city, so moral perplexity, for all its painfulness, is the gift Socrates thinks he is giving Athens. There is an important political lesson to be drawn from these elementary points: if the laws of a city make it possible for citizens to see defects in their early education, then that city will be better governed, by Socratic standards, than a city in which conventional virtue is all that citizens can attain.

Now, how can laws bring individuals to that higher intellectual stage? A statute cannot participate in conversation, nor can a political figure engage in dialectic with a large audience. The hard work of challenging ordinary moral views can only be done by individuals; the best that laws can do is to allow this activity to go on. And that must be the reason why Socrates is more satisfied with the laws of Athens than with the laws of any other city. Athens, like most other cities, encourages the development of conventional beliefs about the virtues—the basic stock without which there could be no further progress. But it has an additional attraction in that it leaves its adult citizens free to make improvements in that ordinary moral training. Because Athenian democracy tolerated unorthodox speech and moral criticism, Socrates was at liberty to stand in the marketplace all day and challenge the conventional wisdom. As Dover has said recently, "Tolerance of the free expression of intellectual criticism was at most times and in most circumstances a predominant characteristic of Athenian society."[63] And of course, Socrates was quite conscious of this feature of Athenian law. He tells Polus, as he tries to restrain him from making a long speech rather than a short reply: "You would be badly treated, my good man, if upon arriving in Athens, where there is more freedom to speak than anywhere in Greece, you alone should fail to get any" (461e1-3, cf. *Meno* 80b4-7). Of course, such figures as Protagoras, Gorgias, Callicles, and Thrasymachus also profited from this freedom and diversity, but Socrates thought there was no great harm in this. He rejects the common idea, espoused by Anytus in the *Meno*, that the sophists are a cor-

---

[63] "The Freedom of the Intellectual in Greek Society," p. 54. Speaking in 341, Demosthenes says (9.3) that many house-slaves in Athens have more freedom to say what they want than do the citizens of certain other cities. Unfortunately, there is no consensus about how much intellectual freedom was really available to the citizens of late fifth-century Athens. Dover, ibid., casts doubt on the evidence that the condemnation of Socrates was part of a general pattern of intellectual persecution in the late fifth century. For a less skeptical attitude toward the ancient testimony, see Dodds, *The Greeks and the Irrational*, pp. 189-192; Kerferd, *The Sophistic Movement*, pp. 20-22. I side with Dover: for if the laws of Athens were being used to stifle intellectual inquiry, as Dodds and Kerferd believe, then why was Socrates so satisfied with the legal system?

rupting influence (91b2-92c6).[64] In fact, Socrates welcomed the visits of Gorgias and Protagoras, for his conversations with them and their disciples allowed him to subject his own moral system to the most rigorous examination.[65] Yet he denied that any of them had the power to make their listeners or students more virtuous. Socrates was convinced that he was the only figure of the day who was giving Athens the medicine it needed—he alone was improving the citizens by cross-examination. As he says in the *Gorgias*, he is the only one to "undertake the real political craft and practice politics . . ." (521d6-8). He thinks that the real job of the politician is to make the citizens better, and he arrives at the conclusion that Athens is the best governed city because it allows someone like himself to go about his business.[66] The freedom Athens gave its citizens, which so horrified Plato in the *Republic* (557b4-558c1), is the very thing that made Socrates prefer it to any other legal system.

This freedom, of course, was not constitutionally guaranteed: there was no law in Athens that even remotely resembled the first amendment of the American Constitution. The intellectual freedom enjoyed by the Athenians consisted in the absence of restrictive law, rather than in the guarantee of a right. That is, there were no laws in Athens, as there were in Sparta and Crete, that stifled the free flow of ideas. It is useful to recall here what the *Crito* says (51d1-e1) about the Athenian's freedom to depart permanently from his native city. This freedom was not guaranteed by some particular law, but merely resulted from the

[64] See too *Protag*. 357e2-8. Socrates thinks that his fellow citizens have no good grounds for refusing to have their sons educated by the sophists. Typically, they reason: "Since wise men like Pericles could not find teachers of virtue for his sons, virtue cannot be taught. And in any case, even if it could be taught, our knowledge of virtue would still be overcome by pleasure." This passage is more fully discussed in VIII.13.

[65] See *Grg*. 486d2-487e7, 527a8-b2. Socrates does not mean in these passages that Gorgias, Polus, or Callicles can pass his strictest tests for wisdom and therefore deserve to be called wise. They cannot rationally sustain their conception of how to live, nor have they even attempted to give satisfactory definitions of the virtues. Nonetheless, when he calls them wise, he is not paying them an empty compliment. They are smart men, by ordinary standards, and that is why Socrates finds it especially valuable to test his views by arguing with them.

[66] For further discussion of *Grg*. 521d6-8, see n. 76 below and Ch. VIII n. 80.

absence of legal prohibitions. What a legal system fails to prohibit is no less important than what it requires, and therefore
the silence of the laws on a given matter may turn out to be
one of their great virtues. Athenian law permitted philosophical
activity and moral criticism to a degree unparalleled by any
other Greek city, and it surely was this "negative" feature of
the legal system that made Socrates one of the great admirers
of his native city.

To summarize: According to Socrates, there were two ways
in which cities fostered the virtue of their citizens. First, they
saw to it that children and adults received a conventional moral
education. This is something achieved by many Greek cities,
including Athens, Thebes, Megara, Sparta, and Crete, although
in this area Sparta and Crete excelled because they achieved a
higher degree of social control. Second, by tolerating the free
criticism of moral ideas, a city could allow its citizens to remedy the defects of a conventional moral education. Here Athens
excelled, while Sparta and Crete did not even try. Socrates is
more satisfied with Athens than is any other Athenian citizen
because he values, exploits, and profits from Athenian intellectual freedom more than anyone else. He prefers Athens to any
other city because its legal system made it easiest for individuals
to recognize their ignorance and to move beyond the elementary stages of their moral education. ". . . The unexamined life
is not worth living . . ." (38a5-6), and the intellectual freedom
Athens allowed its citizens made it the city in which such a life
could most easily be lived. The many would never rid themselves of false beliefs, but someone who will never see the truth
is nonetheless raised to a higher level by entertaining doubts
about his false beliefs. That is why Socrates believes that every
citizen can benefit from the city's tolerance.[67]

[67] My account of Socrates' attitude toward Athens should be compared with
Guthrie's, *History*, Vol. III, p. 413: "Living under a democracy, his principles
made him loyal to its laws, and his native Athens had penetrated too deeply
into his bones to make the choice of emigration possible. How could Socrates,
of all people, desert the most intellectually alive of all Greek cities where he
could meet and argue with men of every shade of opinion, the magnet which
attracted *sophistai* like Protagoras, Gorgias, Prodicus and Anaxagoras, the home
of Euripides and Aristophanes, the place where he could gather around him a
brilliant circle of younger men like Antisthenes and Plato? For preference, he
never went outside its walls (*Phaedr.* 230c-d). That being so, he must obey the

7

Four stages of moral development

In the preceding section, I distinguished two stages of moral development: the acquisition of a conventional moral education, and the recognition of grave defects in that education.

---

laws, a course not inconsistent with a profound disapproval of the way the city was governed in his latter days." Note these differences between Guthrie and me: (A) I do not attribute to Socrates the view that if you have chosen to remain in a certain city, then you must obey its laws. For one may remain without agreeing to every law (see VI.8 and 10), and even when one has agreed to a law, one may break the agreement if it requires injustice (see II.2). (B) Guthrie attributes to Socrates "a profound disapproval of the way the city was governed in his latter days." But he does not try to reconcile this statement with the claim, made by the Laws, that Socrates, more than any other citizen, was satisfied with the city's legal system. Guthrie seems to be saying that Socrates was pleased with the intellectual and cultural preeminence of Athens, but disliked its laws. But the *Crito* forbids such an interpretation, since it says that no one can be satisfied with a city unless he is satisfied with its laws (53a4-5). (See VI.9.) Guthrie makes no attempt to show how Socrates' attitude toward virtue leads to his satisfaction with Athenian law. (C) It is true that Athens attracted such sophists as Protagoras, Gorgias, and Prodicus, and as we have seen (n. 65 above), Socrates values his encounters with these men. But this cannot explain his unusual reluctance to leave Athens, for these itinerant teachers visited many other Greek cities, and if Socrates had wanted to, he could have visited them abroad, or even have followed them from place to place. His refusal to do so is best explained by his native city's unusual tolerance for free speech. Had Socrates lived elsewhere, he still could have talked with the sophists, but his own moral investigations could not have been as openly hostile to popular prejudice. The sophists, being more conventional thinkers, were less hampered by social pressure, and so they could pursue their interests in many more cities. (D) The fact that Athens attracted Anaxagoras meant nothing to the Socrates of Plato's *Apology* (19b4-d7): whether or not he was once interested in natural science (*Phd.* 96a6-d6), he no longer is so. And his derogatory attitude toward poetry (*Ion* 533c4-535a2, 541c10-542b4; *Protag.* 347c3-348a6) must have made him indifferent to the fact that Athens sponsored brilliant dramatic festivals. (E) Socrates did "gather around him a brilliant circle of younger men like Antisthenes and Plato." But would they have followed him if he had left Athens? If so, we still need an explanation of why he did not leave. If they would not have followed him, that hardly seems an adequate explanation of why he did not leave. What is missing from Guthrie's account is a fact about Socrates that stares us in the face when we read the *Apology*: he is devoted to the general improvement of the citizenry, and not merely to the intellectual enlightenment of a coterie of admirers. (See esp. 29d1-30b4, 33a1-b3, 39c3-d8.) His mission is to challenge the moral beliefs of *anyone who will listen*. His refusal to accept exile can only be explained by the fact that if Athens, with all its freedom, is not going to tolerate his open iconoclasm, then neither will any other city. He stays in Athens as much as he can because this is the city which is most likely to be roused and changed by his moral questioning.

Earlier (in Section 4), I claimed that Socrates does not take himself to be a fully virtuous person; in other words, he does not
think that he has reached the final stage of moral development.
So, if we put these two sections together, we have a threefold
division:

(a) Many Athenians have acquired a conventional moral
education, but they do not recognize its deficiencies.

(b) Some Athenians have acquired a conventional moral
education, but they do recognize its deficiencies.

(c) Socrates postulates an ideal of moral development—one
that has not yet been reached—in which one acquires a
standard for resolving even the most difficult moral problems.

It will be useful, however, if we make a further division within
category (b). For (b) is so broad as to include both Socrates and
anyone who has just begun to feel the force of Socratic questioning. And surely the major differences between two such
individuals need to be observed. Someone who has only recently recognized his ignorance will be unable to do many of
the things Socrates can do. Socrates can defend his moral convictions in argument, has subjected them to the criticism of
some of the cleverest people alive, and is adept at discovering
the inconsistencies of others. He has come to understand the
oracle's pronouncement that no one is wiser than he (21a4-7),
and he regards himself as the greatest benefactor Athens has
ever had.[68] Surely we are not distorting matters if we put him
into a special category of his own, at a level below (c), but
above those who have merely escaped from (a). Of course, others
could also be placed in this special category, if they ever accomplished as much good and had as much skill in moral discussion
as Socrates.

This gives us a fourfold division:

(A) A child receives a conventional moral training, as described in the *Protagoras* and endorsed in the *Crito*. He has

[68] *Ap.* 30a5-7, 30d1-31c3, 36d1-37a1. See too Sec. 8 below, esp. nn. 82, 83:
Socrates alone can recognize a moral expert.

many true and many false beliefs, none of them systematically related. He thinks he has knowledge but does not. And he often acts incorrectly.

(B) A person is challenged by Socratic questions and loses his complacency. He sees difficulties in his firmly held beliefs, and may come to realize that his conventional moral training had its deficiencies. He cannot defend his beliefs in argument, and he realizes this.

(C) The stage Socrates has reached. He has systematized many of his beliefs and has rid himself of errors. He can defend many of his views in argument, but he is still afflicted by puzzles, the most important of which are definitional. He realizes that he has a long way to go before he completes his moral education.

(D) The stage of moral expertise. A person can define the virtues, is free from moral perplexity, and can determine how to act even in difficult situations.

In Chapter VIII, I will discuss the textual evidence that has led me to the conclusion that Socrates does not locate himself at stage (D). And I will argue that in his opinion it might well be beyond human powers to arrive at that level. Furthermore, I will try to show that according to Socrates one cannot claim to be virtuous until one reaches stage (C); and even then one's virtue is second-rate in comparison with the virtue of the fully developed person who has reached stage (D).

8
Power and knowledge

Thus far, I have argued that Socrates has two attitudes toward the government of Athens: on the one hand, he values the liberty provided by his native city; on the other, he thinks that the many cannot rule well. Athenian democracy was notable to the ancient world for its liberty and equality;[69] Socrates sees the

---

[69] These two characteristics are prominent in Plato's parody of Athenian democracy (*Rep.* 557b4-10, 558c5-6). Aristotle (*Pol.* 1310a28-34, 1317a40-b17; *N.E.* 1161a6-9, 1161b8-10) also takes them to be the preeminent features of a democracy.

merits of the former quality, but not the latter. Now, doesn't this show that the Laws are not really being accurate when they say that Socrates is greatly satisfied with his city? Shouldn't they have said that he is pleased with *one* prominent feature of the Athenian legal system, but that he is a great critic of the other? Why doesn't Plato have the Laws describe Socrates in this more balanced way? Certainly he is not trying to hide the fact that Socrates is a critic of the many: as we saw in Section 1, they are openly attacked both in the *Apology* and the *Crito*. And yet this antidemocratic side of Socrates is not even mentioned when the Laws say that he has always been greatly satisfied with his native city. Why not?

I think that Plato can be defended against the charge that he is oversimplifying or distorting the attitude Socrates adopts toward Athens. For as I have argued, Socrates thought that neither he nor his followers could have done a significantly better job than the many. He was a critic of democracy in the sense that he criticized the way the many ruled, and saw no theoretical justification for democracy. But at the same time, there was no feasible alternative that he preferred. Athens provided its citizens with precisely the conditions they needed in order to make moral progress, and that gave Socrates an overwhelming reason to be pleased with its legal system. The fact that no one as yet had demonstrated the ability to rule well was certainly not the fault of Athenian law, for laws by themselves cannot turn people into moral experts. Only individuals can discover adequate definitions of the virtues, and such a discovery was more likely to occur in Athens than in any other city, because of its legal system. So it is perfectly understandable that Socrates voices no objection when the Laws tell him that he has been greatly satisfied with the city. He thinks there is no reason why a city should *not* be ruled by the many, if no one has yet become a moral expert. And since he doubts that human beings have the capacity for moral expertise, he is all the more inclined to concede in the *Crito* that he is quite pleased with the city's legal system. It would be absurd to complain that a city does not give all power to moral expertise if one doubts that human beings can be moral experts. So, I do not believe that Plato was being inaccurate when he had the Laws tell Socrates how satisfied he was with his native city.

I take Socrates to believe that if there ever are moral experts, then they alone should have political power; they should give commands to the other citizens, and these commands ought to be obeyed. What is the evidence for interpreting him in this way? To begin with, he thinks that if anyone has definitions of the virtues, then he has a standard for determining how to act even in the most difficult cases (*Euphr*. 6e3-6). It would have been natural for Socrates to assume that anyone who possesses such a standard ought to be in a position of authority. For why should decisions be made by majority rule, when someone already knows what the outcome of those decisions should be? That is what Socrates is suggesting at *Laches* 184e8-9—a passage we looked at earlier, in Section 1. Furthermore, both the *Gorgias* and Book I of the *Republic* talk about a craft of ruling—a science that concerns itself with the well-being of the human soul—and they assume that the only person who merits political power is the one who has mastered this science.[70] Now, the *Gorgias* is generally taken to be a later work among the early dialogues; and *Republic* I, if it was not written at the same time as the rest of the dialogue, can also be plausibly placed among the later works of the early period.[71] Someone might suggest, then, that in these two works we see more of Plato's politics than of Socrates'. According to this interpretation, Socrates envisages no political role for a moral expert; it is Plato who first dreams up the idea of the philosopher-king, and he introduces this idea in the latest of the early dialogues. My own view, by contrast, is that a form of authoritarianism must be attributed to Socrates, and not just to Plato. Like Plato, he believes that if there ever are moral experts, then they will be entitled to obedience from the rest of us. As I will now try to show, this view

---

[70] *Grg.* 463d1-465e1, 503d5-504e3; *Rep.* 341c4-342e11, 345d5-347d8.

[71] On the relation of the *Gorgias* to the other dialogues, see Dodds, *Plato Gorgias*, pp. 18-24; Irwin, *Plato Gorgias*, pp. 5-8. *Rep.* I is taken to be an early dialogue by Friedländer, *Plato*, Vol. II, pp. 50-51. So too Annas, *An Introduction to Plato's Republic*, p. 17; cf. p. 47. Contrast Shorey's introductory essay to his translation of the *Republic*, p. x; and Irwin, *Plato's Moral Theory*, p. 292, point 7.

can be found in the *Apology* and the *Crito*—works that are reasonably taken to be quite early.[72] If I am correct, then we ought not say, as Popper does, that Plato's authoritarianism is a "betrayal" of Socratic values.[73] Though we may not like to admit it, Plato inherited from Socrates the idea that moral experts should rule.

Consider the following statement from the *Apology*: ". . . To do an injustice and disobey a superior [*beltion*], whether divine or human: that, I know, is bad and shameful" (29b6-7). When Socrates says this, he is in the midst of explaining to the jury that his philosophical mission is divinely ordained, and he then goes on to tell them (29c6-d5) that he would have to disobey them if their orders were to conflict with the god's. But what interests me is the fact that Socrates talks about obedience to god and to man in he same breath: the absolute submission owed to an immortal is also owed to a human superior. Now, under what conditions will Socrates say that a human being is superior? Is he thinking of military officers, magistrates, and anyone else who occupies a position of power? Certainly not, if the argument of Chapters I-VI is correct. Neither in the *Apology* nor in the *Crito* does Socrates ever commit himself to the position that political officials or the state deserve absolute submission. And so our passage from the *Apology* must mean that Socrates is prepared to obey someone who is superior to him in virtue. That interpretation fits nicely with my view that Socrates does not take himself to be a moral expert; he thinks there is a stage of moral development that he has not yet reached, and he believes that anyone who reaches that stage would be so far superior to him that he would be entitled to the same level of obedience that human beings owe the gods. Whoever becomes a moral expert will possess moral definitions that tell him precisely what to do, even in difficult situations. So it would be both bad and shameful to disobey him: bad, because it would be contrary to one's own interest; and shameful, because it would show a lack of respect and awe before a superior being.[74]

---

[72] See Ch. VIII n. 24 (the *Apology* and *Crito* were written at about the same time); and Ch. VIII n. 46 (the *Apology* is quite early).

[73] *The Open Society*, p. 194.

[74] I take *Ap*. 29b6-7 to mean that disobeying a superior is one kind of injus-

This hypothetical authoritarianism is also present in a passage from the *Crito*. I used it in Section 1 as evidence of Socrates' low opinion of the many, and now let us look at it again to see his attitude toward moral expertise. Crito is worried about what others will think of him if he does not help Socrates escape, and so Socrates tells him to respect only the opinions of the wise, and to dismiss the opinions of the many (47a2-11). For example, if we don't want our bodies to be ruined, then we must obey a doctor or a trainer; we must fear his censure and be pleased by his praise (47a13-c7). Then Socrates asks (47c9-d2): What if someone has knowledge of justice, the good, and other such matters? Shouldn't we follow him, and feel shame and fear before him? Or should we have these attitudes toward the many? Crito accepts the analogy: just as we obey experts in the non-moral spheres, so too we should obey moral experts, if there are any. Socrates does not say—here or anywhere else—that there already *are* people who have a knowledge of justice that is comparable to a doctor's or a trainer's knowledge of health.[75]

---

tice. Socrates is not mentioning two unrelated acts—doing injustice and disobeying a superior—that happen to be shameful. Rather, he thinks it a matter of justice that a superior (i.e. one who has knowledge of the relevant subject) should rule. Cf. *Grg.* 490b1-c7. Socrates agrees with Thrasymachus that as a matter of justice those who are rulers in the strict sense should be obeyed (*Rep.* 340e8-341a4); but he thinks that Thrasymachus has an inadequate conception of who the true rulers are. Since disobeying a true superior is a form of injustice, it is categorically condemned.

[75] This is also the view of Irwin, *Plato's Moral Theory*, pp. 71, 298 n. 40. Cf. Dybikowski, "Socrates, Obedience, and the Law: Plato's *Crito*," p. 520; and contrast Greenberg, "Socrates' Choice in the *Crito*," p. 56. I find it hard to understand Grote's interpretation of this passage. He says, *Plato*, Vol. I, pp. 308-309: ". . . it is he [Socrates] alone who steps in to act himself the part of professional Expert, though he does not openly assume the title. The ultimate authority is proclaimed in words to reside with some unnamed Expert: in fact and reality, he finds it in his own reason and conscience. You are not competent to judge for yourself: you must consult the professional Expert: but your own reason and conscience must signify to you who the Expert is. The analogy here produced by Plato—of questions about health and sickness—is followed out only in its negative operation: as it serves to scare away the multitude, and discredit the Vox Populi. But when this has been done, no oracular man can be produced or authenticated." Grote does not seem to be saying that in the *Crito* Socrates is portrayed as someone who believes himself to be an expert. Rather, he "steps in to act . . . the part." But what is it to assume that role? The *Crito* says that an expert is someone before whom others should feel fear and shame; he is also someone whose commands should be obeyed. Surely Socrates is not asking Crito to adopt these attitudes. The mere fact that one

He denies that he is an expert,[76] and frequently says that he lacks answers to the definitional questions he takes so seriously; nor does he ever hint that someone else has the definitions he seeks. The point he is making to Crito could be put in this way: "Your fear of what others will think of you is entirely appropriate in certain circumstances, namely, when those others have an expert's mastery of the subject in question. But the many are not experts, either in medical matters or in any other field. So stop looking up to them as though they were wise authorities, and let's discuss this question on its merits." Socrates is certainly not saying, "Take it from me, Crito, since I'm an authority on moral matters: it would be wrong to escape." For nothing in the subsequent discussion rests on an appeal to authority or expertise; even when the Laws enter the discussion, they do not claim the status of moral experts who must be obeyed in all cases. All talk of obedience, fear, and reverence in the face of expertise, so conspicuous at 47a13-d9, is dropped as soon as it has served its immediate purpose, which is to get Crito to realize that his attitude of deference to the many is utterly without justification. Surely Socrates does not think that Crito should look up to him as a moral authority and follow

person reasons toward a conclusion in a conversation with someone else does not mean that he is assuming the role of an expert. Grote is right when he says that the "negative" function of the passage is to "discredit the Vox Populi." Socrates says that Crito's deference is owed to a moral expert—*if there is such a person*. The italicized phrase hardly means "and I am such a person." If we were to read it in this perverse way, we would be forcing Socrates to affirm what he explicitly denies in other early dialogues.

[76] See esp. *La.* 185e4-186c5; the connection between expertise and the ability to defend definitions is suggested at 189e3-190c6. Aside from the *Crito* passage under consideration (47a2-d5), there is one other that might mistakenly be taken to mean that Socrates views himself as a moral expert: at *Grg.* 521c7-522a7, he says that were he brought to court he would be like a doctor who is prosecuted by a pastry cook before a jury of children. Does this mean that Socrates takes himself to be as accomplished in the moral sphere as a doctor is in the medical realm? I think not. Socrates means that he is like a doctor in that he uses painful methods to improve the souls of his listeners, just as a doctor causes pain for the sake of health. But he cannot mean that he has knowledge of virtue, just as medical experts have knowledge of health, since he explicitly denies in the *Gorgias* that he has knowledge of moral matters (509a5). He says that he has *undertaken* the true art of politics (521d7), which means that he has taken steps to turn himself into a political and moral expert, but that his goal has not yet been reached.

his every command. Nonetheless, as the *Apology* tells us, he himself is prepared to follow a certain kind of human being as though he were a god. Subordination of adults to other adults is entirely appropriate when those other adults have an expert's command of moral matters.[77]

But what would happen if a moral expert gave commands that frequently contradicted the legal orders of a state? Socrates says that it is shameful to disobey a moral superior, whether divine or human, and so he is committed to disobeying the law in all such cases. But obviously there is a political arrangement that would make it impossible for a legal official's and a moral expert's authority to be in conflict: the two sources of authority can coincide if the expert rules the state. And thus the *Apology*'s remark about human and divine superiors leads naturally to the notion we find in the *Gorgias* and *Republic* I, that if there are moral experts they alone should have political power. The *Laches* tells the same story: "It is by knowledge that one ought to make decisions, if one is to make them well, and not by majority rule" (184e8-9).[78] At the end of the dialogue, the interlocutors realize that none of them is a moral expert, for none has a satisfactory definition of the virtues. But if Socrates ever found such an expert, he would treat him like a god, and his satisfaction with Athenian democracy would disappear.

The reader should be warned that the interpretation I have been putting forward is rejected by several prominent writers. Popper, for example, takes Socrates to believe that the role of an authority in moral matters is simply to get others to criticize themselves and to make up their own minds.[79] Gulley follows Popper's lead, and says that according to Socrates, ". . . the

---

[77] Those who take the *Cleitophon* to be a genuine and early Platonic dialogue have an additional reason to accept my interpretation. For at 408a7-b5, Cleitophon says that, according to Socrates, it would be better to live as a slave under the direction of a political expert than to live freely without a master. Grube, "The *Cleitophon* of Plato," defends the authenticity of this dialogue. He is followed by Irwin, *Plato's Moral Theory*, p. 293 n. 33, point 4; and Annas, *An Introduction to Plato's Republic*, p. 17. For further discussion, see Friedländer, *Plato*, Vol. II, p. 306 n. 2.

[78] See too *La.* 197e1-2: "It is fitting that those in charge of the most important matters have the most important kind of wisdom."

[79] *The Open Society*, pp. 129-130.

individual must be free to realise his own good."[80] Similarly, Vlastos writes that for Socrates ". . . the role of the specialist and the expert should be only to offer guidance and criticism, to inform and clarify the judgment of the layman, leaving the final decision up to him."[81] But none of these pronouncements tallies with the *Apology*'s undeniable authoritarianism. If, as Socrates says, it is shameful ever to disobey a divine or human superior, then he is not bidding us merely to consult with moral authorities—if there ever are any—and then go off and make up our own minds. After all, Socrates would scoff at the proposal that we should give the commands of the gods a fair hearing, and then decide whether we want to obey them. The divine orders that come to us through dreams, prophecies, and oracles (*Ap.* 33c5-6) must be obeyed, because to do otherwise would be shameful and contrary to our own interests. The same deference should be paid to a human superior, if some human being ever becomes a moral expert and gives the rest of us commands. And of course, if a moral expert ever rules the state— something he will do if he wants to avoid being ruled by worse

[80] *The Philosophy of Socrates*, p. 177.

[81] "The Paradox of Socrates," p. 20. Grote, *Plato*, Vol. I, p. 239, writes in a similar vein when he says that ". . . Socrates requires from no man implicit trust: nay he deprecates it as dangerous. . . . The sentiment of authority . . . is formally disavowed and practically set aside." Here, Grote slides too quickly from (A) the claim that Socrates disavowed the role of a moral authority, to (B) the claim that according to Socrates no one should ever be regarded as a moral authority. The one text he cites to support (B) is *Protag.* 313a1-314b6. But in this passage Socrates is merely telling Hippocrates that he must deliberate much more carefully about whether to entrust his soul to a sophist than he would deliberate about whether to entrust his body to a doctor. The implication of this passage is the very opposite of what Grote reads into it: it is just as rational to subordinate oneself to a moral expert as it is to place one's trust in a medical expert, so long as one exercises due care in the choice of an authority. Entrusting oneself to a moral expert is more dangerous than choosing a doctor, since if one chooses badly it is one's soul, and not one's body, that is ruined. And Hippocrates, who has never laid eyes on Protagoras or heard him speak, has no good reason to take moral instruction from him. But that does not mean that there can be no good reason for anyone to apprentice himself to a moral expert. On the contrary, if Hippocrates knew that what Protagoras had to offer him was good, he could safely take lessons from him (*Protag.* 313e2-5). Socrates does not think it will be easy for nonexperts to assess the credentials of moral authorities (see nn. 82, 83 below), but he never says it is impossible.

men—then commands are what the other citizens can expect to receive.

The question might now be raised: how can someone who is not a moral expert ever recognize that someone else is? I think that Socrates would reply that *he* at least could recognize moral expertise if he ever came across it, for he makes it his daily business to determine whether anyone else can define the virtues. To put the point more generally: if someone has reached a certain level of skill in a subject, he thereby acquires the ability to determine whether certain others have far more skill.[82] As we learn a subject we see what the right questions are, and we take those who answer our questions in illuminating ways to be more advanced than we are.[83] In addition, we frequently take

---

[82] At *Charm.* 171b4–c10, Socrates says that only someone who has studied a certain field can distinguish a charlatan from a genuine expert in that field. He is presumably thinking of the possibility explored at *Grg.* 456a7–c7, 458e3–459a6, 464c3–e2, 521d6–522a7: someone who has rhetorical skill can deceive the ignorant into thinking that he is an expert. However, at *Meno* 91c1–92a6, Socrates says that Protagoras could not have corrupted his followers without their realizing that he was having that effect; similarly, he says, an incompetent shoe repairman will be recognized by his customers when their sandals quickly fall apart. In this passage, Socrates recognizes that the impostor's ability to deceive is limited in two ways: (A) when a craftsman is expected to produce a simple physical object, even the many can recognize bad workmanship; (B) in the case of moral training, the many have enough true beliefs to recognize cases in which one person has corrupted another, i.e. made him far worse than a conventionally virtuous citizen. (For example, if Protagoras had taught his followers to assault their parents and cheat their cities, then even the many would have recognized him as a corrupting influence.) These two points do not conflict with the main thesis Socrates puts forward about the many: they have given so little thought to the virtues that even if a moral expert should appear before them, they would not recognize his superiority. To appreciate his wisdom, they would have to revise their moral code.

[83] At *Ap.* 22d2–4, Socrates says that he assured himself that the craftsmen really knew their special subjects. Presumably, he asked them questions about why they used certain techniques and what they were trying to accomplish; and they answered his questions satisfactorily. (Here I follow Irwin, *Plato's Moral Theory*, p. 296 n. 28.) He realized that, if he had wanted to, he could have learned the crafts from these teachers. Evidently, he is assuming that looking for skilled artisans is a far more straightforward matter than looking for moral experts. Any normal adult already has enough information about (for example) shoes to test the knowledge of those who put themselves forward as skilled craftsmen. That is why Socrates could tell that the artisans knew what they were talking about, when they confined themselves to their specialized spheres. But Socrates does not believe that any adult who has received a con-

others to be experts simply because we have confidence in the institutional framework that certifies that status. Given the proper social setting, certain individuals will come to be looked upon as moral experts, and as they teach others the ethical theory they have mastered, the confidence their students place in them will be confirmed.

At one point, Gulley draws the following contrast between the educational ideas of Socrates and Plato: Plato, he says, "rejects Socrates' belief that education is a personal affair, of individual by individual, and that education of this kind is the only proper education. . . ."[84] But surely this contrast is bogus. Plato never denies that it is individuals who teach individuals, nor does Socrates ever say that the state has no business interfering with education. To my knowledge, no one in classical antiquity even entertained the idea that Sparta was violating the rights of its citizens by controlling education. And if the suggestion I made in Section 6 is correct, Socrates thinks that Sparta is well governed precisely because the city makes it its business to inculcate moral beliefs. He is aware of the ways in which different legal systems contribute to the moral progress of their citizens: thus he praises Sparta for the way it ensures that its citizens reach stage (A); and he prefers Athens because it allows its citizens to move beyond that, to stage (B) in some cases, and to stage (C) in his own case. He presumably thinks that the best legal system would be one that provided a setting in which a few individuals could reach stage (D) of moral development. Of course, no system of laws can by itself guarantee that citizens will reach that stage. But if there are moral experts, then a legal system can institutionalize their moral system and facil-

---

ventional moral training is thereby competent to test others for moral expertise. Contrast Irwin's treatment of *Ap*. 22d2-4, ibid., p. 73. He takes Socrates to believe that a moral expert would be recognized as such by any nonexpert. This is difficult to reconcile with the *Gorgias'* point that the many cannot distinguish a charlatan from a moral expert, since they judge practical questions in terms of pleasure. It is also difficult to reconcile with *Crito* 49c11-d5, where Socrates talks about the contempt the many will always have for those who think that injustice must never be done. Socrates expects a moral expert to adopt this principle, and he expects the many to look upon anyone who adopts it as a fool.

[84] *The Philosophy of Socrates*, p. 176.

itate the transmission of that ethical code from one generation to another. The state, for example, could certify that certain individuals are moral experts, and it could require every citizen to learn as much as possible from such teachers. Gulley thinks that Socrates would have principled objections to such state interference with education, but the early dialogues tell a different story. Socrates thinks that the proper goal of a good ruler is to benefit the citizen (*Rep*. 345e2–347a6) and that there is a no greater benefit than moral development. If the state could provide the conditions in which some citizens could advance as far as stage (D), Socrates would be delighted.

At this point, someone might protest against my interpretation in the following way: "You are completely forgetting about Socrates' most famous philosophical maxim: 'the unexamined life is not worth living' (*Ap*. 38a5–6). If the rest of us just take orders from moral experts and never think for ourselves, then we are not living an examined life. So even if there ever are moral experts, they would just ask moral questions, as Socrates does; they would try to get us to think for ourselves, but they wouldn't tell us what to believe or what to do. Such experts would therefore have no use for political power." But this objection makes an important philosophical mistake, for there is no incompatibility between subordinating oneself to a person and trying to understand why the orders of that person are justified. To lead an examined life one must subject one's moral beliefs to questioning; the false ones, if there are any, must be discovered and rejected, and the true ones must be systematically investigated until one sees why they are true. If you acquire your beliefs from someone you recognize as a moral expert, then you can be fairly sure that nothing you believe is false. But that still leaves a good deal of work for you to do. Just accepting what someone says doesn't give you much understanding of what he says. So I see no conflict between Socrates' statement that we would be wrong to disobey a moral superior and his statement that an unexamined life is not worth living.[85] What Socrates must say is that if moral experts ever

[85] What if someone Socrates takes to be a moral expert orders him to kill his parents, privately disobey Athenian law, and dishonor the gods: would he obey?

rule the state, they should not simply give commands to the rest of the citizens; they must also try to get the others to understand, so far as possible, the ethical theory that lies behind these commands. In such a society, all children could be taught the rudiments of the science of ethics, and as young adults they might be challenged by licensed teachers to go beyond this elementary stage and acquire a deeper understanding of moral theory. Not many would master the complete theory of the virtues, but all could be challenged by experts to defend their beliefs in argument. Such a society is of course a dream-world: Socrates believed it would never come to pass, and he had no interest—as Plato did—in sketching the institutions of his ideal society. This is not because he had no use for politics or institutions, but because his first priority was to discover the ethical theory that would be taught by the expert rulers of such a utopia. When Socrates says that the many will never agree with him that injustice must never be done (*Crito* 49d2), his pessimism about changing the world is evident. Surely he realized that if the state controlled education, as it did in Sparta, then the moral beliefs of the many could be manipulated in accordance with the wishes of the rulers. But he doubted that there would ever be leaders who would rule society in accordance with Socratic principles. He dissuaded his followers from pur-

---

There are several things to say. (1) If there is adequate time for discussion, then surely Socrates would want to learn the expert's reasons for these commands before obeying. If the expert can defend his orders adequately, then Socrates will obey, for in this case following an expert and following one's own reason have the same upshot. (2) If there is adequate time for discussion but the "expert" cannot defend his commands, then Socrates will conclude that he was mistaken in taking this individual to be an expert, or that he had lost his expertise. (3) It is hard to know what Socrates would do if there were too little time for discussion. Several factors are important: (A) How strong were his original grounds for thinking this person an expert? (B) Has it happened before that this individual has given unconventional commands and turned out to be right? (C) How strong a case can Socrates give against committing these acts? (4) Even if Socrates is willing to revise his opinion that someone is an expert, in the light of shocking commands, that does not show that obedience to moral expertise has no place in his thought. He can still look up to certain individuals in the expectation that he will learn a great deal from them, and he can obey their commands whenever his own reasoning ability gives him no decisive advice one way or the other. He can also urge the many to obey certain individuals, even when the commands of those individuals conflict with ordinary notions of good and bad. For further discussion, see the Appendix.

suing a political career before they had mastered the correct ethical theory, and he had severe doubts about whether the complete moral system he sought would ever be discovered. That is why he thinks that the many will always be riddled with error.

If my reading of the early dialogues is right, then there is a connection in Socrates' mind between the unteachability of virtue—i.e. the unreachability of stage (D)—and the justification of democracy. Virtue is teachable if and only if there can be moral experts. And if there are no moral experts, then democracy is, for all its defects, no worse than any other political arrangement. Can we find any passage in the early dialogues that links democracy with unteachability in this way? The answer is yes. Here is what Socrates says in the *Protagoras* when he argues for the unteachability thesis:[86]

> I call the Athenians wise, as do the other Greeks. For I see that whenever we meet in the Assembly and need to take some common action about building, the builders are sent for as advisors, and similarly for shipbuilding and all other subjects they think are learnable and teachable. And if someone else whom they don't consider an expert [*dē-miourgon*] tries to advise them—even if he is quite handsome, rich and nobly born—they don't have a bit more tolerance for him. Rather, they laugh and shout, until having been shouted down he gives up his attempt to speak, or the armed guards, at the request of the presiding officers, drag him away. That is how they treat a subject about which there is expertise [*en technēi*]. But when they must make a decision about governing the city, then all alike stand up and give advice—joiner, smith, cobbler, merchant, shipowner, rich and poor, nobly or ill born. And no one rebukes them, as in the former case, on the grounds that he studied with no one and had no teacher, yet still tries to give advice. It's obvious that they don't think this is teachable. (319b3–d7)

[86] Many scholars refuse to believe that Socrates is serious about the unteachability of virtue, and they would not take him to be endorsing that thesis in the passage cited. This issue will be fully discussed in Chapter VIII.

Socrates wholeheartedly agrees with the idea of his fellow citizens that you should never seek the advice of an amateur when experts are at hand. And he also agrees that since moral experts do not exist, all ideas and speakers should receive an audience in the Assembly. But notice that a highly undemocratic conclusion is lurking in this passage: if there were moral experts—i.e. people who know as much about virtue as other experts know about their own fields—then we should subordinate ourselves to them in the same way we look up to nonmoral authorities. That is precisely the point we saw Socrates making in the *Apology* and the *Crito*.

I hope I have explained why it is inaccurate to portray Socrates as either a simple enemy or a simple friend of democracy. He thinks that the many will always rule badly, and he would prefer a society run by moral experts. But he sees little hope for anything better than democracy, and he values the intellectual freedom provided by this political system. The authoritarianism we find in Plato's *Republic* has its roots in the early dialogues, but those who cherish free critical inquiry justifiably look upon Socrates as their patron saint. If I am right, these apparently conflicting elements in the early dialogues fit together to form a coherent political outlook.[87]

[87] A shorter version of this chapter is to appear in Gregory Currie and Alan Musgrave (eds.), *Popper and the Human Sciences* (The Hague: Martinus Nijhoff).

VIII

DEFINITION, KNOWLEDGE, AND TEACHING

᪐

1

An expert in disguise?

MANY of Plato's early dialogues exhibit a familiar pattern: Socrates raises a question of the form, "What is —— ?" (e.g. "What is courage?" "What is piety?"), and claims that he does not know the answer; he asks his interlocutor if he can do better, and it turns out that he cannot; several definitions are proposed, all are found inadequate in one way or another, and the dialogue ends in failure.[1] According to the interpretation I put forward in Chapter VII, Socrates is being perfectly honest when he says that he cannot define the virtues. Of course, he has many beliefs about the virtues, and he passionately defends his convictions with complex arguments. He holds, for example, that the virtues are necessary and sufficient for happiness,[2] and he believes that they are all branches of knowledge.[3] Nonetheless, he does not have answers to the "What is X?" questions he asks, and so the failure with which so many early dialogues end reflects a real failure on the part of Socrates. This interpretation of the early dialogues is certainly not novel,[4] but neither

---

[1] Thus *Charm.*, *Euphr.*, *H. Ma.*, *La.*, *Lys.*, *Meno*, and *Rep.* I.

[2] *Grg.* 470e8-11, *Rep.* 352d2-354a11.

[3] *La.* 194d1-2, *Protag.* 361b1-2, *Meno* 87d4-88d3.

[4] See Grote, *Plato*, Vol. I, pp. 246-247, 256-257, 270-271; Irwin, *Plato's Moral Theory*, pp. 39-40; Guthrie, *History*, Vol. III, pp. 442-449; Allen, *Plato's 'Euthyphro,'* pp. 6, 89; Woodruff, *Plato Hippias Major*, pp. 142-143.

is it uncontroversial. For some scholars think that Socrates' frequent disclaimers of knowledge should not be taken at face value. He is, on this interpretation, concealing his favored answers behind a mask of irony—a mask he wears to force his audience to discover the proper definition of the virtues on its own.[5] But if we study the early dialogues carefully, we will see that Socrates wants to define virtue in the following way: it is knowledge of good and evil.[6]

I think that this way of reading the early dialogues is misguided, and in the first few sections of this chapter I will examine those passages that seem to support it. As a result of my discussion, the reader should come to have a better idea of what Socrates is looking for when he asks his "What is X?" question. As we will see, the project of defining the virtues is an enormously difficult undertaking—a point about which Socrates had no illusions. He suspected that it might not be humanly possible to find what he was looking for, and in any case he did not pretend to have found it himself. Socrates thought he was embarked on a project whose completion might always remain a long way off.

When we look at those few passages that suggest to some scholars that Socrates could define the virtues, it will be important to bear in mind how strong the evidence against this thesis is. First, there is an abundance of direct textual evidence: Soc-

[5] Thus Cornford, *Plato and Parmenides*, p. 245: "In a whole series of the early dialogues—*Laches, Charmides, Euthyphro, Lysis*—the conclusion that is meant to be accepted is skilfully masked, so that the reader may be forced to discover it by careful study." Similarly, Versényi, *Socratic Humanism*, p. 118, says, ". . . There is hardly a dialogue that does not arrive at solutions to the problems discussed. These conclusions are negated at the end merely to prevent the student from uncritically accepting them instead of going through reflection that would make them his own." So too Teloh, cited in the following note.

[6] Versényi, *Socratic Humanism*, pp. 75-110, discusses each of the virtues and says how Socrates would define them: they are all "nothing but wisdom, the knowledge of good and evil . . ." (p. 108). So too Teloh, *Plato's Metaphysics*, pp. 46-64. ". . . Socrates in each case either turns from this conclusion [that virtue is knowledge of good and evil] at the last moment, or after arguing for it so that it seems to be inescapable, overturns and rejects the identity for intentionally spurious and contrived reasons" (p. 46). The myth that Socrates has answers to his definitional questions goes back a long way. See *Ap.* 22e6-23a5. It is an interpretation put forward by Thrasymachus (*Rep.* 337a4-7), a fact that indicates how little merit Plato saw in it.

rates often affirms his inability to say what the virtues are.[7] In fact, no other point in Plato's early works is made more frequently and earnestly than this. If there is one fact about Socrates that Plato seems most eager to communicate to his readers, it is that Socrates confessed his inability to define the virtues. Second, there is the argument I presented in Chapter VII: Socrates' political outlook makes sense only if he believes that no one has a standard for determining which acts are pious and which impious, which just and which unjust, etc. If he thought that he had such standards, then he would hardly have confessed his great satisfaction with the legal system of Athens. For he says that if anyone has knowledge of the virtues, then he is the one who should make decisions, not the many (*La.* 184e8-9). And he claims that if any mortal has a godlike superiority over the rest of us, then he should be obeyed no less than the gods (*Ap.* 29b6-7). It is undeniable that Socrates would have approved of a state ruled by moral experts; that he thinks the many fall far short of moral expertise; and that he is nonetheless greatly satisfied with the laws of Athens. The only way to explain these facts is to take Socrates at his word when he says that neither he nor anyone else has satisfactory answers to his "What is X?" questions. Those who portray him as an expert in disguise have no good reason to overturn his frequent disavowals of knowledge; and their error is all the worse since they make it impossible to give any coherent account of his political attitudes.

There is another claim I made in Chapter VII that could be challenged. I said that Socrates seriously doubts that virtue is teachable, and I tried to show that these doubts are connected with his attitude toward democracy. On this issue, I seem to be a minority of one, for I have found no other scholar who takes Socrates seriously when he argues, in the *Protagoras* and

---

[7] More generally, he cannot answer his "What is X?" question even when X is not a virtue. See *Euphr.* 5a3-c5, 11b1-5, 11e2-4, 14b8-c5, 15c11-16a4; *Charm.* 165b5-c1, 166c7-d6, 175c8-176b1; *H. Ma.* 286c3-e4, 304d4-e3; *La.* 185e4-186c5, 199e11-12, 200e2-201b5; *Lys.* 212a4-7, 223b4-8; *Meno* 71a5-7, 100b4-6; *Protag.* 361c3-6; *Rep.* 337d3-4, 354c1-3.

the *Meno*, that virtue is unteachable.[8] According to some, Socrates considers himself to be a teacher of virtue;[9] though he denies that he teaches (four times in the *Apology*, once in the *Laches*),[10] this disclaimer is not to be taken at face value. He disavows this role only because he is not doing what his listeners would have expected of a conventional teacher: spewing forth information and dogmatizing. Instead he asks questions and gets his listeners to think for themselves: that is the sort of teacher Socrates thinks he is. Since he realizes that he is a teacher of virtue, he cannot be serious when he claims that virtue is unteachable. The argument he gives for this claim looks quite suspicious; perhaps it is intentionally fallacious,[11] or perhaps it

[8] To treat this argument seriously, one must take Socrates at his word when he says (A) that there are no teachers of virtue, and (B) that it is therefore unteachable. If one takes Socrates to be equivocating on "virtue" or "teaching" in this argument, one is not taking him at his word. Both (A) and (B) are defended at *Meno* 89d6-96c10. I take *Protag.* 319e1-320b5 to be putting forward the same argument. Sometimes the argument is dismissed in an extremely cavalier way. Thus A. E. Taylor says about the *Protagoras'* argument for unteachability: "We must observe that he does not undertake to prove that statesmanship cannot be taught, nor does he commit himself to any of the views he goes on to present. He merely urges that, seeing the quarter from which they come, they cannot simply be dismissed, but have to be met" (*Plato*, p. 242).

[9] Teloh, *Plato's Metaphysics*, p. 51, takes *Grg.* 521d6-e2 to show that Socrates considered himself a teacher. Against this, see Sec. 12 and n. 80 below; cf. Ch. VII n. 76. Others arrive at this conclusion in a more oblique way. Devereux, for example, argues that the point of the *Meno* is to contrast two kinds of teaching: Socratic and sophistical. See "Nature and Teaching in Plato's *Meno*." Similarly Crombie, *An Examination of Plato's Doctrines*, Vol. I, p. 222. I take them to mean that Socrates thinks there is a sense in which he does teach. For if, as these scholars claim, Socrates thinks that to teach virtue is to induce moral progress by asking the right questions, then surely he has to believe that he is a teacher of sorts. I take up Devereux's interpretation of the *Meno* in n. 79 below. Weingartner, *The Unity of the Platonic Dialogue*, pp. 132-133, discusses two kinds of teaching and two kinds of virtue. On his view, Socrates believes that (A) real virtue can be taught in the real way; (B) Protagorean virtue can be taught in the Protagorean way; (C) Protagorean virtue cannot be taught in the real way. But he does not say whether, in his view, Socrates takes himself to teach in the real way. If not, then Weingartner commits Socrates to denying what he affirms at *Meno* 89d6-e3, 96c6-10: that if there are no teachers of a subject it cannot be taught. For another analysis of the *Protagoras* in terms of different kinds of teaching, see C.C.W. Taylor, *Plato Protagoras*, pp. 213-214. As I will try to show, the argument for unteachability is best interpreted without resorting to a distinction between different kinds of teaching or virtue.

[10] *Ap.* 19d8-e1, 20d9-e2, 33a5-6, 33b5-6; *La.* 185e4-187a8.

[11] Thus Irwin, *Plato's Moral Theory*, p. 317 n. 22. He claims that Socrates

is only meant to show that virtue cannot be taught by conventional methods. After all, one of Socrates' deepest convictions is that virtue is knowledge, and he says that if it is knowledge it must be teachable. If we take him to be saying that virtue is *unteachable*, then we commit him to a contradiction. And surely Socrates was too clever to have had inconsistent beliefs!

I will argue that the suggestions made in the previous paragraph lead to dead ends. The idea that Socrates is equivocating when he disavows the status of a moral teacher, and that he is not serious when he argues for the unteachability of virtue, is no better than the idea that he really has hidden definitions of the virtues. In my opinion, those who find an esoteric figure in the early dialogues—Socrates, the moral expert; Socrates, the antiauthoritarian teacher; Socrates, the concealer of definitions; Socrates, the man who is never puzzled by unanswered questions or inconsistencies—are engaged in a project that systematically distorts material that stares us in the face when we read Plato's early works. What we find there is a continual emphasis on the limitations of their protagonist and the deficiencies of human nature. Unless we recognize this pessimistic and negative side of Socrates, and see how it fits together with his remarkable arrogance, we will have missed one of the central features of his personality and philosophy.

2
Euthyphro 14b-c

One of Euthyphro's attempts to state a standard of piety reads as follows:

> . . . If someone knows how to say and do what is gratifying to the gods, in prayer and sacrifice, these things are holy, and such things preserve private households and the public affairs of cities; things opposite to what is gratifying

---

does not seriously believe that if anything is teachable, there are teachers of it. On his view, Socrates has no doubts about the teachability of virtue. See pp. 24, 74, 298 n. 43.

are unholy, and they overturn or destroy everything. (14b2–7)

To which Socrates replies:

> You could have spoken far more briefly, if you had wanted, Euthyphro, and have given me the gist [*kephalaion*] of what I asked for. But you are not eager to teach me—that's obvious. For just now, when you were at a certain point, you turned away. If you had given me that answer, I would have adequately learned from you about holiness. As it turns out, however, the one who asks must follow the one who is asked, wherever he may lead. . . . (14b8–c4)[12]

It certainly sounds as though Socrates already has the answer to his question, and is simply waiting for Euthyphro to come up with it on his own. Why else would he say that Euthyphro was just on the verge of giving the right answer? How could Socrates know that Euthyphro was about to stumble upon the truth, unless he himself had the truth?[13]

My reply is that Socrates' comment at 14b8–c4 is half in jest and half in earnest. Euthyphro's long-winded statement begins with the idea that whoever is pious must know something, and this is the part of his definition that Socrates thinks is profoundly correct. As we see in the *Protagoras* and the *Laches*, Socrates thinks that the virtues are all forms of knowledge.[14] To be pious, then, is to know something-or-other: if Euthyphro had merely said that, he would have made an insightful and unobjectionable statement. Yet, even if Euthyphro had been more brief, and had simply said, "piety is knowledge," we can

---

[12] Following TW rather than B. See Burnet, *Plato's Euthyphro, Apology of Socrates, and Crito*, ad loc.; and Allen, *Plato's 'Euthyphro,'* pp. 57–58 n. 1.

[13] See Allen, *Plato's 'Euthyphro,'* pp. 6–7, against the view, adopted by several editors, that Socrates must have a definition of piety in the light of this passage. But his argument (p. 58 n. 1) against this way of reading 14b8–c4 is disappointingly brief: ". . . This, in context, suggests only that the 'What is it?' question can be answered, not that Euthyphro has succeeded in answering it." This avoids the issue: how can Socrates say that Euthyphro has almost given him the right answer, if Socrates himself does not know the right answer? Teloh, *Plato's Metaphysics*, pp. 59–60, takes 14b8–c4 to be a hint that piety is to be defined as knowledge of good and evil.

[14] See n. 3 above.

be sure that Socrates would have challenged him with a further question: "Precisely what is it that must be known, if one is to be pious?" The statement that piety is knowledge says nothing to distinguish it from farming, geometry, or any other branch of knowledge. Furthermore, "piety is knowledge" does not give Socrates what he is after, in this dialogue. He wants a standard for determining what is the pious thing to do, but if someone is having trouble deciding whether a certain act is pious, he is not going to be helped by being told that piety is knowledge of something-or-other.

This brings me to the ironic part of Socrates' comment at 14b8-c4. When he says, ". . . you are not eager to teach me . . . ," he acts as though Euthyphro really knows how to complete the definition, "to be pious is to know _____," and he complains that his interlocutor is being malicious and contrary by refusing to fill in the blank in a satisfactory way. This irony is present throughout the dialogue, as every one of its readers surely realizes. Socrates plays along with Euthyphro's unjustified assumption that he is an expert about religious matters, and so when Euthyphro's attempts to give definitions fail, Socrates pretends that the cause is his interlocutor's ill will, rather than his ignorance (see esp. 11a6–b5). That is why I say that Socrates' remark at 14b8-c4 is half in jest and half in earnest. He doesn't really believe that Euthyphro already knows how to fill out the idea that piety is knowledge, but he does believe that Euthyphro's statement at 14b2-7 contains an essential ingredient in the correct definition of this virtue. Socrates is convinced that to be pious is to know something-or-other, and so when Euthyphro starts to give a definition of piety in terms of knowledge, Socrates mockingly pretends that he is finally about to get what he has always been searching for.[15]

---

[15] See Vlastos, "The Paradox of Socrates," p. 14, for a different treatment of *Euphr.* 14b8-c4. He takes the passage to show that Socrates "has been doing his best to lead Euthyphro to the point where he could see for himself the right answer. What he positively refuses to do is to *tell* Euthyphro this answer, and this, not because he does not think Euthyphro's soul worth the saving, but because he believes there is only one way to save it and that Euthyphro himself must do the job by finding this one right way, so that he too becomes a searcher" (his emphasis). This suggests that if Socrates had an answer to the question,

I conclude that the *Euthyphro* contains no answer, explicit or implicit, to the question Socrates raises: can we state a standard of piety that will enable us to classify any given act as pious or impious? Nor does any other Platonic work even attempt an answer to this question. Socrates clearly says in the *Euthyphro* that he does not know what piety is, and no passage in this or any other dialogue forces us to take his avowals at less than face value.

3
Knowledge of good and evil:[16] The *Charmides*

It is possible to read this dialogue and come away with the false impression that Socrates has an unstated answer to this question, "What is temperance?" Here is how this misunderstanding can occur.

After several definitions of temperance are proposed and refuted, Critias puts forward the following candidate: to be tem-

---

"What is piety?" that served as an adequate standard, he would nonetheless refuse to tell it to Euthyphro. The truth, in other words, is worth knowing only when one discovers it on one's own, without having first heard it from others. If this is what Vlastos means, I have to disagree. As we saw in Chapter VII, Socrates expects a moral expert to give commands; he does not merely prod others into discovering the truth by their own efforts. Socrates himself—who is no moral expert—does not hesitate to share his moral principles with others. He preaches the doctrine that the improvement of the soul is human-kind's most important task (*Ap.* 29d7-e3); this is not something he hints at, leaving it to his listeners to formulate the discovery on their own. Of course, Socrates would not want his interlocutors to accept his statements on faith, but this does not prevent him from revealing his convictions. For example, he simply tells Crito (49c11-d6) to accept only those Socratic principles that he really believes. It might be asked: "Why then doesn't Socrates just tell Euthyphro that piety is a branch of knowledge? Why doesn't he say that at least that part of his definition is correct?" My reply is that Euthyphro would not have made the least bit of progress if he had merely come away from his conversation with the conviction that piety is knowledge. He would still have had the problem with which he began: he thinks that he has as much knowledge of piety as he needs. Socrates has to show him, not that piety is knowledge, but that Euthyphro lacks the knowledge that piety consists in. The only way to get him to realize this is to ask him to say what piety is knowledge of, and to refute his answers. This of course is precisely what Socrates does.

[16] This translation of *kakon*, though common, can be somewhat misleading. For us, "evil" often suggests contempt for moral considerations; by contrast, *kakon* can easily be applied to acts merely because they are contrary to one's interest. "Bad" is perhaps better than "evil" here.

perate is to have knowledge of oneself (164d2–165b4), and therefore temperance is the branch of knowledge that has itself as its subject matter (165d8–166c3). It is, in other words, the knowledge of knowledge (166e5–8). Whoever has this kind of expertise will be able to examine himself and others to see whether they really have the knowledge they claim for themselves (167a1–7). A city that is governed by temperance would be one in which each citizen confines himself to his field of expertise and leaves to others any activities or subjects about which he is ignorant (171d1–172a5). At first glance, such a community would seem to be quite appealing: people would enjoy better health because only expert doctors would practice medicine; sea voyages would be less dangerous, clothes would be better made, etc. (173b1–d3). But at this point in the dialogue, Socrates asks: does anything we have said about this imaginary city guarantee that its citizens will fare well and be happy (173d3–5)? The answer he gives is no. What the citizens need, if they are to fare well, is the knowledge of good and evil; lacking that, they will be in bad condition, even though their knowledge of knowledge might provide them with excellent health, fine clothes, etc. (173d8–174b10). The *only* study that provides a benefit, then, is the knowledge of good and evil; temperance—if we define it as knowledge of knowledge—will not be of value (175a3–8). But Socrates refuses to concede that temperance is useless; on the contrary, he thinks it a good so great that it is sufficient for happiness (175e6–176a1). So he rejects Critias' definition of temperance, no further candidates are proposed, and as usual, the dialogue ends in perplexity. But the observant reader notices, as the dialogue ends, that there is a way of defining temperance that avoids the objection Socrates makes to Critias' final candidate. Knowledge of good and evil, according to Socrates, is sufficient for happiness. And temperance, he says, is sufficient for happiness. So why not define temperance as knowledge of good and evil? Isn't this the intended conclusion of the dialogue?

It would be wrong to reject this way of reading the *Charmides* merely on the grounds that it goes beyond what the text actually says. Any interpretation must do that. But at least we can demand that an adequate interpretation not contradict the text, and if we say that "knowledge of good and evil" is the intended answer to Socrates' question, "What is temperance?" we *will* come into conflict with the explicit message of the dialogue. For Socrates tells us on three separate occasions in the *Charmides* that he does not have an adequate answer to the question he is raising.[17] And as I pointed out in Section 1, Socrates' political outlook and his frequent disclaimers of knowledge throughout the early dialogues both indicate that he cannot define the virtues. So we have every reason to look for a way of interpreting the *Charmides* according to which "knowledge of good and evil" is not the definition of temperance Socrates is looking for.

The key to understanding the dialogue is to realize that since Socrates has several different ways of showing the inadequacy of a proposed definition, an answer to his "What is X?" question can pass one test and still be a bad definition because it fails another. Here are some of the criteria he uses to disqualify alleged definitions:

(A) A definition must not be too broad or too narrow.[18]

(B) A definition must explain what it is about virtuous acts or persons that makes them virtuous.[19]

(C) The property with which a virtue is identified must be as valuable as the virtue in question.[20]

(D) A definition must be usable as a standard for deciding which acts are virtuous.[21]

---

[17] 165b5–c1, 166c7–d6, 175c8–176b1.

[18] For example, Euthyphro's first definition of piety (5d8–e2) is rejected because it is too narrow; Laches' second definition of courage (192b9–c1) is too broad. In the early dialogues, these are the most common defects of proposed definitions.

[19] *Euphr.* 10a2–11b1. Piety cannot be defined as what the gods love because their loving it is to be explained in terms of the nature of piety.

[20] *Rep.* 332d7–333e2. If justice is helping friends and harming enemies, it is of little use, and this point by itself is enough to defeat Polemarchus' definition.

[21] *Euphr.* 6e3–6. Socrates seeks a statement about piety that will help him sort every act into just one of two categories: the pious and the not pious. If a proposed definition fails to meet this standard—if, for example, it says that one and the same act can be both pious and impious (8a10–b6)—then it will not be action-guiding. It will tell us both to perform and refrain from the act in ques-

In the *Charmides*, Socrates is using (C) to defeat the proposal that temperance is knowledge of knowledge: temperance is an extremely valuable good, but knowledge of knowledge does not benefit us. And as readers have sometimes noticed,[22] the dialogue does point toward a way of repairing this difficulty: if we defined temperance as knowledge of good and evil, then both *definiens* and *definiendum* would be extremely valuable properties. But then why does Socrates continue to deny, at the end of the dialogue, that he has an adequate definition of temperance? What would be wrong with defining this virtue as knowledge of good and evil? My suggestion is that although this proposal would satisfy criterion (C), and would therefore be an improvement over Critias' candidate, it would nonetheless fail to satisfy criterion (D), the hardest test of all.[23] Though

---

tion. At 8b7-9, Euthyphro confusedly tries to show that his definition (piety is what the gods love) does at least help with the case at hand: for all the gods agree that whoever has killed unjustly should pay the penalty. He evidently assumes that in the eyes of the gods his father has killed unjustly, and so even if his definition permits the possibility of actions that are both pious and not pious, that is a technical flaw that is irrelevant to his current undertaking. But Socrates will not let him have even this much. As he points out at 9a1-b3, Euthyphro has no evidence that all of the gods think he should prosecute his father. So his proposed definition is not only a potentially bad standard (since it can give conflicting advice), but it provides no standard in the current situation. Notice that Socrates gives and needs no argument that in fact the gods are split in their attitude toward Euthyphro's legal action. Euthyphro is the one who thinks that the gods have moral and religious disputes, and so if his definition is to provide a workable standard for decision, he is the one who needs some evidence that all the gods approve of what he is doing. At 9c1-8, Socrates emphasizes the point that even if Euthyphro's definition were useful in the present situation, it would still be inadequate on more general grounds. And he then relaxes the requirement that a definition provide a standard for action. He construes "loved by the gods" as a way of putting acts into one of four categories: pious, impious, both, or neither (9d1-5). And he proceeds to show that even if Euthyphro's definition could sort actions into one of these four categories, it nonetheless has serious deficiencies.

[22] Thus Penner, "The Unity of Virtue," pp. 63-64; Irwin, *Plato's Moral Theory*, p. 88; and Teloh, *Plato's Metaphysics*, pp. 54-56. Of these, only Teloh commits himself to the view that Socrates has a satisfactory definition of the virtues. See pp. 46-47, 61-64. Irwin, pp. 39-40, denies this.

[23] Contrast Teloh, *Plato's Metaphysics*, pp. 61-64. He thinks that Socrates refuses to spell out the answer to his definitional questions because he wants "to engage the autonomous resources" (p. 64) of his interlocutor. Thus Vlastos, "The Paradox of Socrates," pp. 14, 20, though he does not clearly say that Socrates knows how to define the virtues. Cf. n. 15 above.

Socrates is convinced that temperance, like any other virtue, is knowledge of something-or-other, he thinks that we must try to specify the object of that knowledge in such a way that it provides a guide to action. This is the task he finds himself unable to perform. We must not insult his intelligence by thinking him unable to invent vague statements about what a virtuous person must know. What he is searching for is a particular piece of knowledge that he can always look to as a definitive guide for the solution of practical problems. That is a standard of definition that "knowledge of good and evil" does not come close to satisfying.

I can imagine two objections that might be raised against this way of reading the *Charmides*. First, it might be asked: if Socrates thinks that "knowledge of good and evil" is a bad definition of temperance because it fails criterion (D), then why doesn't he say so? Why doesn't he say that although "knowledge of good and evil" satisfies one criterion for a good definition, it fails another? To this question, I have no answer; but I do not regard this fact as a telling objection to the interpretation I propose. I do not see why Socrates has to point out the inadequacies of definitions that have not actually been put forward. And in any case, the question, "If that is what he means why doesn't he say so?" could be raised about any interpretation that goes (as it must) beyond the text. But there is a second and more legitimate problem that the reader might want to raise: how do we know that Socrates' conception of a good definition does not gradually develop in the early dialogues? After all, although criterion (D) is invoked in the *Euthyphro*, it is not even mentioned in the *Charmides*. Couldn't that test be a late development? What prevents us from saying that the *Charmides* was written before the *Euthyphro*, and that in the earlier dialogue Socrates has not yet thought of the idea that definitions should provide workable standards for right behavior? In reply: *Some* explanation is needed for the fact that "knowledge of good and evil" is not adopted in the *Charmides* as an adequate definition of temperance. It obviously satisfies condition (C), and so we must try to discover some other Socratic criterion that it fails to satisfy. It is plausible to suppose that "knowledge of good and evil" would pass tests (A) and (B), according to Socrates, but it is hard to believe that, in his opinion, it would satisfy criterion (D). And I see no reason why our attempt to understand the *Charmides* should be restricted to information we can gather about Socrates from that dialogue alone. Furthermore, we must not forget the connection I tried to establish in Chapter VII between Socrates' political outlook and his search for definitions. He says that if someone has knowledge of moral matters, then he should give commands and the rest of us should obey; in such circumstances, rule by the many should give way to rule by expertise. This idea, as we saw, is not confined to any one dialogue: it appears not only in the *Gorgias* (which is late among the early works) and *Republic* Book I (which was written during Plato's middle period or at the end of his early period), but in the *Apology* and the *Crito* as well; and these last two works are reasonably thought to be among the earliest of Plato's early writings.[24] Now, what sort of knowledge would entitle someone to play the role that Socrates assigns to a moral and political authority? That person would have skills and knowledge that far surpass what Socrates can accomplish, for he continually denies that he is a moral expert, equipped with definitions of the virtues. What Socrates can do is formulate such vague statements as "temperance is knowledge of good and evil," or "virtue is knowledge of how to live well." But he refuses to put himself forward as an expert political leader who deserves obedience, since he lacks a workable standard for resolving difficult moral problems. That is a deficiency he would be ready to acknowledge whenever he expresses the authoritarian political outlook we studied in Chapter VII. Therefore, criterion (D) cannot be confined to one dialogue alone—the *Euthyphro*. We have to appeal to that criterion to understand the political outlook Socrates expresses at every point, early and late, within the early dialogues.

[24] On the dates of the *Grg.* and *Rep.* I, See Ch. VII n. 71, Ch. VIII Sec. 8. See n.46 below on the date of the *Apology*. I assume that the *Crito* was written at roughly the same time as the *Apology*, since they have a common purpose: to expound the philosophy that led to the death of Socrates. Guthrie, *History*, Vol. IV, p. 93, makes the same assumption. He takes the *Apology* to be Plato's first written work (p. 72).

I conclude that there is a perfectly good explanation of why
Socrates does not end the *Charmides* with the statement that
temperance is knowledge of good and evil: he does not think
that such a statement provides a solution to the problem he is
raising. It is not as though he thinks that "temperance is knowledge of good and evil" is *false*. Rather, he would say that
"knowledge of good and evil" is a way of relabeling temperance, but that it doesn't tell us what it really is. It does not give
us the standard the temperate person would use in making decisions about how to act.

4

Knowledge of good and evil: The Laches

In this dialogue too, it is tempting—though wrong—to infer
from the textual evidence that Socrates is pointing to a conclusion that he does not want to make explicit. Here, it might be
thought, Socrates is cryptically telling us that he does have a
satisfactory answer to his question, "What is courage?" His secret answer is: knowledge of good and evil. But we will see
that here, as in the *Charmides*, there is a better way of reading
the dialogue—one that does not needlessly come into conflict
with Socrates' emphatic insistence that he cannot solve the
problem he is raising. Unfortunately, giving a satisfactory
interpretation of the *Laches* is complicated by the fact that, on
the surface, the dialogue seems to conflict with the *Protagoras*.
But I will suggest a way of reconciling these two works.

Immediately after raising the question, "What is virtue?" in
the *Laches*, Socrates insists that he and his interlocutors should
first tackle a less general problem: instead of asking about the
whole of virtue, they should select one of its parts (190c8–d8).
Since the part that is most pertinent to their earlier conversation
is courage, the question now becomes: what is courage? Several
definitions proposed by Laches are refuted, and when Nicias
tries to do better, he takes up an idea he once heard Socrates
put forward: anything that makes a man good must be a form
of wisdom (194d1–9). And so courage, according to Nicias, is
knowledge of something. But knowledge of what? As I said in

Sections 2 and 3, that is a question that Socrates finds impossible to answer when it is asked about piety and temperance. The explicit message of the *Laches* is that he can do no better when it comes to courage (199e11–201b5). Consider the proposal that Nicias makes: courage is "knowledge of the fearful and the hopeful" (194e11–195a1). That, of course, is not going to serve as a workable standard for deciding, in particular situations, what the courageous thing to do is; and Socrates is therefore committed to rejecting it. But the objection he decides to bring forward is that the proposal fails a far simpler test for adequate definitions: it is too narrow. To show that "courage is knowledge of the fearful and hopeful" fails this simple test, Socrates gets Nicias to agree that fear and hope are always directed toward *future* goods and evils (198b2–c1); they never concern the present or the past. But nothing can be a branch of knowledge if it is about the future alone (198d1–199a4). There is, for example, no science of future health: one branch of knowledge tells us what was, is, and will be healthy. Therefore, since courage too is a branch of knowledge—a point Socrates wholeheartedly accepts—it cannot be restricted to future goods and evils, and so Nicias' definition must be abandoned.

At this point (199c4–d2), Socrates suggests that they make a change in Nicias' proposal: suppose we consider whether courage might be knowledge of *all* goods and evils, past, present, and future. No one could say against *this* definition that it is too narrow, but as Socrates points out, the new proposal has the opposite fault: it is too broad. Knowledge of good and evil is something that can be identified with virtue entire, but courage, being only a part of virtue, must be identified with something less general (199d4–e9). Since this modification of Nicias' definition is no better then the original, Socrates concludes the dialogue with his usual confession of perplexity. He has not made every objection he has in his arsenal against the idea that courage is knowledge of what is fearful and hopeful, or that it is knowledge of good and evil. But he has said enough to justify his rejection of both candidates. And so the perplexity with which the dialogue ends is real.

Against the interpretation I have just given, it might be said that even though the *Laches* has not found a satisfactory definition of one part of virtue—namely, courage—it has found a satisfactory definition of the whole thing. That is, Socrates has rejected "knowledge of good and evil" as a definition of *courage*, but he hasn't said why this would not be a good definition of *virtue*. He certainly would not claim that it is too broad or too narrow to do that job. So why not say that this is the hidden conclusion of the dialogue: virtue (thought not courage) is the knowledge of good and evil? My reply is that if we read the dialogue in this way, we have to reject too much that is in the text. Socrates insists that he is not an expert about virtue (185e4–186c5), and he requires that such an expert be able to say what virtue is (190a1-c6). So he must mean that he no more has a definition of *virtue* than of *courage*. Of course, that is just what we would expect, since he tells his interlocutors in the *Laches* that discovering a definition of courage is a project they should undertake before they tackle the larger task of defining the whole of virtue (190c8–d1). And it is easy to explain why "knowledge of good and evil" is not a satisfactory account of virtue: it fails to provide a usable standard for making practical decisions.

Another alternative to the interpretation I propose is this: perhaps Socrates does not really mean that courage is just a part of virtue.[25] He thinks that Nicias is being thick-headed in failing to see that if *this* claim is rejected, then they can hang onto the idea that courage is knowledge of good and evil. Courage and virtue, according to this suggestion, are really the same thing for Socrates: knowledge of good and evil. My reaction to this proposal is that it has all the disadvantages of the previous one, and more. For it is Socrates who introduces the notion that courage is just part of virtue, and he is the one who keeps insisting upon it.[26] He thinks that "knowledge of good and evil" is not a satisfactory answer to the question, "What is virtue?" and he thinks it an even worse answer to the question, "What

[25] Penner, "The Unity of Virtue," pp. 60–62, and Irwin, *Plato's Moral Theory*, pp. 88–89, adopt this view. They take Socrates to be hinting that courage is the knowledge of good and evil. In this they are joined by Teloh, *Plato's Metaphysics*, pp. 58–59.

[26] Introduces it at 190c8–d8; insists upon it at 197e10–198b2, 199c3–e11.

is courage?" There is simply no evidence in the *Laches* that Socrates really means to reject his own claim that courage is a part of virtue.

If we look outside the *Laches*, we find further evidence that according to Socrates certain virtues are only parts of the whole: piety has precisely this status in the *Euthyphro*, for example.[27] But if piety and courage are less than the whole of virtue, how can Socrates say, as he does in the *Protagoras*, that all of the words for the virtues (wisdom, justice, piety, courage, and temperance) name one and the same thing?[28] If courage is only a part of wisdom, in what way are they one? Is the *Protagoras* hopelessly at odds with the *Laches* and the *Euthyphro*? I suggest that they can be reconciled if we bear in mind the comparison Socrates makes between the parts of virtue and the parts of gold (*Protag.* 329d6–8). He says that the parts of gold differ from each other and from the whole in size, and he grants that in this fashion the various virtues may be parts of virtue entire. His idea is that courage and piety are not like independent organs (e.g. eyes, ears, nose, etc.) that are connected to each other only because they happen to belong to a larger whole (*Protag.* 330a4–b1). Rather, the particular virtues blend imperceptibly into one another, like subsegments of a continuous and uniform object. What do these similes amount to? My suggestion is that Socrates is thinking of the way in which one vast branch of knowledge can encompass several interconnected subdivisions. We might say, for example, that economics and micro-economics are not two separate disciplines with no overlap between them; rather, they are one and the same field of inquiry, the part dif-

---

[27] 11e4–12e8. The *Meno* (78d1–79c5) also shows that, according to Socrates, it is not the case that each of the virtues is identical with the whole of virtue. Vlastos rightly emphasizes this point in "Socrates on 'The Parts of Virtue.'"

[28] *Protag.* 329c2–330b6, 333b4–5, 349b1–c5, 350c4–5. Vlastos, "The Unity of the Virtues in the *Protagoras*," denies that these passages commit Socrates to the view that the virtue-terms name the same thing. See esp. pp. 227–228. I find this implausible, in the light of the way the issue is posed at 349b1–c5. In this respect, my interpretation is similar to the one advocated by Penner, "The Unity of Virtue"; Irwin, *Plato's Moral Theory*, pp. 86–90; and C.C.W. Taylor, *Plato Protagoras*, pp. 103–108. But I do not infer, as they do, that all of the virtues have precisely the same scope: this obliterates the thesis, which Socrates wants to preserve, that the virtues might vary in size (*Protag.* 329d7–8).

fering from the whole only in size. If my conjecture is correct, then "courage," "piety," and "virtue" name one and the same thing—a certain branch of knowledge—in the same way that "stage right," "front stage," and "stage" name one and the same physical object. If the gold analogy is interpreted in this way, then the *Protagoras'* idea that the virtues form a unity becomes consistent with the plain thesis of the *Laches* and the *Euthyphro* that certain virtues are less than the whole.[29]

5

Courage: *Protagoras* 360d

Near the end of this dialogue, Socrates tries to show the sophist that anyone who is courageous must have knowledge. His strategy is quite simple: he leads Protagoras to the conclusion that "courage is knowledge of what is and is not fearful" (360d1-2), and from this it follows that no one who lacks knowledge

---

[29] Presumably, Socrates is open to the suggestion that his words for temperance and justice name the whole of virtue. For these Greek terms are sufficiently broad to make this thesis plausible. See Irwin, *Plato's Moral Theory*, pp. 19-23. But he obviously thought that courage and piety do not encompass the whole of virtue. Does that mean that courage, piety, and virtue will each have its own definition? Not necessarily, as we will see in Sec. 9. See esp. n. 51. It could be said, against my interpretation, that it does not take the gold analogy seriously: the parts of gold are qualitatively uniform, whereas the parts of a face are not. But I think it would be a mistake to press this analogy (or the face analogy) too far. Roughly, the idea is that virtue is a single systematically connected theory which must be acquired and understood as a whole; we can talk about different parts of it, just as we can point to different parts of a gold bar, but that does not show that it is not a uniform object. By contrast, the parts of a face are connected to each other only because they happen to belong to a single object, the head. Suppose all members of a certain society knew history, geometry, and farming: in that society, these subjects would always be found together (like eyes, ears, and mouth), but that would hardly show that history, geometry, and farming constitute a single branch of knowledge. Courage, piety, and virtue are far more closely connected—they form a single theory—and that is the point of the gold analogy. Notice that this analogy is quite misleading in one respect: gold can be cut into parts, and one can acquire one part without acquiring the rest; but that is precisely what Socrates wants to deny about the virtues. Obviously, the gold analogy is not intended to be exact. The main test for an interpretation of the *Protagoras* is not literal faithfulness to this analogy, but its ability to reconcile the two views that Socrates adopts: (A) some virtues are less than the whole of virtue; (B) all the virtue-terms name the same uniform thing.

can be courageous (360d9-e5). The question I want to ask is this: should we take "courage is knowledge of what is and is not fearful" to be a definition that Socrates is backing in the *Protagoras*?[30] If so, then I must abandon my thesis that he *never* thinks he has a satisfactory definition of a virtue, and I will have to admit that in the *Protagoras*, at least, he does not expect a satisfactory definition to provide a workable standard for making practical decisions. After all, if someone is having trouble deciding what the courageous thing to do is, he will not be helped by being told that courage is knowledge of what is and is not fearful. And if, in the *Protagoras*, Socrates does not expect a definition to provide a standard for decision-making, then perhaps it is wrong to read this criterion into the *Charmides*, where this test for definitions is nowhere stated. In that case, "knowledge of good and evil" might be Socrates' definition of temperance after all, and we might have to discount the passages in which he claims to have no such definition.

On the surface, it does seem reasonable to take "knowledge of what is and is not fearful" to be Socrates' answer to the question, "What is courage?" For he is the one who leads Protagoras to accept it, and he uses this statement about courage to show the sophist that one cannot be courageous without having knowledge. Would Socrates use a statement he does not accept to win victory in an argument? Some scholars find it hard to believe that he ever resorts to such low blows. On the other hand, there is a formidable obstacle to the view that here in the *Protagoras* Socrates has for once found a definition to his liking. For as the dialogue draws to a close, soon after the alleged definition of courage has been discovered, Socrates confesses (360e6-361d6) that he is caught in a dilemma: he began by arguing that virtue is unteachable, but then he tried to show that all of the virtues are forms of knowledge; and if they are branches of knowledge, then surely they are teachable. To resolve this problem, Socrates suggests that he and Protagoras directly confront the question, "What is virtue?" If they solve that problem, they can return to the question of whether it is

---

[30] An affirmative answer is given by Santas, *Socrates*, p. 100. Similarly Vlastos, "What did Socrates Understand by His 'What is F?' Question?" p. 417.

teachable. Yet, if Socrates takes himself to have discovered what courage is, then it is difficult to see what he is getting at when the dialogue ends. For consider: Socrates has argued that courage, like any virtue, is unteachable; he has also argued that it is knowledge, and he infers from this that it is teachable. How to resolve this conflict? By finding out what courage is. But by hypothesis, he has already done so!

Evidently, we must choose between two alternatives: either Socrates isn't serious at the end of the dialogue, when he says that it will be useful to discover what virtue is; or, he doesn't seriously accept "knowledge of what is and is not fearful" as a satisfactory definition of courage. Once we pose the problem in this way, it becomes clear that the second alternative is the right one.[31] By reading the dialogue in the way I suggest, we bring it into line with all the others; and it would be quite odd if Socrates had succeeded in finding the definition of one virtue, but of no others. If someone can define a certain virtue, then according to Socrates he *has* that virtue;[32] and since one cannot have any virtue without having the others,[33] Socrates cannot believe that he has a satisfactory definition of courage but of nothing else. And we must remember the connection between Socratic definition and Socratic politics: to understand his political attitudes, we must assume that he is always hoping for a standard of right action whenever he looks for definitions. Furthermore, we have the straightforward testimony of the *Laches*, where Socrates rejects the view (194e11-199e11) that courage

---

[31] Allen, *Plato's 'Euthyphro,'* p. 89 n. 1, also appeals to *Protag.* 360e6-361d6 to cast doubt on the view that the dialogue contains a definition of courage with which Socrates is satisfied. But I do not accept his view (pp. 95-99) that since Socrates has not defined virtue, he is committed to no positive doctrine in this dialogue. For example, Socrates clearly endorses the doctrine that virtue is knowledge (361b1-2). In Sec. 9 below, we will see why Socrates thinks that the teachability issue can be resolved only when virtue is defined.

[32] See *Grg.* 460a5-b7: knowledge of justice is sufficient for being just. I assume that, according to Socrates, if someone can defend a satisfactory definition of a virtue, then he knows that virtue. But as we will see in Sec. 7, one can have knowledge of virtue, and thereby qualify as a virtuous person, without having a satisfactory definition of virtue. Of course, a good person must be able to pass *some* intellectual tests: see *Ap.* 29e4-30a2.

[33] I take him to deny Protagoras' thesis that some virtues can be acquired in the absence of others. See 329e2-6, 349d2-8, 359a7-b6.

can be defined as knowledge of the fearful and the hopeful. Of course, we could say that the *Laches* comes after the *Protagoras*, and that in the later work Socrates is rejecting a position he had advocated earlier.[34] But there is a better way of explaining the relationship between the two dialogues: in the *Protagoras*, Socrates is not being completely honest with the sophist when he leads him to the conclusion that courage is knowledge of what is and is not hopeful. He does believe that courage is knowledge of something, and whatever that something is, Protagoras will have to concede defeat: it will be impossible to be courageous without having knowledge. But Socrates does not want the discussion to go off on a tangent, and that is precisely what would happen if he argued with Protagoras in a more scrupulous way; if he confessed his doubts about what the courageous person knows, the dialogue would become even more protracted and shapeless than it is. And so the project of finding fault with the statement, "courage is knowledge of what is and is not fearful," is left for another occasion.[35] Socrates wins a victory over Protagoras through a bit of dishonesty, but his sin is venial, since the sophist would have lost the argument in any case had Socrates decided to proceed in a more open and roundabout way.

This way of looking at courage in the *Protagoras* is reinforced by one further consideration: on two other occasions in this dialogue, Socrates' arguments exhibit a similar pattern of excusable dishonesty. The first is well known, though highly controversial. To prove that knowledge cannot be mastered by pleasure or passion, Socrates gets Protagoras to recognize that all of his choices, and the choices of the many, are made on a hedonistic basis (353c9-354c2). That is, what makes one alternative better than another is the fact that it leads to more pleasure or less pain over the long run. Once that concession is made,

---

[34] Santas, "Socrates at Work on Virtue and Knowledge in Plato's *Laches*," p. 202, suggests the reverse interpretation: the *Laches* precedes the *Protagoras*. But how could Socrates first reject a certain definition of courage, and then accept it without giving any explanation of why the earlier objection was misguided?

[35] I have no view about the relative order of the *Laches* and the *Protagoras*. If the *Laches* is earlier, then in the *Protagoras* Socrates is keeping the sophist in the dark about a point he made before; if the *Laches* is later, then in the *Protagoras* Socrates is postponing criticism of the definition in question.

Socrates has an easy time showing that no one knowingly chooses the worse of two alternatives (354e3-358d4), and on this basis he is able to prove that courage is a form of knowledge (358d5-360e5). Now, many have held—and I agree—that hedonism is not Socrates' own position.[36] Although he depends on hedonism to reach important conclusions in the *Protagoras*, he does not in fact accept this premise, as we can see most clearly from his extremely bitter attack in the *Gorgias* on the equation of pleasure and the good.[37] In other words, in the *Protagoras* he argues in a dishonest way, and he redeems himself by setting the record straight in a different dialogue: this is precisely the way he treats courage, as we have just seen. A third instance of

[36] Thus Sullivan, "Hedonism in Plato's *Protagoras*," pp. 24-28; A. E. Taylor, *Plato*, p. 260; Vlastos, "Socrates on Acrasia," pp. 75-78; Santas, *Socrates*, pp. 198-199, 318-319 n. 8; and Zeyl, "Socrates and Hedonism: *Protagoras* 351b-358d." On the opposite side, see C.C.W. Taylor, *Plato Protagoras*, pp. 164-167; Irwin, *Plato's Moral Theory*, pp. 103-108, 308-309 n. 13; Grote, *Plato*, Vol. II, pp. 87-89; Hackforth, "Hedonism in Plato's *Protagoras*"; and Crombie, *An Examination of Plato's Doctrines*, Vol. I, p. 240.

[37] More fully, I hold that: (A) in the *Protagoras* Socrates never clearly embraces hedonism as his own position; (B) nor does he ever deny the truth of hedonism in this dialogue; (C) the *Protagoras*' argument for the power of knowledge and the unity of courage and wisdom rests on the truth of hedonism; (D) but what we find in other dialogues, especially the *Gorgias* (494e9-500e1), makes it difficult to believe that Socrates was ever a hedonist; (E) and therefore, the most likely interpretation is that in the *Protagoras* he is using his opponents' underlying commitment to hedonism to subvert their own position. In view of (B) and (C), we would be fully justified in taking Socrates to be a hedonist in the *Protagoras*, if we had no other information about him.

Notice that in the *Gorgias*, Socrates rejects not only (1) the view that pleasure is the good (495a3, d4), but also (2) the view that all pleasures are to some extent good (495a3-4, b3-4, 499c7; contrast *Protag.* 351c2-6), as well as (3) the view that the virtuous life happens to be the most pleasant life (497e3-499b3). It is hard to believe that he could have adopted any of these propositions in the *Protagoras* only to deny them *with such great contempt* in the *Gorgias*. (And if the latter gives us Plato's position rather than Socrates', it would still be hard to believe that Plato suddenly had such disdain for the doctrine of his revered teacher.) The *Gorgias* says that politicians, orators, and sophists can acquire power ony if they make decisions solely on the basis of pleasure and pain. See 464b2-465e1, 518a7-c7, 521d6-522a7. Accordingly, in the *Protagoras*, Socrates brings out the underlying hedonism of Greece's leading sophist; he is not bringing Protagoras over to a doctrine that is alien to him. In assenting to Socrates' questions at 351b4-7, Protagoras shows that he is a hedonist, but he is reluctant to accept that position when boldly stated, at b7-c2. Similarly, the many mask their underlying hedonism (351c2-3, with 353c9-354e2). For details, see Zeyl, "Socrates and Hedonism: *Protagoras* 351b-358d."

this pattern is not widely recognized, but I will dwell on it in Section 11: to show that virtue is unteachable, Socrates claims that the wisest and best of the Athenians have not been able to teach it (319d7-320b5); and his star example of a wise man is Pericles (319e3-320b1)—the same Pericles who is attacked in the *Gorgias* for his lack of concern with virtue, properly conceived (515c4-519c2). It would be a mistake to think that for some mysterious reason Socrates changed his mind about Pericles somewhere between the *Protagoras* and the *Gorgias*.[38] He believes in the former no less than in the latter that this popular leader has only the lowest level of wisdom and virtue; but he thinks that his argument for the unteachability of virtue still works even though one of its premises—that Pericles is wise— is false. Later, we will see more clearly how this argument for the unteachability of virtue works, and why it is an excusable form of dishonesty. For now, I think it is safe to conclude that "knowledge of what is and is not fearful" is not really Socrates' candidate, in the *Protagoras*, for a satisfactory definition of courage.

6
Socratic epistemology: Two apparent contradictions

I have done all I can to defend a thesis put forward in Chapter VII: Socrates should be taken at his word when he says that he cannot answer his own "What is X?" questions. As we have seen, the passages that seem to conflict with this interpretation do not really do so. Now I want to prepare a defense of two other claims of Chapter VII: (A) Socrates took himself to be quite distant from the discovery of satisfactory moral definitions; (B) in fact, he had no confidence that this discovery is humanly possible. The evidence for (A) is to be found in the *Apology*, where Socrates announces that the only form of wis-

---

[38] Dodds, *Plato Gorgias*, p. 21 n. 3, takes the *Gorgias* and the *Protagoras* to conflict over the issue of hedonism, and charges that other scholars, who want to reconcile the two works, have an irrational zeal for finding unity in Plato's thought. Would he want to say, therefore, that these two dialogues differ over the merits of Pericles? Why not? Didn't Socrates and Plato ever change their minds?

dom he has consists in knowing how little his wisdom is worth. The evidence for (B) consists primarily in Socrates' argument for the unteachability of virtue. (A) tells us that Socrates saw a huge gulf between his accomplishments and those of a moral expert; (B) goes even further, and tells us that he suspected the gulf to be unbridgeable. Taken together, (A) and (B) make Socrates' satisfaction with the laws of his native city all the more significant. He thought that, in principle, moral experts should rule in an authoritative manner, but that in the meantime Athenian democracy provided the best conditions for the discovery of the correct moral system. What (A) and (B) tell us is that this *meantime* might be a very long time indeed. Socrates thought it would be hard—perhaps impossible—to improve on Athenian democracy; that is why he cannot be considered, as he too often is, a simple antidemocrat.

My defense of (A) rests on an interpretation of the *Apology*, but before we confront the relevant passages, it is best to become aware of two apparent inconsistencies between this work and several early dialogues.

(1) Socrates thinks that virtue is a branch of knowledge, and this entails that whoever is virtuous must possess some knowledge. Of course, what it is that the virtuous person knows—what it is that makes him virtuous—is a question Socrates cannot answer, as we have seen. But nonetheless, he can say in various rough ways what a good person must understand: the good person must know how to make decisions and how to live his life well; and he must have knowledge of the virtues. However, it seems paradoxical that according to Socrates of all people a virtuous person must have knowledge of virtue: for he considers himself to be a virtuous man,[39] and yet he denies that he has knowledge of virtue. He holds in the *Meno* (71b3-4) that if one does not know what virtue is, then one can know nothing further about it. Now, *he* does not know what virtue is, since he cannot answer his "What is X?" questions when they are asked about the virtues. Therefore he should conclude that

---

[39] *Ap.* 30c8-d1 and 41c8-d2 are best interpreted in this way. *Ap.* 20d6-8 and *Grg.* 521b4-6 put the matter beyond doubt. *Ap.* 20d6-8 will be more fully discussed in Sec. 7 below.

he is not virtuous. He should take himself to be a walking counter-example to the thesis that virtue is knowledge. How could he have missed this internal contradiction?[40]

(2) To make matters worse, there is at least one passage in which Socrates most definitely claims to know something about virtue. Recall the line that played such an important role in Chapter VII: ". . . To do an injustice and disobey a superior, whether divine or human: that, I know, is bad and shameful" (*Ap.* 29b6-7). Earlier, I called attention to the authoritarian implications of this statement. Now I want to emphasize the point that Socrates claims to *know* that it is true.[41] We cannot dismiss this claim to knowledge as a careless remark tossed off at an unguarded moment, for it is spoken just after Socrates has told his judges that he never makes unsupportable claims to knowledge. Death, he says, is something no mortal knows to be an evil, and so the fear of death is sheer presumption on our part (29a4–b6). Then he adds: but the shamefulness of disobeying a superior—that is something I *do* claim to know. Clearly, Socrates is being quite careful and self-conscious here about his epistemology.[42] But his claim to knowledge contradicts his statement in the *Meno* that one cannot know anything about virtue if one cannot say what it is. Socrates cannot say what justice or injustice are, but he claims to *know* that disobeying a superior is unjust. How did this contradiction escape him?

Both of our problems could be solved if we said that Socrates *does* have a satisfactory definition of the virtues, for then he would be entitled to consider himself a good man, and he would

[40] Here I am indebted to Gregory Vlastos for raising this problem. See "The Paradox of Socrates," p. 7. His solution (pp. 10-12) is to distinguish senses of "knowledge" and to read Socratic disavowals of knowledge as equivocations.

[41] Again I am indebted to Gregory Vlastos (this time to unpublished writing) for calling this passage to my attention. See too Irwin, *Plato's Moral Theory*, p. 58.

[42] Two other passages in the *Apology* support this interpretation: (A) In the immediately following sentence, Socrates says (29b7-9), "I will never fear or flee, in the place of bad things which *I know* to be bad, such things as, for all I know, might be good . . ." (B) When considering a counter-penalty to death, Socrates asks (37b7-8), "Instead of this, should I choose something that *I know* is bad, and propose that as my penalty?" (my emphasis in both cases). Cf. Ch. II n. 21.

also be entitled to claim that he knows disobedience toward superiors to be an injustice. But I have already given my reasons for resisting this interpretation. In the next two sections, I will propose a better solution to the problems that have just been raised. Having done that, we will be able to see the evidence for theses (A) and (B).

7

Socratic wisdom and ignorance

If we want to understand how Socrates can consider himself to be virtuous, we have to take a careful look at the *Apology*, for that is the work in which he plainly admits that he has a certain form of wisdom—a wisdom that is unsurpassed by that of any other human being. Yet, paradoxically, we will also see how small that wisdom is, in Socrates' own eyes, and how distant he takes himself to be from the full possession of moral knowledge.

After pointing out that he does not claim to teach virtue, as others do, Socrates tries to explain why some have started referring to him as a wise man:

> (i) My fellow Athenians, I am called by this name for no reason other than a certain wisdom on my part. What sort of wisdom is this? That which might be called human wisdom. . . . (20d6–8)

In explanation, he tells the story of Chaerephon's visit to the Delphic oracle. The priestess is asked whether anyone is wiser than Socrates, and replies that no one is. When Socrates hears of this, he is greatly puzzled:

> (ii) . . . Whatever does the god mean? What is his riddle? For I know myself to be wise in neither a great nor a small way. . . . (21b3–5)

But after searching for wiser men than he, Socrates begins to see what the god is getting at. A politician with a reputation for wisdom cannot satisfactorily answer the philosopher's questions, yet refuses to acknowledge his own ignorance. So Socrates infers:

(iii) . . . I am wiser than this man. It seems likely that neither of us knows anything grand [*kalon kagathon*], but he thinks he knows something even though he does not, whereas I neither know nor think that I know. It seems, then, that I am wiser than he in this one small way: whatever I don't know, I don't think I know. (21d2–7)

Investigations of the poets and the craftsmen reach the same results, and so finally Socrates concludes:

(iv) It is likely, my friends, that the god is the one who is really wise, and what he means by his oracle is this: "Human wisdom is worth little or nothing." And it seems that in referring to Socrates, he is only using my name and making me an example, as though to say: "Mankind, this one among you is wisest, who, like Socrates, has come to know that he is in truth worth nothing, in regard to wisdom." (23a5–b4)

Two points about these passages should be noticed. First, in (iii) and (iv), Socrates is significantly modifying something he said in (ii). His initial reaction to the oracle is that he has no reason whatsoever to be considered wise. But in (iii) he concedes that he is wise after all—though in a small way. The completely unconditional disavowal of (ii) is rejected, and so Socrates has learned something important about himself through his search for a wiser man: he now thinks he has a certain form of wisdom, whereas before he did not.[43] He comes to see that

---

[43] I see no reason to doubt that the oracle was a turning point in Socrates' life. Before that event, he must have distinguished himself in moral debate with major figures; that is what prompted Chaerephon's question. But up until that time, Socrates could not have considered his dialectical skill or his interest in moral discussion to be the key to a virtuous life. He thought of himself as someone who lacked wisdom, and he thought that the specialized craft-skills of his fellow citizens gave them a *bona fide* form of wisdom. But then, when the oracle says that no one is wiser than Socrates, he is forced to discover the mark that distinguishes himself from others, and he locates it in his knowing how little he knows about virtue. Because of the god, he now sees moral discussion as an intrinsically worthwhile activity, even when it does not lead to definitive solutions; and he realizes that the peculiar form of wisdom he has acquired through moral discussion is the only existing form that is intrinsically worthwhile. For further discussion, see Brickhouse and Smith, "The Origins of Socrates' Mission."

his initial reaction to the oracle, as reported in (ii), was a mistake.[44] Second, nothing Socrates says in (i), (iii), or (iv) entails or even suggests that he thinks of himself as someone who has absolutely no moral knowledge whatsoever. He says in (iii) that whenever he does not know something, he does not claim to know it: that of course leaves him free to claim some knowledge. And earlier in (iii) he says that neither he nor his conceited interlocutor "knows anything grand." This does not disavow all knowledge claims whatever, but only belittles whatever Socrates does claim to know. And (iv) of course tells the same story: human wisdom is worth little or nothing, not because wisdom is an unimportant goal, but because our knowledge of virtue and the good is so severely limited. Whatever we know is shamefully small in comparison with what we don't know, and that is why we are "worth nothing, in regard to wisdom."

So Socrates is describing himself in the following way:

(A) He knows some truths about virtue and the good.

(B) The number of truths he knows about virtue and the good is greatly outweighed by the number he does not know.

(C) He never claims to know what he does not know.

(D) His small wisdom—the only wisdom that a human being can achieve—consists in knowing that (B) is true, and in never claiming to know what he does not.

Proposition (A) is never denied by (i), (iii), or (iv); on the contrary, it is suggested by the claim that Socrates knows nothing grand (i.e. what he knows is nothing grand), and by the claim that human wisdom is worth little or nothing (i.e. what any of

[44] Having finally understood what the oracle means, Socrates presumably realizes that his initial reaction to it, as recorded in (ii), is self-contradictory. You cannot know that you have no knowledge, and similarly you cannot know that you are not wise even in a small way; for to know something is to have a small amount of wisdom. By putting his initial reaction to the oracle into the form of a self-contradiction, Socrates is telling his audience that he should have realized from the start that he was wrong to disavow all claims to knowledge and wisdom. When Socrates goes on, in (iii) and (iv), to correct his initial impression, he avoids making self-contradictory claims about his wisdom.

us knows comes to little). But of course, the best piece of evidence for (A) comes later, when Socrates insists that he does have some moral knowledge: he knows that disobeying a better is bad and shameful (29b6-7). Obviously, (iii) and (iv) have to be interpreted in the light of that later claim, and so it is best to take the *Apology* to be conceding that Socrates does know something—though not much—about virtue and the good. His claim to wisdom is not based on his knowing those few moral truths, but rather on his knowledge of how little he knows.[45]

A serious problem could be raised for Socrates at this point: what is the difference between *knowing* that one knows little about virtue, and *truly believing* that one knows little? This is no idle question, for it is connected with the issue of how easy or difficult it is to become a virtuous person. Consider someone who has no interest in moral problems, and who gladly admits that he has no knowledge in this area. Suppose he is told that ethics is a vast subject, embracing many truths that have yet to be discovered, and he accepts this claim on faith. I think that Socrates would not want to attribute *any* knowledge or wisdom to such an individual—not even the second-order wisdom that he himself has. The individual in question may have a true and justified belief that he knows nothing about ethics, but he does not *know* it. But why not? What is it about knowledge that would allow Socrates to say this? Socrates has no answer to this question, for he has no interest in epistemology. Perhaps he is

---

[45] See too *Symp.* 175e2-3: Socrates' wisdom is a paltry thing (*phaulē*), and beset by difficulties (*amphisbētēsimos*), as though he were in a dream. In the *Meno*, after the distinction between knowledge and right opinion is made, Socrates says (98b3-5), ". . . If I should say that I have knowledge—and I should say this in few cases—I would lay this down as one of the things I know." The explicit distinction made here between knowledge and right opinion is Platonic rather than Socratic, but nonetheless it is significant that the *Meno* repeats the *Apology*'s portrayal of Socrates as someone who confesses his epistemic mediocrity: he does make some knowledge claims, but not many. This conflicts with *Euthyd.* 293b7-8, where Socrates says that he knows many things, though they are small. I take this to mean that he knows what any ordinary person knows—e.g. that it is hot in the summer, dark at night, etc.—but that none of this amounts to much when it is compared with what he doesn't know. So the conflict with *Meno* 98b3-5 is superficial: whether Socrates claims to know a lot of things or only a few, the important point is that such knowledge and wisdom as he has is minute in comparison with what remains to be discovered.

tacitly relying on the assumption that any claim to wisdom must be backed up by some genuine skill, and the individual in question has no such skill. Socrates can successfully defend himself in argument, and so he is entitled to claim a second-order form of knowledge. But those who recognize their ignorance do not, by virtue of that fact, have any skill that would support a claim to knowledge. Unable to pass a Socratic cross-examination, they may justifiably and correctly believe that they have no knowledge, but they do not yet know it. I do not claim that this is a satisfactory defense of Socrates' position, but it may be the assumption that lies behind his claim to moral preeminence.

In any case, the solution I propose to the first problem of Section 6 should be clear by now. Socrates is being perfectly straightforward when he claims that he knows of no satisfactory definition of the virtues. Although he does need to claim some knowledge and wisdom in order to qualify as a virtuous man, he has no need to claim any first-order knowledge of propositions about virtue and the good. What he does know is how little his first-order moral knowledge comes to, when it is compared with what he doesn't know. That is the form of wisdom that allows him to claim in the *Apology* that he is a good man and cannot be harmed.

8

An epistemic retreat

The *Apology*, as I have interpreted it, portrays Socrates as someone who has some moral knowledge, but very little. In certain places, however, his epistemology is more radical: for example, having argued in Book I of the *Republic* that justice is a virtue and that the just are happy, Socrates insists that he doesn't *know* that these things are so (354c1-3). For he doesn't yet have a satisfactory account of what justice is, and in the absence of such an account, he thinks he is not entitled to claim knowledge of justice. Here Socrates is appealing to the restrictive epistemic principle put forward in the *Meno* (71b3-4), and his adherence to that principle prevents him from claiming to know even those propositions in which he has great confidence. He is as certain of the point that justice is a virtue as he is of anything. It is a claim he has argued for, and he sees nothing wrong with the case he has made. But if he has no doubt about the proposition that justice is a virtue, why does he refuse to say that he knows it to be true? Why does he think that he needs an account of what justice is before he can issue any knowledge claims about it? I suggest that he is making the following two assumptions:

(i) If someone knows the correct definition of X, he is in the best possible position for making true claims about X.

(ii) No one is entitled to claim any knowledge about X unless he is in the best possible position for making such claims.

With definition comes expertise (*La.* 190a1-c2), and of course the experts in any field are the ones who are in the best position to make true claims about their subject. So it is not difficult to believe that Socrates always assumed the truth of principle (i). On the other hand, (ii) is a principle that he cannot always have believed throughout the early dialogues. For as we have seen, in the *Apology* he confidently and deliberately claims to know that disobeying a superior individual is bad and shameful (29b6-7). He has no definition of justice, and yet he claims to know something about it; since (i) is an assumption he has every reason to make, it follows that he is not committed to (ii) in the *Apology*. Now, it is reasonable to hold that the *Apology* is one of the earliest, if not the first, of Plato's works, whereas the *Meno* comes at the end of his early period.[46] Book I of the *Republic* may well have been composed during Plato's middle pe-

---

[46] The chronological place of the *Apology* among the early works is unfortunately a matter of guesswork and subjective impressions. Guthrie, *History*, Vol. IV, pp. 71-72, briefly reviews the range of opinions that have been held on this issue, and is "inclined . . . to agree that it was Plato's first work, written not long after the event" (p. 72). The *Meno*, by contrast, is generally agreed to be a transitional work between the early and the middle dialogues. See Guthrie, ibid., p. 236; Bluck, *Plato's Meno*, pp. 108-120; Dodds, *Plato Gorgias*, pp. 23-27. The philosophical discrepancy between the *Apology* and the *Meno*, to which I have been calling attention, is a good reason for ascribing the former work to the earlier part of Plato's early period. Where there is conflict between his works, it is plausible to assume that they are separated by a significant period of time.

riod, along with the rest of that dialogue; but even if it was written at an earlier time, it is plausible to believe that it belongs to the latest group of early dialogues.[47] So I suggest that as Plato continued to write about Socrates, he made a modification in his teacher's epistemology: at first, (ii) is not a principle that Socrates accepts, but at a later point it is. If the *Apology*, being considerably earlier than the *Meno*, is the more accurate portrait of the historical Socrates, then that philosopher never disavowed *all* claims to first-order moral knowledge. Principle (ii) is a Platonic scruple that gets foisted on to Socrates.

This principle is evidently at work in another dialogue that was written at a late point in Plato's early period: the *Gorgias*. After arguing, against Callicles, that injustice must be avoided at all costs, Socrates says:

> Since these things have appeared in our previous arguments to be so, they are—so I claim—held down and secured by arguments of iron and adamant, if I may use such a rough expression. So at any rate it seems. If you or someone more feisty cannot undo them, then no speaker contradicting what I now affirm can be right. Yet I always make the same statement: I don't know how these things stand, but of all those I've encountered none—including you—have been able to contradict [me] without being ridiculous. (508e6–509a7)

Why doesn't he claim to have knowledge,[48] if he has "arguments of iron and adamant"? After all, in the *Apology* he did

---

[47] See Ch. VII n. 71.

[48] At *Grg.* 486e5-6, Socrates says he knows that if he and Callicles manage to agree about something, then the agreed-upon proposition is true. And this could be taken to mean that if he and Callicles agree upon *p*, then Socrates knows that *p*. But how could he have knowledge about virtue before he acquires a satisfactory definition—something he is not even looking for in the *Gorgias*? My response is to take his remark at 486e5-6 as a piece of irony. As in the *Euthyphro*, Socrates' first maneuver in confronting an interlocutor is to inflate his opponent's credentials; and it becomes clear as we read beyond *Grg.* 486e5-6 that this is what he is doing to Callicles. For example, at 487e1-5, Socrates says that if he and Callicles agree upon something, he will never have to test it in argument again, for Callicles could never concede a point through lack of wisdom or excess of shame. Obviously, Socrates isn't seriously saying that he would refuse to reexamine a statement merely because he and Callicles had

claim to know that superiors deserve obedience, and presumably the arguments he used to support this position were not stronger than those of the *Gorgias*. The most plausible answer, I suggest, is that Plato is by this point subscribing to principle (ii). Socrates has no definition of justice, and therefore he cannot claim any knowledge about it. So when he says in the above passage that he always makes "the same statement: I don't know how these things stand," he is ignoring a way in which the *Gorgias* departs from the *Apology*. It is quite true that he always issued disclaimers of knowledge, and that is what he is getting at above. But it is equally true that he once claimed some small amount of moral knowledge. So the early dialogues give us two conflicting pictures of Socrates' epistemology: according to one, he merely insists on the smallness of his knowledge about the virtues; according to the other, he becomes more extreme and disavows all first-order moral knowledge whatsoever. Nonetheless, whenever Socrates claims to have knowledge or claims to lack it, he is being unequivocal and sincere. When he says that he knows of no satisfactory account of the virtues, he is being perfectly honest: there is no esoteric definition hidden between the lines of the early dialogues. Again, when he says in the *Apology* that he knows that superiors deserve obedience, he is to be taken at his word, for he does not yet subscribe to principle (ii). That principle comes into play in the *Gorgias*, and so in this dialogue Socrates exercises even more epistemic caution than before.

The early dialogues, taken as a group, do contain a contradiction, for the epistemic principle laid down in the *Meno* and followed by both the *Gorgias* and *Republic* I is violated in the *Apology*. But it is hardly surprising to discover that Plato's description of Socrates changes, as he begins to develop his own views. Socrates has always been an epistemological conservative, priding himself on the fact that he claims to know no more than he really does. So the new Socrates of the *Gorgias* is really continuous with the old Socrates of the *Apology*: one claims to

---

agreed to it; similarly, we don't have to take him seriously when he says, at the beginning of his speech, that he will have knowledge of whatever he and Callicles agree upon.

know little, the other nothing. And that must have struck Plato as a minor modification in his portrayal of Socrates. Nonetheless, this alteration may have posed the following problem in his mind: if someone has true beliefs rather than knowledge, does that show that he is not a virtuous person? Suppose Socrates had said in the *Apology*, not that he knows little, but that the number of moral truths he has come to *believe* is just a small proportion of the moral truths there are. And suppose he had said, not that he knows, but that he believes there are many more truths waiting to be discovered. If in fact he has no knowledge of this sort, but only hard-earned belief, would he have to admit that he is not a virtuous person at all? According to the *Meno*, no such concession is necessary, since virtue does not require knowledge.[49] It can hardly be a coincidence that when Plato starts rejecting Socratic claims to knowledge, he also rejects the principle that without knowledge one cannot be virtuous. In the *Meno*, Plato is not giving up all hope that moral knowledge can be acquired and that virtue can be taught. But since he has become more fastidious about when knowledge claims are justified, he compensates by lowering the old Socratic standard of what it takes to be a virtuous person.

One further point. We should realize that the *Meno*'s epistemic restriction goes significantly beyond what has been said earlier, in the *Protagoras* and the *Laches*. In the *Protagoras*, Socrates says that he would like to find out what virtue is, and then return to the question of whether or not it is teachable (361c2–6). It is plausible to take this to mean that the perplexity into which he and Protagoras have fallen will never be resolved until they determine what virtue is. But notice that this is quite a limited claim, when compared with the *Meno*'s principle that we can know no quality of X until we know that X is. That principle prevents Socrates from claiming any knowledge whatsoever about virtue, but nothing in the *Protagoras* limits him so severely. Similarly, nothing in the *Laches* prevents him from knowing something about virtue. He says in this dialogue that

---

[49] See 96e4–97a7, 98b7–c10. In Sec. 12, we will take a closer look at the *Meno*'s rejection of the thesis that knowledge is necessary for virtue. See esp. nn. 81, 82 below.

since he lacks a definition of the virtues, he cannot advise anyone about the best method of becoming virtuous (190a1–c6,
200e1–201b5). But that is a far cry from the claim that he can
know nothing about the virtues.[50] It is a mistake to take the
Meno's epistemic principle to be the tacit assumption guiding
Socrates throughout the early dialogues. The claim he makes to
knowledge in the *Apology* shows that this cannot have been so.
The *Meno*'s epistemic severity is something Plato attributes to
Socrates rather late in the game.

9
Socratic definition revisited

Someone might say that Socrates is naive to think that so much
good will come of definitions. How, for example, can a brief
sentence about justice help us resolve all our political problems?
How can a simple statement about piety serve as a standard for
deciding whether any given act is pious? To see what is wrong
with these questions, we should recall one of the points I made
about the *Apology*: Socrates believes (in fact, he says he knows)
that the truths about virtue that he has yet to discover far out-
number the few truths he knows. So he can hardly be criticized
for thinking that all he needs is one magical sentence about the
virtues (or perhaps a separate one for each), and suddenly per-
fection will be achieved. Rather, he must believe that the search
for a proper account of the virtues will require the discovery of
a large series of moral truths, and that after we systematically
explore these truths, we will be able to single out one statement
about virtue (or perhaps one corresponding to each virtue)[51]

---

[50] As we will see in the following section, Socrates has good reason, quite
apart from the *Meno*'s epistemological scruple (71b3–4), to say that the dilemma
of the *Protagoras* cannot be resolved unless we know what virtue is. Similarly,
we will see that the claim of the *Laches*—that one cannot teach virtue without
having a definition—is defensible quite apart from the *Meno*'s epistemology.

[51] The fact that courage and piety are sub-theories of a larger discipline (see
Sec. 4) does not mean that each will provide its own standard for action. To
decide what is the courageous thing to do, we might need to look at the definition of virtue, and there might be no separate definition of courage. Socrates
has no way of telling whether this will be the case until he actually discovers
what the virtues are.

that will serve as our definition. That definition will form the most important part of our new theory, but it need not be understandable apart from its relation to all the rest. Notice that the definitions of the virtues in the *Republic* have this character: though they are couched in familiar terms, we cannot fully understand them without also understanding the psychological and political assumptions that lead up to them. I see no reason to think that, according to Socrates, definitions can be discovered and understood in a simpler way.[52]

Earlier, in Sections 2-5, I emphasized the point that Socrates expects a good definition to provide a workable standard for making practical decisions. Such statements as "virtue is knowledge of how to live well" or "virtue is knowledge of good and evil" might pass certain tests for satisfactory definitions, but they fail to provide the standard Socrates is looking for. But now it might be asked: does Socrates have good reason to reject such vague statements as these, if he concedes that the search for definitions must uncover a whole series of ethical truths before it achieves success? Granted, "knowledge of good and evil" *by itself* won't tell us what to do in particular cases; but perhaps it will provide a workable standard if it is combined with a good deal more. So, it could be charged, Socrates should concede that "knowledge of good and evil" might turn out to be a perfectly adequate definition of virtue after all. His rejection of such vague generalities seems to be premature.

I think that Socrates can be defended against this charge. Even if no single statement can by itself provide a criterion for action, we can still recognize a distinction between vague, general statements and those that embody a substantive moral conception. An example might help here. Consider the claim that ". . . institutions are just when no arbitrary distinctions are made between persons in the assigning of basic rights and duties and when the rules determine a proper balance between competing

---

[52] Contrast Teloh's conception of Socratic definition, *Plato's Metaphysics*, pp. 34-35, 46, 65. He takes Socrates to believe that discovering how to act involves introspection into one's soul, and he rightly criticizes this position (p. 65) for its vacuousness. ". . . In the early dialogues we are never given clear directions for introspection, nor are we really ever told what such an inward glance would yield."

claims to the advantages of social life."[53] In a sense, that statement tells us what justice is, but it does so in too general a way, for the purposes of political theory. As Rawls puts it, such a statement articulates the *concept* of justice, but it does not give us a definite *conception* of this social virtue.[54] Even before one develops a full political theory, one can justifiably believe that such a vague way of expressing the notion of justice will never serve as the substantive core of one's theory of a just society. And this lesson can be applied directly to the early dialogues: Socrates is entitled to his assumption that "virtue is knowledge of good and evil" will never be the central claim of a full theory of the virtues; one can tell, even before one has the full theory, that such a statement has too little substance to form its pivotal point.[55] Socrates, in other words, is not trying to express the concept of virtue (courage, piety, etc.),[56] but is looking for a

---

[53] Rawls, *A Theory of Justice*, p. 5.

[54] Ibid., p. 5.

[55] The view I am putting forward should be distinguished from Irwin's idea in *Plato's Moral Theory*, pp. 72–73, that according to Socrates a definition of virtue must "eliminate disputed terms." Both this criterion and mine will rule out such statements as "virtue is knowledge of good and evil." But according to Irwin, the presence of the word "good" is objectionable to Socrates, whereas I see no reason why he should hold that the presence of disputed terms by itself prevents statements from having sufficient substance. In any case, the presence of disputed terms does not always produce a disputed statement: to use the familiar example, "that is a good watch" contains a disputed term, but it need not be a disputed statement. More important, I see no reason why Socrates should think the less of a purported definition if it is disputed. As we have seen, he is convinced that the many will never give up certain conventional moral beliefs; and this could easily prevent them from recognizing the truth of definitions, if ever they are discovered. Definitions, of course, must be *capable* of resolving disputes. But they will do so only if they and their associated moral theory are accepted and understood by the parties to the dispute. A theory that is full and detailed enough will pass this test, even if it is centered around definitions that contain disputed terms.

[56] Here I differ from Vlastos, "What did Socrates Understand by His 'What is F?' Question?" He says, pp. 412–413, that Socrates' definition of speed at *La.* 192a1–b3 looks very much like conceptual analysis. But here Socrates is merely emphasizing the point that a definition of X must apply to all and only X's. His question about speed no more calls for a semantical investigation than does the question, "What do all red objects have in common?" Vlastos thinks that at *La.* 191c7–e7 Socrates is appealing to his interlocutor's "linguistic intuitions" about courage (p. 411 n. 3). What does this amount to, if—as Vlastos admits in this same note—Socrates is not bothering with "contemporary Greek usage"? Why not say that at 191c7–e7, Socrates is appealing to his interlocutor's *moral*

particular conception of virtue (courage, piety, etc.).[57] That is, he wants a substantive theory, organized around a small number of core statements, that tells us how to decide all practical questions.[58] When Socrates asks, "What is it that a virtuous person knows?" he is looking for these core statements. Once he finds them, he will be able to spell out the property that all

beliefs? Irwin makes the same point, *Plato's Moral Theory*, pp. 63–64. I agree with Vlastos that Socrates is not trying to understand linguistic usage, but it is little improvement to say he that he is trying to understand "concepts named by those words" (p. 411 n. 3). It is best to say that Socrates is looking for a moral theory, i.e. a systematic body of sentences that will enable him to resolve practical questions.

[57] Penner, "The Unity of Virtue," pp. 41, 45, 56–57, says that if we want to understand what Socrates is getting at when he asks such questions as "What is bravery?" we should think of Freud asking, "Well, what is hysteria, really?" rather than Ryle asking, "Well, what is a feeling, really?" That is, Socrates is trying to discover that inner motive-force which causes men to act virtuously; he is not doing conceptual analysis. I agree with Penner to this extent: Socrates identifies an individual's virtue with a certain psychological state, namely, his knowledge of something or other. But I also find Penner's analogy misleading, for when Socrates asks the question, "What is courage knowledge of?" he is looking for an ethical theory, and his search is therefore not merely a psychological investigation. He is more like Kant or Mill asking, "What is justice?" than Freud asking, "What is hysteria?" Of course, he differs from Kant and Mill, since he believes that knowledge of the correct ethical theory will by itself motivate virtuous action: that is why Socrates' search for an ethical theory is at the same time a search for a virtuous person's motive-force. My position is close to that of Julia Annas, *An Introduction to Plato's Republic*, p. 23, who says of Plato's project in Book I of the *Republic*: "What he is doing is investigating *what justice is*; and this is a comprehensible task, one undertaken in books like Rawls's *A Theory of Justice*, but one not usefully described as giving a definition of justice" (her emphasis). Notice that, if we wanted to, we could give the fundamental kernel of Rawls's theory in a fairly short statement (the two principles of justice: ibid., p. 60). Similarly for utilitarianism.

[58] A core statement will not by itself provide a standard for decision, but will do so only when combined with more peripheral parts of a full ethical theory. One of the points Socrates makes against Euthyphro is that his definition of piety—"what the gods love"—cannot be combined with his other beliefs to provide an adequate standard for action. For Euthyphro believes that the gods differ in their loves and hates (6b7–c7, 7c10–e5), and this allows the possibility that a single act will be both required and forbidden (8a10–b6); furthermore, Euthyphro has so little information about the attitudes of the gods that he cannot use his definition as a standard in the present situation (9a1–b3). So the inadequacy of "loved by the gods" as a standard is demonstrated when Socrates shows how poorly it combines with Euthyphro's other beliefs. Furthermore, this alleged definition does not strike at the heart of piety (11a6–b1), since the gods love pious people for the knowledge they have of central moral truths. Those substantive truths are the ones that will be put into a definition of piety.

virtuous acts have in common, and that makes them all virtuous acts: each would be chosen by someone who has knowledge of those core statements.[59]

When we look at Socratic definition in the way I suggest, we can make good sense of his idea (*La.* 189e3–190c6) that one cannot tell others how to acquire the virtues unless one can say what they are. At first sight, this notion might seem to be absurd. Why can't one teach the virtues, even if one cannot define the concept of virtue? What does one's skill as a moral educator have to do with one's ability to give definitions of moral concepts? But once we realize that Socrates is looking for a full theory of right action, centered on a few statements about what virtue is, the connection he makes between teaching and definition is not easily dismissed. He thinks that the conventional moral training we all receive as children is partially false and radically incomplete, and that before one can advise others about how to remedy these deficiencies, one must discover the correct theory. That is what he means when he requires a moral teacher to define the virtues.

Now, finally, I am in a position to explain why I said, in Chapter VII, that Socrates takes himself to be quite distant from the discovery of adequate definitions of the virtues. (This is also thesis [A] of VIII.6.) My point, quite simply, is that Socrates thinks he will have to uncover a great many moral truths before he is ever able to say what the virtues are. He realizes that what he needs is not just one statement about virtue, or a few statements about the virtues, but an entire moral theory, of which

[59] "Would be" is important here, since as yet no one has such knowledge. Penner, "The Unity of Virtue," p. 41, takes Socratic bravery to be "the psychological state which explains the fact that certain men do brave acts." But whatever it is that causes men to do brave acts now, it is certainly not the knowledge that Socrates is looking for, since no one yet has that knowledge. This is what is misleading in Penner's suggestion, pp. 56–57, that Socrates' "What is X?" question is a request for causes. Once one knows what virtue is, then of course that knowledge will cause one to behave in certain ways. But Socrates was not asking what it was that caused his contemporaries to be so virtuous. Notice that on my interpretation, there is no significant difference between asking what all virtuous *acts* have in common, and asking what all virtuous *people* have in common. All virtuous acts would be chosen by someone who knows that . . . ; all virtuous individuals know that. . . .

he possesses only the elementary fragments.[60] I know of no more plausible way to explain his statement that ". . . he is in truth worth nothing, in regard to wisdom" (*Ap.* 23b3-4).[61]

An optimistic philosopher might think that he is bound to make steady progress toward some intellectual goal he sets himself. And if the many problems that perplex him yield, one by one, to satisfactory solutions, he might have good grounds for his optimism. But what if a philosopher finds that as he discovers new truths and corrects old errors, he also becomes aware of vast areas of ignorance? The greater his superiority over conventional wisdom becomes, the more he realizes how far he falls short of real wisdom. That, I suggest, is the intellectual situation of Socrates. I also suggest that a philosopher in this situation could raise legitimate doubts about whether the discoveries he wants to make are humanly possible. After all, there is no reason to assume that human beings have the intellectual ability to discover everything they would like to know. And there is also the counsel of traditional piety: mankind knows itself when it recognizes how limited its powers are, as compared with those of the gods. For Socrates, this typically Greek notion has to be interpreted in a special way: the gods are the ones who are really wise, because they have the full and correct moral theory; the wisdom of human beings—i.e. the moral theory we have—is fragmentary. Should any human being ever make the moral discoveries Socrates wishes he could make, then he would attain the status of a god.

[60] Cf. Nagel, "The Limits of Objectivity," p. 136: "Even the most civilized human beings have only a haphazard understanding of how to live, how to treat others, how to organize their societies. The idea that the basic principles of morality are *known*, and that the problems all come in their interpretation and application, is one of the most fantastic conceits to which our conceited species has been drawn. (The idea that, if we cannot easily know it, there is no truth here, is no less conceited.) Not all of our ignorance in these areas is ethical, but a lot of it is. And the idea of the possibility of moral progress is an essential condition of moral progress. None of it is inevitable" (his emphasis). This conception of ethics is alien to Aristotle.

[61] There is one further indication that, in the eyes of Socrates, the discovery of definitions would not eliminate the need for a comprehensive moral theory: in the *Crito*, a fair bit of moral theory is brought to bear on the question whether Socrates should escape, and surely he realized that a definition could not eliminate the need for this theory. A definition of justice would shed further light on this practical issue, but it would not on its own prove the injustice of escape.

This is why Socrates makes just the right point when he says, at the end of the *Protagoras*, that we cannot know whether virtue is teachable or unteachable until we can say what it is. If one can define virtue, then one must have a full theory of right action, and whoever has such a theory can teach it to the few who will be able to learn it. But if one does not have such a theory, then the issue of virtue's teachability must remain moot. Virtue can be taught only if it can be discovered. And can it be discovered? Well, how can one tell ahead of time? As Socrates sees it, there are grounds for pessimism, since the wisest man there is—namely, himself—never gets closer to moral definitions, even as he learns more about the virtues. Perhaps, then, the gods have not given to even a few human beings the intelligence they need to discover a full moral theory. (Hence thesis [B] of VIII.6: Socrates has no confidence that moral definitions are humanly possible.) Nor should one expect, as a matter of course, that if one only works hard enough and has enough native talent, one will eventually become godlike. On the other hand, Socrates is convinced that virtue is a branch of knowledge, and it is therefore the sort of thing that should be reachable through thought and discussion. So he is caught in a dilemma: experience and piety combine to make him doubt that virtue is teachable, yet his own intellectualist conception of virtue suggests otherwise. This is precisely the dilemma he describes in the *Protagoras*.

10
Perplexity in the *Protagoras*

What are we to make of the inconsistent triad with which the *Protagoras* closes? Socrates is of course correct in claiming that these three propositions cannot all be true:

(A) Virtue is unteachable.[62]

(B) Virtue is knowledge.

(C) If virtue is knowledge, it is teachable.

[62] It is possible to challenge the common assumption that the *Protagoras* is concerned with the teach*ability* of virtue. For the Greek term that is rendered by "teachable" is *didaktos*, and this can mean "is taught" as well as "is teacha-

But which does he wish to reject? The credentials of (B) as a genuine Socratic principle are impeccable. He endorses it not only in the *Protagoras* (361b1-2), but in the *Meno* (87c11-89a4) and the *Laches* (194d1-3) as well; in the *Charmides* (165c4-6) and the *Euthyphro* (14c5-6), the search for temperance and piety eventually leads to the idea that these qualities are forms of knowledge; and if we wish to look outside the early dialogues, we can find Aristotle (*N.E.* 1144b28-30) and Xenophon (*Mem.* III ix 5-6) attributing (B) to Socrates. Furthermore, he never rejects (C);[63] in the *Protagoras* it is taken for granted, and the real tension is attributed to (A) and (B) (361a5-c1). And when the *Meno* calls attention to the conflict between (A) and (B), (C) is once again left undisturbed (87c1-7, 99a7-8). Evidently, Socrates believed that the way to resolve this problem is to reject either (A) or (B). Now, since the evidence for his allegiance to (B) is so impressive, are we forced to the conclusion that he rejected (A)? Does he introduce and defend (A) only for the sake of discussion? Does he think that his arguments for (A) at *Protagoras* 319a8-320b5 are totally without merit?

---

ble." Perhaps, then, Socrates is saying that since no one teaches virtue, it is not taught. However, the text shows decisively that he is making the more adventurous move from "no one teaches virtue" to "virtue is unteachable." At 319e1-3, he says, "The wisest and best of our citizens *are not able* to pass along to others [*ouch hoioi te allois paradidonai*] the virtue they have" (my emphasis). Surely, if they are *not able* to teach virtue, then the intended conclusion is that it *cannot* be taught. So *didaktos* is properly translated "teachable," after all. This defense of the common translation is equally applicable to the *Meno*, which also raises the question whether virtue is *didaktos*. See 99b7-9.

[63] At *Euthyd.* 282c1-8, Socrates asks Cleinias whether wisdom (*sophia*) can be taught. Cleinias replies that it can, and then Socrates, pleased with this answer, says that Cleinias has saved him the trouble of going through a long inquiry. Why does Socrates think that it would be hard to show that wisdom can be taught? Do his remarks betray any hesitation about Cleinias' answer? It is possible that he foresees the following problem: (1) He thinks that there is a good deal of support for the view that (A) if X is a branch of knowledge then X can be taught. For all of the recognized crafts are teachable. (2) He is committed to the view that virtue is a branch of knowledge. (3) He has doubts about whether virtue can be taught. (4) And so, in the light of (2) and (3), he sees problems for (A). If this speculative reconstruction of the thought behind the text is correct, then the *Euthydemus*—unlike the *Protagoras* or the *Meno*—reflects a willingness to question the view that if virtue is knowledge, it is teachable. But since Socrates accepts Cleinias' answer as satisfactory, he must think that (A) should be accepted, when all is said and done.

I wish to give negative answers to these questions. I believe that Socrates was genuinely undecided about how to resolve the conflict among (A), (B), and (C). He thinks that good reasons support each of the three propositions, yet he recognizes that they cannot be true together. So he is faced with a contradiction and fails to see any easy way out of it. True, he does think that his real choice is between (A) and (B); the *Protagoras* and the *Meno* indicate that (C) is not the source of his problem. But once (C) is assured, a choice must be made between (A) and (B), and in the *Protagoras* Socrates honestly confesses that he sees good arguments for both. We should not assume *a priori* that he was too brilliant to have believed in two opposing propositions. On the contrary, it would be absurd to suppose that no great philosopher was ever torn between conflicting views. When a philosopher tells us that he believes (A), believes (B), and believes that they conflict, why should we not take him at his word?[64]

I can think of two objections to this way of reading the *Protagoras*. First, it might be said that when Socrates presents his two arguments against the teachability of virtue, he is merely being ironic. He really believes that those two arguments are without merit, but he propounds them to provoke Protagoras into discussion. Second, it could be argued that Socrates con-

[64] Notice that at the end of the *Gorgias* (527d2–e7) Socrates says that neither he nor his interlocutors are sufficiently advanced in virtue or rational ability to pursue political careers. For all of them are caught in contradictions about the most important matters. About this remarkable confession, Dodds, *Plato Gorgias*, ad loc., says, ". . . This reproach applies of course to Callicles only . . . but Socrates politely includes himself in the condemnation, thus disguising the positive character of his conclusion. . . ." An odd form of politeness, and a peculiarly thin disguise! Is it normal Socratic practice to accuse himself, at the end of dialogues, of faults he does not possess? Why can't we take Socrates at his word here? He *is* someone who is caught in dilemmas about the most serious issues: both the *Protagoras* and the *Hippias Minor* end with such confessions. And as I have argued in Chapter VII, the withdrawal from politics that Socrates advocates at the end of the *Gorgias* is perfectly sincere. It is hard to believe that he is making up a phony reason for his claim that he is inadequate to the political task. Just as he must be taken seriously when he laments his ignorance at the close of the definitional dialogues, so too we should take him at his word when he confesses that he is torn between contradictory positions. There is simply no reason to explain away an aspect of Socrates so clearly advertised in three dialogues: the *Gorgias*, the *Protagoras*, and the *Hippias Minor*. (For my analysis of the latter dialogue, see the Appendix.)

siders himself to be a teacher of virtue—thought not a teacher
in the conventional fashion. He does not pour information into
his students, but nonetheless he asks the right questions and
gets them to learn. Since Socrates thinks that he teaches virtue,
he obviously cannot believe that it is unteachable. What he means
in the *Protagoras* is that virtue cannot be taught in the conventional way; but he believes that it *can* be taught in Socratic fashion. That, it might be said, is the intended lesson of the *Protagoras*. When Socrates says at the end of the dialogue that he has
backed contradictory propositions, he is only pretending to be
confused.[65]

But as we will see, neither of these objections can be sustained. There is no good reason to believe that the arguments
for the unteachability of virtue totally misrepresent Socrates'
real view; nor is it plausible to hold that the intended conclusion
of the dialogue is nowhere stated in the text. When Socrates
confesses his confusion at the end of the *Protagoras*, he must be
taken at his word, for this is just what we have come to expect
from a Socratic dialogue. Honest perplexity is his hallmark, and
attempts to interpret it away falsify Plato's picture of the man.

11
Can virtue be taught?

Consider the second argument Socrates gives in the *Protagoras*
for the unteachability of virtue (319e1–320b5): the wisest and
best citizens are unable to pass along to others the virtue they
have. Pericles, for example, had his sons educated in those subjects of which there are teachers, but he did not educate them
in those matters about which he was wise, or hand them over
to others for such training. Nor could he find someone to teach
virtue to Cleinias, of whom he was the trustee. And, Socrates
says, many more examples could be produced of good men
who could not make the members of their household, or anyone else, into superior individuals. Reflecting on these facts, he
has come to the conclusion that virtue is unteachable.

As many have noticed, this argument moves from the claim

---

[65] See nn. 8, 9, and 11 above.

that virtue *has not* been taught to the conclusion that it *cannot* be taught, and to some this seems an obvious fallacy.[66] But I think there is a plausible way of defending this inference. Consider an analogy. A large group of strong men are trying to shatter a certain metal, and they keep attacking it with various instruments and materials. A long period of time goes by, and no one succeeds in shattering the metal, so someone suggests that it is unbreakable. Here we have a move from "has not been shattered" to "cannot be shattered," but surely this is no obvious mistake. Repeated and unsuccessful attempts can provide powerful evidence that something by its very nature cannot be done. Of course, such a hypothesis is highly vulnerable to disconfirmation: all it takes is one shattering blow, and the unbreakability thesis must be abandoned. But until such a blow occurs, the unbreakability thesis is a reasonable one.[67]

Now, Socrates' argument for the unteachability thesis takes this same form. The "wisest and best citizens" (319e1-2) have been unable to teach virtue, or to find someone else who could. Surely virtue is something the Greeks wanted to teach or have

[66] Koyré, *Discovering Plato*, p. 17. He claims that the *Meno* is not seriously backing the idea that virtue is unteachable. Rather, Plato is telling us that Meno is too stupid to see through the obviously fallacious move from "it is not taught" to "it cannot be taught." The real lesson of the dialogue, on Koyré's reading, is that virtue is teachable—though not to Meno.

[67] Here I follow R. Bluck, *Plato's Meno*, p. 22. He makes the point that the absence of teachers provides "a *reasonable ground*" for the unteachability of virtue, but does not "*entail*" that virtue cannot be taught (his emphasis). Unfortunately, he spoils the point when he adds, p. 24, that Socrates only wants to show that "*existing* virtue is not teachable . . ." (his emphasis). Socrates is not confining himself to the mild assertion that no one has been able to teach virtue *up to now*. He projects from our past and present inability into the future: his hypothesis is that no one will *ever* be able to teach virtue, since it is unteachable. He recognizes that this hypothesis is refutable by future events (100a1-2), but this does not mean that he makes no claims about the future. Like any educated Athenian of the late fifth century, Socrates would admit that mankind has made great *technical* progress (see e.g. *Antigone* 332-375), but this does not make him optimistic about *moral* progress. He refuses to comfort himself with the naive assumption that although genuine moral teachers and experts do not yet exist, this is a merely accidental deficiency that will be remedied in the fullness of time. Surely he is not being superficial here: there is a striking and depressing contrast between our technical know-how and our paltry moral knowledge, and Socrates' hypothesis—that this moral inexpertise is a natural deficiency of the species—cannot easily be dismissed.

taught to their children (*Meno* 93c5-94e1), yet even Socrates himself—so I hold—was not able to do so. Repeated efforts have been made by the wisest men to teach virtue or to find such teachers, and no one has yet succeeded: surely that is a reasonable basis for the hypothesis that it cannot be taught. Of course, Socrates does have his doubts about this hypothesis. Since virtue is knowledge, it is the sort of thing that we should be able to acquire through teaching. Virtue is like a metal whose internal structure has the properties we associate with breakability, but which resists our best efforts to break it. Furthermore, in the *Meno* it is explicitly recognized that the unteachability hypothesis can be easily refuted. All it would take is one political expert (*politikos*) who is able to turn someone else into a political expert (100a1-2).[68] The *Meno* is evidently reaffirming the claim Socrates makes in the *Protagoras* that the political craft, so far as we can judge from present and past evidence, cannot be taught. The men who rule us are far from being real political experts, for they cannot give what political wisdom they have to others.

We should recall, at this point, the highly pessimistic statement Socrates makes in the *Crito* about the many: he claims to *know* that they will never agree with his unconditional opposition to treating others unjustly (49d2). I suggest that this statement is of a piece with the hypothesis that virtue cannot be taught. Neither entails the other, but nonetheless the same methodology underlies both. Socrates made a serious attempt to convert the many to his way of thinking—he challenged the craftsmen as well as the political leaders—but he met with no success, and thereore he is pessimistic about the future. Past failure is seen as a reliable guide to human limits, and that is precisely the thought pattern we find in the unteachability argument of the *Protagoras*. Furthermore, my interpretation of the unteachability argument brings this dialogue into line with the traditional piety Socrates manifests in the *Apology*. According to Protagoras, Zeus has decided to share his political wisdom

---

[68] The *Meno* contains no evidence that Socrates thinks of himself as that *politikos*. As usual, he denies that he knows what virtue is (71a5-7), and this disqualifies him from being a moral or political expert (*La.* 186c5, 190a1-c2).

with human beings: just as we are like Hephaestus and Athena in that we practice the handicrafts, so we are godlike in our ability to live virtuously in a community with others (320c8-322d5). But as we see in the *Apology*, Socrates is convinced that there is a great gulf between the wisdom of the gods and the wisdom of men. He says, with obvious sarcasm, that those who claim to teach virtue "are wise with a wisdom more than human . . ." (20e1). And he takes the Delphic oracle to mean that ". . . human wisdom is worth little or nothing" (23a6-7); the only wisdom a human being can attain by his natural abilities is the recognition of how small his wisdom is (23b2-4). The oracle is not saying that Socrates is the wisest human being that has yet come into existence; rather, it is saying that his highly limited form of wisdom is the most that human nature can accomplish. Human beings are deficient by their very nature, and the god is using Socrates as a sign (*paradeigma*: 23b1) of this deficiency. If, contrary to all expectation, a mere mortal ever acquired the wisdom that comes with moral definitions, this would be what we now call a miracle: at the instigation of the divine, something in the physical world would have escaped the limitations inherent in its nature. A human being would have become a god, because he would have acquired a skill that nature normally reserves to gods.[69] Now, I do not claim that this expectation of unteachability is the whole story about Socrates. For he is also convinced that virtue is knowledge and that every branch of knowledge can be taught. Perhaps some day there will be a godlike human being after all—the possibility cannot be dismissed dogmatically. In any case, the only way to determine whether the natural limits of human knowledge can be surpassed is to make every effort to know more and more.

[69] See *Meno* 99d7-e1. Socrates is not just making the point that whoever acquires the science of good and evil will deserve to be called divine. As *Ap.* 20e1, 23a6-7, 23b1-4, and the unteachability argument show, he thinks the evidence indicates that something in our constitution limits us, and if these limits are not removed, we cannot acquire the knowledge we need. To put it paradoxically, he believes that full moral development is beyond human nature. There is nothing absurd in the idea that what would fully satisfy us and remedy our deficiencies is beyond our grasp, given the way we are currently constituted.

Socrates is pessimistic about the possibility of acquiring the political craft, but he never gives up his quest. He never warns
his fellow citizens, as Pindar does (*Isthm.* v.18–20), against trying
to become like the gods, but he seriously doubts that we will
continually learn more and more about how to live.

The reader might still protest, however, that something is
fishy about Socrates' unteachability argument. He claims that
the wisest and best citizens have been unable to teach virtue;
but isn't he being ironic when he refers to Pericles to support
his thesis? Surely he cannot seriously believe that Pericles is the
best Athens has to offer, for in the *Gorgias* he tells us that this
politician was a failure, by Socratic standards. He was concerned solely with external projects (walls, ships, etc.) and failed
to make his fellow citizens more virtuous (515c4–516d5, 519a1–
c2). Doesn't the fact that Pericles failed to make his sons good
merely show that he was not so wise after all? He failed to use
the Socratic method of teaching: isn't *that* the point Socrates is
really getting at?

I entirely agree that, according to Socrates, Pericles, along
with nearly every other political leader of fifth-century Athens,
does not deserve his reputation for wisdom. Socrates' low opinion of this group is evident enough from the *Apology*: he says
that they are thought wise by many, and by themselves as well,
but they cannot defend their beliefs when they are cross-examined. So, he concludes, he is wiser than any of them, since
he recognizes how little he knows (21b9–22a8). Yet Socrates
also tells us in the *Apology* that he cannot teach virtue to others;
in spite of the fact that he considers himself the wisest man
Athens has produced (20e6–23b4), he does not have the super-
human wisdom that would be needed to teach the virtues (19d8–
20e2). Now, these facts about the *Apology* suggest that Socrates
seriously believes that the unteachability argument of the *Protagoras* is a strong one. He thinks that Pericles is not nearly so
wise as people assume, but he is genuinely committed to the
unteachability argument in spite of the compliment it pays to
that popular figure.[70] For he believes that the "wisest and best"

[70] It is not uncommon for Socrates to make a serious philosophical point at
the same time that he ironically mocks a contemporary. The clearest example
of this occurs in the *Euthyphro*: Socrates praises Meletus (2c8–3a5) for being the

Athenian—namely, himself—is unable to teach virtue, despite his lifelong effort to acquire the science that would enable him to do so. And he considers this good evidence that virtue cannot be taught. This is an incredibly arrogant argument, of course, but that is as it should be, since Socrates was an incredibly arrogant man. He is convinced that he is the wisest man he has ever met, though this does not prevent him from realizing how distant he is from the full wisdom he would like to acquire. Now, if all of this is true, then why doesn't Socrates just say so? Why does he pick Pericles as his star example of a wise man, rather than himself? The answer is obvious: Socrates cannot expect Protagoras and his entourage to take it on faith that he is wiser than they. So, for the sake of argument, he considers a politician for whom the sophists and their students have the greatest respect, and he proves his point nonetheless.[71] If Pericles was the wisest Athenian, it is significant that he couldn't teach virtue even to his own sons: what the wisest man cannot teach perhaps cannot be taught at all.[72]

---

only politician whose first concern is the proper education of the young. It would be a complete mistake to take the irony in this passage to mean that, according to Socrates, politicians shouldn't interfere with the lives of the citizens. At his trial, he never attacks the law against corrupting the young; he only claims that he is innocent of this charge. So the only irony in our *Euthyphro* passage is personal: Socrates doesn't think Meletus has the slightest idea of how to improve young people (*Ap.* 25c1–4). This same combination of seriousness and irony occurs in the unteachability argument: Socrates thinks that Pericles is no paragon of virtue, but nonetheless he seriously suspects that virtue cannot be taught. Similarly, at the end of the *Meno* (99b5–d5), Socrates is serious when he says that virtue without wisdom can come through a divine gift. Again, the only irony in this passage is personal: he doesn't think that the prominent politicians of the fifth century had such a divine allotment. For further discussion, see n. 82 below.

[71] According to a later tradition, Pericles invited Protagoras to draw up a constitution for the colony of Thurii. See Guthrie, *History*, Vol. III, pp. 263–264. For further discussion, see Muir, "Protagoras and Education at Thourioi."

[72] Suppose someone replied to Socrates' argument in the following way: "True, the wisest man (i.e. Pericles) can't teach virtue, and that is odd. But to show that virtue can be taught, we need find only one person—he doesn't have to be the most virtuous—who has taught virtue to someone else. And there is such a counter-example: Mr. X here has taught virtue to his son, Mr. Y. Therefore virtue can be taught." Socrates would have to defeat this counter-example by questioning Y and showing that he is not virtuous after all, when he is judged by rigorous intellectual standards. He thinks that no matter which Y is chosen,

This way of reading the argument for the unteachability of virtue is similar to the way many (though certainly not all) have read the *Protagoras'* argument for the power of knowledge (351b3–358d4).[73] By using hedonism to show that knowledge is an unconquerable force that we need in order to make right choices, Socrates is able to argue from a false but widely shared assumption to a powerful and paradoxical conclusion. He exploits the defective standards of the many for his own argumentative purposes—and this is precisely what he was doing earlier, in the unteachability argument. There is nothing wrong with using Pericles as an example of a wise man, so long as citizens wiser than he are also unable to teach virtue; similarly, there is nothing wrong with using a hedonistic premise to show that knowledge is unconquerable by passion, so long as Socrates can reach the same conclusion by appealing to a higher standard of value. Of course, those who think that the text commits Socrates to hedonism will reject my idea that these two arguments have a similar structure. Nonetheless, the antihedonistic interpretation and my reading of the unteachability argument reinforce each other: each is made more plausible by the fact that there is another passage in the *Protagoras* that lends itself to the same treatment.[74]

12

Does Socrates think that he teaches?

It is not easy to accept the idea that Socrates is serious about the unteachability of virtue. After all, he believes that he has

---

he will not pass the tests, for Socrates has spent a lifetime looking for such a person. (Suppose he had discovered some Y who had a completely defensible, systematic, and detailed moral theory; and suppose Y learned the theory because his father, X, had told him all these truths. Assuming that X and Y really understood the theory in question, Socrates would have no qualms about admitting that X had taught virtue to Y. He would not insist that since X told Y what is the case, this does not count as genuine teaching. For further discussion of this issue, see Sec. 12 below.)

[73] See the first group of scholars listed in n. 36 above.

[74] And if I am right about courage in the *Protagoras* (Sec. 5 above), there is all the more reason to read Socrates' hedonistic premise and the unteachability argument in the way I suggest.

benefited his fellow citizens. Some of them, like Crito, have with great reluctance come to accept Socratic principles; and many of those who reject the central tenets of Socratic morality have nonetheless lost their complacency and dogmatism. As we saw earlier (VII.6), Socrates does not regard himself as someone who tried but failed to benefit his contemporaries. Rather, he thinks he has done more for their well-being than anyone else, and he feels entitled to a great reward for his fine work (*Ap.* 36b3–37a1). Admittedly, he has not turned the citizens into fully virtuous men. But hasn't he brought many of them closer to that goal? Hasn't he improved their souls to some extent, and doesn't he therefore believe that he is, in his unconventional way, a teacher of virtue? Of course, he denies that he is a teacher,[75] but perhaps this is because he thinks that his audience conceives of a teacher as a mere supplier of information. *That* sort of teacher he certainly is not, since his method of instruction proceeds by way of question and refutation, rather than advice and exhortation. This distinction between two methods of teaching is made explicit in the *Sophist* (229d1–230d4); clearly, by the time Plato wrote that late dialogue, he was prepared to classify Socrates as a teacher of virtue. Furthermore, if we look at the *Meno*, we find Socrates insisting that he is not teaching the slave how to double the area of a square (82e4–5, 84c10–d2). He means, of course, that he is not *merely telling* the slave how to do so. But surely he is helping the slave to recollect, and Socrates must be aware of the important role his questions play in getting the slave to learn. So perhaps we should read some ambiguity into Socrates' frequent denials that he teaches virtue. He is not telling people how to live, and in that sense he is not a teacher; but he is asking the right questions, and since those questions benefit the souls of the listeners, he is in a sense a moral teacher after all. Therefore, when Socrates argues in the *Protagoras* that virtue cannot be taught, he must be playing on an ambiguity in "teachable." If you try to make men better by teaching them in the conventional fashion, you will never succeed; the endeavors of "wise" citizens like Protagoras show as

---

[75] *Ap.* 19d8–e1, 20d9–e2, 33a5–6, 33b5–6; *La.* 185e4–187a8.

much. But the Socratic method is a proven success, and in this sense virtue *is* teachable. Surely Socrates must believe that it is teachable, since he is convinced that virtue is a form of knowledge, and that all forms of knowledge are teachable.[76]

To see what is wrong with this approach, we must recall a point made earlier (VII.6): Socrates does not have the slightest doubt that a conventional moral education—the training in music and gymnastics that many Athenian boys received—is enormously valuable. As the Laws say in the *Crito*, anyone who is educated in this way owes both his parents and his city a debt of loyalty—a debt that might even require the citizen to die (50d5-51d1). Socrates applauds this point, and in the *Apology* he agrees with Meletus that the laws of Athens improve the young (24d10-e2). So, if "teaching virtue" means "bringing it about that someone is closer to virtue than he was before," then Socrates believes that many Athenian parents, himself included, are teachers of virtue. When he argues in the *Protagoras* that virtue is unteachable, he cannot mean that traditional methods of education fail to bring the youth any closer to virtue. On the contrary, that is something Socrates thinks the laws and parents of the city most definitely accomplish.[77]

Now, if we look at the relevant texts, we will see that "teaching virtue" does not mean "bringing it about that someone is closer to virtue than he was before." Rather, it means "bringing it about that someone *is virtuous*." Recall the *Protagoras*: the sophist "promises to make men good citizens" (319a4-5), i.e. he promises to produce a certain result. And Socrates is dubious about whether this result can be produced. He doesn't ask Protagoras whether he delivers lectures or uses the method of question and answer; he is not curious about *how* Protagoras manages to do it, but about whether he in fact succeeds. That is why his unteachability argument focuses on results: the best and wisest citizens of Athens have not been able to produce children of a certain sort. Furthermore, when Socrates denies in the *Apology* that he teaches virtue (19d8-20c3), he means that he cannot produce a virtuous person. He recalls a remark (20a5-c3) he made

---

[76] See n. 9 above.

[77] Contrast Irwin, *Plato's Moral Theory*, p. 298 n. 43: ". . . Protagorean methods are entirely useless for teaching virtue. . . ."

to Callias, the man who has spent more money on sophists than anyone else: if Callias had horses to train, rather than sons, he would bring them to a farmer or horse trainer, and that expert would produce in them the virtues of a horse. But, he asks, is there anyone who knows enough to do the same for human beings, i.e. to give them political virtue? Callias nominates Evenus; and Socrates replies that he wishes *he* had that craft. Evidently, when he denies that he teaches others, he means that no one becomes virtuous as a result of listening to his questions and arguments. The same point is made in the *Laches*. He says that if someone has mastered the craft by which the virtues are produced, he should be able to point to "certain Athenians or foreigners, freemen or slaves, who have clearly become good men because of that person . . ." (186b3-5). Once again, Socrates denies that he has such a craft (186c5): no one who has listened or talked to him has thereby become virtuous.[78]

So there is a world of difference between Socrates' denial in the *Meno* that he is teaching geometry and his denial in the *Apology* and the *Laches* that he teaches virtue. In the *Meno*, he knows the solution to the mathematical problem he has given the slave, but he is not telling him the answer; that is why he says he is not teaching the slave.[79] But, as we have just seen, he

[78] At times, Socrates poses the question of teaching in these terms: has anyone become *superior (beltion)* through your influence? See *Grg.* 515a1-5. But as the immediately following lines (5-7) show, by "superior" he means "a superior sort of person," i.e. someone who is completely virtuous. He does not mean "someone who is closer to being virtuous than he was before." Similarly in the *Laches*: compare 186b1-187a8 with 189d4-e1. Recall that *beltion* is used in this way at *Ap.* 29b6-7. See VII.8.

[79] Devereux, "Nature and Teaching in Plato's *Meno*," argues that in the *Meno* Plato is only trying to show that virtue is not teachable in some narrow and debased sense of "teachable." According to this interpretation, the dialogue presents us with two opposed conceptions of teaching: the sophistical sort, in which one person merely tells another what is the case; and the Socratic sort, in which one person asks questions that induce recollection. Devereux's evidence for this reading is as follows: (1) Socrates says at 82a1-2 that there is no such thing as teaching, but only recollection. As Devereux sees it, we can understand what Socrates means if we take him to be presupposing the narrow and sophistical conception of teaching. According to that conception, all knowledge comes from without, since it is always transmitted from one person to another; but in fact all knowledge comes from within, and Socrates puts the point by saying that there is no teaching (in the narrow sense). (2) Throughout the geometrical experiment (82b6-7, 84d1-2; cf. 85e3-6), Socrates says that he is not teaching the slave. But, according to Devereux, he realizes that this is a dubious dis-

has a different reason for denying that he teaches virtue. I argued earlier (VII.3) that Popper was misled by the geometrical experiment of the *Meno*: since Socrates shows that even a slave can be taught a mathematical truth, Popper wrongly inferred that, according to Socrates, everyone can be taught every moral

---

claimer. This disavowal is credible only if Socrates is once again relying on the debased sense of "teaching." That is, he would admit that he *is* teaching the slave, since he is inducing recollection. (3) When Socrates turns again to the question whether virtue can be taught, he "gives a signal that it is the sophistical conception of teaching which is operative throughout the argument" (p. 123). For he asks whether virtue can be transmitted (*paradoton*) or taken over (*paralēpton*) from one person to another (93a6-b6), and these terms are at home in the sophistical conception of teaching.

In reply: (i) Socrates' claim that he is not teaching the slave may strike *us* as dubious, but nothing in the *Meno* suggests that he is less than serious. I take him to be presupposing the truth of this principle: whenever A teaches B, A assures B of the truth of at least some proposition. Since Socrates has assured the slave of nothing, he is not teaching him. The principle just invoked (that teaching involves some telling) is never attacked in the *Meno*, nor does it conflict with the theory of recollection. For if I assure you that *p*, this can cause you to recollect that *q*; in fact, it can cause you to recollect that *p*. (Suppose you can't recall someone's name; I supply it; then you remember it—you actually remember, and don't just take my word for it.) The *Meno* merely claims that knowledge can be acquired without one person telling something to another; it never says that telling someone is incompatible with his coming to know it, nor does it say that a good teacher will never make assertions. (ii) The evidence cited in (3) is weak, for if all teaching involves some telling, then verbs that suggest the handing over of knowledge are not out of place. More important, Socrates explicitly assures Meno (87b8-c1) that when they investigate the question whether virtue can be taught, they will be using "teach" in a way that is compatible with the theory of recollection. (iii) When Socrates says that there is no teaching but only recollection (82a1-2), his meaning cannot be that no one learns anything by being told; for as we have seen, he relies on the teaching-involves-telling principle. I suggest that what he is getting at is this: if we once knew everything and if "A taught B" entails "B did not know before," it follows that there is no teaching. Equivalently, as Socrates puts the point at 81d2-3: what men call "learning" is better called "recollection"; he is assuming that what we learn we didn't know before. Now, these qualms about the normal use of "teaching" are suspended during the geometrical experiment, for that passage tries to prove, and therefore cannot presuppose, that we once knew everything. After the experiment is over, Socrates serves notice (87b8-c1) that henceforth whenever they talk of teaching, the word is to be taken in a way that fits with the theory of recollection. In other words, the normal inference from "A taught B" to "B did not know before" is to be dropped. When Socrates argues that virtue cannot be taught, his conclusion is far more radical than Devereux will allow. He doesn't merely mean that incompetent teachers (i.e. sophists) with ineffective teaching techniques are unable to teach virtue. His claim is that since *no one* has been able to teach virtue—whatever the technique—it must be unteachable.

truth. We will be making a similar mistake if we assume that Socrates is a moral teacher in the same way that he is a geometry teacher in the *Meno*. He knows the answers to the geometrical questions he asks, but he does not have answers to his moral questions. The *Meno*'s geometrical experiment is obviously an illustration of the Socratic method, but we should not naively assume that every feature of the illustration has ethical significance. Nor does the *Sophist* give us any illumination about the early dialogues. Clearly, Plato came to believe that Socrates deserved to be called a teacher of virtue, but this hardly shows that in the early dialogues Socrates accepts that label. He thinks that whoever has the craft that teaches virtue should have results to show—i.e. virtuous students—and since he fails this simple test, he denies that he is a teacher.[80]

Now, suppose someone insists that he does have the ability to teach virtue, and points to several students, whom he claims as his finished products. Obviously, his credentials as a teacher will be substantiated only if his students really are virtuous. But what standards does Socrates want us to use, when we decide whether or not those students really have the virtues? Clearly, if we use Protagorean standards, then everyone under the sun will be entitled to call himself a teacher of virtue. Recall the method Socrates uses to impugn those ridiculously low standards: he argues that the virtues are branches of knowledge. Protagoras assumes that virtue requires no special intellectual skill or independence of thought; a good man is just someone who follows the prevailing social conventions. But once virtue is shown to be knowledge, a good person will have to prove himself by passing rigorous intellectual tests. To show that one is fully virtuous, one would have to state and defend the moral definitions that Socrates continually seeks. Without such defi-

---

[80] I don't agree with Teloh, *Plato's Metaphysics*, p. 51, that *Grg.* 521d6–e2 provides good evidence that Socrates considers himself a teacher of virtue. Socrates says here that he has undertaken the political craft and practices politics. He means that he alone has been engaged in the project of moving others beyond the elementary stage of moral development; and this is the proper role of the political craft. But teaching virtue is a matter of moving individuals to stage (D), or at the very least to stage (C), and this is something Socrates has not been able to do. See VII.7 on the stages of moral development. Cf. Ch. VII n. 76.

nitions, one could not claim to have the measuring science of right and wrong that is mentioned in the *Protagoras* (356c4–357c1), for one would have no standards for resolving moral issues in difficult cases. Now, as we have seen, Socrates conceded that one can be virtuous without having definitions of the virtues, though in this case one will be less than fully virtuous. If one has the intellectual skill and moral accomplishments of a Socrates, then one has a reduced form of wisdom, and therefore a reduced form of virtue. Notice that Socrates never claims to have produced a single person of this sort. Not one of the admirers that fill the pages of Plato's text—Crito, Critias, Alcibiades, Laches, Nicias, etc.—could have defended himself in moral argument as Socrates could. Since he has produced no virtuous man even in this reduced sense, Socrates thinks he is completely justified in refusing to call himself a teacher of virtue. But what if he had produced another Socrates? Would he then change his tune and concede that he had become a teacher of virtue after all? I suggest that even in this case he would have had grave misgivings about calling himself a teacher. Consider an analogous situation in the crafts: suppose someone claims to be a teacher of architecture, but can only make his students aware of how little they know in this area; though they know a bit more than the ordinary person, neither teacher nor student can build a satisfactory building, or say what it is that makes buildings well-designed. Surely it could be argued that such a person does not deserve to be called a teacher of architecture. Similarly, I suggest that Socrates would have called himself a teacher of virtue only if he had known enough to turn some of his fellow citizens into fully virtuous individuals. For he says that the issue of teachability can be resolved only by finding a definition of virtue (*Protag.* 361c2-6). Had Socrates produced another Socrates, and had he inferred that he was therefore a teacher, this link between teachability and definition would have to be broken.

One further text suggests that Socrates is quite serious when he puts forward the claim, in the *Protagoras*, that virtue is unteachable: the *Meno* confronts the same dilemma as the *Protagoras*, but rather than abandon the unteachability thesis, it solves the problem by modifying the claim that virtue is knowledge. Virtuous men are those who serve as useful guides, and someone can offer correct guidance in either of two ways: because he has knowledge, or because he believes (but does not know) the truth (96e7–97c2). Either type of person will be useful, and so both will qualify as good. ". . . It is not only through knowledge that men are good and useful to their cities . . . but also through right opinion . . ." (98c8–10).[81] Here, the *Meno* takes an important step away from the early dialogues: never before had Socrates been prepared to give up his conviction that virtue is knowledge and that virtuous men must therefore have something better than true belief.[82] Of course, the *Meno*, as we

[81] Cf. 96e1–97a7. The *Meno* is not merely adopting the weak principle that a right action can flow from a right opinion even when the holder of the opinion lacks knowledge. Such a principle falls far short of the claim that right opinion is sufficient for being *a good person*. I take Plato to be saying that if someone has enough true beliefs to serve as a beneficial guide to others, then he is a good man even if he lacks knowledge. (This should be distinguished from the absurd idea that having one true belief can make someone good.) Furthermore, Plato is probably assuming that mere guesswork cannot bring us the large number of true beliefs we would need to be beneficial guides. In other words, whoever has enough true opinions to be a good man must have acquired many of those opinions through reasoning. Recall that the *Meno*'s example of someone who has true belief without knowledge is the slave, and presumably at the end of the geometrical experiment the slave has acquired not only a true belief but some reason for his belief. For the point of the experiment is to exhibit the process of recollection, and recollection involves reasoning, not the chance acquisition of true beliefs. Therefore, when Plato says that a good man need not have knowledge, he is probably thinking of someone who, like the slave, has begun to recollect, but who has not yet acquired the definitions that would give him knowledge. Notice the distinction Plato makes at 99a3–5 between right actions that occur through chance, and right actions that are guided by right opinion or knowledge. It is doubtful, then, that he is thinking of a good man as someone who luckily and frequently makes correct guesses.

[82] Irwin, *Plato's Moral Theory*, p. 317 n. 22, says that the *Meno* does not abandon the position that knowledge is necessary for virtue. But if he were correct, it would be hard to understand what Plato is trying to accomplish from 96d1–100c2 (a sizable stretch of the dialogue, given the brevity of the whole work). He argues as follows:

(1) At 100a6–7, ". . . Socrates says that someone with knowledge would be the only one with real virtue. . . ." The passage cited says that if there ever were a political expert who could teach virtue, then he would be like Teiresias in the underworld: he would be the real thing (*alēthes . . . pragma*) with respect to virtue. But the meaning of this comparison is elusive. Would a political expert have real virtue in the sense that he alone would be virtuous, or in the sense that he alone would be truly (i.e. fully) virtuous? Plato is not saying that

saw earlier, affirms the view that someone who has knowledge will be far superior to those who merely have true belief (100a1–7); so Plato does not abandon the Socratic doctrine that knowledge of the virtues is the goal of moral development. The *Meno* allows virtue without wisdom, but it reaffirms the *Apology*'s

---

the political expert would be to the rest of us as a flesh-and-blood man is to a ghost. For Teiresias is no flesh-and-blood man in *Odyssey* 10.493–495 (from which the *Meno* quotes); he is just one shade among many. "His wits hold fast/ To him even in death Persephone gave wisdom [*noos*] / So that he alone is sensible, while the others flit about as shadows." Obviously, what Plato likes about this passage is the contrast between a superior state of mind that holds fast, and some lesser intellectual state that is vulnerable to fluctuation. That is precisely how he characterizes the differences between knowledge and belief (97e2–98a8). Notice that after comparing the true political expert to Teiresias, Plato goes on to reaffirm his proposal that virtue comes to us as a divine allotment (100b2–3, reaffirming 99e6). This suggests that the Teiresias passage is not meant to subvert the claim that there is a way to be virtuous without having knowledge. Nor is he overturning that claim when he says that a teacher of virtue would be "the real thing with respect to virtue." In the *Apology*, Socrates says that the god is the one who is really wise (*tōi onti . . . sophos*: 23a5–6); he means that the god has a higher order of wisdom, not that human beings are devoid of wisdom.

(2) ". . . The comparison with the inspired ignorance of diviners is recognized as unflattering to statesmen, 99b11–e2. . . ." Similarly Guthrie, *History*, Vol. IV, p. 262. In reply:

(A) I entirely agree that when Socrates says that the fifth-century politicians admired by Anytus were divinely possessed, he should not be taken seriously. He says this only to set matters straight between Anytus and himself. For at an earlier point in the dialogue (93a5–b7), he had allowed Anytus to think that they had no disagreement about the wisdom of such men as Themistocles: the only question was whether these politicians could teach the virtue they had. Now, at 99b5–e2, he wants Anytus to realize that he ascribes no wisdom to such men, and he expects Anytus to resent the comparison between great political figures like Pericles and mere poets.

(B) But there is no reason to think that Plato is retracting his earlier statements that one can be good without having knowledge (96e4–97a7, 98c8–10). He clearly indicates that to be virtuous one must have true beliefs that benefit one's fellow citizens. The ordinary politicians of the fifth century fail even this relaxed test of virtue, and so there is no reason to suspect that Plato views it as an invalid test.

(C) Furthermore, Plato's statement that virtue comes to us—when it does come—as a divine allotment (*theia moira*: 99e6, 100b2–3) should be taken seriously. For Socrates has already said in the *Euthyphro* (15a1–2) that ". . . there is no good for us that they [i.e. the gods] do not give us." In other words, whenever we achieve anything worthwhile, we ought to thank the gods for their cooperation with our success. When Plato says that virtue comes to us by a divine allotment without *nous* (99e6), he should not be taken to mean that a virtuous person has no reasons for what he believes. In this passage, to lack

doctrine that there is a way of being virtuous that falls far short of full moral development.

What consequences do these facts have for an interpretation of the *Protagoras*? To begin with, we cannot assume that the *Meno*'s solution to the teachability dilemma is the one that is intended by the *Protagoras*. As most scholars agree, the *Meno* is a transitional dialogue, containing some material that stays within the compass of the earlier dialogues, and some that moves beyond it.[83] For example, we can see the influence of Pythagoreanism on the *Phaedo* and the *Republic*, and this same influence is obviously present in the *Meno*'s geometrical experiment and doctrine of recollection. Those aspects of the dialogue can therefore be attributed to Plato rather than Socrates. And since Socrates had never rejected the claim that virtue requires knowledge, we can safely say that this too is a Platonic innovation. In other words, the *Meno* takes over a problem that had afflicted Socrates and proposes a solution that Socrates had never

---

nous is merely to lack knowledge or wisdom. That is how *nous* is used at *Meno* 88b5, 7 and 8. (Cf. *La.* 188b4, *Grg.* 466e10, 13, *Rep.* 506c6-9.) The fact that Socrates says in the *Ion* that the rhapsode has a divine allotment (542a4) does not mean that whoever has such a gift must be as devoid of rational ability as Ion is. Finally, we should recall the religious inspiration of the *Meno's* theory of recollection. Plato tells us (81a5-b2) that he derives the doctrine from what he has heard from certain divine poets, priests, and priestesses. No one doubts the fact that Plato was influenced by Pythagorean or Orphic religious doctrines. Why then should we suspect irony when he says that a virtuous man has a divine gift?

(3) One further argument—advanced by Guthrie, not Irwin—should be considered: The *Meno* closes with the reminder (100b4-6) that Socrates still does not know what virtue is; this is the question he wanted to pursue, but Meno prevailed on him to ask instead whether virtue can be taught. Guthrie infers (Vol. IV, p. 264) that Plato is disavowing his claim that virtue does not require knowledge. "The message is clear," he writes. "The present conclusion is *not* the correct one, because Meno has made Socrates ask the wrong question. Virtue *is* knowledge . . ." (his emphasis). In reply, we should remember that Socrates never adopts the absurd position that before we know what virtue is, we can never deploy any sound arguments about its qualities. It is only *knowledge* of its qualities that we are said to lack. (See *Meno* 71b3-4). The *Gorgias* contains no definition of virtue, but that does not prevent Socrates from giving arguments of "iron and adamant" (509a1) for his belief that virtue is essential to happiness. Similarly, Plato is entitled to claim in the *Meno* that he has good reason for thinking that virtue is available to those who lack knowledge.

[83] See Bluck, *Plato's Meno*, pp. 108-120; Irwin, *Plato's Moral Theory*, p. 291 n. 33; Dodds, *Plato Gorgias*, p. 23; Guthrie, *History*, Vol. IV, p. 236.

endorsed. I think these points make it most unlikely that the *Protagoras'* arguments for the unteachability of virtue are meant to be without merit. For the *Meno* takes that argument so seriously that it abandons the doctrine that virtue is knowledge. Since the *Meno* takes the unteachability argument to be a good one, it is hard to believe that the *Protagoras* does not.

13
Political expertise and the Athenian Assembly

The *Protagoras* has two arguments for the unteachability of virtue, and thus far we have focused entirely on the second of them. Let us now turn to the first (319b3–d7). The Athenians are a wise people, Socrates says, and they are so regarded by the other Greeks. Now, when they meet together in the Assembly and need advice about buildings or ships, they allow only those who are proven experts to speak. Anyone who has not studied the subject in question or who has had no teachers in it is immediately hooted down, and if he continues to speak he is thrown out. But when the Athenians need advice about managing the city, they allow anyone to speak, whatever his trade, income, or social status. No speaker is expected to have made a special study of virtue, or to have had moral teachers. Evidently, the Athenians do not think this subject can be taught, and that is why they open the floor to general discussion.

How are we to understand this passage? I suggest that it follows the same pattern exhibited by the second argument for unteachability. Socrates is endorsing an Athenian belief, even though he is not telling Protagoras his real reasons for thinking that belief true. He merely gives an argument for attributing to the Athenians the view that virtue cannot be taught: they do not demand expertise of those who speak on political subjects, and therefore they must believe that politics is not a subject that can be mastered through intellectual study. But why should we take this belief of the Athenians to be true? Because they are wise, Socrates says (319b3–4); but that is a lame response, and he knows it. He hardly supposes that everything the Athenians believe is true, and he hardly thinks that the many are the best judges of whether or not political experts exist. Now, as we saw earlier, Socrates is masking his real reasons when he gives his second argument for the unteachability thesis. He says that Pericles is one of the wisest of citizens, and that even so he could not teach or find teachers for the young members of his household. But Socrates' *real* argument is this: "Even *I* can't teach virtue, despite all of my efforts; and no one is wiser than I. So perhaps virtue simply cannot be taught." Similarly, Socrates thinks that the Athenian people do not completely deserve their reputation for wisdom, and his first argument for unteachability—were he to express it forthrightly—would be this: "Even *I* have far less knowledge about political virtue than an expert craftsman has in his own area. And I alone of all the Greeks have made a serious attempt to become an expert about the virtues [*Grg.* 521d6-8]. So the Athenians have hit upon the truth, in their belief that they cannot demand political expertise of their speakers. For that kind of expertise seems to be unteachable." Since Socrates does not want to claim, in front of Protagoras, that he is the wisest of the Greeks, he offers a weak reason ("the Athenians are wise") instead of the one that is in the back of his mind. He thinks that the Athenians are not well equipped to determine whether they have any political experts in their midst, just as they are in a poor position to tell whether their children will become virtuous through the teaching of Protagoras and men of his ilk. It so happens that their negative opinion is correct; for if they had as much wisdom as Socrates has about virtue, they would see more clearly that there are no political experts. That is, there is no one who knows enough to teach others how to become virtuous.

Later in the *Protagoras*, after Socrates has shown that being overcome by pleasure is really an intellectual error, he returns to his unteachability thesis:

> So this is what being weaker than pleasure is: the greatest form of ignorance, a condition which Protagoras here and Hippias and Prodicus say they cure. But because you think that it is something other than ignorance, you neither send yourselves nor your sons to those who teach these mat-

ters—the sophists. For you don't think it can be taught,
and so out of concern for your money you keep it from
them—a bad practice, both for individuals and the city.
(357e2-8)

Here he is criticizing the assumptions that lead the many to
deprecate the sophists. Of course, he is not seriously advocating
that they send their children to such individuals as Protagoras:
we have plenty of evidence to the contrary. The many assume
that there is no room for improvement in their moral beliefs.
They think that they know as much as they need about moral
matters, and that no one can improve their souls in any way.
So even though they are right not to go to the sophists, they
refuse to do so for the wrong reasons—and they are the losers
for having such reasons. (Compare *Meno* 91b7-92d5, where
Socrates criticizes Anytus' unthinking antagonism toward the
sophists.) Similarly, Socrates thinks that the many have an inadequate basis for their belief that virtue cannot be taught. The
men they take to be wise are not; and the ability of the many
to determine whether there are political experts is quite defective. But the above passage should not be taken as evidence
that, according to Socrates, the many have a false belief when
they claim that virtue is unteachable; no more is it evidence
that, according to Socrates, the many have come to the wrong
conclusion when they deny that the sophists teach virtue. In
both cases, they have come to the right conclusion in spite of
their inadequate reasoning: virtue *is* unteachable, and the sophists are *not* moral teachers.

Socrates and the many agree on an important principle:
whenever we need advice about a particular subject, we should
listen only to an expert, and not to those who lack knowledge.
That is just the point he makes in his discussion with Crito: we
should pay no attention to popular prejudice, but should always
follow the advice of someone who knows—if, in fact, someone
does have knowledge (47a2-d5). A corollary of this principle is
that if there were political experts, we should be ruled by them
rather than by the many. Letting the common man contribute
to political decisions would make as little sense as allowing

everyone, expert and amateur alike, to speak and vote about the design of buildings and ships. In both cases, only the experts should be allowed to make decisions. But as it has turned out, there are to date no political experts, and Socrates suspects that this is one field into which human reason cannot penetrate. Should such an expert ever arise, the many would not recognize him, since they assess another person's wisdom by purely conventional standards.[84] In any case, so long as such experts do not exist, democracy is a satisfactory political arrangement. No one deserves, by reason of his intellectual credentials, to rule the city, and so no serious objection can be made against allowing all citizens to voice their opinions in the Assembly. Of course, that does not mean that all opinions are true or reasonable; even the many would resist that extreme form of relativism. Nor does it mean that the popularity of a belief is a sign of its truth. Socrates tolerated the equal distribution of power among citizens only because he thought that no political alternative would be a significant improvement, in the absence of political experts. Had he believed that he himself was such an expert, or had he believed that his circle of students was qualified to teach the virtues to other citizens, he would never have declared himself satisfied with the legal system of Athens. So the political assumptions of the *Protagoras* and the *Crito* are perfectly in tune: in each dialogue, we find that Socrates sees no feasible alternative to Athenian democracy.

14
Final remarks

Throughout this study, I have been guided by the assumption that no early work of Plato's should be studied entirely on its own, apart from its relationship to the other early works. Thus, in Chapters II through VI, I have offered an interpretation of the *Crito* that makes it consistent with the *Apology* and with the objective, absolutist conception of ethics that Socrates everywhere presupposes. In Chapters VII and VIII, I have tried to

---

[84] See Ch. VII nn. 82, 83; Ch. VIII n. 55.

show that the political themes of the early dialogues—e.g. Socrates' satisfaction with Athenian law, his criticism of rule by the many, his withdrawal from conventional politics—have to be seen against the background of his unsuccessful search for definitions and his pessimism about human limits. To be sure, I hold that Plato's early works are not entirely consistent with each other: the claims to knowledge in the *Apology*, as we have seen, conflict with the *Meno*'s epistemic severity. Nonetheless, when the early dialogues are read with care, they form a remarkably coherent unit. They are best viewed as chapters from an intellectual biography, no part of which is entirely self-contained. Each contributes to our understanding of the rest; none can be fully appreciated on its own.

That the *Crito* is one of the central chapters of this biography, few would deny. That it is a good piece of philosophical work is far from self-evident, but I hope that the arguments of Chapters II through VI will change some minds. In the last two chapters, I have tried to show that the *Crito* provides several important clues for our general understanding of the early dialogues: (A) Socrates relies heavily on certain conventional beliefs. He holds that one must never treat one's parents with violence, and his inability to define the virtues does not make him the least bit hesitant to exploit this traditional assumption when he makes life-and-death decisions. For all the importance of definitions, Socrates thought he could live a just life—so long as he remained a private citizen—without them. (B) More generally, Socrates' attitude toward traditional Greek moral training is far from hostile. He thinks that it contains serious errors, and that it is radically incomplete; but he also takes conventional *paideia* to be a benefit so great that it secures his loyalty to Athens even to the point of death. It is not surprising that Xenophon emphasizes the conventional and innocuous side of Socrates: gratitude for traditional education was part of Socratic philosophy, and it was the part to which Xenophon responded. (C) Though Socrates was a severe critic of Athenian democracy, he also loved his city, not because of its architecture or its dramatists (they left him cold), but, of all things, because of its laws. He says that Athens is the city that allows the greatest freedom of speech (*Grg.* 461e1-3), and he thinks that he, more than anyone else, has profited from this liberty. Speculative though it is, I know of no better way to explain his great satisfaction with the Athenian legal system. (D) Once we realize that, even in the *Crito*, Socrates is committed to disobeying a civic order that requires injustice, we are in a better position to recognize the real authoritarianism in his philosophy. His statement that he would never disobey a divine or human superior (*Ap.* 29b6-7) means that he would never disobey a *moral* superior, i.e. someone who has a complete ethical theory. Since moral experts alone deserve absolute obedience, Socrates' search for definitions, as he realized, had the potential for founding a new political order. Every Socratic conversation was, in this sense, a revolutionary act—a point Meletus and Anytus perhaps grasped all too well. (E) But we must not lose sight of the fact that although the seeds of antidemocratic authoritarianism lay dormant in Socratic conversation, they were held in check by his strong sense of human limits. As the *Crito* shows, his doubts about the unteachability of virtue cannot be interpreted as an expression of contempt for conventional methods of teaching. He accepts unjust treatment from Athens partly because he values the traditional moral training the city gave him. The unteachability thesis means that political expertise is beyond human nature, and therefore when Socrates seeks definitions, he hardly expects to succeed. His search has value even when it fails to find a standard, since it is intrinsically worthwhile to know how small a grasp one has of the correct moral theory. The founding of a new political order was not the sole or even the most important aim of Socratic conversation. To fulfill such a utopian fantasy, the limits of human nature would have to be transcended.

APPENDIX

Perplexity in the *Hippias Minor*

I ARGUED in Chapter VIII that when Socrates talks about his intellectual limitations, he is being completely straightforward and honest. We should not look for ambiguity or irony when he denies that he teaches the virtues and when he claims that he cannot define them. Furthermore, there are several passages in which Socrates confesses that he believes inconsistent propositions: in the *Gorgias*, he merely asserts this (527d7-e1) without elaborating;[1] in the *Protagoras*, he claims that his thesis that virtue is knowledge conflicts with his earlier statement that it is unteachable; and in the *Hippias Minor*, he carefully argues for some highly paradoxical conclusions, and then confesses that he is sometimes of the opposite opinion. In this appendix, I want to suggest that these confessions in the *Hippias Minor* should be taken at face value, since they fit into the larger pattern of honest self-deprecation that we have observed throughout the early dialogues. Conversely, by showing that Socrates can be taken at his word in the *Hippias Minor*, I hope to lend further support to my thesis that he is serious about the unteachability of virtue. If Socrates thinks he is faced with a genuine dilemma at the end of the *Hippias Minor*, and if he admits to such problems in the *Gorgias*, then we have all the more reason to take him at his word when he argues that virtue is unteachable.

Socrates says in the *Hippias Minor*:

(A) . . . Those who harm men, do injustice, lie, deceive, and go wrong voluntarily—rather than involuntarily—are better than those [who do these things] involuntarily. (372d4-7)

But he immediately adds: "Sometimes, however, I believe the opposite of this, and I vacillate about these matters—obviously

---

[1] See Ch. VIII n. 64.

because I do not have knowledge" (372d7–e1). Later in the dialogue, he says:

> (B) Therefore, Hippias, the one who voluntarily goes wrong and does shameful and unjust things, if there is such a man, would be none other than the good man. (376b4–6)

Hippias says he cannot agree, and Socrates replies that neither can he agree with himself, even though the argument has led him to (B) (376b7–c1). "As I said before, I go back and forth on these matters, and it never seems to me the same . . ." (376c1–3). It would be a mistake to think that with these expressions of confusion, Socrates is entirely disassociating himself from (A) and (B); the path to these conclusions has been laid with great care, and there is no indication that he is less than serious. But it would be equally wrong to ignore the fact that he has expressed doubts about the very propositions for which he has argued.[2] The best interpretation is that Socrates really feels himself to be trapped by a dilemma. Let me say what I think his problem is.

Consider two singers: although both occasionally sing out of key, the first does so voluntarily, the second involuntarily. That is, whenever the first sings out of key, it is because he chooses to do so, for whatever reason. Had he wanted to, he could have stayed perfectly in tune. By contrast, when the second singer goes out of key, he is trying but failing to sing properly; he wants to hit the right tone, but cannot. Which is the better singer? Obviously, the first. And the same holds true in any field of expertise, branch of knowledge, craft, or skill. The astronomer who voluntarily gives false information about the stars is someone who knows the truth but chooses to speak otherwise. He is better at astronomy than someone who makes involuntary errors in his subject. The archer who voluntarily misses

---

[2] Penner, "Socrates on Virtue and Motivation," pp. 139–143, takes Socrates to believe that (A) and (B) are only apparently paradoxical. As he reads the *Hippias Minor*, Socrates thinks these two propositions are perfectly acceptable, since no one voluntarily does injustice. So too Irwin, *Plato's Moral Theory*, pp. 77, 299 n. 48. This interpretation refuses to take Socrates at his word when he says that he keeps changing his mind about (A) and (B). But neither Penner nor Irwin explains why we should dismiss these confessions of ambivalence.

the mark is better than the one who misses it involuntarily. In general:

(C) Someone who voluntarily goes wrong in the practice of a craft is better at it than someone who involuntarily goes wrong.

But now comes the surprising step in the argument. According to Socrates, the virtues are crafts, and so (C) must apply to them no less than to astronomy, music, archery, etc. To go wrong in music is to sing out of key; to go wrong in archery is to miss the target; and to go wrong in the realm of good and evil is to do what Socrates and the many would least expect of a virtuous man: to harm others, do injustice, lie, and deceive. This gives us:

(A) . . . Those who harm men, do injustice, lie, deceive, and go wrong voluntarily—rather than involuntarily—are better than those [who do these things] involuntarily. (372d4–7)

It might be thought, however, that (A) is not so terribly shocking. Perhaps it is better to be a voluntary rather than an involuntary perpetrator of injustice, but that still allows us to say that both sorts are far inferior to someone who never does any injustice, voluntary or involuntary. However, I do not think that Socrates intends (A) to be so tame. For he tells us that sometimes he rejects (A), and why would he do so unless he found it difficult to accept? Furthermore, he finds himself committed, like it or not, to (B), and this further proposition tells us that if anyone voluntarily does injustice, he "would be none other than the good man." He is not merely better than the involuntary perpetrator of injustice: he is actually a virtuous individual, in spite of his willing malfeasance. How can Socrates be serious about this?

An important clue is provided by the fact that in the *Protagoras* (345d9-e4) and the *Gorgias* (509e2-7), Socrates puts forward another highly paradoxical thesis about voluntary injustice: he says there is no such thing. For an individual wants to perform actions only on the assumption that they are good for him; if he is mistaken in this assumption, then he is not doing what he wants, and in this sense his action is involuntary.[3] In the *Protagoras* and the *Gorgias*, Socrates expresses no doubts about the idea that injustice is always contrary to the agent's interests, and that is why he characterizes all unjust action as involuntary. But in the *Hippias Minor*, he gives an argument against himself and honestly admits that he has reached no settled way of answering it. In all of the nonmoral crafts, an expert cannot be characterized as someone who would never do such-and-such; rather, he is someone who has a certain skill, and he might use that skill in ways that others would not expect of an expert. Similarly, in the moral realm, we should characterize the good man as someone who always acts voluntarily when he makes decisions about how to lead his life. He pursues his own good, gets what he wants, and achieves happiness. What makes him an accomplished expert—what makes someone an expert in any field— is the voluntariness of his choices, and not the kind of act he chooses. Just as a good singer could sing out of key and still remain an expert, so long as he did so voluntarily, so a good man could do what Socrates would least expect of him—commit unjust acts—and still remain a moral expert, so long as his injustice was voluntary. That, at any rate, is where the argument leads Socrates in the *Hippias Minor*. But as he says, he is sometimes of the opposite opinion. At times, he thinks that the virtues are unlike the crafts in this one respect: if we see someone committing an unjust act, we can immediately infer that he is not a moral expert; but in the nonmoral realm, we cannot conclude that someone lacks expertise merely because he acts in a way that is typical of bad practitioners of the craft.

A concrete example will help explain what the *Hippias Minor* is worried about. Suppose Socrates comes across several men kicking their father, and starts to interrogate them. As he quickly discovers, they know full well that the man is their father; and they have not been forced into kicking him. Can Socrates immediately infer that these brothers are evil men, or at least that they fall short of perfect goodness? Sometimes he follows com-

---

[3] See *Grg.* 467c5–468c8. This is the argument to which Socrates alludes when he claims at 509e2–7 that all injustice is involuntary.

mon sense and thinks he is entitled to make this judgment straightaway. For their act is voluntary, by ordinary standards;[4] he is convinced that a good man will never voluntarily do injustice; and he thinks that any good man will realize that violence against one's parents is always unjust. But at other times, as in the *Hippias Minor*, he sees the force of the opposite point of view. What if he further interrogates these brothers, and they respond brilliantly to his moral questions? They defend definitions of the virtues, skillfully trace connections between their moral beliefs, and cogently defend the view that sometimes one should unjustly use violence against one's parents. Haven't they passed Socrates' tests for moral expertise? In fact, don't they know far more than he about the virtues? Can he deny that they are good men merely because they have acted in a way that neither he nor the many would have expected of virtuous individuals? By his own admission, Socrates is no moral expert, and he concedes the possibility that he might come across someone who knows virtue far better than he. Can he reject someone's credentials as a moral expert merely because that person rejects a Socratic moral principle?[5] If not, then the good man is best characterized as someone who achieves his good and always acts voluntarily—even if he voluntarily chooses injustice.

It is to Socrates' credit that he is bothered by these questions, for they are not easily answered. He sees no way to construct a moral theory except by building on conventional belief, yet he knows there is risk in this, since conventional opinion contains serious errors. His hope is that he has rooted out these imperfections, but nothing can assure him of success except daily conversations with highly imperfect interlocutors. If he ever came across a more skillful talker than himself, how radical a change would he be willing to make in his moral system? Would he deny someone the status of a moral expert merely because

---

[4] See *Crito* 49a4: there would be no point in condemning *voluntary* injustice unless ordinary tests of voluntariness were presupposed. Cf. *Ap.* 25e4–26a7, 37a5–6; *Grg.* 488a2–4.

[5] See Ch. VII n. 85. Anyone who is willing, as Socrates is, to take orders from a moral superior should ask himself such questions.

this person maintained that injustice must sometimes be done? In the *Hippias Minor*, as in so many other early dialogues, we see the depth of Socrates' questions and the honesty with which he confronts them. Here as elsewhere, we should resist those interpretations that deny this fundamental feature of the man.

BIBLIOGRAPHY

Adkins, Arthur W. H. *Merit and Responsibility: A Study in Greek Values*. Oxford: Clarendon Press, 1960.

Allen, R. E. *Plato's 'Euthyphro' and the Earlier Theory of Forms*. London: Routledge & Kegan Paul, 1970.

———. *Socrates and Legal Obligation*. Minneapolis: University of Minnesota Press, 1980. (This contains a translation of the *Crito*.)

Annas, Julia. *An Introduction to Plato's* Republic. Oxford: Clarendon Press, 1981.

Audi, Robert. "On the Meaning and Justification of Violence." In *Violence: Award-Winning Essays in the Council for Philosophical Studies Competition*, edited by Jerome A. Shaffer, pp. 45-99. New York: David McKay Co., 1971.

Aune, Bruce. *Kant's Theory of Morals*. Princeton: Princeton University Press, 1979.

Barker, Andrew. "Why Did Socrates Refuse to Escape?" *Phronesis* 22 (1977): pp. 13-28.

Barker, Ernest. *Greek Political Theory: Plato and His Predecessors*. London: Methuen & Co., 1918.

———. *The Political Thought of Plato and Aristotle*. New York: Russell & Russell, 1959.

Bennett, John G. "A Note on Locke's Theory of Tacit Consent." *The Philosophical Review* 88 (1979): pp. 224-234.

Bluck, R. S. *Plato's Meno*, edited with introduction and commentary. Cambridge: Cambridge University Press, 1964.

Brickhouse, Thomas C., and Smith, Nicholas D. "Socrates and Disobedience to the Law." Abstract published in *Proceedings and Addresses of the American Philosophical Association* 54 (1981): p. 513.

———. "Socrates' Proposed Penalty in Plato's *Apology*." *Archiv für Geschichte der Philosophie* 64 (1982): pp. 1-18.

———. "The Origin of Socrates' Mission." *The Journal of the History of Ideas*, in press.

Burnet, John, ed. *Platonis Opera*. Vols. I-V. Oxford: Clarendon Press, 1900-1907.

———. *Plato's Euthyphro, Apology of Socrates, and Crito*, edited with notes. Oxford: Clarendon Press, 1924.

Burnyeat, M. F. "Socratic Midwifery, Platonic Inspiration." *Bulletin of the Institute of Classical Studies* 24 (1977): pp. 7–13.

Burtt, J. O., trans. *Minor Attic Orators*. Vol. II. Cambridge: Harvard University Press, 1962.

Bury, J. B., and Meiggs, Russell. *A History of Greece to the Death of Alexander the Great*. 4th ed. New York: St. Martin's Press, 1975.

Church, F. J., trans. *Euthyphro, Apology, Crito*. Indianapolis: The Bobbs-Merrill Co., 1948.

Cohen, Marshall. "Liberalism and Disobedience." *Philosophy & Public Affairs* 1 (1973): pp. 283–314.

Connor, W. Robert. *The New Politicians of Fifth-Century Athens*. Princeton: Princeton University Press, 1971.

Cornford, Francis MacDonald. *Plato and Parmenides*, translated with introduction and commentary. Indianapolis: The Bobbs-Merrill Co., n.d.

Croiset, Maurice, trans. *Platon Oeuvres Complètes*. Vol. I. Paris: Société d'Édition "Les Belles Lettres," 1963.

Crombie, I. M. *An Examination of Plato's Doctrines*. Vol. I, *Plato on Man and Society*. London: Routledge & Kegan Paul, 1962.

Devereux, Daniel. "Nature and Teaching in Plato's *Meno*." *Phronesis* 23 (1978): pp. 118–126.

Dodds, E. R. *The Greeks and the Irrational*. Berkeley and Los Angeles: University of California Press, 1951.

———. *Plato Gorgias*, a revised text with introduction and commentary. Oxford: Clarendon Press, 1959.

Dover, K. J. *Greek Popular Morality in the Time of Plato and Aristotle*. Oxford: Basil Blackwell, 1974.

———. "The Freedom of the Intellectual in Greek Society." *Talanta* (*Proceedings of the Dutch Archaeological and Historical Society*) 7 (1976): pp. 24–54.

Dybikowski, J. "Socrates, Obedience, and the Law: Plato's *Crito*." *Dialogue* 13 (1974): pp. 519–535.

Feinberg, Joel. "Duty and Obligation in the Non-Ideal World." In *Rights, Justice and the Bounds of Liberty: Essays in Social Philosophy*, by Joel Feinberg, pp. 252–264. Princeton: Princeton University Press, 1980.

Frankena, William K. *Ethics*. 2nd ed. Englewood Cliffs, N.J.: Prentice-Hall, 1973.

Fried, Charles. *Contract as Promise: A Theory of Contractual Obligation*. Cambridge: Harvard University Press, 1981.

Friedländer, Paul. *Plato*. Vol. II, *The Dialogues: First Period*, translated by Hans Meyerhoff. New York: Bollingen Foundation, 1964.

Green, Thomas Hill. *Lectures on the Principles of Political Obligation*. London: Longmans, Green, and Co., 1941.

Greenberg, N. A. "Socrates' Choice in the *Crito*." *Harvard Studies in Classical Philology* 70 (1965): pp. 45-82.

Grote, George. *Plato, and the Other Companions of Socrates*. Vols. I and II, 3rd ed. London: John Murray, 1875.

Grube, G.M.A. "The *Cleitophon* of Plato." *Classical Philology* 26 (1931): pp. 302-308.

————, trans. *The Trial and Death of Socrates*. Indianapolis: Hackett Publishing Co., 1975.

Gulley, Norman. *The Philosophy of Socrates*. London: Macmillan, 1968.

Guthrie, W.K.C. *A History of Greek Philosophy*, Vol. III, *The Fifth-Century Enlightenment*. Cambridge: Cambridge University Press, 1969. Vol. IV, *Plato The Man and His Dialogues: Earlier Period*. Cambridge: Cambridge University Press, 1975.

Gutmann, Amy. *Liberal Equality*. Cambridge: Cambridge University Press, 1980.

Hackforth, R. "Hedonism in Plato's *Protagoras*." *Classical Quarterly* 22 (1928): pp. 39-42.

Harrison, A.R.W. *The Law of Athens*. Vol. I, *The Family and Property*. Oxford: Clarendon Press, 1968.

Holmes, Robert L. "Violence and Nonviolence." In *Violence: Award-Winning Essays in the Council for Philosophical Studies Competition*, edited by Jerome A. Shaffer, pp. 101-135. New York: David McKay Co., 1971.

Hume, David. "Of the Original Contract." In *Essays: Moral, Political, and Literary*, Vol. I, by David Hume, pp. 443-460. New York: Longmans, Green, and Co., 1898.

Irwin, Terence. *Plato's Moral Theory: The Early and Middle Dialogues*. Oxford: Clarendon Press, 1977.

————. *Plato Gorgias*, translated with notes. Oxford: Clarendon Press, 1979.

Kadish, Mortimer R, and Kadish, Sanford H. *Discretion to Disobey: A Study in Lawful Departures from Legal Rules*. Stanford, Calif.: Stanford University Press, 1973.

Kerferd, G. B. *The Sophistic Movement*. Cambridge: Cambridge University Press, 1981.

Kessler, Friedrich, and Gilmore, Grant. *Contracts: Cases and Materials*. 2nd ed. Boston: Little, Brown and Co., 1970.

Koyré, Alexandre. *Discovering Plato*, translated by Leonora Cohen Rosenfield. New York: Columbia University Press, 1945.

Kraut, Richard. "Plato's *Apology* and *Crito*: Two Recent Studies." *Ethics* 91 (1981): pp. 651-664.

Krentz, Peter. *The Thirty at Athens*. Ithaca, N.Y.: Cornell University Press, 1982.

Lacey, A. R. "Our Knowledge of Socrates." In *The Philosophy of Socrates*, edited by Gregory Vlastos, pp. 22-49. Garden City, N.Y.: Anchor Books, 1971.

Liddell, Henry George, and Scott, Robert. *A Greek-English Lexicon*. 9th ed. Oxford: Clarendon Press, 1968.

Lloyd, G.E.R. *Magic, Reason and Experience: Studies in the Origin and Development of Greek Science*. Cambridge: Cambridge University Press, 1979.

Locke, John. *The Second Treatise of Government*. Edited by Thomas P. Peardon. Indianapolis: The Bobbs-Merrill Co., 1952.

Lyons, David. *Forms and Limits of Utilitarianism*. Oxford: Clarendon Press, 1965.

MacDowell, Douglas M. *The Law in Classical Athens*. London: Thames and Hudson, 1978.

Maidment, K. J., trans. *Minor Attic Orators*. Vol. I. Cambridge: Harvard University Press, 1968.

Maier, Heinrich. *Sokrates: Sein Werk und Seine Geschictliche Stellung*. Tübingen: J.C.B. Mohr, 1913.

Martin, Rex. "Socrates on Disobedience to Law." *The Review of Metaphysics* 24 (1970): pp. 21-38.

McLaughlin, Robert J. "Socrates on Disobedience: A Reply to Gary Young." *Phronesis* 21 (1976): pp. 185-197.

Morrow, Glenn R. *Plato's Cretan City*. Princeton: Princeton University Press, 1960.

Muir, J. V. "Protagoras and Education at Thourioi." *Greece & Rome* 29 (1982): pp. 17-24.

Murphy, Jeffrie G. "Violence and the Socratic Theory of Legal Fidelity." In *Violence and Aggression in the History of Ideas*, edited by Philip P. Wiener and John Fisher. New Brunswick, N.J.: Rutgers University Press, 1974.

Nagel, Thomas. "The Limits of Objectivity." In *The Tanner Lectures on Human Values*, Vol. I, edited by Sterling McMurrin, pp. 77-139. Salt Lake City: University of Utah Press, 1980.

Nelson, William N. *On Justifying Democracy*. London: Routledge & Kegan Paul, 1980.

Ostwald, Martin. *Nomos and the Beginnings of the Athenian Democracy.* Oxford: Clarendon Press, 1969.

Pangle, Thomas L. *The Laws of Plato,* translated, with notes and an interpretive essay. New York: Basic Books, 1980.

Penner, Terry. "The Unity of Virtue." *The Philosophical Review* 82 (1973): pp. 35–68.

————. "Socrates on Virtue and Motivation." In *Exegesis and Argument: Studies in Greek Philosophy Presented to Gregory Vlastos,* edited by E. N. Lee, A.P.D. Mourelatos, and R. M. Rorty, pp. 133–151. Assen, The Netherlands: Van Gorcum & Co., 1973.

Popper, Karl R. *The Open Society and Its Enemies.* Vol. I, *The Spell of Plato.* 5th ed. rev. Princeton: Princeton University Press, 1966.

Rawls, John. *A Theory of Justice.* Cambridge: Harvard University Press, Belknap Press, 1971.

Raz, Joseph. *The Authority of Law: Essays on Law and Morality.* Oxford: Clarendon Press, 1979.

Romilly, Jacqueline de. *La loi dans la pensée grecque, des origines à Aristote.* Paris: Les Belles Lettres, 1971.

Ross, W. D., ed. *The Works of Aristotle Translated into English.* Vol. IX, *Ethica Nicomachea,* translated by W. D. Ross. Oxford: Oxford University Press, 1915.

————. *Plato's Theory of Ideas.* Oxford: Clarendon Press, 1951.

Santas, Gerasimos. "Socrates at Work on Virtue and Knowledge in Plato's *Laches.*" In *The Philosophy of Socrates,* edited by Gregory Vlastos, pp. 177–208. Garden City, N.Y.: Anchor Books, 1971.

————. *Socrates: Philosophy in Plato's Early Dialogues.* London: Routledge & Kegan Paul, 1979.

Sealey, Raphael. *A History of the Greek City-States ca. 700-338 B.C.* Berkeley and Los Angeles: University of California Press, 1976.

Shorey, Paul, trans. *Plato The Republic.* Vol. I. Cambridge: Harvard University Press, 1963.

Siewert, P. "The Ephebic Oath in Fifth-Century Athens." *Journal of Hellenic Studies* 97 (1977): pp. 101–111.

Simmons, A. John. *Moral Principles and Political Obligations.* Princeton: Princeton University Press, 1979.

Singer, Marcus George. *Generalization in Ethics: An Essay in the Logic of Ethics, with the Rudiments of a System of Moral Philosophy.* New York: Alfred A. Knopf, 1961.

Singer, Peter. *Democracy and Disobedience.* New York: Oxford University Press, 1974.

Smyth, Herbert Weir. *Greek Grammar*. Cambridge: Harvard University Press, 1963.

Sorabji, Richard. *Necessity, Cause and Blame: Perspectives on Aristotle's Theory*. London: Duckworth, 1980.

Strang, Colin. "What If Everyone Did That?" In *Ethics*, edited by Judith J. Thomson and Gerald Dworkin, pp. 151-162. New York: Harper & Row, 1968.

Sullivan, J. P. "The Hedonism in Plato's *Protagoras*." *Phronesis* 6 (1961): pp. 10-28.

Taylor, A. E. *Socrates*. New York: D. Appleton and Co., 1933.

————. *Plato: The Man and His Work*. New York: The Dial Press, 1936.

Taylor, C.C.W. *Plato Protagoras*, translated with notes. Oxford: Clarendon Press, 1976.

Teloh, Henry. *The Development of Plato's Metaphysics*. University Park: The Pennsylvania State University Press, 1981.

Tredennick, Hugh, trans. *The Last Days of Socrates*. Harmondsworth, England: Penguin Books, 1954.

Ullman-Margalit, Edna. "The Generalization Argument: Where Does the Obligation Lie?" *The Journal of Philosophy* 73 (1976): pp. 511-522.

Versényi, Laszlo. *Socratic Humanism*. New Haven: Yale University Press, 1963.

Vlastos, Gregory. "Socrates on Acrasia." *Phoenix* 23 (1969): pp. 71-88.

————. "The Paradox of Socrates." In *The Philosophy of Socrates*, edited by Gregory Vlastos, pp. 1-21. Garden City, N.Y.: Anchor Books, 1971.

————. "Socrates on Political Obedience and Disobedience." *Yale Review* 63 (1974): pp. 517-534.

————. "The Unity of the Virtues in the *Protagoras*." In *Platonic Studies*, 2nd ed., by Gregory Vlastos, pp. 221-265. Princeton: Princeton University Press, 1981.

————. "Socrates on 'The Parts of Virtue.' " In *Platonic Studies*, 2nd ed., by Gregory Vlastos, pp. 418-423. Princeton: Princeton University Press, 1981.

————. "What did Socrates Understand by His 'What is F?' Question?" In *Platonic Studies*, 2nd ed., by Gregory Vlastos, pp. 410-417. Princeton: Princeton University Press, 1981.

Wade, Francis C. "In Defense of Socrates." *The Review of Metaphysics* 25 (1971): pp. 311-325.

Wasserstrom, Richard. "The Obligation to Obey the Law." In *Today's Moral Problems*, 1st ed., edited by Richard Wasserstrom, pp. 358–384. New York: Macmillan Publishing Co., 1975. (This paper does not appear in the second edition. It was originally published in *The U.C.L.A. Law Review* 10 [1963]: pp. 780–807.)

Weingartner, Rudolph H. *The Unity of the Platonic Dialogue: The Cratylus, The Protagoras, the Parmenides.* Indianapolis: The Bobbs-Merrill Co., 1973.

Winspear, Alban D., and Silverberg, Tom. *Who Was Socrates?* New York: The Cordon Co., 1939.

Wolff, Robert Paul. *In Defense of Anarchism.* New York: Harper & Row, 1970.

Wood, Ellen Meiksins, and Wood, Neal. *Class Ideology and Ancient Political Theory: Socrates, Plato, and Aristotle in Social Context.* New York: Oxford University Press, 1978.

Woodruff, Paul. *Plato Hippias Major*, translated, with commentary and essay. Indianapolis: Hackett Publishing Co., 1982.

Woozley, A. D. "Socrates on Disobeying the Law." In *The Philosophy of Socrates*, edited by Gregory Vlastos, pp. 299–318. Garden City, N.Y.: Anchor Books, 1971.

————. *Law and Obedience: The Arguments of Plato's* Crito. London: Duckworth, 1979. (This contains a translation of the *Crito*.)

Young Gary. "Socrates and Obedience." *Phronesis* 19 (1974): pp. 1–29.

Zeyl, Donald J. "Socrates and Hedonism: *Protagoras* 351b–358d." *Phronesis* 25 (1980): pp. 250–269.

GENERAL INDEX

adikein, 25, 27 n. 4, 28 n. 6, 50 n. 31
Adkins, Arthur W. H., 5 n. 3, 128
 n. 10
agreements: implicit, 152–161, 171–
 177, 183–184, 188, 191; as independent civic ties, 33 n. 12, 47,
 52–53, 110–111, 114, 143, 190; to
 do injustice, 29, 36, 58–59, 68; if
 just, to be carried out, 29–35; require persuasion when broken, 58–
 59, 68; and unjust treatment, 35–
 39, 188. *See also* oaths of allegiance
akrasia. See knowledge, power of
Allen, R. E., 4 n. 1, 5 n. 3, 6 n. 5,
 11 n. 21, 19 n. 32, 26 nn. 2–3, 27
 n. 4, 32 n. 11, 37 n. 17, 42 n. 23,
 53 n. 32, 56, 85 n. 41, 137 n. 16,
 156 n. 4, 157 n. 5, 178, 209 n. 38,
 245 n. 4, 250 nn. 12–13, 264 n. 31
Annas, Julia, 11 n. 19, 233 n. 71, 237
 n. 77, 282 n. 57
apodidraskein, 120–121
Arginusae, battle of, 19, 223
aristocrats, 201–203, 208, 214
Athens: benefited by Socrates, 225,
 227, 230, 295; jury system of, 14,
 79–80, 84; law and virtue in, 79,
 131, 219–228; Socrates' concern
 for, 212, 214, 229 n. 67; Socrates
 treated unjustly by, 28, 45–46, 66,
 130; tolerance of criticism in, 166,
 226–228, 229 n. 67, 231–232, 308–
 309
Audi, Robert, 104 n. 11
Aune, Bruce, 136 n. 14
authoritarianism: alleged in Socrates,
 5–6, 23 n. 38, 36–39, 55–57, 108–
 110, 127, 151, 161–171, 189; and
 moral expertise, 10, 23 n. 38, 194,
 233–244, 247, 257, 306–307, 309

Barker, Andrew, 5 n. 3
Barker, Ernest, 5 n. 3, 37 n. 17, 195
 n. 4

Bennett, John G., 160 n. 8
Bluck, R. S., 27 n. 5, 275 n. 46, 289
 n. 67, 303 n. 83
Brickhouse, Thomas C., 13 n. 24, 89
 n. 49, 271 n. 43
Burnet, John, 18, 19 n. 31, 93 n. 2,
 250 n. 12
Burnyeat, M. F., 27 n. 5
Burtt, J. O., 34 n. 14
Bury, J. B., 18 n. 29

Chaerephon, 125, 195 n. 2, 270, 271
 n. 43
children, 94–103, 154–157. *See also*
 parents
chronology of dialogues, 4 n. 1, 13
 n. 22, 234, 256–257, 265, 275–276,
 303–304
Church, F. J., 26 n. 3
civil disobedience, 61, 73–76, 125–
 126, 146
Cohen, Marshall, 61, 76 n. 33, 85 n.
 41
Connor, W. Robert, 224 n. 62
Cornford, Francis MacDonald, 10 n.
 17, 246 n. 5
courage, 254 n. 18, 258–267, 279 n.
 51
craft analogy. *See* expertise, moral
 and political
Crete, 177–181, 215–216, 222–223,
 227–228
Croiset, Maurice, 177
Crombie, I. M., 10 n. 17, 248 n. 9,
 266 n. 36

definitions: allegedly concealed to
 promote autonomy, 9–10, 246, 251
 n. 15, 255 n. 23; discoverable in
 Athens, if anywhere, 232, 268;
 embedded in theory, 279–285; how
 shown inadequate, 254–256; and
 knowledge, 251, 256, 258, 265,
 274–277; needed in difficult cases,

harm. *See* virtue, and invulnerability to harm
Harrison, A.R.W., 91 n. 1, 97 n. 5, 98 n. 6, 113 n. 17, 212 n. 44
hedonism, 265–266, 294
Holmes, Robert L., 104 n. 11
Hume, David, 185 n. 14, 200

idiōtēs, 43, 115–123. *See also* privacy of escape
implicit agreements. *See* agreements, implicit
inconsistency: Socrates aware of his own, 285–288, 311–316; in Socratic epistemology, 269, 274–278; value of recognizing, 225, 228
injustice: resistance to, 36–39, 86 n. 43, 94 n. 4, 184 n. 13, 189, 215; suffering better than doing, 37–38, 210–211. *See also* agreements, and unjust treatment; justice
irony: alleged, 9, 10 n. 17, 246, 287–288, 302–303 n. 82, 311–312; disclaimed, 16; genuine, 27 n. 5, 219 n. 58, 250–251, 276 n. 48, 292 n. 70, 302 n. 82
Irwin, Terence, 11 n. 19, 205 n. 32, 207 n. 36, 208 n. 37, 209 n. 38, 211 n. 40, 213 n. 45, 233 n. 71, 235 n. 75, 237 n. 77, 239 n. 83, 240 n. 83, 245 n. 4, 248 n. 11, 255 n. 22, 260 n. 25, 261 n. 28, 262 n. 29, 266 n. 36, 269 n. 41, 281 n. 55, 282 n. 56, 296 n. 77, 301 n. 82, 303 n. 83, 312 n. 2

justice: as inviolable principle, 11–12, 22–28, 107–108; as standard for legitimate disobedience, 57–58, 65–69, 80 n. 39, 111–112; and the whole of virtue, 262 n. 29. *See also* injustice

Kadish, Mortimer R., 64 nn. 17–20
kakōs poiein, 26–27, 45 n. 28, 50 n. 31
kakourgein, 26–27, 28 n. 6, 45 n. 28, 50 n. 31
Kerferd, G. B., 226 n. 63
Kessler, Friedrich, 153 n. 2

knowledge, power of, 265–266, 294, 305–306
knowledge of good and evil, 246, 250 n. 13, 252–262, 280–283
knowledge of virtue: claimed in *Apology*, 269, 272–276; elsewhere disclaimed, 209, 245–247, 268–269, 275–279; and true belief, 273–274, 278, 301–303. *See also* definitions; expertise, moral and political; virtue
Koyré, Alexandre, 289 n. 66
Kraut, Richard, 13 n. 23, 23 n. 38, 31 n. 9, 60 n. 13, 75 n. 32
Krentz, Peter, 18 n. 29

Lacey, A. R., 4 n. 1
law: allegedly must be just, 5 n. 3, 21 n. 36; contrasted with decrees and orders, 20–21; effect on character, 218–228, 239–241, 296; and satisfaction, 178, 181–184, 190–191; upheld by Socrates, 221–222. *See also* Athens, law and virtue in
Laws: distinguised from laws, 81–82; not representative of common opinion, 66, 78–79; why personified, 40–41
Leon of Salamis, 12, 17–23, 29, 33 n. 13, 38–39, 81 n. 39, 124, 125 n. 6, 196 n. 7
liberty. *See* freedom
Liddell, Henry George, 26 n. 3, 115 n. 1, 203 n. 21, 203 n. 23
Lloyd, G.E.R., 105 n. 13
Locke, John, 145 n. 19, 160–161, 190
Lyons, David, 43 n. 24

MacDowell, Douglas M., 14 n. 25, 20 n. 34, 34 n. 15, 49 n. 29, 80 nn. 36–37, 154 n. 3, 212 n. 44
Maidment, K. J., 125 n. 6
Maier, Heinrich, 5 n. 3, 214 n. 49
many, the: cannot detect moral expertise, 239 nn. 82–83, 304–306; have permanent defects, 8, 22, 196–198, 205, 209, 242–243; improved by Socratic questioning, 201–202, 225–228, 229 n. 67, 242;

INDEX OF PASSAGES

Library of Congress Cataloging in Publication Data

Kraut, Richard, 1944–
Socrates and the state.
Bibliography: p.
Includes index.
1. Socrates—Political science. I. Title.
JC71.S62K72 1984   320'.01'0924   83–17113

ISBN 0–691–07666–9
ISBN 0–691–02241–0 (pbk.)